ON STALIN'S TEAM

ON STALIN'S TEAM

THE YEARS OF LIVING DANGEROUSLY IN SOVIET POLITICS

SHEILA FITZPATRICK

PRINCETON UNIVERSITY PRESS

PRINCETON AND OXFORD

press.princeton.edu
Cover photograph: *Molotov, Khrushchev, and Stalin on
the rostrum of Lenin's tomb,* 1936 © ITAR-TASS / Sovfoto

Third printing, and first paperback printing, 2017
Paperback ISBN 978-0-691-17577-5
The Library of Congress has cataloged the cloth edition
of this book as follows:

Fitzpatrick, Sheila.
On Stalin's team : the years of living dangerously in
Soviet politics / Sheila Fitzpatrick.
pages cm
Includes bibliographical references and index.
ISBN 978-0-691-14533-4 (hardback : acid-free paper)   1. Stalin, Joseph,
1879–1953.   2. Stalin, Joseph, 1879–1953—Friends and associates.   3.
Soviet Union—Politics and government—1936–1953.   4. Politicians—
Soviet Union—Biography.   5. Soviet Union—History—1936–1953—
Biography.   6. Political culture—Soviet Union—History.   I. Title.
DK268.S8F593 2015
947.084'20922–dc23   2015002745

British Library Cataloging-in-Publication Data is available

This book has been composed in Eurostile and Arno Pro

Printed on acid-free paper. ∞

Printed in the United States of America

3 5 7 9 10 8 6 4

CONTENTS

EXPLANATORY NOTE

I HAVE FOLLOWED LIBRARY OF CONGRESS TRANSLITERATION RULES, except for substituting "y" for the final "ii" in male proper names, dropping the extra "i" that strict transliteration would require in names like Maria and Evgenia, and using "y" instead of "i" in front of vowels in names like Vyacheslav and Nadya to make pronunciation easier. Where there is a familiar Anglicization of a proper name, like Allilyueva or Alexander, I have used it, and I have rendered Iurii as Yury and Iosif as Joseph. For women, I have kept the feminine version of Russian last names: for example, Molotova (Molotov), Krupskaya (Krupsky).

Before the Second World War, ministries in the Soviet government were called "People's Commissariats" and the ministers were called "People's Commissars." For clarity, I will use the term "ministry" and "minister" throughout. For convenience, I call the Council of People's Commissars (Sovnarkom) "the government." I use the term "Supreme Soviet" for the body that until 1938 was called the Executive Committee of the All-Union Congress of Soviets. Its chairman was the title "head of state," sometimes referred to as "president," of the Soviet Union.

When I cite visits to Stalin's Kremlin office, no reference is given in the endnotes because they always come from his office log, published as *Na prieme u Stalina: Tetradi (zhurnaly) zapisei lits, priniatykh I. V. Stalinym (1924–1953 gg.)*, ed. A. A. Chernobaev (Moscow: Novyi Khronograf, 2008). (I used the earlier journal version, "Posetiteli kremlevskogo kabiineta Stalina," ed. A. V. Korotkov, A. D. Chernev, and A. A. Chernobaev, published in *Istoricheskii arkhiv*, 1994, no. 6–1997 no. 1.)

A useful summary of this data for the 1930s (Politburo members and Central Committee secretaries only) may be found in Oleg V. Khlevniuk, *Master of the House: Stalin and His Inner Circle* (New Haven: Yale University Press, 2009), appendix 2, 266–71. Data on Politburo attendance in the 1930s are from the table in *Stalinskoe Politbiuro v 30-e gody: Sbornik dokumentov*, comp. O. V. Khlevniuk et al. (Moscow: AIRO-XX, 1995), 183–255. My quick reference for the Secretariat of the Central Committee of the Soviet Union was http://en.wikipedia.org/wiki/Secretariat_of_the_Central_Committee _of_the_Soviet_Union, but I have tried to check this information against other sources.

Russian archival locations are identified by *fond* (collection), *opis'* (inventory), *delo* (file), and *list* (folio), but I have rendered this in abbreviated form. Thus, RGASPI, f. 17, op. 1, d. 100, l. 1 appears as RGASPI 17/1/100, l. 1.

Regarding dates, in February 1918, Russia switched from the Julian calendar to the Gregorian, thirteen days ahead. I give dates in the Julian style before the switch and Gregorian after. This means that the Bolshevik Revolution occurred in October 1917, not early November (as in the Gregorian calendar).

GLOSSARY

BOLSHEVIK: Name of the group (later party) that split from the Russian Social-Democratic Labor Party in 1903; in the first decades after the October 1917 Revolution, it was used as the party name jointly with "Communist," which ultimately replaced it.

CENTRAL COMMITTEE OF THE COMMUNIST PARTY: Elected by Communist Party congresses, it was nominally the party's leading organ, although in practice the Politburo became the decision-making body.

CHEKA: Security police in the Civil War period (later known as GPU, OGPU, NKVD, MVD/MGB, KGB).

CIVIL WAR: Fought in 1918–20 between the Reds (Bolsheviks) and the Whites, the latter with foreign support from Western "interventionists."

COMINTERN: International organization of Communist Parties set up in 1919 and run from Moscow.

COMMUNIST: Name of the ruling party from October 1917; *see* Bolshevik.

COUNCIL OF PEOPLE'S COMMISSARS OF THE SOVIET UNION (Sovnarkom): Highest organ of the government before the war, renamed Council of Ministers after the war.

DACHA: Weekend place outside town.

FEBRUARY REVOLUTION: Event that resulted in the abdication of Tsar Nicholas II in 1917 and that established the Provisional Government, which was then overthrown by the Bolsheviks in October 1917.

GKO: State Defense Committee, key wartime body.

GPU: *See* Cheka.

GULAG: The chief administration of camps under the NKVD, which applied to the entire labor camp system.

JAC: Jewish Anti-Fascist Committee (1942–48), headed by Solomon Mikhoels, under the supervision of Solomon Lozovsky.

KOMSOMOL: Communist youth organization.

KULAK: Prosperous peasant, regarded by the Bolsheviks as an exploiter of the poor.

LEFT OPPOSITION: Groups headed by Trotsky (1923–24) and Zinoviev (1925–26) that were in political struggles with the Stalin team.

LENINGRAD: Capital of the Russian Empire (under the names of Saint Petersburg and Petrograd [1914–24]); renamed after Lenin's death, now again Saint Petersburg.

MENSHEVIKS: The larger group (party) produced by the split in the Russian Social-Democratic Labor Party (RSDLP) in 1903.

MGB: Ministry of State Security in the 1940s (*see also* Cheka).

NEP: New Economic Policy of the 1920s.

NKVD: The name of the security police from 1934 to the war; the initials stand for Narodnyy Komissariat Vnutrennikh Del (People's Commissariat of Internal Affairs) (*see also* Cheka).

OCTOBER REVOLUTION: Bolshevik seizure of power in 1917.

OGPU: *See* Cheka.

OLD BOLSHEVIK: Term used informally for party members who had joined before the revolution.

ORGBURO: One of two bureaus of the party's Central Committee (the other being the Politburo) in charge of organizational functions.

PALE: Area in Ukraine and Belorussia to which the Jewish population was restricted in imperial Russia.

PETROGRAD: Capital of the Russian Empire/Soviet Russia until 1918, so named in 1914–24; previously Saint Petersburg (*see also* Leningrad).

POLITBURO: Bureau of the party's Central Committee, consisting of full and "candidate" (nonvoting) members elected by party congresses; top Soviet decision-making body (*see also* Presidium).

PRESIDIUM OF THE CENTRAL COMMITTEE OF THE COMMUNIST PARTY:
Name given to the Politburo in 1952–66 (note that, confusingly, other
institutions also had presidia).

RAPP: Russian Association of Proletarian Writers, headed by Genrikh
Yagoda's brother-in-law Averbakh; closed down by the Central Committee in 1932.

RIGHT OPPOSITION: Strictly not an opposition but a tendency ("Rightism"), personified in 1929–30 by Rykov, Bukharin, and Tomsky.

RSDLP (RUSSIAN INITIALS: RSDRP): Russian Social-Democratic Labor
Party, founded in 1898; split into the Bolsheviks and the Mensheviks in
1903.

SHAKHTY AFFAIR: Show trial, in 1928, against nonparty experts and
Communist industrial administrators in the Shakhty region of Ukraine.

SOVNARKOM: *See* Council of People's Commissars.

STALINGRAD: Volga city and site of a crucial battle during the Second
World War in the winter of 1942–43; previously known as Tsaritsyn,
now Volgograd.

THERMIDOR: Month of the fall of Robespierre in 1794 during the French
Revolution; used by Bolsheviks as shorthand for the degeneration and
waning of revolutionary vigor.

USSR: Union of Soviet Socialist Republics established in 1924. Constituent
republics were the Russian Federation (RSFSR), Ukraine, Belorussia,
and the Transcaucasian Federation (later split into Georgia, Armenia,
and Azerbaijan); the Central Asian republics of Kazakh, Uzbek, Kirgiz,
Tadjik, and Turkmen, which were established at various times before
the war; and the Baltic republics (Latvia, Lithuania, and Estonia) and
the Moldavian Republic, added in 1940.

VOKS: Soviet society for cultural ties with foreign countries, headed by
Olga Kameneva in the 1920s and Alexander Arosev in the 1930s.

VOZHD': Exalted term for leader, applied to Stalin from the 1930s onward.
The plural *vozhdi* was applied to the whole Stalin team.

ON STALIN'S TEAM

INTRODUCTION

WHEN STALIN WANTED TO TEMPORIZE IN DEALING WITH FOREIGNERS, he sometimes indicated that the problem would be getting it past his Politburo. This was taken as a fiction, since the diplomats assumed, correctly, that the final decision was his. But that doesn't mean that there wasn't a Politburo that he consulted or a team of colleagues he worked with. That team—about a dozen persons at any given time, all men—came into existence in the 1920s, fought the Opposition teams headed by Lev Trotsky and Grigory Zinoviev after Lenin's death, and stayed together, remarkably, for three decades, showing a phoenixlike capacity to survive team-threatening situations like the Great Purges, the paranoia of Stalin's last years, and the perils of the post-Stalin transition. Thirty years is a long time to stay together in politics, even in a less lethal political climate than that of the Soviet Union under Stalin. The team finally disbanded in 1957, when one member (Nikita Khrushchev) made himself the new top boss and got rid of the rest of them.

I've used the term "team" (in Russian, *komanda*) for the leadership group around Stalin. At least one other scholar has also used this term, but alternatives are available. You could call it a "gang" (*shaika*) if you wanted to claim that its activities—ruling the country—had an illegitimate quality that made them essentially criminal rather than governmental. You could call it "the Politburo" (that is, the executive organ of the Communist Party's Central Committee, elected by periodic party congresses), which is semicorrect since the membership was very similar but, owing to Stalin's preference for informal working groups, never quite the same. Or you could call it a "faction," another pejorative term in Soviet discourse. The reader who prefers "gang" or one of the other alternatives is welcome to make the mental substitution. It was, in any case, a collective entity whose members had individual responsibilities but met regularly as a group, and who were united by loyalty to Stalin and, initially, to one another. Formed to fight other teams competing for leadership after Lenin's death, its function shifted with victory into governing the country.[1]

Like most teams, this one had a captain, Joseph Stalin, a figure of great authority over the others, who might also be described as a playing coach. His prerogatives in practice, though this was nowhere written down, included the politically crucial power of selecting and dismissing the other players on the team. In the early years, most of the team addressed Stalin, as well as one another, by the familiar form *ty*, and the convention was that he was just the first among equals. But the reality that he was more than that was increasingly visible, and by the postwar period only a couple of old hands were still using the familiar form with Stalin. It was a team apparently defined by its leader—Stalin's team (*stalinskaia komanda*)—which, when he died, managed something nobody expected, namely, to function as a leadership team without him.

In the scholarly world, where Stalin has long existed as a singular subject of political biography, the introduction of a team may be wrongly understood to imply a claim that Stalin's power was less than has been supposed. This is not what I am arguing. Indeed, in researching the book, I was struck by how great his authority was with the rest of the team, and how unchallenged his preeminence, even when circumstances seemed to call for a challenge, as in June 1941. The big policy initiatives were his, while the team's contributions (often hard to ascertain exactly, since the convention was to attribute *all* initiative to Stalin) were generally in their fields of particular expertise and institutional responsibility, on issues that Stalin considered secondary. But the fact is that, unchallenged top dog though he was, Stalin preferred—as his contemporaries Mussolini and Hitler did not—to operate with a group of powerful figures around him, loyal to him personally but also operating as a team. These men were not competitors with him for leadership, but neither were they political nonentities or simply "entourage," like his secretaries or secret policemen. They ran important sectors like the military, railways, and heavy industry, often with great competence. They were advocates within the Politburo for whatever institutions they headed at any given time. Most important policy issues were discussed by them (and Stalin) as a group in their frequent formal and informal meetings. Stalin did not need their agreement for his initiatives, but when he sensed it was lacking or lukewarm, he sometimes backed off or simply (for example, in cases of political outcasting) waited for them to come around.

There were changes in the team's composition over the thirty years. Three members (Sergei Kirov, Valerian Kuibyshev, and Sergo Ordzhonikidze) died in the mid-1930s, and another (Mikhail Kalinin) just after the war. Four new recruits (Andrei Zhdanov, Khrushchev, Georgy Malenkov, and Lavrenty Beria) joined the team in the second half of the 1930s. The Great Purges removed some marginal members, notably, three working in Ukraine (Stanislav Kosior, Vlas Chubar, and Pavel Postyshev), and after the war, the Leningrad Affair claimed a fast-rising recent recruit (Nikolai Voznesensky). But a core group—Vyacheslav Molotov, Lazar Kaganovich, Anastas Mikoyan, Klim Voroshilov, and, until 1952, Andrei Andreev—remained constant, and it was this group, together with the 1930s recruits, who constituted the team ("collective leadership") that took over upon Stalin's death.

The extent of the team members' powers of independent action in their own spheres varied over time, as did the degree to which they felt themselves a collective rather than simply a band of rivals. Interestingly enough, the two variables tended to move together and in the same direction. Both independence and team spirit were high in the early 1930s, and both were much reduced in the late 1930s as a result of the Great Purges. They rose again during the war, and remained high, though in a perilous context, in the postwar period until Stalin's death in 1953. The last period is particularly interesting in that Stalin was then at his most volatile and suspicious of his colleagues, but at the same time was no longer capable of continuing the huge workload of earlier years. He could still make initiatives that the rest of the team had to go along with (such as the anti-Semitic campaign of the late 1940s and early 1950s), but in matters he hadn't tagged as his own, the team members were working *around* him as much as with him by the end. When he wanted to drop Vyacheslav Molotov (long his no. 2 man) and another old-timer, Anastas Mikoyan, from the team in October 1952, the rest of the team resisted. He couldn't even stop the two in disgrace from showing up uninvited at his dacha, because the other team members were tipping them off.

How this struggle would have ended up is unknowable, because at the crucial point, Stalin died. Not surprisingly, under the circumstances, rumors circulated that his death was helped along, but nobody has ever been able to prove it. His death probably saved the lives of Molotov and Mikoyan, and perhaps security chief Lavrenty Beria and the others, too. Even before the leader had breathed his last breath, the team had their post-Stalin collective leadership up and running. The Stalin team, it turned out, could manage quite well—indeed, compared to the last few years of Stalin's life, substantially better—without Stalin. Everyone had predicted anarchy when Stalin died, and the team themselves feared it, but they actually carried out a successful transition with minimal (in Soviet terms) loss of life and a remarkably wide-ranging and radical reform program. The fact that reforms were initiated immediately strongly suggests that an unspoken consensus on the desirability of change, combined with recognition of its nonfeasibility as long as Stalin was around, had developed in the team in the years *before* Stalin's death.

My subtitle is "The Years of Living Dangerously in Soviet Politics," and danger is a crucial aspect of the story. The team as a whole was in danger at the beginning of the 1930s, when the reckless and wildly ambitious combination of collectivization of peasant agriculture and forced-pace industrialization could have ended in disaster. The Great Purges of the late 1930s was another high danger point, both for Stalin (since the terror could have got out of control and turned on its initiator) and the team members, perpetrators along with Stalin but constantly reminded they could become victims. In fact, most of the core team survived, politically as well as physically: Stalin proved to be a loyal patron to them, though with relatives and trusted subordinates dropping like flies around them, they couldn't be sure of that in advance. Fear of Stalin was not the only thing that held the team together, but it was certainly never absent after the early years.[2]

The team, the regime, and the country were at risk during the Second World War, with one and a half years of almost uninterrupted defeats and retreats until the tide turned in the winter of 1942–43. In what should have been triumphant years of victory after the war, individual members of the team were again in danger. In the post-Stalin transition, the team quickly eliminated one member, Beria, because of his evident ambition and disdain for collective rule, as well as out of fear, because he was thought to

have compromising files on them. Otherwise, the team remained more or
less intact until 1957, when Khrushchev was the one whose ambition and
noncollegiality led the others to try to rein him in—a plan that misfired
and led to the ousting of Molotov, Kaganovich, and Malenkov, and, effectively, the end of the Stalin team. But the age of living dangerously in Soviet politics was already over by 1957. Neither side in that conflict thought
of arresting or killing its rivals but simply of removing them from power.

The idea of writing this book came to me in the early 1990s, when the
Stalin archive (*fond Stalina* in RGASPI, successor to the old party Central
Committee archive) first opened, disclosing a large amount of correspondence between Stalin and other team members. The subject was initially
going to be just Stalin and Molotov, Molotov being vice-captain and Stalin's alter ego for much of the period under discussion, but then I became
conscious of the team dimension. This occurred to me in the context of
another archival research project in which I encountered team member
Sergo Ordzhonikidze not only running heavy industry with entrepreneurial flair and initiative but also vigorously representing the industrial
interest in the Politburo—which made me realize that this was how the
Politburo must have operated. In addition, I had always felt that there was
a book to write about Soviet high politics that put political science models
aside and focused on individuals and their interactions, my sense of which
was based on the vivid personal portraits my Soviet friend and mentor
Igor Sats, who had known most of the party leaders in his capacity as secretary to a People's Commissar (minister) in the 1920s, painted for me in
our conversations in the late 1960s.[3]

With the Soviet party and government (but not secret police) archives
opened, rich collections of papers of most of the leaders—Stalin, Molotov, Kaganovich, Mikoyan, Malenkov, Voroshilov, Ordzhonikidze, Kalinin, Kirov, Andreev, and Voznesensky—became available. Khrushchev
was a partial exception in the 1990s because of his awkward status as a deposed leader, while Beria, the team member who was shot in 1953, was and
remains archivally inaccessible. Since the 1990s, many Stalin biographies
and publications of source materials have been helpful to me in writing
this book. One of them, Simon Sebag Montefiore's lively biography, shares
my interest in the milieu in which Stalin lived, though not specifically the
political team in which he played. There have been fine scholarly studies
of Stalin's political "inner circle" by the Russian historian Oleg Khlevniuk,

whose knowledge of the sources is unequaled, and his British collaborator, Yoram Gorlizki, and an important quantitative analysis of the team by
Stephen Wheatcroft.[4]

It is not surprising that Stalin should largely have monopolized public
attention and even that of scholars, since great dictators always exert a
special fascination. In the case of the Stalin team, however, there are other
reasons. It was the convention within the team and in the world outside to
stress *Stalin's* contributions, not anyone else's. If in the 1930s the Soviet
press often wrote admiringly not just of the leader (*vozhd'*) but of the
leaders (*vozhdi*), meaning the team, this changed after the war, when the
team's public profile was largely restricted to flanking Stalin on the receiving stand in Red Square at May Day parades and the like. In addition, personal relations within the team had taken a sharp turn for the worse. The
kind of collegial friendships that existed in the early 1930s had largely vanished by the early 1950s, partly as a result of Stalin's encouragement of mutual suspicion and animosity, and attempts to reestablish closer personal
and family relations after Stalin's death were short-lived and not particularly successful.

After 1953, when Beria was executed, 1956, when Stalin was denounced,
and 1957, when Khrushchev banished the rest of the team after labeling
them an "anti-Party group," it was in nobody's interest to remember that
they had long worked together as a team, including Beria, and with and
without Stalin. Beria became the general scapegoat after his disgrace, with
his former colleagues competing with one another to deny any kind of
collegial, let alone friendly, contact with him in the past. With de-
Stalinization in 1956, team members were anxious to distance themselves
from what were now labeled as his crimes, as well as to point the finger at
their colleagues. Later, when survivors, family members, and former associates started to write memoirs, they not surprisingly produced highly
partial accounts focused on the one member of the team who, in their version, got things right. Stalin, and the subject's individual relationship with
him, were central in these accounts, with the rest of the team playing subordinate roles and generally cast in an unflattering light. While the team
members themselves acknowledged a degree of past teamwork, they did
so in passing and often grudgingly, while their children ignored it almost
entirely. This is not surprising, given that all these accounts were written

after the definitive and bitter breakup of the team in 1957, when Molotov, Malenkov, and Kaganovich went one way (but not together, to avoid any suggestion of plotting), and Khrushchev—with Mikoyan and a battered Voroshilov in tow—another.

After the archives opened and the memoirs were published, it became clear that, to a degree unusual among political leaders, Stalin's political and social life were intertwined. He socialized largely with the team, in their Kremlin apartments or out at his dacha. This was true in the early days of the team, when his wife Nadya was alive and he and many of his colleagues had young children, and continued after Nadya's suicide in 1932, when the team and his in-laws from two marriages provided virtually all of his social life, which focused around his dacha. He was a lonely man after Nadya's death, and even lonelier after the Great Purges broke up his surrogate family of in-laws. His daughter, Svetlana, was left for company, but that ended when she grew up and married during the war. The company of the team became all the more important to Stalin after the war, and participants have left memorable accounts of the awfulness of enforced nightly socializing at the dacha (now, in contrast to the 1930s, without wives and children) and the burden it imposed on the team.

In the old days, our picture of Stalin and his team came largely from Trotsky, who thought Stalin was a second-rate nonentity and the team worse than third-rate, hardly worth discussing. Trotsky scoffed at Molotov and lost no opportunity to ridicule and humiliate most of the others. Since Trotsky was deported from Moscow at the end of 1927, and from the Soviet Union two years later, he knew the team members very early in their careers, if at all. Clearly, he was wrong about Stalin, who, whatever he was, wasn't a nonentity or just a creature of the party machine. About the team, he was right about one thing: they weren't cosmopolitan intellectuals like him, or for that matter like Lenin. But they were far from the indistinguishable, faceless men that Trotsky, and others following him, assumed.

Stalin's closest associate, Molotov, nicknamed "stone-bottom," had a seemingly endless work capacity; nobody ever called him charismatic, but after you observe his stubborn perseverance over thirty years, you can't help but develop a certain admiration for his sheer ability to take it—not just the work but also the abuse—and his almost invariable refusal to apologize. Ordzhonikidze, on the other hand, was charismatic, hot-tempered, and much liked by his colleagues; in charge of heavy industry in the peak years of the industrialization drive, he did a phenomenal job, fighting tooth and nail for "his" plants and "his" people. Beria, another Georgian, is the hardest to come to grips with, because in the wake of his 1953 disgrace, everyone dumped on him, and he ended up being seen as a totally corrupt sex offender, as well as repressor in chief; it's something of a shock to see him through the eyes of his son as someone whose beautiful and highly cultured wife was a scientific researcher and who preferred the company of intellectuals. With Kirov, it's the opposite problem: his early death turned him into a martyr, by definition the nice guy, whom everyone remembered as his best friend. The pudgy Malenkov seems the quintessential apparatchik: Who would have thought that after his fall from power he would have immersed himself in biology (his son's specialty) and cowritten a scientific article on antigravitational pull? Andreev, the former worker, traveled to purging missions in the provinces while listening to Beethoven on his portable gramophone. Kaganovich, the bully with an inferiority complex about intellectuals, was notable for physical bravery; his onetime protégé Khrushchev masked a sharp brain and a decisive personality under a misleadingly "simple peasant" exterior.

The team's wives and children were part of their lives and mutual interaction, and are thus part of my story. Stalin's own family ties were attenuated: a wife who killed herself in 1932; an elder son by his first marriage, Yakov, of whom he was dismissive; a wastrel second son, Vasily; and Svetlana, his favorite, who in 1967 was to do the unthinkable for a team offspring and defect to the West. Half of the members of the team were "uncles" to Svetlana. Vasily and Svetlana grew up with the other Kremlin brats, notable among whom were the five rambunctious Mikoyan boys, two of whom got themselves arrested and exiled for some years during the war. Molotov's wife, Polina Zhemchuzhina, whom he deeply loved, was also arrested for Zionism and sent into exile for eight years while he remained a member of the Politburo: an emancipated strong woman, she founded the Soviet cosmetics industry. Beria and Zhdanov each had one cherished son who, with their parents' encouragement, became intellectuals, like many of the team's offspring. The "Kremlin children," as they grew up, almost all followed their parents' wishes and stayed out of politics, most of them receiving a higher education; Svetlana's wartime and early postwar generation fell in love with America, and a number, including Svetlana, majored in American studies at Moscow State University. With the notable exception of Svetlana, the Kremlin children remained close to their parents and, in later decades, tended the flame of their memory.

If you paint a group portrait, especially including the social and domestic context, you almost inevitably humanize your subjects, including Stalin. Some people may find this outcome in principle unacceptable, as tending to detract from recognition of their essential evil. But to yield to this objection means deciding to leave Stalin and his men out of history, ghettoizing them in a special "essence of evil" sector not subject to examination. Arendt wrote in the context of Nazi perpetrators about the banality of evil, which is another way of saying that evil is committed by human beings who are only life-size when you see them up close. As long as we keep them more than life-size and extra-human, we can't see the world from their perspective, and therefore it becomes very difficult to understand why they acted the way they did. Of course, understanding how they saw the world always carries with it the danger of justifying their actions. But for a historian, the opposite danger—that of simply failing to grasp what was happening because of a lack of understanding of what the historical actors thought they were doing—is even greater.

In any case, I can't say that my own experience confirms the notion that doing research on people makes you like them better. You certainly get a feeling of familiarity—with Molotov's blank, impassive expression in response to needling and his stillness, except for the drumming of his fingers; with Beria's combination of smarmy deference to Stalin, boundless energy, and malicious wit; with Ordzhonikidze's explosions and Mikoyan's ability to duck trouble and keep going. As far as Stalin is concerned, the person who has emerged in recent scholarship, starting with the Soviet historian Dmitry Volkogonov during perestroika, is a whole lot cleverer and better-read than we thought before the 1990s. He could be charming as well as cruel. His team feared him, but they also admired and respected him, seeing him (correctly) as in a different league from themselves, particularly in terms of boldness and cunning. From an outsider's point of view, of course, the boldness meant indifference to killing people, and the cunning, which often had a sadistic edge, meant skill at deceiving them. "You tricky bastard" was one of my commonest private reactions while reading Stalin's papers.

Some readers may think that nothing but sustained outrage is appropriate for writing about a great evildoer like Stalin. But I think the historian's job is different from that of prosecutor, or, for that matter, counsel for the defense. Your first task as a historian is to try to make sense of things, and that's a different brief from prosecution or defense. This is not to deny that there are problems with assuming a stance of objectivity: hard as we might try, we all have biases and preconceived opinions, and it's a physical impossibility to paint "the view from nowhere." In my own reading of historical work, I find that I either come to trust the authors (on the basis of their handling of sources and presentation of evidence) or to distrust them, in which case I usually stop reading. I hope my readers come to trust me, but if not, the other option is always available.[5]

This still leaves the question of where my point of observation derives from, since it can't be from nowhere. For social historians of the Soviet Union, including me in one of my earlier books, *Stalin's Peasants*, that point is generally with the victims. But that doesn't work well for political history: the peasants in my book had strong opinions about Stalin but very little reliable information and no opportunity to observe at close quarters. In this book, I have made my point of observation on Stalin (who, like it or not, is the center of this story) from *within his team*. It's a different perspective from usual, and I think it gives new insights. The team knew more about him than anyone else, having unparalleled access to information and opportunity to observe. In addition, they saw him in the complex way that goes with simultaneously being comrades in arms and potential victims, and in later life, given Stalin's dethronement in 1956, they had to come to terms with that complexity. I must admit that there is also a personal reason that I like this point of observation. It was always Stalin's fear that a spy would sneak into his milieu and observe him from up close. In this book, I am that spy.

A word about sources is in order. The Politburo record is relatively thin, partly because of that body's disinclination to have minutes taken of its deliberations (originally, back in the 1920s, because they couldn't stop the leaks, not only domestically but internationally). The correspondence with team members is a wonderful source for most of the prewar period, but the personal side disappears after the war, though fortunately at that time Stalin's absences from Moscow became ever greater, which resulted in a large corpus of letters and telegrams between him and the Politburo collectively. Soviet history is full of myths that became part of Sovietological as well as Moscow folklore. I approach these with a mixture of skepticism and recognition that sometimes the myths turn out to be right. For the 1950s, I use another kind of folklore, the letters about current affairs from Soviet citizens to leaders, as a kind of Greek chorus commenting on the transition and its aftermath.

The profusion of memoirs and late-life interviews was one of the pleasures and challenges of this project. Naturally, they are all, to varying degrees, self-justifying and self-serving, and many of them are written long after the event, or by children (Beria's, Malenkov's, Khrushchev's) who were relating what they remembered their father telling them at the time. You feel, as a historian, that such sources are like lobbyists, all clamoring to make their pitch, yet a book like this couldn't have been written without them. I couldn't help being aware that the people who left the most detailed record (Khrushchev and Mikoyan) are thereby privileged in establishing their version of events. Another inbuilt bias of the sources that needs to be mentioned is that for the purpose of memoirists and Soviet historians, political outcomes turned some people into villains and others into saints. Beria, executed in 1953, is in the first category. The second category includes Kirov, murdered in 1934, along with Kalinin, who in Soviet times was designated as the people's favorite on the team. (I suspect, by the way, that this is wrong and that the people's favorite was the genial and somewhat dashing military man, Voroshilov.)

Stalin's personal archive is rich, but it is also a work of art, carefully pruned and shaped by a variety of hands, starting with his own. Stalin, a master of manipulation who could easily take two sides of an argument in different contexts (which is not to say that he didn't have principles, in his way, as well as purposes), was capable of the most brazen lies but also of unexpected, if no doubt calculated, truth-telling. He had a lively, creative imagination that had once, back in his Georgian youth, made him a poet and in Soviet times led him to take great satisfaction in thinking up scenarios for show trials. He was also, it turns out, an excellent professional-standard editor of other people's texts, including for grammar and punctuation. He is disadvantaged in the memory stakes by leaving no account of his own and being the only team member whose memoirist-child, Svetlana, was not on his side.

Although this book has been researched in archives and primary sources like a scholarly history, it has not been written as one. It seemed a waste to flatten all that high drama and leave out the personal detail, which, for me, made the team come alive. Moreover, the Stalin era is still important to a broader public, especially those who went through the Cold War. In the past I have written extensively about the social, cultural, and everyday aspects of the Soviet experience, but this is my first large-scale foray into high politics or biography. Since it is conceived as a popular book, I have generally not highlighted scholarly controversies. My bibliography includes only such secondary works as are cited, usually as factual sources, in the text. But scholarly readers are also part of my intended audience, which is why I have included detailed notes that enable them to see where I got my information (though to avoid an overabundance of note numbers in the main text, rather than citing each direct quote, I've chosen to group together sources for the quotes, including them under boldface subject lines in the notes section). The conclusion highlights the book's contributions to scholarly debates.

Readers who know my earlier work will recognize some themes from the past, notably, the emphasis on institutional interest in high politics, patronage networks, and everyday interactions. In a way, what I have written is an *Everyday Stalinism* moved from the popular, urban milieu of that earlier book to the strange, isolated world of the Kremlin. But there were unexpected discoveries in the course of my research—things that surprised me, which I hope will also surprise my scholarly colleagues. When I started, I knew the 1930s much better than the postwar and post-Stalin period, and I expected the most interesting and lively period of the team, qua team, would occur then. It seemed plausible that the Great Purges should have snuffed the life out of the team. I spent some time with the Politburo archives for 1939–40 and noted that, while Stalin seemed to be functioning normally, the rest, though functioning and indeed working hard repairing purge damage, were keeping their heads well down. But was this a temporary or permanent change?[6]

Mikoyan made the case in his memoirs that it was the Second World War that was the high point of team effectiveness, the team's finest hour.

That, of course, was incompatible with the hypothesis that the vitality of the team had ended with the Great Purges. Moreover, there was the anomaly in the postwar period of Stalin's failure to remove Molotov and Mikoyan from political power and his social circle, evidently because of resistance from the team. A team that could encroach on Stalin's old, previously unchallenged prerogative of exclusion was surely a team that was still alive and kicking, or at least pushing back. Then, when I started focusing on the post-Stalin chapter, I was struck by how extraordinarily well the team managed the transition, for all their apprehension that without Stalin everything would fall apart. As if it were the most natural thing in the world, the Stalin team without Stalin metamorphosed into a collective leadership—and a reforming one to boot.

Time was when the portraits of team members were carried by marchers on May Day, along with Stalin's, and their names were lavishly bestowed on cities, factories, collective farms, and cultural institutions throughout the country, apparently ensuring their immortality. Then came Stalin's partial dethronement in 1956 and 1961; the ousting of Molotov, Malenkov, and Kaganovich in 1957 and then of Khrushchev, in 1964; and finally the collapse of the Soviet Union in 1991. The city of Molotov reverted to its earlier name of Perm in 1957. During perestroika, team names were removed from a string of North Caucasian and Ukrainian cities, including Lugansk/Luhansk (Voroshilovgrad) and Mariupol (Zhdanov). In Russia, the wartime capital of Kuibyshev resumed the name of Samara in 1991. Only Kalinin and Kirov remained in the atlases, probably by serendipity. Kirov was the luckiest, retaining not only the city and province of Kirov (formerly Vyatka) in the Urals but also the Kirov Ballet, though it is now in Saint Petersburg rather than Leningrad. Kalinin was half lucky, losing Tver in Central Russia but retaining Kaliningrad, the name given to Königsberg when it was acquired by the Soviet Union at the end of the Second World War.[7]

Stalin also lost out in the matter of place-names. In 1961, Stalingrad was renamed Volgograd, and the same fate befell Stalino in Ukraine (now Donetsk) and the Tajik capital Stalinabad (now Dushanbe). There is still contestation in Putin's Russia about whether Volgograd should change its name back again, the better to emphasize its heroic past as the site of the battle of Stalingrad in the Second World War. Stalin's name is in no danger of disappearing from Russian consciousness. But the team's names, except perhaps for Molotov and Voroshilov, will probably be forgotten by the next generation. Nobody is ever going to propose turning Perm back to Molotov, and the recently proclaimed Lugansk People's Republic in Eastern Ukraine, though looking to Russia, has not thought of calling itself Voroshilovgrad again.

The team wouldn't necessarily complain about this neglect. With the exception of Khrushchev (and Beria, if he had had the chance), they were not looking for a separate place in history but were by and large content to be Stalin's comrades in arms in the great work of building socialism—a project that they thought was on the side of history, though that is not the way it looks from the perspective of the twenty-first century. The team used to say, modestly but correctly, that Stalin was the lynchpin of the whole thing, implying what was to them self-evident, namely, that they couldn't have done it without him. But the corollary is also true: he couldn't have done it without them. Let that, for good or ill, be their epitaph.

ONE

THE TEAM
EMERGES

In the beginning, it was Lenin's team. Vladimir Ilyich Lenin was the captain, as he always had been since the days of the split among Russian Marxist revolutionaries between Bolsheviks and Mensheviks back in 1903. Lenin's lot took the title *bol'sheviki*, or majority group, leaving the minority label (*men'sheviki*) to the Opposition. But actually it was the other way around: it was the Bolsheviks who were the minority and Lenin—the most intransigeant and least conciliatory of the party's leaders—who provoked the split. There was no room for argument about who should be captain of the Bolsheviks. If you didn't want to play under Lenin, you had to go elsewhere. Lenin and many other revolutionaries were living in emigration in Europe in the years before the First World War, escaping the attention of the tsarist secret police; and his team included fellow émigrés like Grigory Zinoviev and the young Nikolai Bukharin brash enough to argue with Lenin about the theory of imperialism and state capitalism. But his party had supporters in the Russian revolutionary underground too, the so-called committee men, veterans of prison and exile, like the Georgian Josef Stalin and the Russian Vyacheslav Molotov.

The old underground people were a rougher lot than the émigrés, less well educated and several notches lower on the social scale. Many of them, like the Russian Mikhail Kalinin and the Latvian Jan Rudzutak, were workers, as befitted a self-styled "proletarian" party. Russia was a multinational empire, and the Russian revolutionary movement, includ-

ing the Bolshevik Party, had as many non-Russians as Russians in its
ranks, which reflected the resentment of national minorities against the
Russification policies of the Old Regime. Jews—including Zinoviev, Kamenev, and Stalin's future henchman Lazar Kaganovich—were one of the
largest contingents, with substantial groups from the Caucasus, particularly Georgians and Armenians, and the Baltics, particularly Latvians, as
well as Ukrainians and Poles. The Bolshevik Central Committee elected
in August 1917 consisted of eight Russians, six Jews, two Latvians, two
Ukrainians, a Pole, a Georgian, and an Armenian.[1]

A liberal Provisional Government had taken over in Russia after the
February Revolution, but its grip was precarious. Popular unrest increased as it failed to pull the country out of the First World War despite
defeats, huge casualties, and, by the summer, mass desertions from the
front. Spurred on by the impatience of radicalized soldiers, sailors, and
workers, the Bolsheviks seized power in Petrograd in October. The main
organizer of the coup was a former Menshevik émigré, Lev Trotsky, who
joined up with his old opponents, the Bolsheviks, when he realized that
Lenin was the man who was serious about taking power. But it was Lenin,
of course, who led the new government. It was almost entirely Bolshevik,
in line with Lenin's rooted dislike of cooperating with revolutionaries
outside his own party. But even single-party rule was not immune from
internal disagreements.

During the Civil War that raged from 1918 to 1921, various factions
formed in the party, one around Trotsky, but Lenin was determined to
squash them. His way of doing so was a learning experience for Stalin
and a number of those who ended up on the Stalin team. What Lenin
wanted, and actually achieved in 1921, was a ban on factions within the
Bolshevik Party. The way he did it was to create a faction of his own,
much more tightly organized than those of his opponents, particularly
Trotsky, who was more interested in his policy issue of the moment
(labor conscription in the wake of the Civil War, fiercely resisted by the
trade unions) than forming a faction. Lenin's faction was complete with
conspiratorial arrangements, secret meetings, and lists of Opposition
candidates to be voted down in the elections of provincial delegates to
the forthcoming national party congress. He even suggested calling in
an old comrade from underground with an illegal hand printing press to
run off leaflets. As a veteran conspirator, Lenin greatly enjoyed the whole

process and teased Stalin, his right-hand man for party organizational matters, for his qualms about so blatantly engaging in factionalism in order to pass a ban on factions. Molotov, future no. 2 man on Stalin's team, was proud to be "part of Lenin's plot against Trotsky in 1921." Out in the provinces, two young Bolsheviks, both future team members, caught Lenin's and Stalin's eye by their sterling service on the side of Lenin's faction: twenty-two-year-old Armenian Anastas Mikoyan and twenty-seven-year-old Lazar Kaganovich, Jewish working-class from the Pale, who were organizers of victory in tough local factional fights in the Volga city of Nizhny Novgorod and Turkestan, respectively. Sergo Ordzhonikidze, a Georgian whose ties with Lenin went back to 1911, was another who fought for the Lenin faction against lively opposition down in the Caucasus.[2]

The brilliant and arrogant Trotsky was the second man in the country at this point, thanks to his Civil War achievements as creator and leader of the Red Army. Forty-two years old in 1921, thus Stalin's near contemporary and Lenin's junior by nine years, he was a member of the Politburo, the party's top decision-making body, along with Lenin, Zinoviev, Kamenev, Stalin, and a trio of junior "candidate" (nonvoting) members, Molotov, Bukharin, and Kalinin. As Trotsky later told the story, he and Lenin remained close despite the 1920–21 conflicts. On Lenin's side at least, it was a wary closeness. Not only had Trotsky been a vigorous opponent in various prerevolutionary polemics about Marxist theory, he was also the charismatic hero of the 1905 Revolution, the October Revolution of 1917, and the victorious Civil War. In other words, he was serious competition for Lenin, regardless of whether he had any intention of challenging his leadership. For the Bolshevik young, especially those who had served in the Red Army during the Civil War, Trotsky was something of a cult figure. But those who had been in the Bolshevik Party before 1917—"Old Bolsheviks," as they came to be called—tended to view him with suspicion as a Johnny-come-lately.

Stalin, by comparison, was still a shadowy figure. A cobbler's son from the Georgian provinces with an unfinished seminary education, he was one of the underground "committee men" for whom conspiracy, prison, and exile were formative experiences. His connection with Lenin went back before the revolution—he had visited him in Poland in 1912, earning the sobriquet of "marvelous Georgian"—but they had worked closely together only since Lenin's return in April 1917. Initially taken aback, like other Russia-based Bolsheviks, by Lenin's intransigeance and unwillingness to cooperate with other revolutionary parties, he soon hewed to Lenin's line, supporting him on the controversial issue of seizure of power (which Zinoviev and Kamenev opposed). Serving in Tsaritsyn (later, Stalingrad) during the Civil War, he and his friend Klim Voroshilov had such serious conflicts with Trotsky, head of the Red Army, that Lenin had to mediate. A bit of a loner, Stalin's social connections in the Bolshevik movement were improved by his second marriage during the Civil War to Nadya Alliluyeva, the young daughter of a well-known revolutionary from the Caucasus. He was a behind-the-scenes man, rarely in these early years expressing an opinion in the Politburo. Where he shone was in party organization and personnel management, keeping tabs on which local party branches needed propping up and which delegates could be relied on to vote for the Lenin faction at the annual party congresses.

Neither a good public speaker nor a prominent participant in the party's theoretical debates, Stalin didn't look much like a contender in the early 1920s, and assessments from this period are almost uniformly negative. "Mediocrity," "nonentity," and "small-town politician" are among the condescending characterizations from Trotsky and other party intellectuals. Nikolai Sukhanov, a revolutionary intellectual who knew everyone who was anyone in the Bolshevik Party, despite not being a member, retained only "the impression of a grey blur, looming up now and then dimly and not leaving any trace." Another cosmopolitan intellectual remembered Stalin in 1919 as "frightening and banal, like a Caucasian dagger"—but perhaps everything but "banal" was hindsight. To a fellow worker in the Central Committee in the early 1920s, Stalin seemed self-disciplined, secretive, and cautious, conscious of being less educated than many of his Politburo colleagues, and had a vindictive streak. The proud and touchy Stalin knew what the others thought of him, and resented it. But Lenin turned to Stalin "whenever toughness or underhandedness were needed."[3]

Then, in only the fifth year of Soviet power, disaster struck. Lenin had his first stroke on 24 May 1922, followed by a second in December of the same year, which ended his active participation in political life. For more than a year, as Lenin lay dying, the party was in the grip of a leadership crisis. Running the party and, by extension, the country in Lenin's absence were Politburo members Trotsky, Stalin, Zinoviev, Kamenev, Mikhail Tomsky, and the newly elected Alexei Rykov, who had been Lenin's deputy at the head of the government and now succeeded him in that capacity. Stalin was general secretary of the party, Kamenev headed the Moscow Soviet, Zinoviev headed the Leningrad party organization, Trotsky was in charge of the military, and Tomsky of the trade unions. Sidelined by illness, Lenin developed a critical and almost hostile attitude to the entire team, accusing them of "oligarchical" tendencies. Whether or not this represented a belated conversion to democracy, as some have claimed, Lenin was clearly upset at being effectively excluded from decision making by his illness. A week after his second stroke, Lenin produced a rather incoherent document, known in retrospect as his "Testament," surveying the field of potential successors—all negatively. The two "outstanding leaders" were Stalin and Trotsky, he wrote, but their personal qualities were such that they might "inadvertently lead to a split" in the party. Stalin had "concentrated enormous power in his hands" as the party's general secretary, but might not always use it prudently, while Trotsky, "personally the most able man" in the leadership, was overconfident and prone to rule by command. A few weeks later, Lenin added a postscript, very damaging to Stalin: he was "too rude," Lenin wrote, and should be replaced as general secretary by someone who is "more patient, more loyal, more respectful and attentive to comrades, less capricious, and so on."[4]

Part of Lenin's annoyance had to do with his disagreements with Stalin about nationalities policy, the only field in which Stalin claimed special expertise. The newly formed Soviet Union included territories in the Caucasus—the future republics of Georgia, Armenia, and Azerbaijan—which had been part of the old Russian Empire, incorporated in the new revolutionary state with various degrees of willingness. Georgia had been the biggest problem, and the touchy issue of the early 1920s was whether it should retain the status of a separate republic or be incorporated into a Transcaucasian Federation. Stalin was the strongest advocate of the Federation, which Lenin supported, but with more sensitivity than Stalin to the concerns of the Georgian Bolsheviks who opposed it. When it was reported that Stalin's ally in the region, Sergo Ordzhonikidze, had actually struck one of his local opponents, Lenin was outraged. It was as if, in his illness, he had reverted to the code of honor and decorum of his respectable, provincial upbringing in the 1880s.

Lenin's curiously non-Bolshevik reaction on the Caucasus question was matched by his fury with Stalin for the latter's rudeness to his wife, Nadezhda Krupskaya. Stalin, an only partially reconstructed Georgian macho man in his personal relations, was never at his best with wives like Krupskaya, uncompromising women who were party veterans themselves, who disliked being bossed around and scorned feminine wiles. When Stalin was landed by his Politburo colleagues with the unpleasant task of seeing that Lenin followed doctors' orders to rest and not work, he was almost bound to come into conflict with Krupskaya. As a loyal wife (or, as she would have put it, comrade), she was systematically flouting the doctors' orders, at Lenin's urgent request, by bringing him newspapers, taking messages to colleagues, and generally keeping him informed. Stalin rudely abused her for this, and when Lenin heard of it, some months after his second stroke, in March 1923, he wrote icily that he considered an insult to his wife to be an insult to him—another reversion to the norms of his upbringing, since Bolsheviks did not talk about their wives in such terms. He threatened to break off relations unless Stalin apologized. Stalin was devastated to be turned on by the man who, as he told Lenin's sister, he "loved with all his heart." Still, he offered only the most grudging apology: he thought Lenin was being totally unreasonable and Krupskaya was the one in the wrong. To Molotov, he said resentfully, "So because she uses the same toilet as Lenin, I'm supposed to value and respect her like Lenin?" The better-brought-up Molotov, though no great admirer of Krupskaya, thought this crass.[5]

Lenin died on 21 January 1924. At his funeral on 27 January, all the Politburo members—Stalin, Kamenev, Zinoviev, Tomsky, and candidates Molotov, Bukharin, and Rudzutak—were pallbearers, along with Felix Dzerzhinsky, the respected Polish Bolshevik who had been the founding head of the Cheka (security police). Trotsky, bruised by political struggles with his Politburo colleagues and recuperating from illness in the South, declined to return to Moscow for the funeral—a strange personal decision in light of his declared attachment to Lenin, and a politically suicidal one.

Jockeying for succession was well under way. It was an odd kind of contest. In the first place, there was no formal position of party leader to fill. The remaining leaders were unanimous in saying, and probably for a time feeling, that nobody could replace Lenin. The Politburo had never had a formal head; it was understood as a group of equals, although among these equals Lenin was definitely first. The second oddness, a consequence of the first, was that what historians call the succession struggle was not overtly a struggle for leadership. Rather, it was a struggle for unity against "factionalists," whose resistance to majority rule was held to cover (illegitimate) personal ambitions to assume the role of leader. Factionalism, although formally banned, remained a bugbear in the party: "we had the thinnest stratum of party leadership," Molotov later recalled, "and in that very thin stratum cracks were appearing all the time." Like the Jacobins in the French Revolution (a precedent of failed revolution very much on the minds of the party's leaders), the Bolsheviks could be undone by factionalism. Their tenuous grip on power could fail and the whole revolution be overthrown, no doubt with the aid of hostile "capitalist" powers of the West who had already tried to achieve this once by their intervention in the Civil War.[6]

Trotsky was the obvious threat. He was not an Old Bolshevik; he had been considered a factionalist in 1920 on the basis of policy disagreements, and on top of that—always remembering that the French Revolutionary analogy loomed large—his leadership of the Red Army leadership during the Civil War made him easy to cast as a potential Bonaparte. In fact, he was not a natural organizer of factions, being impatient, opinionated, sarcastic, and contemptuous of people of lesser intellect. He was probably not even interested in becoming party leader. But he liked to have his own way, loved arguing about policy, and considered himself the party's foremost Marxist theoretician. It's not surprising that his Politburo colleagues, to whom he showed little respect, thought he was out for the leadership, especially those who may have wanted the top job for themselves, namely, Zinoviev and Stalin.

Lenin was not the only one to worry about a withering of revolutionary democracy. To be sure, all Bolsheviks were in favor of centralized control by a single party, but they were accustomed to a fairly freewheeling situation that accommodated lots of arguments within the party and, in practice, considerable independence at the local level. Making revolution was what the Bolshevik Party was used to, but now that it was a ruling party, its modus operandi had to change. The process was called "bureaucratization," and all Bolshevik leaders professed themselves to be against it and blamed one another for its emergence.

There were other problems to argue about. One was economic policy. During the Civil War, the Bolsheviks had tried full-fledged nationalization in the cities, failed, and backed off with a partial relegalization of the market known as the New Economic Policy (NEP). Bruising confrontations over Civil War requisitions with the peasantry, still 80 percent of the population, had forced them to leave agriculture as it was, which was not only nonsocialist but precapitalist ("backward," to use the Bolsheviks' favorite term of abuse). But the Bolsheviks were socialist modernizers as well as revolutionaries. If they didn't produce socialist modernization of the economy, their revolution would have failed. The question was how to do it, and when.

The year 1923, the interregnum, was a time of intensive self-examination within the party. Trotsky wanted bolder economic policies. Others wanted more democracy within the party. The leadership agreed to a wide-ranging discussion of the big issues. It was a sign of the party's strength, Stalin said—making the best of it—not its weakness or disarray. Of course, there were limits: the party was an instrument of struggle, not a talkshop (Stalin again), and as Zinoviev frankly admitted, when push came to shove, "every revolutionist says: to hell with 'sacred' principles of 'pure' democracy." Trotsky and his supporters were among the most energetic discussants, and when he issued a manifesto calling for a "New Course" to revive the revolutionary spirit, reverse the party's ossification, and rally the young, his Old Guard colleagues in the Politburo were not amused.

The discussion turned into a kind of election campaign in the winter of 1923–24, since it coincided with the selection of delegates to the upcoming XIII Party Conference by local party committees. The Opposition, as it was beginning to be called, sent its speakers around to the local committees—not Trotsky himself, since he was ill, as he often was in a crisis, but his supporters, as well as advocates of more party democracy (a separate faction, not represented in the Politburo). The Opposition's opposition, which was starting to call itself "the Central Committee majority," was out in force as well, Zinoviev being the most visible spokesman. How much support the Opposition had is hard to gauge, since its early successes in Moscow were generally reversed after the arrival of Central Committee majority strongmen, whose persuasive powers were backed up with the behind-the-scenes disciplining that was Stalin's specialty.

Still, the "majority" probably had more right to the title than Lenin's Bolsheviks had had in 1903, and their victory was decisive. Out of 128 voting delegates to the party conference that met in January 1924, only three belonged to the Opposition. In a powerful speech to the conference that marked his emergence into a more publicly visible leadership role, Stalin mocked Trotsky's late conversion to democracy—he having been a harsh disciplinarian during the Civil War and a notorious centralizer—and accused him of factionalism and, by implication, leadership ambitions: he had "counterposed himself to the Central Committee and put about the idea of himself as a superman standing above the Central Committee," Stalin said.

It was the beginning of the end for Trotsky, though he remained a voting member of the Politburo, and a powerful and insistent voice in its debates for several more years. At the XIII Party Congress that followed in May, his speech went down badly. Trying to add a touch of humility, he said that "the party is always right" because it was on the side of history. A few years later, that would have sounded unremarkable, but in 1924 it was still over the top, and from the self-willed Trotsky—a fierce critic of the Bolsheviks until he joined them in June 1917—it just sounded hypocritical. Lenin's widow, Krupskaya, mocked him for it.[7]

If the convening of the XIII Party Congress in May 1924 was a bad moment for Trotsky, it wasn't good for Stalin either. Krupskaya brought the letter that became known as Lenin's Testament along a few days before the congress opened, and the party leaders—none of whom received a favorable review—had to decide quickly what to do. They decided not to make it known to the congress (which is what Lenin had asked) but to circulate it to a select group of leaders of provincial delegations. Stalin offered to resign as general secretary, but no one took him up on it. It was a tense, unhappy time for him. According to one account, he ran away from Moscow in the middle of the congress and locked himself up at a dacha (weekend cottage), refusing to admit anyone except Tomsky's wife, Maria, "who sat with him for two days and nights, fed him with a teaspoon and looked after him like a child" before he could be persuaded to come back to Moscow. "People had insulted him undeservedly," he complained. Maria was a friend of his own wife, Nadya, whose absence from this episode is notable. Stalin and Nadya were not getting on.

Other signs of an unusually vulnerable Stalin appear at this time as well. A few months later, he received a letter from a seventeen-year-old Komsomol member from the northern provinces, who expressed his ardent political commitment and asked for Stalin's permission to take his last name, since Stalin was Lenin's true disciple. Stalin himself replied (surprisingly, as this would normally be left to a secretary), and his response sounds almost like a cri de coeur from a lonely man grateful for a kind word: "I have no objections to your taking the name Stalin; on the contrary, I will be very pleased, as that will give me the chance to have a younger brother (I have no brothers and never had)." This letter was written just a few weeks after Stalin had asked to be relieved of his duties as Central Committee secretary, his excuse being that he needed to go away and recover his health. He requested an assignment "to Turukhansk District [in the frozen North, Krasnoyarsk Province, the site of his last pre-revolutionary exile] or to Yakutsk Province or somewhere abroad in some unobtrusive posting." In other words, as far away as possible, and—since he asked the Central Committee to decide the matter in his absence—without him even having to see the colleagues before whom he had lost face.[8]

The Central Committee didn't send him to Turukhansk, of course. They didn't even remove him from the position of general secretary, and by autumn, after a vacation, he was back in harness. But Stalin's friends and associates remembered that he had a bad time in these years, with a lot of bruising of the ego. It's generally assumed that Stalin already saw himself as the future leader and was pursuing a systematic strategy of getting rid of the competition one by one. This may be true, but it's only with hindsight that we know who was going to win. The way Stalin remembered it later, *they* had been out to get *him*, not vice versa.

Embattled though he felt himself, Stalin was beginning to gather a group of supporters around him, as were his rivals Trotsky and Zinoviev. By comparison with the others, Stalin's team was short on intellectuals, cosmopolitans, Jews, and former émigrés, but had more former workers and Russians, as well as a substantial contingent from the Caucasus. Its proletarian, as well as Russian, character was important to the team's legitimacy. Polemicizing with Trotsky, Molotov boasted of "the true Russian" proletarians like Kalinin, Voroshilov, and Tomsky on his team, in implicit contrast with the Jewish intellectuals of the Opposition. Stalin

welcomed the growing self-confidence of "our proletarians," adding Rudzutak to Molotov's list. Bolshevik "toughness" (*tverdost'*), seen as a quality
natural to workers but not to intellectuals, was particularly esteemed in
the Stalin team, a number of whose members had bonded working together at various fronts during the Civil War. But Stalin also valued competence, energy, and a capacity for hard work. The ambience in the team
has been described as one of "conspiracy, companionship and crude mas-
culine humour."[9]

Vyacheslav Molotov was the first notable recruit to Stalin's team. Personally, they were not particularly close friends, though they had known
each since 1912. There were some frictions in 1917, as Stalin and Kamenev's
return from exile pushed Molotov out of the leadership of the Petrograd
Committee. Molotov had a less distinguished Civil War than Stalin, but
he did manage to marry an interesting and strong-willed woman: Polina
Karpovskaya, known by her party name Zhemchuzhina, a tailor's daughter, who was serving as a political commissar in the Red Army when they
met (Molotov's respectable Russian provincial family wouldn't have anything to do with her, a Jewish nobody). Molotov had a notable promotion
in 1921, when Lenin moved him into the position of party secretary. This
didn't last long, however, as Lenin soon decided that Molotov, though a
good organizer, wasn't a shrewd enough politician for the job, and got Stalin appointed over his head to the new position of general secretary. Molotov may have had some resentment about this, and his tone in a private
exchange with Stalin about Marxist theory a few years later suggests that
he was still insisting on a presumption of equality. Still, Molotov was
twelve years Stalin's junior—the youngest ever member of the Politburo
when he joined it as a candidate in 1922 at at the age of thirty-two, as he
later proudly recalled—whereas Stalin had been on it as a full member
since the body's establishment in 1919. With his pince-nez and a neat little
moustache, Molotov didn't look much like a revolutionary even in his
youth; he could have been a clerk in a government office, a position for
which his high school diploma (acquired when he was already a professional revolutionary) qualified him. Not brilliant or quick-thinking, according to his own and other accounts, he was well organized and extremely hardworking. Trotsky, whom he loathed, once castigated him in
the Politburo as one of "the Party bureaucracy without souls, whose stone
bottoms crush all manifestations of free initiative and free creativity." Ad-

justing his pince-nez and looking crushed, Molotov stuttered, "We can't all be geniuses, comrade Trotsky." The epithet "stone-bottom" stuck.

Klim Voroshilov, the jaunty cavalryman better known for his personal bravery than for scintillating intellect, went back quite a way with Stalin: near contemporaries, they had found themselves roommates at the underground party's Stockholm conference in 1906 and then worked together in Baku. But it was at Tsaritsyn in the Civil War, when Stalin was political commissar for the Southwest and Voroshilov head of the Southwestern Army, that they had bonded, partly in antagonism to Trotsky, whose military orders Voroshilov used Stalin's protection to defy. Born an ethnic Russian in a poor proletarian family in Ukraine, Voroshilov started his working life in the Donbass mines as a ten-year-old. By age fifteen, he was working in a factory, and at seventeen he joined the revolutionary movement. His wife, born Jewish Golda Gorbman (she was later baptized and changed her name to Ekaterina), was a fellow revolutionary who Voroshilov married in exile before the revolution. Despite his subsequent reputation as a military man, Voroshilov did not serve in the Russian Army in the First World War; it was only after the February Revolution that, as a professional revolutionary, he established contact with soldiers in Petrograd and was elected their delegate to the Petrograd Soviet (of Workers' and Soldiers' Deputies). After forming a partisan resistance unit in Ukraine during the Civil War, he created and led the First Cavalry Army, participating in the war with Poland in 1920–21. After the war, he remained associated with the military, becoming defense minister (a position earlier held by Trotsky) in 1925. At the end of the same year, he became a member of the Politburo.[10]

Lazar Kaganovich, a decade and a half younger than Stalin and three years younger than Molotov, worked with the two of them in the party Central Committee in the early 1920s, though at a lower level in the hierarchy. They were secretaries, whereas he was just a department head, though admittedly it was an important department in terms of Stalin's rise to power: personnel. Jewish and born in the Pale (restricted area of Jewish settlement) in Ukraine, the teenage Kaganovich worked in a shoe factory and followed his elder brothers Mikhail and Julius into the revolutionary movement. During the Civil War, he was a political commissar in the Red Army, serving at various locations, including Voronezh (where he had his first meeting with Stalin) and Turkestan (where he fought local rebels and internal party factions with another future member of Stalin's team, Valerian Kuibyshev). It was probably on the recommendation of Kuibyshev, who had just moved to Moscow as a Central Committee secretary, that Stalin invited Kaganovich to work in the secretariat in 1922. One of his fellow workers found him quick and energetic, humble, and conscious of his lack of education. Later it was his toughness and tendency to bully and physically intimidate subordinates that was more often noticed than humility. But he certainly remained humble as far as Stalin was concerned; he was the most devoted of all Stalin's team (a "200 percent Stalinist" according to Molotov), who, even in the days of casual camaraderie in the 1920s, could never bring himself to use the familiar form of address (*ty*) to Stalin, as the rest did. He and Molotov rubbed along in the secretariat, never friends but able to work together. Molotov thought he always had a chip on his shoulder, apt to complain, "It's easy for you, you're an intellectual, but I come from the workers." He became a candidate member of the Politburo in 1923, but for the second half of the 1920s, he was mostly absent from Moscow as Stalin's man in Ukraine, where he held the position of first secretary of the party.

To Trotsky, Zinoviev, and Kamenev, and no doubt to the party elite in general in the mid-1920s, what distinguished the Stalin group was that it consisted mainly of people who worked or had worked in the office of the party Central Committee. This was true not only of Stalin, Molotov, and Kaganovich, but also of Valerian Kuibyshev, Jan Rudzutak, and Andrei Andreev, all of whom were party secretaries at some point in the first half of the 1920s.

Kuibyshev, a Russian like Molotov and about the same age, was one of the best educated of those who ultimately joined Stalin's team; Molotov counted him as a cut above himself, culturally and socially. The son of a Russian military man who, like Lenin's father, was of noble status, he had been a cadet at a military academy when he dropped out to join the revolutionary movement. He headed an important city soviet on the Volga in 1917–18, then became a political commissar in the Red Army, and ended the Civil War in Turkestan. A candidate member of the Politburo from 1921, his main field of activity turned out to be industry and state planning, but in the 1920s he had two stints of party work: first as party secretary (along with Stalin and Molotov) in 1922, and then in the mid-1920s as head of the party Control Commission, where he was a useful ally for Sta-

lin in dealing with the Trotskyists. But he was neither one of Stalin's closest political allies nor one of the group of team friends who socialized together. He preferred mixing with artistic people, and had a somewhat
tumultuous private life in the 1920s: while he stuck to the Old Bolshevik
milieu for marriages, his young third and fourth wives came from the next
generation.[11]

The Latvian Jan Rudzutak, nine years younger than Stalin and a Bolshevik since 1905, had been a factory worker in Riga. Despite his proletarian origins and lack of formal education, he became notable after the revolution for his strong cultural interests and contacts with the artistic
world—part of the reason, no doubt, that Molotov judged him in the
1930s to have gone a bit soft. After a stint as party secretary in 1923–24, he
was put in charge of the railways. Although Stalin liked him, they didn't
socialize together, and he was not always seen as a strong Stalin man. At
one point, there was talk of putting him forward, as a nonaligned candidate, to take over from Stalin as general secretary. A candidate member of
the Politburo from 1923, he became a full member in 1926, but Molotov remained concerned about his wavering. Stalin told him not to worry: "He
is 'playing politics,' thinking that's how to be a 'real politician.'"

Andrei Andreev, seventeen years Stalin's junior, was another of the
proletarians. One of the youngest members of the team, he was a candidate member of the Politburo from 1926. Son of a Russian peasant, he became a munitions worker and joined the Bolsheviks as a teenager. He met
his wife, Dora Khazan, during the First World War when both were working at the Putilov factory and active in the revolutionary movement; later
she was a friend and fellow student of Stalin's wife Nadya. As a supporter
of Trotsky's faction in 1920, Andreev had something to live down politically, but he was "our friend" despite that, according to Molotov. Distinguished by his absolute and unquestioning execution of instructions,
which was to make him a feared hatchet man during the Great Purges, he
was treated a bit condescendingly by colleagues in the 1920s: even Voroshilov, not the team's most polished and cogent public speaker, felt he
could give "Andryusha" tips on clear exposition at a Central Committee
meeting in 1928. Throughout the 1920s, Andreev was working his way
through a secondary education with tutors in his spare time. Always un-
assuming, Andreev was liked and respected as a mentor of up-and-
coming young functionaries in the 1930s.[12]

Of the worker group, Mikhail Kalinin was the oldest and the most senior. He had actually been a foundation member in 1898 of the Russian Social-Democratic Labor Party from which, five years later, the Bolshevik Party emerged. Sporting a little goatee, he had a slightly mischievous look, but even in his forties, he was already being referred to (with degrees of condescension, respect, and affection) as the elder (*starosta*) of the revolution. A peasant by origin, he became a wageworker in Saint Petersburg in adolescence. His subsequent varied career, both as a worker (metalworker, railway worker) and as a semiprofessional revolutionary, took him to various parts of the empire, including Georgia, where he became friends with Stalin's future father-in-law, Sergei Alliluyev, and Riga, where he met and married a young Estonian worker of similar revolutionary persuasion, Ekaterina Lorberg. From 1919 until his death in 1946, he was titular head of the Soviet state and one of the party's most popular figures; at party congresses the applause for him was second only to that for Stalin. Presenting himself as a wily old peasant, he liked to play the comedian at party meetings, trading on his age and popularity, and usually got away with it. In the debates of the 1920s, he was generally a moderate and took the role of defender of peasant interests, an anomaly in a "proletarian" party that suspected peasants of bourgeois acquisitive instincts; in 1928, he annoyed Stalin with his cheeky remark that he spoke "as a peasant," not as a member of the party leadership. Although Kalinin ended up on the Stalin team, Trotsky (with whom Kalinin and his wife shared a communal apartment in the Kremlin during the Civil War) claimed that he had done so only with the greatest reluctance, quoting him as saying "that horse [that is, Stalin] will some day drag our wagon into a ditch." Perhaps he was so prescient—but more likely he didn't want to join anyone's faction until he had to.

The Georgian Grigory Ordzhonikidze, always known by his revolutionary name of Sergo, was another veteran of the revolutionary movement as a founding member of the Bolshevik Party in 1903 and was long acquainted with Lenin. He was elected to the Bolshevik Central Committee in 1912, a status shared only by Lenin and Zinoviev in the 1920s leadership, though Stalin was later co-opted and Kalinin was a candidate member. A leader of the Bolsheviks' Caucasian Bureau in the early 1920s, along with Kirov, he was a close ally of Stalin's in Caucasus politics, but the two of them got into big trouble with Lenin on the nationality issue in 1922, which probably explains the delay in bringing Ordzhonikidze into the center. Loyal, and generous, Ordzhonikidze had many friends, including Stalin, Voroshilov, and Mikoyan. Regarded on the team as a typical Georgian, "a man of heart and feelings," as Molotov put it, he was volatile and easily offended. Ordzhonikidze was finally summoned to Moscow in 1926 to take over from Kuibyshev as head of the party Control Commission, a key position in the faction fights, though he was not a faction-fighter by temperament. For Trotsky, Ordzhonikidze was the only one of the Stalin team to warrant individual comment: agreeing with Molotov about his loyalty, he granted him "forcefulness, courage and firmness of character," despite a certain "uncouthness"—but then, from Trotsky's standpoint, the entire Stalin team was uncouth.[13]

The Armenian Anastas Mikoyan was the youngest of a trio of friends, the others being Ordzhonikidze and Sergei Kirov, who came up from the Caucasus in 1926 to join Stalin's team in the center. A seminary dropout, like Stalin, but seventeen years younger, Mikoyan was famous for his association with the legendary 26 Baku Commissars executed during the Civil War. A personable and gregarious young man, he became friends with Kuibyshev in Turkestan during the Civil War, and a few years later bonded with Voroshilov and Ordzhonikidze when the two of them looked after his young wife, Ashken, and their newborn baby in his forced absence on party business. With Stalin, Mikoyan was on familiar terms (using *ty*) since 1923. The young Mikoyan cut a dashing revolutionary figure, dressed, as was the custom of those years, in semimilitary dress: high boots, belted field jacket, and peaked cap. After a stint on the Volga in the early 1920s, distinguishing himself as a supporter of the Lenin faction, he went back South as party secretary in Rostov on Don before being summoned to Moscow in 1926 to head the trade ministry. He resisted this transfer, despite the candidate membership of the Politburo that went with it, because he liked the South and wanted to stay in party work, considering trade bourgeois. But he did so well at it that he remained the party's top internal and external trade specialist for forty years; with the passage of time, it came to seem natural that, as a cunning Armenian, he should know how to trade. Mikoyan turned out to be the great survivor of Soviet politics, though he was in trouble with Stalin many times. He was notable in the team for his resistance to killing and outcasting individuals—not that he opposed it in principle, but in practice he tried to avoid it as much as possible. With his strong sense of family loyalty, he also repeatedly broke the team rules about looking after victims' families.

The last of the "Caucasus" trio, Sergei Kirov, was actually Russian, born in Vyatka Province in the Urals and educated in Kazan, but had spent much of his adult life in the South. Drawn into revolutionary activity as a student, he spent time in prison (Kuibyshev was a fellow prisoner in Tomsk in 1909), but seems to have taken something of a break from revolutionary activity in his prerevolutionary years in the North Caucasus. There he worked as a journalist and married Maria Markus, who shared his interests in theater and literature. The revolution brought him back into the fray, and he and Ordzhonikidze, almost exact contemporaries, became friends when they worked together on the Caucasus Front during the Civil War and then in the Bolshevik Caucasus Bureau, which Ordzhonikidze headed with Kirov as his deputy. His friendship with Mikoyan also dates from this period. He was Ordzhonikidze's and Stalin's ally in the fight about Georgia's future status at the beginning of the 1920s (though it was the other two who got the rough side of Lenin's tongue). From 1921 to 1926, he headed the party committee in Azerbaijan, continuing his close cooperation with Ordzhonikidze in Georgia, and then came up North—very unwillingly, as he loved Baku—to head the Leningrad party committee after Zinoviev's ouster. Because of the circumstances of his death (he was murdered in 1934), there has been a tendency to canonize him as the liberal on the Stalin team. There is no real evidence for this, but he was not one of the more enthusiastic shedders of blood, by all accounts an attractive man who, childless himself, liked children and was popular with his peers. Stalin and his wife both became very attached to him. They used the intimate *ty* with one another from at least 1922, Kirov calling Stalin by his Caucasus nickname, "Koba."[14]

The Stalin who these men saw and accepted as their leader was very different from Trotsky's nonentity. He was a "very strong character," Molotov remembered, talking to Felix Chuev decades later: decisive, talented, and full of initiative, with a clarity of vision others didn't have. There were good people around him but none at the same level: "we were milk-drinkers" by comparison. Above all, he was the man the revolution needed after Lenin's death: it was the party's "great good fortune" that Stalin was there to take over. "Many revolutions collapsed. In Germany, in Hungary. In France—the Paris Commune. But we held on." "He was iron, tough, calm," Kaganovich said, "a person that was internally under control, mobilized all the time. He never let a word fall from his lips that he hadn't thought about. . . . I always saw him thinking. He would be talking to you but at the same time thinking. And purposeful."

Purposeful sounds right for Stalin, but what were his purposes? His team wasn't gathered on the basis of policy choices. This made it different from the group forming around Trotsky (the "Left," as it came to be called), who wanted to develop central planning and push forward with industrialization. It also distinguished it from "the Right," those inclined toward moderate policies and caution in dealing with the peasantry, including Politburo members Bukharin, Rykov, Tomsky, Kalinin, and often Voroshilov. In the mid-1920s, a "Rightist" policy orientation was quite compatible with membership of Stalin's team, which Trotsky perceived as a policy-neutral bloc of "party bureaucrats." Nikolai Bukharin, the most visible spokesman for moderation, was a close friend of Stalin's in the mid-1920s, treated for a while as his no. 2 man, on a level with Molotov. When Trotsky and his supporters attacked Bukharin for his "softness" on the peasantry, Stalin famously interjected, "You demand Bukharin's blood? We won't give you Bukharin's blood." In other words, Stalin could look and sound like a Rightist himself.[15]

With Trotsky's defeat, tensions soon emerged in the Central Committee majority. Each successive party congress added new members to the Politburo—Molotov, Voroshilov, and Kalinin at the end of 1925, then Kuibyshev and Rudzutak in 1927, with Andreev, Kaganovich, Kirov, and Mikoyan as new candidates—and almost all the new members were Stalin supporters. None were linked to Zinoviev, the other Politburo member who could be regarded as a leadership contender. This reflected Stalin's dominance of the party's secretariat, which in turn controlled the selection of delegates to the party congresses that elected the Central Committees and, ultimately, the Politburo. Zinoviev, who had already flubbed one chance to insert himself into this process, remained unhappy about Stalin's control of the party machine but let it happen, except in his own bailiwick of Leningrad, where he built up a machine of his own. A vain man, he was no doubt confident that his visibility as an orator and his position as head of the Soviet-led international Communist organization, the Comintern, as well as the Leningrad party organization, would keep him at the top. Stalin and his group cordially disliked Zinoviev, whom they referred to as Grisha, in a spirit of disrespect, not affection. He was a show-off and a coward, Molotov said; his ally Yury Kamenev, head of the Moscow Soviet and a former underground committeeman, was the one with character, for all that Zinoviev thought he was boss in their alliance. Stalin used the familiar form *ty* with Kamenev. Yet it was Kamenev who at the end of 1925 denounced Stalin as aspiring to be the party's *vozhd'*, a leader above all others.

Supreme personal power is certainly an answer to the question about Stalin's purposes, and it is the answer that is usually emphasized to the exclusion of all others. But it's rare that anyone's purposes are so simple, and Stalin was not a simple man. He wanted power to achieve revolutionary purposes, because he believed in the particular kind of party-led, state-controlled, socialist modernization that Lenin had espoused. In addition, he and his team regarded themselves in the 1920s as playing a *defensive* game, however aggressively: their purpose was to defeat the factions and preserve the unity of the party. This is not to say that Kamenev may not have correctly discerned Stalin's private ambitions, but the factional issue was the immediate one. For Stalin and Molotov in the 1920s, fighting the factions was a single-minded preoccupation, exhilarating to the point that other concerns were temporarily sidelined. It was not until about the end of the decade, after the defeat of the Left Opposition, that government, as opposed to politics, gained their serious attention.[16]

Stalin and his team didn't seem like the wild men of Soviet politics during this period. Stalin and Molotov favored a public style that one historian aptly refers to as "militant moderation," tough but never as strident as their opponents. They generally left others—Zinoviev and Kamenev in the fight against Trotsky, Rykov and Bukharin in the later fight against Zinoviev and Kamenev—to wield the hatchet most violently. No doubt this was a calculated tactic, but it won them many admirers in the party. Nikita Khrushchev, who first encountered Stalin as a junior Ukrainian delegate to party congresses in Moscow in the mid-1920s, was struck by his commitment to party unity and his relatively tolerant way of dealing with his opponents, which compared favorably to the shrill polemical style of the Opposition; he thought Stalin had "a democratic spirit." From his perch down in Rostov, Mikoyan admired Stalin's adroitness in debate: he would wait until the Opposition had put all its cards on the table, jousting with other Stalin team members, and then take the floor, "calmly and with dignity, not in a tone of sharpening the conflict but, on the contrary, damping it down." He wasn't arrogant, didn't hector, and always managed to make his opponents look like the aggressors.

The decisive moment in the fight with Zinoviev came in the winter of 1925–26, when the Stalin group, having officially split with Zinoviev and Kamenev at the recent party congress and gained majority support, dislodged Zinoviev from Leningrad. Molotov headed the high-powered team, including Kirov, Voroshilov, Kalinin, Andreev, and Bukharin, that swept into Leningrad to break the machine and get the Leningrad party to condemn Zinoviev and his men as breakers of party unity. It was a matter of "taking" the key factories' party organizations one by one, as Molotov, with a nice use of military metaphor, wrote to Stalin. Voroshilov was like an old warhorse sniffing battle; it was as if he were back in 1905 again, he wrote exultantly to his friend Ordzhonikidze: "I literally got younger." Kirov, the designated successor to Zinoviev, was still hoping to avoid the Leningrad job and complained bitterly in private letters about his "terrible" mood, the "very very difficult" situation, the twenty-four-hour workday, and the hostility of the Leningraders. It was a "desperate fight, unlike any we've had before," and at first he wasn't at all sure they would win. But they did, and he was stuck with Leningrad, which, after a while, he came to love.[17]

The great faction fight was something that went on in the capitals, Moscow and Leningrad (as Petrograd was renamed after Lenin's death), with relatively little provincial involvement, and ex-provincials like Kirov, Mikoyan, and Ordzhonikidze had to be persuaded to take it seriously. Ordzhonikidze hated faction-fighting: back in 1923–24, he had been so depressed by the quarrel with Trotsky that he told his friend Voroshilov privately that "whoever ends up on top . . . , it will be a defeat for our party." The sharpness of Rykov's attack on Zinoviev and Kamenev at one Politburo meeting upset him to the point that he burst into tears and walked out. Voroshilov had to work hard to make him see that there was no alternative to bashing the "splitters." Even after he accepted this necessity, agreeing that "We're not going to let them build another party, and we'll send them to the devil out of our party," he remained much less willing than Stalin to break personal relations with political opponents. True, he had more friends to lose in the first place.

Mikoyan was another who had to adjust his perspective once he moved to Moscow. Down in the North Caucasus, the economy was booming, the party was united, and things seemed to be going just fine. But in Moscow he found that people were constantly talking as if there was a crisis. Kamenev, whom he personally liked and whose job as trade minister he was inheriting, was terribly pessimistic and discouraged, feeling the revolution had entered a new and potentially catastrophic phase. No doubt Kamenev's pessimism owed a lot to his recent political defeats, but the Stalin people were not overflowing with optimism either. They and the Opposition were starting to trade accusations about responsibility for the "degeneration" of the revolution and disillusionment of youth, agreeing about the phenomenon although disagreeing about who was to blame. "We are meant to be going forward economically," Kuibyshev (who headed the supreme economic council, Vesenkha) told his Politburo colleagues in 1928, "but we're not: the economic figures are just terrible, and we're actually going backward." If they wanted to press ahead with industrialization, the Politburo agreed, they just *had* to get foreign credits. But was any capitalist country going to extend them? The prospects looked grim, especially as diplomatic relations with Britain, intensely suspicious of Soviet espionage and Communist subversion, had just been broken off.[18]

Trotsky's and Zinoviev's Oppositions united after Zinoviev's defeat in the winter of 1925–26, but it didn't do them much good. Neither group could forget the abuse hurled by the other in past years, and neither leader had a real power base. Zinoviev lost his Leningrad job at the beginning of 1926 and was dropped from Politburo membership six months later on the pretext that a supporter had organized an illegal conspiratorial meeting. Kamenev, removed from the Politburo, was sidelined directing the Lenin Institute. Trotsky, who had been pressured to resign from the defense ministry in January 1925, had since that time held relatively minor economic positions. He remained a member of the Politburo until October 1926, however, outlasting Zinoviev by a few months ("It's better to hit them separately," Stalin explained to Molotov).

Bukharin once said that in dealing with his enemies, Stalin was a master of "dosage," meaning that he undermined them step-by-step rather than cutting them off with one stroke. For Politburo members, the first step was to be excluded from the leadership meetings where the *real* business was conducted, a technique first used against Trotsky in 1924–25 when a so-called Group of Seven, consisting of all the Poliburo members except him, met regularly every Tuesday. Molotov, with his disciplined civil-service mind, assumed this was a temporary expedient, but Stalin, who understood the power of exclusion, thought otherwise: Groups of Seven, Five, Eight, or whatever the magic number was at any given time, with a shifting membership close to but not identical with that of the Politburo, continued to meet throughout the Stalin period. The next stage was formal removal from the Politburo, followed by removal from the Central Committee, and finally from the party. (That was considered the ultimate sanction until the end of the 1920s, when things got substantially nastier.) No doubt this incremental approach was a product of Stalin's caution: the team, after all, might balk at a particular exclusion, as sometimes happened, or some drawback to the plan might become evident. But at the same time it had a tinge of sadism: the defeated hung twisting in the wind for a long time, begging for clemency and reinstatement. Molotov and other more straightforward faction-fighters would probably have ousted Trotsky from the Politburo long before this point, but Stalin's tactic was to isolate him and other Oppositionists until they ended up as total outcasts, if not gibbering wrecks.

The dosage approach was aimed at getting the Stalin team on board, as well as undermining the victims. Not all members of the team were as keen as Stalin and Molotov on outcasting old comrades; they may, for example, have drawn the line at dropping Kalinin in 1930. Earlier, when Stalin wanted to get Zinoviev and Trotsky off the Central Committee, he let Molotov take the heat while he went on vacation. As Molotov reported, Kaganovich and Kirov were fully on board, but Kalinin, Ordzhonikidze, and Rudzutak were dubious, and Mikoyan had evaded the issue by staying away from the meeting. Stalin expressed surprising equanimity about Rudzutak's and Mikoyan's wavering, but he was annoyed about Ordzhonikidze's lack of active support ("Where was Sergo . . . Why was he hiding? Shame!"). When it turned out that Voroshilov was hesitating too, Molotov told Stalin he needed to come back from vacation early and quell the incipient rebellion. Stalin agreed to do so, but added that he wasn't too disturbed about the waverers, for reasons that "I'll explain when I come." Alas, we don't know what those reasons were, but it sounds as if he thought he had some leverage—perhaps a spot of implicit blackmail about past sins—to get the errant team members back in step.[19]

By 1926, the relative courtesy of public exchanges between Oppositionists and the Central Committee majority, characteristic of earlier years, had long gone. At party congresses, Oppositionists were now mercilessly heckled. Even in Central Committee meetings, Trotsky said he was "constantly interrupted by whistling, shouts, threats, [and] swear words"; it reminded him of the tumultuous days in Petrograd between the February and October Revolutions. In the Politburo, too, exchanges grew sharper. Trotsky was not bashful about expressing his opinions and launching ad hominum attacks, and he and Molotov had a shouting-match in May in which the infuriated Molotov called him a "natural-born insinuator"—a strange, bookish word to use, perhaps an attempt to show Trotsky that he was an educated man, too. There was more angry backbiting in Politburo meetings in 1926 and 1927. Voroshilov told Zinoviev he wouldn't trust him with a kopek. Trotsky sneered at Rudzutak's allegedly limited intellectual gifts, which, he gratuitously added, even Stalin made fun of in private, which prompted a furious Rudzutak to call Trotsky a "specialist in slander."

Stalin and Trotsky went after each other hammer and tongs in September 1927, when the Politburo and the Central Control Commission met to discuss the Opposition. Trotsky, present by invitation though no longer a Politburo member, responded to an interjection from Stalin with a sharp rebuke: "Comrade Stalin, don't interfere, you will have the final word, as always," and when Stalin objected, he added, "You always take the floor at the end in order to put forward some new lie, tale-bearing, and slander and send it out through the party office." It only got worse from then on:

> STALIN: You are telling lies because you are a pitiful coward, fearing the truth.
> TROTSKY: If I was so awful, why did the party keep me in charge of [the] army[?]
> STALIN: You are a pathetic person, deprived of an elementary feeling for truth, a coward and a bankrupt, a brazen and insolent fellow,

allowing yourself to say things that have absolutely no relationship
to reality. That's my answer.

TROTSKY: That's him alright: coarse and disloyal as ever.

It was unusual for Stalin to lose his cool to that extent, but Trotsky had
that effect on people. Normally, especially in national party meetings,
Stalin was able to take the high road. After letting Rudzutak and Bukharin do the hatchet job on Zinoviev at one party conference, he came in
with some gentle mockery: Zinoviev, he said, "once claimed he could put
his ear to the ground and hear the footsteps of history, but now, since he
hasn't noticed that party has turned its back on the Opposition, he should
go and have his ears checked." The delegates—virtually all Central Committee majority men by now—loved it; not only was there "stormy and
prolonged applause" for Stalin's jest but he got a standing ovation at the
end.[20]

The Opposition was not the team's only concern at this time. The
Comintern's policy of cooperation with the Kuomintang in China, advocated by Stalin and Bukharin against criticism from Trotsky, ended in a
debacle when the Kuomintang massacred their Communist allies in
Shanghai in April 1927. The British broke off diplomatic relations in May,
leaving the Soviet leaders wondering if this was a prelude to a new Western war of intervention. Increasing nationalist resistance in the border regions of Ukraine and Georgia, with active foreign support, was reported
by the Soviet internal security agency, the OGPU (security police force).
Soviet alarm came to a head when the Soviet envoy to Poland was assassinated by a Russian émigré monarchist at a Warsaw railway station in June,
and simultaneously a bomb was thrown in a party club in Leningrad. Of
the assassination, Stalin wrote to Molotov: "One feels the hand of England. They want to repeat Sarajevo [the assassination of Archduke Franz
Ferdinand, which was the trigger for the First World War]." The OGPU's
response, obviously approved by Stalin, was to conduct mass arrests of
suspected traitors (former aristocrats and so on) and summarily execute
twenty of them as a warning. "London's agents sit deeper in us than we
thought," was Stalin's comment to OGPU chief Vyacheslav Menzhinsky.
The OGPU must be strengthened, military intelligence beefed up, and
more security precautions put in place in the Caucasus. The British espionage network should be rooted out and their spies put on show trial.

The Soviet leaders were telling the public to brace themselves for a new military intervention by the capitalist powers, who were eager to finish the job they had begun during the Civil War. Whether they literally believed this is debatable, but they were certainly extremely jittery, especially Voroshilov, the defense minister, who repeatedly warned his colleagues that the military was underfunded, and there would be hell to pay "if our enemies [abroad] find out" about the army's parlous state. One of the things that was really bothering the security-minded Stalin was that their enemies were indeed receiving such information, because the Politburo was leaking like a sieve. This was not a paranoid fantasy but attested to by the treasure trove of Politburo and OGPU documents from the late 1920s found by historians in German archives. Politburo documents were meant to have limited circulation, with rules requiring return of materials after reading, but the rules were often flouted. No wonder there was constant uneasiness in the Politburo about keeping official minutes of their meetings: when they did, the minutes were leaked, not only within the party but also abroad. Stalin seems to have thought that Oppositionists were slipping the documents to old Menshevik friends, who in turn sent them out covertly to German Social Democrats, but it looks as if another, more direct route led from the Kremlin (by whose hands is not known) to the German Embassy in Moscow.[21]

The tenth anniversary of the October Revolution came around in early November 1927. According to the OGPU, the Opposition planned a coup attempt during the celebrations that was called off only at the last minute because of Trotsky's doubts. No confirmation of this has been found in the Trotsky archive at Harvard, and Menzhinsky's extremely alarmist reports to the Politburo may be taken with a grain of salt, all the more given his assertion that, despite the enormity of the threat, it could be completely eliminated if the Politburo would just allow the OGPU to arrest a few ringleaders. Stalin, who probably encouraged Menzhinsky to sound the alarm, dissociated himself from his most extreme positions while basically endorsing the need for radical measures against the Opposition. Some Oppositionists, though as yet none of the leaders, had already been arrested—a new departure in Soviet political practice—and Menzhinsky suggested that it might be necessary to "arrest them all overnight." Stalin did not endorse this, but proposed expelling the Opposition leaders from the party. The trouble they were causing was undermining Soviet foreign policy, because in London and Washington, "the view is held that our present government is on the verge of collapse, that the Opposition is about to take the helm, and that, therefore, it is pointless to conclude any agreements with us."

The Oppositionists' actions would be considered "high treason" in capitalist states and would therefore be punishable by death, Stalin wrote to the Central Committee and Central Control Commission sometime toward the end of 1927, "and I see no reason why we should not protect the dictatorship of the proletariat with the strictest measures." The "high treason" argument was predicated on the idea that the Soviet Union was essentially in a war situation because of the acute foreign threat, and the Stalinists made much of the fact that Trotsky had said that even war would not lead him to abandon his criticism of the Stalin regime. No wonder Trotsky had started thinking about the guillotine. In the French Revolution, he said, the Jacobins had used it first against the enemies of the revolution, just as the Bolsheviks had, and that was no problem, a revolutionary necessity. But then the Jacobin Robespierre (read: Trotsky) had been guillotined, and that was another matter, for it was done by counter-revolutionary Thermidorians (read: Stalin) and marked the end of the revolution.[22]

Trotsky wasn't guillotined, at least not yet, but he might have felt he was about to be lynched at a joint meeting of the Central Committee and party Control Commission in October, when, in addition to the constant heckling, "inkpots, heavy volumes, and a glass" were flung at Trotsky's head as he spoke, and he was shoved off the podium. One of the book-throwers was Emelian Yaroslavsky, an Old Bolshevik member of Ordzhonikidze's Control Commission, who wrote to Ordzhonikidze, not too shamefacedly, that Trotsky and his supporters had "behaved so outrageously and were so insulting to us Bolsheviks, that, despite having vowed to myself not to lose my temper, I lost it and threw *The Control Figures of Gosplan* at him." Stalin was the only one to stay calm, according to Trotsky. Members of the team refrained from physical violence, but none of them publicly dissented from the condemnation of Trotsky, which doesn't mean they were all happy about it. Bukharin, who broke the news of the expulsion to Trotsky in a telephone call, expressed sympathy ("Things must not stay like that. You must return"), without mentioning that he had spoken against him in the discussion. Ordzhonikidze, despite his position as head of the Control Commission, managed to be absent for health reasons through the crucial month of October. Stalin, expressing warm concern for his health and keeping him informed about the fight with the Opposition, did not urge a speedy return, which suggests there may have been something to the rumors that Ordzhonikidze was being kept out of the way intentionally because he was uneasy about the expulsions. "Maybe it's just as well you weren't there," as Yaroslavsky put it.[23]

The formal decision to expel Trotsky and other Opposition leaders from the party was ratified the next month by an obedient (but also enthusiastic) party congress. It had been decided not to charge Trotsky with treason, Menzhinsky said, because "we found a much more skillful solution," namely, deportation of Opposition leaders to remote areas of the Soviet Union far from the big cities. Menzhinsky spoke of this explicitly as an alternative to the death sentence, which might otherwise have been imposed. Trotsky and his household were sent off to Alma-Ata in Kazakhstan in January 1928.

Trotsky remained defiant and unapologetic, but Zinoviev and Kamenev capitulated, not renouncing their opinions but accepting the will of the majority and promising not to split the party or try and organize outside of it. They were expelled nonetheless, and Kamenev's dignified attempts to be conciliatory without groveling were met with jeers. The Stalin team laid into the Opposition with a will: What does it matter losing a bunch of intellectuals from the party, said Rudzutak; they have no credibility except with the international bourgeoisie. They are nothing but troublemakers, said Kaganovich: at their expulsion, "a sigh of relief burst forth from the breasts of hundreds of thousands of party members and millions of proletarians." Hypocrites, said they all, and lucky to have been treated as gently as they had been (Lenin wouldn't have "nannied" them like we have done, said Rykov, generally thought of as a moderate). If they've fallen off the cart of history, who cares, said Stalin, it only means we don't have to trip over them as we march forward.[24]

Internal deportation, it turned out, was not enough to eliminate Trotsky as a political presence. An underground Opposition organization remained active, though thanks to the dispersal of its leaders and the necessity for written correspondence, the OGPU knew as much about its activities as Trotsky did. The team regularly received large dossiers of intercepted Opposition materials from the OGPU, which must have made curious reading for these veterans of prerevolutionary conspiracy, especially because the subjects of surveillance were people they knew well. The OGPU gave Trotsky an ultimatum to desist from oppositional activity, but he refused. Stalin was for expelling him from the country, an expedient Lenin had used on political opponents (but not his fellow party members) back in 1922. There were waverings about this on the team: in the decisive vote, Kuibyshev voted against it, as did Tomsky and Rykov (the last saying he was afraid Trotsky would be assassinated by counterrevolutionaries). Bukharin, who had been one of Trotsky's most savage attackers earlier, had had a change of heart and voted against expulsion, but then at the last minute, when Trotsky was already on his way under OGPU escort, he switched his vote to side with the majority.

Expelling Trotsky turned out to be not altogether simple: Stalin might think he had betrayed the party, but for Europe, Trotsky personified the Communist threat, and Germany, his preferred destination, refused to take him in. The fallback position was Turkey. Trotsky was taken across the Soviet border en route to Istanbul on 11 February 1929, leaving his homeland forever. It was a ruthless way of dealing with him, if less extreme than the Menzhinsky option of execution as a traitor. As Molotov explained to an admirer long after, Trotsky couldn't have been killed in 1929, as it would have been a stain on the party's reputation. But at least he and the other Oppositionists were out of the way. Stalin and his team had won the factional struggle that had preoccupied them for the past five years. Power was theirs. The question was: What were they were going to do with it?[25]

TWO

THE GREAT BREAK

STALIN'S ANSWER TO THE QUESTION OF WHAT TO DO WITH POWER WAS simple and surprising: make a revolution. That wasn't what most people had expected of him. Perhaps he had not even expected it of himself before victory over the factions emboldened him. It was a revolution from above rather than from below, of course, though not without substantial popular mobilization. The point of the revolution was to "build socialism" in the shortest possible time, which in practice meant a crash modernization program. The whole urban economy, including trade, was to be taken into state hands and to become subject to centralized planning. The First Five-Year Plan was to launch rapid industrialization. Peasant farming was to be collectivized, and the allegedly voluntary aspect of the process was not to be taken too seriously. The "class enemies" of socialism, at home and abroad, would be fearlessly confronted: let them understand once and for all that the Soviet regime was not to be trifled with. Stalin called the whole package "the great break."

If much of this sounded like Trotsky and the Left's program, Stalin didn't really care. It was the maximal version of the options that had emerged from the policy debates of the 1920s, and now that he had power, he was going to be a maximalist. At some point during these years, the idea must have taken root in Stalin's mind that by launching Russia's second revolution, the economic one, he could put himself up with Lenin, the leader of the political revolution in 1917, in the history books. He had no doubt that this would require the same uncompromising toughness and willingness to use force as the first revolution; indeed, he probably welcomed this. Even before he had decided to take the plunge, he was very clear that socialist modernization would mean breaking heads. The core question about proceeding to Russia's second (economic) revolution, he suggested in 1926, was whether the Soviet Union had the strength, and presumably the will, to take on and defeat its internal class enemies. By 1928, he had decided that the will was there.

In introducing the New Economic Policy (NEP) back in 1921, Lenin had stressed that the retreat from the maximalism of the Civil War period was "serious and for a long time." By this, he meant to convince doubting Communists, who wanted to keep on making revolution, that the change had to be for real if the new state was going to survive. Nevertheless, it was a tactical retreat, not a change of objective, and at some point, if the party stayed revolutionary, the retreat would have to end. "Not tomorrow, but in a few years" was Lenin's last utterance on the question of when "NEP Russia would become socialist Russia." Six years had passed since then, and the economy had strengthened. As Stalin would tell the Central Committee in July 1928, "the position of permanent retreats is not our policy."[1]

Outsiders looking at NEP hoped that, after going through its revolutionary turmoil, Russia was slowly returning to normality; it was assumed that as time passed, common sense would increasingly prevail and utopian revolutionary ideals be forgotten. This would indeed happen in time, but not yet. The general population—"philistines," as the Bolsheviks liked to call them—were in favor of a return to normality, but the party activists were still raring for a fight. The activists in the party and its youth branch, the Komsomol, had not been happy with the socially conciliatory policies of NEP, which required them to refrain from pushing peasants around, let the backward masses go to church, and respect the greater knowledge of "bourgeois specialists," that is, the intelligentsia. They wanted more "class struggle," as they had known it during the Civil War, so that they could show priests, traders, kulaks (prosperous peasants), and the bourgeoisie who was in charge now. The outsiders' hope of a return to normality was the Bolsheviks' fear: they called it Thermidor, after the month of Robespierre's defeat in the French Revolution, and worried immensely in the second half of the 1920s about whether signs of revolutionary "degeneration" were already visible. Trotsky taunted Stalin with aspiring to be a Thermidorian, but he was wrong. The role to which Stalin evidently aspired was the same one as Trotsky: the Robespierre of the Russian Revolution.

The Bolshevik Party called itself a workers' party, but in the 1920s it was also a party of Civil War veterans. For the large proportion of party members who had fought or served as political commissars in the Red Army, the Civil War was the great formative and bonding experience. This was the source of the macho culture in the party, a fellowship of hardened male veterans who liked to drink and smoke together, and who still usually wore a version of military uniform, with belted tunic and high boots, in civilian life. The Stalin team shared this culture and dressed in this way in the 1920s. Most of them had been at the fronts during the Civil War, often bonding with each other when they served together.

A new willingness, even gusto, for using force against enemies was noticeable in the Stalin team's demeanor in the wake of the Left Opposition's defeat. Two categories of class enemies came immediately under fire in the first months of 1928. The first were kulaks, who were supposed to be hoarding the grain necessary to feed the towns and the army. Despite a good harvest in the autumn of 1927, peasant grain sales fell far below expectations. One response on the part of the leadership might have been to raise prices as an incentive for peasants to bring their grain to market, but at a time when the state was planning to make major investments in industry, this was an unattractive option. Stalin came up with a different solution. In a rare trip outside the capital, Stalin visited Siberia in the spring of 1928 and decided that sales were down not because producers were holding out for a better price but because bad peasants ("kulaks") were withholding the grain, their motive being to sabotage Soviet power. Since this was in essence counterrevolutionary behavior, the answer was to use force to get the grain out of the villages and hit the hoarders with prison terms.

This was the beginning of an escalation of hostilities between the state and the peasantry that ended up in general forced collectivization, which gave the state more leverage in ensuring that the peasants accepted low prices and kept up grain deliveries. To make collectivization stick, the Stalinists introduced a ruthless intimidatory measure (their own innovation, not part of the playbook of the Left), namely, the arrest and deportation of kulak households. Kulaks were hard to define exactly, since exploitation of other peasants and anti-Soviet attitudes, as well as comparative prosperity, were criteria, and the term became a catchall for peasant troublemakers. It is estimated that four million peasants were uprooted in 1930–31, though many of these fled from their villages on their own rather than being deported by the state. The intimidatory and traumatic impact was also felt by the peasants remaining in the village, most of whom signed up, however unwillingly, in collective farms within a few years. The campaign against kulaks was combined with a savage campaign against churches and mass arrests of priests. While Stalin's wager that massive force from the OGPU and, where necessary, the army would prevent major peasant revolt proved correct, peasant disturbances were registered all over the Soviet Union. The collectivization campaign launched in the winter of 1927–28 was the beginning of a five-year battle with the peasantry that Stalin told Churchill was the greatest challenge the revolution ever faced and Molotov later described as a "more significant victory" than the Second World War.

It was Stalin who took the initiative in these great struggles, showing a firmness and boldness that inspired the rest of the team and convinced them of his outstanding qualities as a leader. The rashness of Stalin's new policies sometimes took their breath away, not to mention his penchant for coercion, but they admired him for it (and so, after a while, did some of the former Left Oppositionists). Of the team members, Molotov was Stalin's closest ally in launching the Great Break, his unfailing supporter on the need for toughness, and the one most privy to his sometimes remarkably devious machinations against opponents and allies. In later life, it was a matter of pride to Molotov that the harsh measures he used to get out the grain on a trip to Ukraine early in 1928 had inspired Stalin to go off to Siberia a few months later and come up with something even harsher: prosecution of "hoarders" under the criminal code.[2]

The OGPU was an indispensable player in the struggle with the peasantry, but this was not the only field in which its activities were expanding. From the late 1920s, it had been drawn into the party's factional fights on the Stalin side, exiling Oppositionists and keeping their underground organizations under surveillance. Private traders and middlemen had been arrested and their property confiscated. The foundation of the future Gulag empire was laid, as camps were established for a new influx of peasants and urban traders; soon, the OGPU would be supplying new

industrial construction projects with convict labor. The OGPU and Stalin worked well together, though the assumption that the OGPU leaders
were Stalin's men seems—with regard to the period before 1937—premature. After the departure of Dzerzhinsky, a major political figure in his
own right who was usually a Stalin ally, the OGPU was headed by people
who were neither of Politburo status nor known for any particular ties to
Stalin. Vyacheslav Menzhinsky, who headed the agency after Dzerzhinsky, was a cultured aristocrat and intellectual of Polish origins, a former
émigré Old Bolshevik and speaker of many languages with whom Stalin
had little in common, though this did not prevent them from setting up
an effective "good cop/bad cop" routine on the issue of punishing the
Opposition. As Menzhinsky's health declined, his deputy Genrikh Yagoda increasingly took over, efficiently organizing the kulak deportations. But he was so little Stalin's man that he was rumored to have
Rightist sympathies.[3]

Rapid industrialization on the basis of a state economic plan was the
cornerstone of the new program, the sine qua non in Bolshevik eyes for
moving toward socialism. Economic planning may not sound exciting
now, but it was trailblazing stuff in the 1920s, when *Man masters the economy* carried the emotional punch of *Man conquers space* forty years later.
What such an economic plan would look like had been debated since the
early 1920s, but the discussion was on hold for a few years in the mid-1920s
as the party's theoreticians and economic specialists argued about how it
could be paid for. Massive investment would be required, and it didn't
look as if loans and credits would be available from the West. The alternative of raising the money domestically seemed unpromising: there were
no real capitalists left, and "squeezing" the peasantry via taxation or terms
of trade was considered politically risky. Various versions of a First Five-
Year Plan were drafted and hotly discussed in 1926–27, the minimalist
coming from the State Planning Commission (where non-Communist
economists were influential), the maximalist from the Supreme Economic
Council, headed by team member Kuibyshev. Stalin himself barely participated in the debates on industrialization planning, but from 1924 the
top economic authority (Vesenkha) was always headed by a major figure
who was a Stalin ally or team member—Dzerzhinsky in the mid-1920s,
then Kuibyshev after Dzerzhinsky's death, and later Ordzhonikidze—so
we can assume Stalin shared the general opinion that it was a key post. By

the autumn of 1927, Kuibyshev was claiming that the Soviet economy was entering "a new phase of development which has no precedent in our history or in the history of other countries." They were about to embark on centralized state economic planning.

When the First Five-Year Plan was brought for approval of the XV Party Congress in December 1927 (the same congress that marked the defeat of the Left Opposition), the industrial ministry's maximalist line was in the ascendant, with Kuibyshev speaking in terms of much more ambitious industrialization targets than had been hitherto contemplated. Among his most enthusiastic supporters was Voroshilov, in charge of the military, who wanted a strong defense industry to support the Red Army. The threat of war seemed sufficiently real for the planners to be told to prepare a contingency First Five-Year Plan for the eventuality of armed attack, given "the probability of foreign intervention." For Stalin, rapid industrialization was nothing less than a matter of survival in the inevitable battle with the capitalist West. For all of Russian history, in Stalin's reading, Russia had been "beaten" and humiliated by foreign powers, and the capitalists were waiting to try it again as soon as opportunity presented. They would fail, but only if the Soviet Union brought off its ambitious industrialization plan. "To slacken the tempo would mean falling behind ... We are fifty or a hundred years behind the advanced countries. We must make good this distance in ten years. Either we do it or we shall go under."[4]

The Stalin team did not find a conventional economic solution for the problem of how to raise the money for the industrialization drive. Instead, they almost ignored it, apart from pushing grain exports regardless of domestic consumption needs. If investment capital was in short supply, cheap labor was plentiful, thanks to the stream of peasants fleeing collectivization to work in the towns and industrial construction sites and the availability of convict labor to work in inhospitable parts of the Soviet Union where free labor wouldn't go. Planning was still rudimentary, consisting largely of identifying priority projects, setting production targets, and punishing those who failed to meet them. It was a "crash through or crash" approach, powered by large doses of coercion and smaller ones of enthusiasm on the part of activists and the young. For the young enthusiasts, the experience was exhilarating, leaving lasting memories of comradeship, adventure, and struggle against the odds. The team felt something of the same exhilaration, along with a burden of responsibility and occasional stabs of panic. Stalin rose to the occasion, projecting unflinching purpose and the concentration of a general in battle.

Cultural Revolution was the order of the day, a precursor of China's better-known movement of the 1960s, which similarly involved mobilization of radical youth against class enemies, Rightists, and bureaucrats. In the countryside, kulaks and priests were the major victims; in the cities, non-Communist intellectuals and professionals. Alarm was whipped up about the untrustworthiness and potential for treason of "bourgeois specialists," as white-collar professionals were called. The message was dramatized by the Shakhty trial, held in the spring of 1928 in Moscow and given extensive press coverage. The anti-Soviet conspiracy of mining engineers in the Shakhty region of the North Caucasus was the discovery (or invention) of the local OGPU, but the elaboration of a narrative involving treasonous contacts with foreign intelligence and lax oversight by "Rightist" bureaucrats was done in Moscow under Stalin's close supervision. On a national scale, this was the first in a new genre of political theater in which anti-Soviet "wreckers" were accused of sabotage and other subversive activities on behalf of foreign intelligence. Some of Stalin's team were a bit bemused about the whole thing: Molotov suggested to Stalin after a few months of saturation press coverage that people were probably getting sick of it. But Stalin loved these trials, which clearly allowed the creative aspect of his personality (after all, he was a former poet) full rein. Whether he believed the literal truth of the accusations or simply understood them as symbolically true and politically useful is unclear, but he certainly took a keen interest in shaping the scenario.[5]

It might seem odd to go after engineers at the same time as launching an industrialization drive. Whereas it could be argued that the drive against kulaks, another class enemy, was a misplaced response to a real threat in the form of falling grain deliveries, it's hard to see how arresting engineers could be thought to increase industrial production. But anti-intellectualism always had popular appeal in Russia, and hostility to "bourgeois" engineers was widespread among factory workers, who saw them as representing old-style management. These attitudes were reflected in the Bolshevik Party, whose rank-and-file membership included many workers, especially the class-conscious kind. When the implications of the Shakhty Affair were discussed in the Central Committee in April

1928, the general mood was enthusiastically against "bourgeois" specialists; sixty speakers signed up to take part in the discussion. Stalin explained the political stakes: it was just like the Civil War, when "whole groups of military specialists, generals and officers, sons of the bourgeoisie and landowners" were ready to help military interventionists bring down Soviet power. Then the capitalists had launched a military and political intervention, whereas now it was an economic one. "They [the Western capitalists] want us to give up our revolutionary policy, and then they will be 'friends' . . . What do you think, comrades, can we go along with that?" There was a resounding cry of "No!"

The Stalin team, however, had varying reactions. Apart from the message of antibourgeois vigilance going out to the public, the specific policy implications were quite complex. Not fully articulated, but unmistakably present as a subtext, was the proposition that if things went wrong in industry, as they were bound to do given the ambitious targets of the Five-Year Plan, the proper response was to arrest people, more or less regardless of culpability, and charge them with "wrecking." Since industrial administrators (some of whom went on trial along with the engineers) had failed to detect the conspiracy, and were generally being accused of letting bourgeois specialists pull the wool over their eyes, they were in defensive mode, especially those from Ukraine, with its own coal mines. Kuibyshev, head of the industrial ministry, was worried by the shadow cast on engineers, a key component of his industrialization efforts. Kaganovich had no problems with arresting engineers or stepping up OGPU activities but, as party boss in Ukraine, he was uneasy about the implication that Ukrainian party officials had been lax. Andreev eagerly endorsed the need for more vigilance against enemies, and a future team member, Andrei Zhdanov, still out in Nizhny Novgorod but already buttering up Stalin in hope of promotion, took such a holier-than-thou posture about the need for vigilance that one of the Ukrainian delegates interjected sourly, "Is it wrecking when the people on duty are asleep?" Rykov, although the official rapporteur on the Shakhty Affair, clearly had reservations about blowing up its significance. Alone of the team, Tomsky, the trade unionist, struck an openly skeptical note, being inclined to see bad management and wasted money rather than intentional sabotage and conspiracy.[6]

The team response was complicated by the fact that a heated bureaucratic fight was under way between the industrial and education ministries about which of them should control higher technical education. This seemingly trivial issue was invested with all sorts of political overtones, because the education ministry was run by party intellectuals suspected of bourgeois liberal tendencies. Although Stalin unambiguously took the side of the industrial ministry at the April 1928 plenum of the Central Committee, a long and passionate discussion ensued, in which Molotov, Kaganovich, and, of course, Kuibyshev (as minister for industry) followed Stalin's lead, but Ordzhonikidze and Andreev were opposed; Tomsky and Rykov equivocated. Nadezhda Krupskaya, deputy head of the Russian education ministry, was one member of the education group who argued strongly against the Stalin/Molotov position, citing Lenin as her authority. The issue was sufficiently unresolved to require more discussion at the next Central Committee meeting in July. At this meeting, with Molotov as rapporteur strongly supporting transfer of higher technical schools from education to industry, no team member publicly opposed him, and the final vote recorded only seven dissents. But the leaders of the Russian and Ukrainian education ministries put up such spirited resistance that the ultimate adjudication was left to the Politburo, which duly voted for the transfer. It was the last occasion when team members publicly took different sides on a policy issue. Members of the team would disagree with one another and with Stalin in the future, but only within the confines of the Politburo.[7]

The team kept up an inhuman pace of work in the years of the Five-Year Plan. Core members of the Stalin team were constantly on the road, fighting (and sometimes laying fires) all over the nation, sending daily reports on local collectivization and industrial construction back to Moscow. It was a level of peripatetic activity unprecedented since the Civil War, and undoubtedly recalled those glorious days for the participants. Molotov, Kaganovich, and Mikoyan crisscrossed the country, particularly the main grain-growing regions, several times a year, pushing local officials to push the peasants. In the spring they were monitoring the sowing, in the autumn the harvest and grain deliveries. In 1928 alone, Molotov traveled to Ukraine, Russia's Central Black Earth region, and the Volga; Kaganovich went to the Central Black Earth region and the Lower Volga; and Mikoyan was in the North Caucasus, Ukraine, and the Central Black Earth region. Ordzhonikidze was also frequently on the road. Kalinin, the party's recognized peasant expert, was sent out less often, presumably because he was considered soft on peasants: these jobs were for the really tough members of the team. The pattern was repeated for years. Of course, as Molotov noted, they didn't know much about the village, but that was not the point: their task was to force local authorities to get maximum deliveries from the peasants, jolt them into a revolutionary and "vigilant" frame of mind, and back them up in tough measures, including mass arrests and deportations. Molotov was to claim in later life—contrary to most contemporary grassroots descriptions—that the party's efforts aroused a great positive response: "the country rose at once to collectivization. A stormy process began, which we hadn't expected. It turned out much better, much more successful."

Agriculture was one of the few major sectors of government without a specific team member in charge, probably because in the first stormy years of collectivization, Stalin and Molotov were so deeply engaged. They were assisted by Yakov Yakovlev, a bright young Jewish protégé of Stalin's, minister for agriculture from 1929 to 1934, who seems to have functioned almost as a team member for some years but was never appointed to the Politburo. Other team members were also closely involved. Mikoyan's baptism by fire as a team spokesman to the Central Committee was his report on grain procurements in April 1928. Andreev, sent down to the North Caucasus as regional party secretary early in 1928, had a similarly testing experience in November. Although he knew nothing about agriculture (he had "not yet completely liquidated my agronomic illiteracy," he admitted to the Central Committee), his task was to demonstrate the potential for rapid growth in agricultural output, despite the resistance of the class enemy, on the basis of the experience of his major grain-growing region. Stalin himself stayed in Moscow, after his memorable Siberian excursion, but was at his warmest encouraging the troops. "I could kiss you for how you acted there," Stalin told Molotov after he got back from cracking the whip in Ukraine in his January 1928 trip. When Mikoyan showed signs of flagging under the strain of the grain procurements battle, Stalin wrote supportively, "In a word, hold on and don't get depressed—our team must win."[8]

Industry became more and more central to the team's concerns after the adoption of the First Five-Year Plan in spring 1929, which inaugurated a crash program of industrial expansion throughout the Soviet Union. It wasn't just Kuibyshev, as industrial minister, who was intimately involved on a day-to-day basis. Ordzhonikidze was as well, since the state arm of his Control Commission had started an intensive investigation of the state of factories and industrial authorities, which produced a series of highly critical reports. As head of the government, which included both the state planning authority and the industrial ministry, Rykov had a lot to do with decision making on industry. For Kirov in Leningrad, Stanislav Kosior in Ukraine, and other republican and regional party secretaries, industrial development was a major preoccupation. Indeed, Kuibyshev, Stalin, and the Politburo as a whole were encountering an unexpected by-product of the economic plan: intensive lobbying for industrial investment from the heads of different industries and regions, Ukraine being particularly forceful. Kuibyshev started noticing the lobbying phenomenon after the XV Party Congress, when he found himself visited by a stream of party secretaries from the big industrial regions—Ukraine, the Urals, Western Siberia, Baku—hoping to persuade him to back big new projects. Correspondence between Stalin and Molotov during Stalin's yearly vacations started to be peppered with the names of particular industrial plants and construction sites. From 1929 onward, the Politburo regularly discussed the situation in particular sectors of heavy industry, on several occasions with Stalin as rapporteur, and every such discussion and subsequent resolution was preceded by heavy lobbying.[9]

At the same time, a new split in the leadership was in the making, this time with the Right. It was scarcely a surprise that those most closely associated with moderate policies in the 1920s—notably, Rykov, Bukharin, and Tomsky—should have reservations when Stalin switched to radical ones. They had weight in the leadership and visibility in the country, with Rykov heading the government, Tomsky the trade unions, and Bukharin the Comintern (as well as editing *Pravda*); in addition, all three were ethnic Russians, which was useful in terms of public opinion. (Kalinin, titular head of the Soviet government, was similarly inclined to moderation, though he ended up on the Stalin team, not with the Right.) Given that a comparative openness to debate still prevailed in the Politburo, they no doubt hoped to stay in as a moderating influence, awaiting the inevitable time when things settled down again, but in the meantime prepared to accept and publicly endorse decisions that went against them. Certainly, they had no thought of organizing an Opposition faction, having seen what happened to the last one, and never made the slightest move to do so. But it didn't suit Stalin to have internal dissenters on the team, however loyal. Mikoyan reports a curious conversation early in 1928, while riding back from the dacha one evening with Kirov and Ordzhonikidze, in which Stalin remarked casually that there were a few moderates who would doubtless drop out of top positions in the next few years, to be replaced by up-and-coming, hard-driving men like them. They were all shocked, Mikoyan says, being still in unity mode. But there were other warning signs, notably a very sharp attack on Rykov by Molotov in a discussion of the First Five-Year Plan in March 1928, which Tomsky later remembered as the beginning of the campaign against the Right.

While Rykov had always been an ally of Stalin's, rather than a member of Stalin's team, Bukharin and Tomsky had both been personally and politically close to Stalin in the mid-1920s. Indeed, during his vacations in 1925–26, Stalin addressed many of his communications jointly to Molotov and Bukharin, as acting team captains in his absence. Rykov and Tomsky were near contemporaries of Stalin's, Bukharin a decade younger. Rykov and Bukharin were among the party's intellectuals, educated men with connections to Lenin going back to the 1910s; Tomsky was a worker, a former printer who had worked with Lenin's wife Krupskaya in Saint Petersburg back in the 1890s and remained friendly with her after Lenin's death. Lenin had called Bukharin "the favorite of the party" in his "Testament," and this is broadly attested: just about everyone on the team used the intimate form of address with him. People often referred to him by diminutives of his surname—Bukharchik, Bukhashka—which were both affectionate and a shade condescending: his volatility and tendency to weep in public made his colleagues not take him entirely seriously, though he was recognized as a powerful orator, theorist, and polemicist. At the XV Party Congress, his standing, as measured by strength of applause recorded in the published minutes, was high: he came in third (along with Voroshilov) after Stalin and Kalinin, the popular "old man" of the party.

Bukharin became a close friend of Stalin's in the mid-1920s; he called him "Koba," Stalin's conspiratorial pseudonym from the prerevolutionary underground in the Caucasus, a name reserved for his intimates. Bukharin and his then wife, Esfir Gurvich, had a daughter, Svetlana, not much older than Stalin's own daughter, Svetlana, and the family was invited for lengthy stays at Stalin's dacha in Zubalovo; in 1927, at Stalin's suggestion,

Bukharin (though not Esfir, who was an emancipated career woman) moved into an apartment at the Kremlin, and they thus became neighbors. Their wives, both enrolled as students in Moscow higher educational institutions, were friendly, too. Tomsky and his wife were Kremlin neighbors whom Stalin often visited at home. Both Tomskys called Stalin Koba, as their son remembered, and Tomsky had a photo affectionately inscribed to "To my pal Mishka Tomsky."[10]

The increasingly militant tone of the party at the April and July plenums in 1928 alarmed the Right. They were worried about the escalating confrontation with the peasantry and what they saw as unrealistic targets in the First Five-Year Plan industrialization drive. Tomsky, as trade-union leader, was alarmed at the talk of working-class sacrifices in the cause of rapid industrialization and the strengthening of management powers vis-à-vis labor. At some point in the late 1920s, Tomsky and Stalin had a serious quarrel that brought their friendship to an end: as Tomsky family legend has it, Stalin's last friendly visit, bottle in hand, ended with Tomsky throwing him out with the words, "You're a bastard, a real bastard! Get out and take your bottle to the devil!"

Bukharin also reportedly had a shouting match with Stalin around this time, after which they did not speak for several weeks. Bukharin's unhappiness came to a head at the Central Committee plenum of July 1928. At the end of the meeting, he left the Kremlin with Grigory Sokolnikov, an Old Bolshevik intellectual of the Zinoviev faction with whom he had been friendly since childhood. Exactly what happened next is a matter of dispute. Bukharin (who tended to tell fibs when he was in trouble) told Anna Larina, his future third wife, that he and Sokolnikov had run into the disgraced Oppositionist Lev Kamenev by chance on the street and fell into a conversation that became emotional on Bukharin's part, but was in no way conspiratorial. Kamenev said that Bukharin and Sokolnikov showed up at his place unexpectedly after the plenum, but that he had had a meeting with Sokolnikov earlier in the day, where Bukharin's unhappiness with Stalin and the possibility of the Right's rapprochement with the Zinovievites had been discussed. This suggests that on Sokolnikov's part, at least, the affair had a conspiratorial aspect. From Stalin's point of view, it was clearly a conspiracy—a secret meeting whose purpose was the formation of a block between the old Zinovievite Opposition and the Right. Whatever the exact circumstances, it was an act of incredible political folly on Bukharin's part, as he later admitted ("What a boy I was, what a fool!").

The Stalin interpretation certainly looks plausible in light of Kamenev's notes on the meeting, whose basic accuracy Bukharin later did not deny. In a state of high emotion during his conversation with Kamenev, he spoke of Stalin in a "tone of absolute hatred" and seemed to have no doubt that a split was inevitable. Identifying Rykov, Tomsky, and himself as a bloc, he said that "we consider Stalin's line ruinous for the revolution," and moreover described Stalin as "an unprincipled intriguer, who subordinates everything to keeping power" and was likely to put a knife in your back at any time. Stalin had instilled a "Genghis Khan culture" in the Central Committee. He was spying on them: the GPU was following them and tapping their telephones. Bukharin and his allies had come to see Zinoviev and Kamenev as infinitely preferable to Stalin. Kamenev pressed him on just who those allies were, and Bukharin implied that it was most of the Politburo, although not all were willing to come out and say so. The "blockhead Molotov, who gives me lessons in Marxism and whom we call 'stone-bottom,'" was a hopeless case, of course. But Rykov and Tomsky were absolutely committed, along with Bukharin, in opposition to Stalin; Andreev was with them, and police chief Yagoda was on board. The Leningrad people (that is, Kirov) "are in general with us, but took fright at the idea of the possible removal of Stalin." Voroshilov and Kalinin were sympathizers, but "betrayed us at the last minute," evidently because Stalin had some kind of hold over them. Ordzhonikidze was another sympathizer who had let them down, despite having "come round to my place and cursed out Stalin."

All this was duly noted by Kamenev and typed up by his secretaries for transmission to Zinoviev. As Bukharin should surely have anticipated, given his remarks about surveillance, Stalin soon had the report in his hands—he immediately gave it to Rykov to read, who was appalled at Bukharin's folly—and within a few months it had ended up in the hands of the outlawed Trotskyist Opposition, which put it into underground circulation. This was brought up for discussion and condemnation at a joint meeting of the Central Committee and the party Control Commission in April 1929.[11]

Stalin was furious when news of this betrayal reached him. In a handwritten note he passed to Bukharin at the Central Committee plenum in

April 1929, he wrote angrily (still using the familiar form of address), "You won't force me to be silent or hide my opinion . . . Will there ever be an end to the attacks on me?" Bukharin could have made the same complaint: from the standpoint of anybody but Stalin, *he* was the person being hounded at the meeting. Bukharin is said to have been shocked when Stalin publicly repudiated their friendship, saying that "the personal element is a triviality, and it's not worth taking time with trivialities. Yesterday we [he and Bukharin] were still personal friends, but now we have parted company with him on politics." The repudiation shouldn't have been a surprise. Not only had Bukharin, in fact, betrayed Stalin both personally and politically, but Stalin's statement about the "triviality" of personal ties was an axiom for the Bolsheviks, and indeed all Russia's revolutionaries going back to the nineteenth century. When Stalin said, "This is not a family circle, not a company of personal friends, but a political party of the working class," he was saying something completely obvious and unexceptionable in party terms—which is not to say that he was telling the whole truth about his feelings about the matter. The team was indeed "a company of personal friends," among other things, and Stalin had just heard that one of those friends had claimed to hate him and think his leadership disastrous, while others, including Kirov, to whom Stalin was particularly attached, and his old friends Ordzhonikidze and Voroshilov, were said to hold similar opinions.

Bukharin was remarkably slow to recognize the irreversible train wreck he had brought about, but he certainly noticed the semipublic campaign against him, orchestrated by Molotov, that was undermining him in the Comintern, attacking his writings on economics, and punishing his young disciples. One of the charges brought against him was that he was a hypocrite who publicly supported the party's collectivization policies but actually privately opposed them. This was of course true, but it was also a function of the rules of the game: once a decision was made within the Politburo, all members were supposed to support it outside. The alternative was to go public with disagreement and thus issue a factional challenge, as the Left had done. But Bukharin and his allies were desperate to avoid anything that could be construed as factional activity: they believed that Stalin was trying to paint them as splitters, as he had earlier done with the Left. "You're not going to get a new opposition!" Bukharin shouted at Stalin at the April 1929 plenum. "You're not going to get it. And not one of us is going to head [it]!" In an article in *Pravda*, "Notes of an Economist," Bukharin had published an Aesopian critique of industrialization policies, thus breaking the rules in what he hoped was a minor and deniable way, but he had also been maneuvered into public endorsement of policy that he privately opposed and, more embarrassing still, into public denunciation of the unnamed villains who sought to undermine it. It was an untenable position, and Stalin and Molotov gleefully made the most of Bukharin's discomfiture.[12]

True to Stalin's principle of dosage, the three Rightists were ousted from their positions gradually, and according to separate timetables, but it was clear to the team long before the final departures that they were on their way out. "Rykov and his gang must be driven out," Stalin wrote to Molotov in the autumn of 1929. *"But for the time being this is just between ourselves"* (italics in the original). Bukharin was formally removed from the editorship of *Pravda* in June 1929 and the leadership of the Comintern a month later, but, in fact, feeling himself undermined, he hadn't been going to work at either place since his return from summer vacation the year before, thus leaving himself open to accusations of slacking because of injured vanity. Tomsky, similarly, stopped going to work at the trade union office after Kaganovich was sent in as a watchdog, and was officially removed in June 1929. Rykov, a more prudent and slippery customer than the other two, soldiered on as head of the government, but the Stalinists made it increasingly difficult for him to get anything done. On New Year's Eve, December 1929, the three of them made a last-minute attempt at peacemaking, arriving unexpectedly at Stalin's apartment in the early hours, bearing a conciliatory bottle of Georgian wine. But it was too late. While they were not cast into outer darkness like the Left, having not in fact organized anything approaching a faction, they were dropped one by one from the Politburo—Tomsky in July 1929, Bukharin four months later, and Rykov in December 1930. After his removal as head of the government at the end of 1930, Rykov got a second-tier position—minister of communications—while Bukharin and Tomsky were given third-tier positions in economic administration.[13]

In the early stages of the parting of ways with the Right, the team—or at least some of its members—was inclined to hope for a reconciliation. "We honestly did not want to cut off Rykov, Tomsky and Bukharin," Mikoyan recalled, without clarifying exactly who "we" were. Molotov, as usual, was staunchly backing Stalin and, in his absence, monitoring the reliability of the rest of the team. Quite a few "friends [are] inclined to panic," he warned Stalin in August 1928, and he seemed to expect that some of these "political weathervanes"—perhaps a larger group than the three who ended up in disgrace—would have to be dropped from the team. Stalin was afraid that Mikoyan and Kuibyshev might be susceptible to Tomsky's arguments, so dropped a word to Kuibyshev that Tomsky was "a malicious person and not always honest," who, despite the appearance of friendship, was "planning to hurt you." Molotov was doing a bit of undermining of his own, as Kaganovich later remembered: "he would say [of Bukharin] he is a cunning fox; he is the Shuisky of our time." (Vasily Shuisky was a noble who played both sides in the seventeenth-century Time of Troubles and had a brief stint as tsar before being deposed in his turn.)

Ordzhonikidze, never an enthusiast for cutting off his friends, was at first strongly opposed to any further splits in the leadership. "We need to leave this behind us," he told Rykov in the autumn of 1928, using the intimate form of address. He was sure that there were no fundamental disagreements between the Rykov group and the rest of the team; it was just that last year's grain procurements problem had rattled everyone. He begged Rykov to do what he could to bring about a reconciliation between Bukharin and Stalin (though he knew enough about their estrangement to know that this would be difficult) and avoid at all costs getting into a fight on any policy issue. Dropping Rykov, Bukharin, and Tomsky from the team would be "ridiculous," "just madness." A month or so later, he was glad to be able to tell Voroshilov that "Misha [Tomsky] ... had conducted himself quite diplomatically," but expressed unhappiness about the covert critique of Politburo policy that Bukharin had published in "Notes of an Economist": "It's not good with Bukharin's article.Poor Bukharin is getting quite a hard time at the meetings. He shouldn't have written such an article. Have you read it? It's quite confused: Bukharchik didn't dare to come out and say openly what he wanted to say in that article, and therefore had a go both at the left and the right; as a result everyone is dissatisfied."

But once the content of his conversation with Kamenev became known to the team, sympathy with poor Bukharchik sharply declined. He had tarnished or insulted virtually everyone on the team, and for those who were his friends, the whole affair was peculiarly embarrassing. Indeed, Bukharin could scarcely have delivered a crueler blow to the team waverers (if such they were), or one more likely to have sent them scurrying back into the fold. Probably they had in fact been somewhat disloyal on occasion in private conversation, as who has not? Most likely none of them really wanted to see the Right cast out. Their wavering may have come as no surprise to Stalin, if OGPU surveillance of the leaders was as good as is claimed. But by sanctioning the release of Kamenev's notes, albeit only for the limited public of the Central Committee, Stalin had not only blown Bukharin out of the water but also sent a warning shot across the bows of Ordzhonikidze, Voroshilov, Andreev, Kirov, and Kalinin, and they reacted accordingly. "To hell with him [Bukharin]," Ordzhonikidze wrote to Voroshilov, who had complained to him after Bukharin's perfidy. "To our complete surprise, he turned out not to be a particularly decent person. He will do everything he can to create the impression that people are insulting and suppressing him, and at the same time he himself will pour shit on us."[14]

Deteriorating personal relations were evident at the Central Committee's April 1929 meeting, where the Bukharin-Kamenev conversation was discussed. Bored by Bukharin's long theoretical disquisition on the economy, and picking up on his use of the metaphor of winding a screw, Rudzutak interrupted with a scornful "Wind on, wind on," to which Bukharin responded, "I suppose you think that's very funny." Ordzhonikidze laughed, which further angered Bukharin. "So now laughing is forbidden?" Ordzhonikidze riposted, which led Bukharin to shoot back with a reference to Ordzhonikidze's notoriously volatile temper: "I know nobody forbade you to bash chauffeurs in the mug." When Bukharin baited him at a Politburo meeting, Voroshilov completely lost his temper, calling Bukharin a liar and a bastard and threatening physical violence. Voroshilov was embarrassed by his own behavior, as he told his friend Ordzhonikidze, but Bukharin was too much to bear: he was "just trash, a man capable of telling the most awful fibs in your face, putting on a particularly innocent and holy-bastardly expression on that Jesuitical face of his."

Voroshilov made a speech attacking the Right, along with their international capitalist sponsors, which he thought was a total flop ("I tortured the Leningraders with my speech and they won't ask me again"), but Stalin was ready with reassurance: "It was a good, principled speech. All the

[Herbert] Hoovers, [Austen] Chamberlains and Bukharins got hit where it hurts." But not everyone was getting encouragement from Stalin. When Kalinin was named in one of the (fake) confessions of experts accused of wrecking and sabotage—extracted by the secret police in 1930—Molotov, upon receiving the transcript, assumed it should be edited out, but Stalin quickly set him right: "*All* confessions without exception should be sent out to members of the Central Committee . . . That Kalinin has sinned cannot be doubted. Everything that they say about Kalinin in the confessions is the unvarnished truth." The Central Committee needed to be informed "so that in future Kalinin won't get mixed up with scoundrels." In other words, let Kalinin understand that, however high the respect in which he was held in the party, his position was not unassailable.[15]

Nevertheless, Kalinin stayed on the team, perhaps because the majority never came round to excluding him. The same was true of other "waverers" like Voroshilov and Ordzhonikidze, although it was the unwavering Molotov and Kaganovich who became Stalin's closest political confidants. Out in the provinces, future team members were being tested in battle, ready to be brought into Moscow as Mikoyan, Ordzhonikidze, and Kirov had been a few years earlier. Andrei Zhdanov was working in Nizhny Novgorod on the Volga, the site of a major new auto plant. A young man with intellectual pretensions ("I was always the best student in my school and graduated with top honors," he wrote in a 1922 résumé), Zhdanov was more notable for his obedience to changes in the party line than any particular efficiency in meeting First Five-Year Plan targets, but Stalin liked him. Lavrenty Beria was in the Caucasus, rising from head of the Georgian GPU to the head of the Transcaucasus party committee and, through his patron Ordzhonikidze, angling for promotion to Moscow, preferably in a party position, not a security one. He kept Ordzhonikidze and Stalin up-to-date on the intricacies of Caucasian politics, in which both retained a keen interest, and took advantage of Stalin's regular vacation trips to the South to curry favor. Beria's local leadership performance, both in the agricultural and industrial realm, seems to have been superior to Zhdanov's; he was efficient as well as tough, and, if his son is to be believed, managed to secure a First Five-Year Plan for Georgia that encouraged citrus and tea growing—implying a milder form of collectivization than elsewhere—as well as quell anticollectivization uprisings in Azerbaijan "with maximum cunning and minimal firepower."[16]

Stalin and others had initially expected future leaders to come out of the Institute of Red Professors and Sverdlov Communist University, which were set up in the early 1920s as Communist elite training institutions in the social sciences. But these students proved a disappointment. Highly politicized, they were prone to spend their time in ideological debate and factional politics—and, worse, the wrong kind of factional politics, as the students' favorite was the popular and approachable young theorist Bukharin. With the Cultural Revolution, Stalin and the team switched to a strong "class" policy in elite recruitment, favoring proletarians and party members and violently hostile to students from the old upper classes: "Throw them out of Moscow on their necks," Stalin wrote to Molotov, "and put in their place young lads, our people, Communists."[17]

Along with this policy of proletarian affirmative action went an abrupt shift in higher educational priorities toward engineering (now under the jurisdiction of the Stalinist industrial ministry, not the Rightist intellectuals from education), which in the 1930s became the most desirable credential for political as well as professional careers. Looking toward the future, almost all the Brezhnev-Kosygin team in power from the mid-1960s to the 1980s were engineering graduates, but they had precursors in two who joined Stalin's team in the mid-1930s: Georgy Malenkov and Nikita Khrushchev. Malenkov, from a noble Russian family and related by marriage to an Old Bolshevik contemporary and friend of Lenin's (Gleb Krzhizhanovsky), was a student in the early 1920s (after fighting in the Civil War) at the most prestigious of all Russian engineering schools, the Bauman Higher Technical School. According to his son, he was doing well enough for his professor of electrical engineering to encourage him to go on to graduate school, but he chose instead to go to work in the Central Committee office and rose under Stalin's patronage. Khrushchev, ethnically Russian, though spending his youth in Ukraine, was the son of a peasant who worked seasonally in industry, and Khrushchev himself was a factory worker from the age of fifteen. He joined the party in 1918, was mobilized into the Red Army during the Civil War, went into local party work in Ukraine in the 1920s, and became a protégé of Kaganovich's. He moved to Moscow in 1930, as a mature-age student—a beneficiary of proletarian affirmative action—with significant political experience behind him. His place of study was the Industrial Academy, academically less distinguished than the Bauman but with the special profile of providing higher education to working-class Communists like Khrushchev, who had missed out on it earlier. Fellow students included Dora Khazan (Andreev's wife) and Nadya Alliluyeva, whose friendship with Khrushchev may have first drawn him to Stalin's attention. At thirty-five, Khrushchev was probably too old and too busy with politics to learn much engineering, but he made his mark as the academy's party secretary, leading the battle against the Right. He was quickly rewarded by an appointment as second secretary to Kaganovich in the Moscow Party Committee.

In addition to the new men in the wings, there were some old ones renouncing past errors and making a comeback, albeit at a level below the Politburo. For some of the former Left Oppositionists, Stalin's industrialization drive had great appeal, not just because the policies had their origin in the Left but also because their implementation during the First Five-Year Plan period was such an exciting challenge. As of 1930, the Stalin team was riding high, with opposition defeated, strong support in the party rank and file, and launched on the kind of bold, aggressive program of social transformation that, seen from within, seemed natural for a revolutionary party. Foremost among the former Leftists who successfully applied for readmission to the party was Yury Pyatakov, once a close associate of Trotsky, who was soon serving as a key deputy to Ordzhonikidze at the ministry of heavy industry.

"The heroic period of our socialist construction has arrived," Pyatakov exulted. It was a sentiment shared by the team and enthusiastically embraced by the young Communists who served as the "shock troops" of collectivization, the industrialization drive, and the Cultural Revolution. Kaganovich, one of the team's most effective orators, told a Komsomol congress in 1931 that the future was theirs. The First Five-Year Plan had started "a gigantic thrust forward which will show the whole world that the hour is not far off when we shall catch up and surpass the most advanced country—the United States of North America [sic] . . . Socialism will be victorious . . . You will be masters of the whole world."[18]

THREE

IN POWER

"WHAT WONDERFUL TIMES THOSE WERE," EKATERINA VOROSHILOVA wrote in the 1950s, nostalgically remembering the social life of the team back when Nadya Alliluyeva, Stalin's young second wife, was alive. "What simple, genuinely good, comradely relations. And it's incomprehensible almost to the point of pain how, as time passed, life in the party became more complicated, and our mutual relations too." Kaganovich looked back on the early 1920s, when he first got to know Stalin, with equal affection. He and the others used to work until midnight at the Central Committee offices on Old Square and then go home to the Kremlin together. Kaganovich remembered walking home one winter night with Stalin, Molotov, and Kuibyshev—a cheerful bunch of young revolutionaries, still thin and hungry, with full heads of hair and moustaches. Kaganovich particularly remembered the moustaches, Kirov being the only one of the team without one, until hairless and moustache-less Khrushchev and Beria joined in the 1930s. There was no security detail back then. Stalin, in a fur hat with the earflaps dangling, was laughing and talking along with the rest, cracking jokes. They were a brotherhood of free men, Kaganovich said, using the Russian expression from the days of serfdom, *vol'nitsa*, which could also mean a gang of outlaws. Although they lived in the Kremlin, like the tsars, they did not see themselves as heirs to the tsars, and had trouble even seeing themselves as rulers.

"Old Bolsheviks" was the term coming into use for the select few who had joined the party before 1917. They were linked by memories of shared underground organization, exile, prison, emigration, and, above all, struggle. Within Stalin's team in the 1920s, relations were comradely, often friendly. The familiar form of address (*ty*) was often used even in official correspondence. This was a break with the conventions of the Lenin team, where the familiar form of address was less dominant, notably with regard to Lenin: none of his comrades appears to have addressed him with the familiar form in business correspondence, nor he them. But Lenin was older and more upper-class than the Stalin team, and, moreover, in the 1920s Stalin was not a Lenin to his circle. Many of them used the familiar form in writing to him, as they did to one another, and continued to do so well into the 1930s. According to Mikoyan, those who were on familiar terms with Stalin were himself, Ordzhonikidze, Kalinin, Molotov, Voroshilov, Bukharin, and Kamenev. Molotov and Voroshilov often addressed Stalin as Koba in letters, Mikoyan as Soso, a Georgian diminutive for Joseph.[1]

By the early 1930s, some of the team had put on weight and a few were losing hair, but the casual military mode of dress remained in fashion for a few more years, and so did the informal habits within the team. To subordinates, the team favored a quasi-military tone of command, gruff and peremptory, sometimes abusive (Kaganovich was the past master of this); with common people, the preferred manner was simple, kindly, and approachable, a style set by the homespun Kalinin; and with one another, they behaved as comrades and in many cases as friends. Stalin's repudiation of friendship in politics (in connection with his fight with Bukharin) should not be taken too seriously. Friendship meant a lot to him (which is not to say that he couldn't be disloyal), and in the beginning, it was one of the things cementing his team. This changed after the deaths of Kirov (in 1934) and Ordzhonikidze (in 1936), and under the impact of the Great Purges, which inhibited and corrupted personal relations within the team. Yet even after the purges, Stalin continued to rely on team members for companionship, and would do so until the end of his life. Like most of the team (Rudzutak and Kuibyshev, preferring the artistic milieu, were exceptions), his own friendships and social contacts were primarily with other Old Bolsheviks, in addition to family, and after his wife's death at the end of 1932, he relied on the team all the more.

The social core of the team in social terms were the "Caucasians," comprising two Georgians (Stalin and Ordzhonikidze) and one Armenian (Mikoyan), plus two (Voroshilov and Kirov) who had served on the Southern Fronts and bonded with the ethnic Caucasians during the Civil

War. These five were personally close in a way none of them were to Molotov, an uxorious man to whom male camaraderie did not come naturally, although the Stalins and the Molotovs had got on well when they shared an apartment together in the Kremlin in the early 1920s. The Ordzhonikidzes, along with Bukharin and his 1920s partner Esfir Gurvich and the Georgian Avel Enukidze (Nadya's godfather), seem to have been the closest family friends of the Stalins in the later 1920s, along with Leningrad-based Kirov, whose presence was less frequent.

Ordzhonikidze, a man with a warm personality and a gift for friendship, was a general favorite. Almost everyone on the team used the familiar form with him, and his particularly close friends, such as Kaganovich and Mikoyan, often added an endearment. He was punctilious about remembering to ask about the welfare of wives and children, and to send greetings to them. The other general favorites were Kirov, Mikoyan, and, until the great bust-up, Bukharin. Kirov was friendly with Kuibyshev (whom he knew from prison in Tomsk in 1909), Bukharin, and Tomsky, as well as Ordzhonikidze and both Stalins (he had known Nadya from childhood, being an old friend of her father's). The Voroshilovs were friendly with the Kaganoviches and Andreevs, as well as the Mikoyans, and Bukharin and Voroshilov were close. The bachelor Rudzutak was friendly with Rykov and Tomsky, and sometimes went hunting with Voroshilov. Kuibyshev had been friends with Mikoyan and Kirov since the Civil War; he was also on good terms with the Andreevs, particularly after their daughter married his son. Andreev was close to Kalinin (who was also a favorite of Mikoyan's) and quite friendly with Ordzhonikidze and Voroshilov.[2]

In the early 1920s, much of the team's socializing took place in the Kremlin, where the erstwhile revolutionaries and their wives and children were in and out of one another's modest quarters, much as they had been in the old days of share-flats and casual bunking wherever there was a bed or a floor. The Molotovs were an exception to this pattern; other wives sometimes had cutting things to say about Polina's bourgeois inclinations. Later, dachas became centers of team social life, particularly Stalin's at Zubalovo, which was not far from the dachas of the Mikoyans, Voroshilovs, and Svanidzes (Alyosha Svanidze was Stalin's brother-in-law by his first marriage). Stalin welcomed the company, both for himself and his young children, Vasily (Vasya) and Svetlana. The Ordzhonikidzes were often at Stalin's dacha, along with the Mikoyans (with their five young sons, a major social presence), the Voroshilovs, the Kaganoviches, the Andreevs, and the Molotovs. Bukharin was often there after he became an intimate of Stalin's and friend of Nadya's in the mid-1920s. So was Avel Enukidze, who in addition to being Nadya's godfather was an old friend of Stalin's from the prerevolutionary Caucasus underground who had known him back in seminary days. Kirov came when he was in town, as did Pavel Postyshev, a hero of the struggle in the Far East during the Civil War who worked with Stalin as a Central Committee secretary in the early 1930s, and his wife, Tatyana.

The Stalins and their guests played tennis, billiards, bowls, and chess; skied; went horseback riding; danced to the gramophone; sang; drank Georgian wine; and played with their own and other people's children. Kirov and Molotov danced Russian dances with their wives; Voroshilov danced the Ukrainian hopak. Athletic young Mikoyan performed the Caucasian *lezghinka*, "kicking his legs in front of [Stalin's wife] Nadya, trying to persuade her to join him," while she "shyly covered her face with her hand" as the dance demands (but she really was shy and demure). Stalin was not much of a dancer, but he liked acting as DJ and putting the records on.

There were lots of Georgian relatives around, in-laws from both of Stalin's marriages: Svanidzes from the first (his young first wife, Ekaterina Svanidze, died after only a year of marriage in 1907), Allilyuevs from the second. Ekaterina's brother Alyosha Svanidze, deputy chairman of the State Bank, was a particular friend of Stalin's; in the 1930s he often used to stay overnight with Stalin at the dacha to keep him company. Svanidze had a son called John-Reed (named for the famous American Leftist who wrote *Ten Days that Shook the World*) with his wife Maria, a former actress with a worshipful and proprietorial attitude toward Stalin, whose diary carefully chronicled who was at his dacha. In November 1934, for example, it was Kaganovich, Molotov, Ordzhonikidze, and the new team member Andrei Zhdanov, plus "the kids," Vasya and Svetlana Stalin, Tomik Sergeev (Stalin's adopted son and Vasya's companion), and John-Reed (Johnny) Svanidze. The next month, Stalin's fifty-fifth birthday was celebrated at the dacha with "all his close friends, that is, people with whom he not only works with but meets informally," including the Molotovs, Voroshilov, Ordzhonikidze, the Andreevs, Enukidze, Mikoyan, the

Ukrainian Vlas Chubar and wife, Beria (up from the Caucasus), and Kalinin, along with a bunch of Stalin's relatives: Maria, with husband and son; Nadya's sister Anna Alliluyeva, with husband Stanislav Redens, head of the Moscow NKVD; and Nadya's brother Pavel Alliluyev, a military man, and his wife Zhenya. Mikoyan was toastmaster for the first half of the evening, Ordzhonikidze for the second; the Caucasians harmonized on some melancholy songs, with "the boss" on tenor. [3]

Wives and children were an important part of this lively company. Most of the long-established partners were Old Bolsheviks themselves, with their own jobs and professional interests. A number (Polina Zhemchuzhina-Molotova, Maria Kaganovich, Ekaterina Voroshilova, Dora Khazan-Andreeva, Evgenia Kogan-Kuibysheva, Maria Markus-Kirova) were Jewish, although all except Kaganovich's wife were married to Slavs. A few had substantial careers of their own. Polina Molotova, usually called by her party name Zhemchuzhina, worked in a perfume factory in the 1920s, rose from party secretary to director, went on to build an entire cosmetics industry in the 1930s, and later served as deputy minister of light industry and minister for fisheries. Mikoyan thought highly of her abilities, as did Stalin, and she was the only one of the wives allowed to attend formal receptions, when such things started to matter in the years before the war. Maria Kaganovich headed the garment workers' trade union.

Kalinin's wife Ekaterina Lorberg was a manager in the textile industry in the 1920s, and later worked in the Russian Supreme Court. Industrial management jobs also awaited Dora Khazan and Nadya Alliluyeva when they finished their studies at the Industrial Academy. Nadya didn't live long enough to graduate, but Dora rose to head a wool industry body, becoming, like Polina Zhemchuzhina, a deputy minister of light industry. Bukharin's 1920s partner, Esfir Gurvich, graduated from the Institute of Red Professors and later became a doctor of economics. Kuibyshev's second wife, Evgenia Kogan, held senior positions in the Moscow Party Committee; his fourth wife (Olga Lezhava) ended up as deputy director of an industrial research institute. In the younger cohort joining the team in the mid-1930s, two had serious professional careers. Malenkov's wife Valeria Golubtsova became director of the Moscow Power Institute after graduating in engineeering, while Beria's wife Nina was a chemist who, after their move to Moscow in the late 1930s, held a scientific research position at the Timiryazev Agricultural Academy.[4]

A number of Bolshevik leaders' wives worked in the Russian education ministry, but the most senior of them—deputy ministers Nadezhda Krupskaya and Varvara Yakovleva, along with Zinoviev's first wife, Zlata Lilina, who headed the Leningrad education department—were Zinovievites, not members of Stalin's team. Kamenev's first wife, Olga Kameneva, similarly, had a higher status in cultural administration as head of VOKS, the Society for Cultural Ties Abroad, than any of the wives of the Stalin team. But a number of those wives did hold humbler positions in the "soft" employment sectors like cultural administration, propaganda and party history, women's departments, and museums, where women tended to congregate. Ekaterina Voroshilova worked for many years in the Higher Party School (Stalin's daughter, Svetlana, remembered that in the postwar period, when Zinaida Zhdanova was working there too, young people joked that they were there as "visual aids to learning the history of the CPSU"). But her job was important to Voroshilova: as she wrote late in life, she worked "for moral comfort, so as not to seem just a housewife." Teaching had been the prerevolutionary profession of a number of Old Bolshevik wives, including the two housewives among the team wives in the 1920s, Zina Ordzhonikidze and Ashkhen Mikoyan. Nina Kucharchuk-Khrushcheva, also a former teacher, went into party work in a factory after the Khrushchevs moved to Moscow but gave it up when her youngest son Sergei was born in 1935.

The wives had their own social connections, partly interwoven with those of their husbands, partly separate. Zina Ordzhonikidze and the younger Ashkhen Mikoyan, like their husbands, seem to have been general favorites and centers of social life. Nadya Alliluyeva is widely claimed and reported as a friend—of Polina Zhemchuzhina, Zina Ordzhonikidze, Ashkhen Mikoyan, and Dora Khazan, among others—but this is probably more a function of Stalin's status and the Stalins' dacha as a center of socializing than of Nadya's character, which was reserved and not given to warmth. She wrote to her sister-in-law Maria Svanidze in 1926 that "it's strange, but I haven't made any good friends [in Moscow] after all these years," adding that as far as women were concerned, she preferred those who were not party members. The bossy and elegant Polina Zhemchuzhina was not particularly popular with the other wives, and Nina Beria didn't fit in well with the women either: "she was young and beautiful and all the other Politburo wives hated her." On the other hand, Stalin really liked her, and so did his daughter, Svetlana, as she grew up, despite an aversion to Nina's husband.[5]

The wives were not prudes, or at least hadn't been once, as they were of the revolutionary generation that saw marriage as a bourgeois patriarchal convention. Marriages were not necessarily registered: that exemplary couple, the Mikoyans, never registered their marriage despite five children, and neither did Bukharin and his second and probably third wives. Stalin and Nadya lived together for several years before registering their marriage; Khrushchev and his wife Nina were together from the early 1920s but didn't register until the 1960s. Polina Zhemchuzhina was one of the most emancipated of the Stalin team's women: she and Molotov probably had an open marriage, though a devoted and long-lasting one, and she had a daughter from another relationship. Even those wives who later became extremely respectable "Soviet ladies," like Ekaterina Voroshilova and Zinaida Zhdanova, had had their own sexual and marital adventures earlier. But as mores tightened up in the 1930s, affairs on the part of the wives—though not necessarily the husbands—became rarer. Even in the relatively liberated 1920s, there was usually a degree of censoriousness when an Old Bolshevik man left an Old Bolshevik wife for a younger woman, as Kuibyshev, Bukharin, and Kamenev did. In Kuibyshev's case, the first of the younger women, his second wife, Galina Troyanovskaya, was the daughter of Stalin's old friend Alexander Troyanovsky, and Stalin was furious when he heard that Kuibyshev had walked out on her after she became ill.[6]

Many of the team's children were born after the revolution, and, as was normal in Russia in this period of upheaval, their households also included adopted children. Often these were the offspring of fallen comrades, like Artem (Tomik) Sergeev, taken into Stalin's household as a companion for his son Vasily, or the sons of martyred Baku Commissar Sergei Shaumyan, whom the Mikoyans adopted, or the son and daughter of military commander Mikhail Frunze, Timur and Tatyana, who were consigned to the Voroshilovs' care by the Politburo after their parents' death in the mid-1920s. The Ordzhonikidze's daughter Eteri, the Voroshilovs' Petr, and the Tomsky's Yury were adopted too, and the Kaganoviches' Yury was reportedly selected in an orphanage by their teenage daughter Maya.

The Kremlin children grew up together, though not always in harmony. It was said that Polina Zhemchuzhina feared the bad influence of the noisy Mikoyan boys on her delicately raised Svetlana, one of the best students in the group. The Mikoyan boys and Andreev's son and daughter went to School No. 32 (under Krupskaya's special patronage and famous for its educational progressivism), mingling there with children of intelligentsia luminaries and foreign Communists. The two Svetlanas, Stalina and Molotova, went to the equally famous and admired School No. 25, where their fellow schoolmates included the American singer Paul Robeson's son. Vasya went there too, causing distress to his teachers, whom Stalin urged to forget he was Stalin's son and to discipline him severely. The team members were "uncles" to the Kremlin children, often with affection on both sides: Sergo Beria had fond memories of both Stalin and Kirov from his youth. Svetlana Stalin, whose postdefection memories were in general less fond, acknowledged that Kaganovich, Molotov, and Ordzhonikidze had been "uncles" to her in childhood, and Mikoyan and Khrushchev were also fond of her and tried to look out for her in later life. As a child, Svetlana and her father played a game in which he called her "the boss" (*khoziaika*) and assumed the role of her "secretary." Kaganovich also played this game with Svetlana ("I made a report to our boss-girl today," he wrote to Stalin in Crimea when Svetlana, left back in Moscow, was nine. "It seems that Svetlana found our activity satisfactory. She is in a good mood. Tomorrow she will start school").[7]

In the real world, where Kaganovich, as party secretary, answered to Stalin, not Svetlana, the team was relatively stable in the years after the jettisoning of the Right, despite the strains put upon it by the Great Break. The Politburo elected in July 1930 had Stalin, Molotov, Kaganovich, Kirov, Kalinin, Kuibyshev, Stanislav Kosior (general secretary of the Ukrainian party), and Rudzutak as full members. Ordzhonikidze was temporarily off the Politburo because he was head of the party Control Commission and you couldn't hold both jobs, but he came back on once he began working in industry at the end of the year, at which point Andreev took over the Control Commission for a few years. In such cases, nonmembership of the Politburo was something of a formality: the nonmembers attended its meetings anyway, though not voting. Andreev, along with Mikoyan and the Ukrainians Grigory Petrovsky and Chubar, were candidate members; so also was a new but short-lived young favorite of Stalin's from Siberia, Sergei Syrtsov. None of the Ukrainians, occupied with their jobs in Ukraine, were regular attendees of Politburo meetings in Moscow. Nor was Leningrad-based Kirov, but his status as team member was much firmer than the marginal Ukrainians. Pavel Postyshev, a Central Committee secretary in the early 1930s, was a regular attendee at formal Politburo meetings, as well as the informal ones in Stalin's office, when he was in Moscow, and thus functioned as a team member during this period. Yakov Yakovlev, the agriculture minister, was also a regular attendee at Politburo meetings and in Stalin's office.

As always under Stalin, Politburo membership and team membership were closely related but not identical categories. Stalin stuck to his old habits of gathering an inner circle—"the Five," "the Seven," and so on—that included only a chosen group from the Politburo. This offended the newcomer Syrtsov, and he complained that Kuibyshev, Rudzutak, and Kalinin, as well as himself, were excluded from inner-circle consultations. He called it "factionalism," but that's probably not the most accurate way of seeing it: the "in" faction could change, so it was basically a way of Stalin exerting control via the power of inclusion/exclusion over his associates. Kuibyshev was actually a fairly frequent visitor to Stalin's office at this time, about on a par with Ordzhonikidze and Mikoyan, so it's not clear that Syrtsov's picture was accurate. Stalin's closest associates, judging by how often they were in his office, were Molotov and Kaganovich, with Voroshilov in third place. Molotov was indispensable, clearly the team's assistant captain in these years. Stalin got worried when Molotov planned to go on vacation at the same time that he would be gone in the summer of 1933: evidently, he thought that Kaganovich, who also had Moscow to run, was not enough of a heavyweight to manage alone, and Kuibyshev "might go on a drinking spree."

Stalin valued his team, as did all its members. This wasn't necessarily a matter of democracy, though the democratic instinct was not absent. These men had been professional revolutionaries since their teens in most cases; politics was their lives. They were bonded in the team like footballers, embracing in victory, swapping painful reproaches, and putting up with tongue-lashings from the playing coach after defeats. Although Stalin was capable of dressing down team members and playing them off against each other, he nevertheless valued the team and did not want to see its spirit eroded. When Ordzhonikidze had a particularly passionate disagreement in the Politburo with Molotov and Kuibyshev when Stalin was on vacation in the South, Stalin strongly condemned his behavior: the team (he called it "our leading group") could fall apart that way. "Does he really not understand that on that path he will get no support from our side?" he wrote to Kaganovich, using even more underlinings than usual. "What stupidity!"

In the 1920s, Stalin's associates, like Stalin himself, had generally had jobs in the party Central Committee office. The government, by contrast, was headed after Lenin's death by a non-team member, Alexei Rykov, who at the end of the 1920s was part of the Rightist bloc with Bukharin and Tomsky. By the autumn of 1929, Stalin was becoming noticeably unhappy with this situation, especially because, by convention, Politburo meetings were chaired by the head of the government. "Why do you allow this comedy?" Stalin wrote angrily to Molotov from his vacation spot in the South when he noticed that Rykov was still chairing the Monday and Thursday meetings. Yet, true to his principle of dosage, he let the situation drag on for another year. It was not until the autumn of 1930 that he pointed out the obvious: that with Rykov politically disgraced, the government that he headed had become "sick with a fatal illness." Stalin claimed that it was "paralyzed by Rykov's insipid and essentially anti-party speeches," but the truth was such paralysis was the fate of every institution headed by someone in political disfavor. Obviously, however, it was an unacceptable situation, regardless of the truth of Stalin's allegation that the government was becoming a Rightist factional headquarters "*opposing* itself to the Central Committee." The government included the economic ministries that were the keystones in implementation of the First Five-Year Plan. "It's clear that this cannot go on," Stalin told Molotov—and indeed, in a few months, Rykov was formally removed.[8]

But if Rykov was to go, who should head the government? To some members—probably a majority—of the Stalin team, it seemed obvious that Stalin should take over. Mikoyan and Voroshilov both wrote to Stalin urging him to do so, saying that Molotov, Kaganovich, and (with some reservations) Kuibyshev agreed. Lenin had headed the government as well as leading the party and the Comintern, they argued, and Stalin should too—"the leadership is in your hands anyway." But Stalin had

other ideas. He wanted Molotov to take over the job. With Molotov running the government and Stalin running the party in tandem, "we will be
able to have complete unity of soviet and party leaderships, which will undoubtedly double our strength." Molotov was a bit nonplussed by this, uncertain whether he had the necessary authority. Actually he, like Voroshilov, thought Stalin should take over because "that's what is expected,
that's how it was under Lenin," who had combined party and state leadership. But Ordzhonikidze, whom Stalin evidently consulted, said it was
"rubbish" about the team not accepting Molotov—"we will all support
him"—and Molotov thus took over the position that he would hold with
distinction for a decade. Molotov was never quite sure why Stalin had
balked at assuming Lenin's mantle at this point: perhaps he wanted to
keep up the appearance of separation of party and government, or perhaps he thought the government should be headed by a Russian. In any
case, it was a good decision on Stalin's part, not only because Molotov was
an excellent organizer, a hard worker, and a details man, but because Stalin was impatient with administrative detail of the kind the job required.

With Molotov running the government and Ordzhonikidze moving
from party control to heavy industry ministry, two of the most senior
members of Stalin's team moved their sphere of activity from party to
government. It was an important shift, confirming a trend that had started
four years earlier with the appointment of Mikoyan, Rudzutak, and Kuibyshev to major government positions. Now the chief branches of government—industry, economic planning, railways, the military—would all be
headed by members of the Politburo, and, conversely, the majority of
Politburo members now held government positions. Ordzhonikidze was
in charge of heavy industry, Mikoyan of food supply, Kuibyshev of economic planning, and Voroshilov of the military. Railways were under
Rudzutak, then Andreev, and later Kaganovich.[9]

Having specific government responsibilities changed the political behavior of Politburo members. As the drafters of proposed legislation in
their areas, they acquired substantial, if circumscribed, power in policy
making. Moreover, in budgetary and a host of other discussions, they became advocates of the institutional interests they represented. Ordzhonikidze took the lead, becoming almost overnight a passionate and effective
advocate of the needs of heavy industry. But the others behaved in just the
same way: Mikoyan represented the interests of supply and defended the

food ministry when it was attacked, while Kaganovich did the same for railways. "The industrial people" (*khoziaistvenniki*) became a frequent term of reference in Stalin and Molotov's discussions, meaning the industrial lobby in the Politburo and Central Committee. "The military people" (*voennye*) had a similar valence: Voroshilov was a dedicated defender of the interests of the military within the Politburo, periodically threatening to resign if its budget was cut. There were other kinds of institutional loyalties too, for a number of team members headed key regions and cities rather than ministries (Kosior the Ukraine; Kirov, Leningrad; Kaganovich and later Khrushchev, Moscow), and represented their interests in the Politburo with the same vigor as the industrialists and the military. Sometimes the cities and regions competed with each other, but they could also present a united front, for example, asking for more money for urban services. When Politburo members changed their government jobs—as Kaganovich, for example, did several times—they switched seamlessly from one advocacy position to another.

Only three members of Stalin's team were outside this pattern of institutional representation. Molotov and Kalinin, respectively, headed the government (Council of People's Commissars, later Council of Ministers) and the executive committee of the Soviet parliament (later called the Supreme Soviet). Stalin was general secretary of the party. Being above the institutional interests, adjudicating their conflicts, and taking the broader view were central components of Stalin's leadership in the Politburo. In the early 1930s, when his own attention and that of his team was focused very strongly on rapid economic development requiring major investment, Stalin took on the additional role of budget overseer. When he was out of Moscow, he sent a stream of instructions to Kaganovich to hold the line on budget and resist "special interests" pressure from other members of the team: "You gave too much foreign currency to Vesenkha [the supreme economic council] . . . If you behave like this, its greed will have no end"; anyway, the industrial people "are rolling in money." Nor was it only industry that felt Stalin's razor. He told Kaganovich to limit the military budget for 1933, saying that Voroshilov's estimate for army expansion was appallingly inflated.

The bureaucracies, in Stalin's view, were always going to ask for more than they needed. The industrial ministry wanted to "squeeze the state treasury" instead of making its own bureaucracy work better. The agricultural ministry was no better: the aim of local officials was naturally "to squeeze out of the government *as much money as possible*," and the ministry was giving in to them. The "bureaucratic self-esteem" of Mikoyan's supply ministry was boundless. Stalin frequently had to remind Kaganovich to ignore "wailing and hysterics" from the team members when their bureaucratic interests were affected. "You'll see," he said, "if we refuse them they will still find ways and possibilities of satisfying their needs."

Stalin found it natural that people would defend the interests of the institution or branch of the economy they led; indeed, if they had not behaved in this way, he would have lost some of his edge as the team leader who was *above* special interests. He found it natural, also, that bureaucracies would give false information to protect themselves (though he considered it the duty of the Communists at their heads to sort this out before it reached the Politburo); it was part of the job description for bureaucrats to "lie and play games" and to practice "thin end of the wedge" tactics. If you once gave in to their demands, that became a precedent that they would then use "as a means of *pressure*" on Moscow." Stalin was proud of his skill at seeing through the stratagems of bureaucracies and local officials. He regarded himself as a master decoder, able to see through the smokescreen to the real interest that was being prettified or concealed.

When a lower official or even a member of his own team with an institutional interest told Stalin that something was impossible, his immediate response was to suspect the speaker of trying to protect his institution from too much exertion. He saw bureaucracies as naturally prone to entropy, falling back into inertia, retreating from radical policies into moderate "opportunistic" ones if not constantly watched and prodded. To borrow from the Bolshevik lexicon during collectivization, the main danger in policy implementation was not "bending the stick too far" but failing to bend it far enough. Confronted with an example of the latter, the suggestion that kulaks might have the chance to get their civil rights back, Stalin sighed: "I just knew that asses from the petty bourgeoisie and philistines would have to creep into that mouse hole." In other words, if the officials and politicians were pushed into a radical policy like dekulakization, after a while they inevitably tried to water it down.

Defense of institutional interest was never described as anything but an evil, but in practice it was an important modus operandi within the Politburo and Soviet government. Stalin was suspicious of disagreements within the leadership that stemmed from ideology, and disapproved of those where a personal or family interest was involved, but he took it for granted that team members would defend the interests of the institutions they headed. He might rebuke team members for pushing too hard for his institution, but in his eyes, it was a venial sin—not even a sin, really, but behavior that went with the job. Stalin could even joke about it, as when in 1934, in a convivial mood at the dacha and wanting to persuade his friend Kirov to come over from Leningrad, he called him to say that he had better come immediately to defend Leningrad's interests after the recent abolition of rationing and consequent likely rises in the price of bread.[10]

The early 1930s was the time when a Soviet version of the entrepreneurial spirit—the can-do, risk-taking, flamboyant style personified by Ordzhonikidze—ruled in industry. Leadership of this kind included the capacity for energetic and effective advocacy of one's institutional interest (factory, branch of industry, industrial ministry), the ability to get it on to the endlessly contested priority lists that were crucial in the distribution of Soviet goods. Ordzhonikidze personified this ability, and it was in large part thanks to his dynamic leadership that Soviet industry developed so dramatically in the first half of the 1930s. Of all the team members, he was the most likely to insist on getting his own way and the most capable of throwing fits if he didn't. Molotov and Stalin often reminded each other to tread carefully because of his volatile temperament and easily injured vanity. But Molotov, after he became head of the government, had frequent problems with Ordzhonikidze's tendency to act as if his ministry was a totally independent institution; he once protested that it was acting as "a state within a state." When, in Stalin's absence, these conflicts led to open hostilities between Ordzhonikdze and Molotov in the Politburo, Stalin was indignant at Ordzhonikidze's "hooliganism": Who did he think he was to override policy directives from the government and the Central Committee? Equally, why couldn't Molotov and Kaganovich stop him?

There were limits, of course, to Stalin's tolerance of overassertiveness on behalf of their bailiwicks by individual team members, and Ordzhonikidze came close to those boundaries. Probably his very success came to annoy Stalin: by the mid-1930s, Ordzhonikidze was worshipped by "his people" in industry, and industrial plants and projects under his jurisdiction were clamoring to be named after him. Relations with Stalin soured in the last years of Ordzhonikidze's life, and his suicide in 1937 occurred immediately after a serious disagreement with Stalin. These disagreements involved institutional interest but also something to which Stalin paid particular attention: personnel. Ordzhonikidze had long annoyed Stalin by his habit of vigorously defending any of his subordinates who fell under NKVD suspicion, and in 1936 this was happening increasingly often, notably with the arrest of his indispensable deputy, the former Oppositionist Yury Pyatakov. Worst of all, from Stalin's point of view, Ordzhonikidze would not accept the team convention that you didn't defend your own family members. When his brother was targeted by the NKVD, he defended him with passion, and was furious when Stalin refused to rescue him.[11]

Stalin was a suspicious man. He was suspicious even of his own team, particularly those who were not at a given moment at the core of the inner circle. He kept tabs on them, encouraged informing, liked to keep them off balance, and sometimes set traps for them. He often told them (particularly Molotov and Kaganovich) what he was up to in his many political intrigues, but this could not be relied on. When he felt like it, Stalin was a master of the blatant lie. During collectivization, for example, he blamed lower officials ("dizzy with success") for the excesses of collectivization that the center had pushed them into, and a year or so later, in the midst of an unprecedented population outflow from the villages to escape collectivization, he could calmly announce that under Soviet power the peasant no longer felt a need to flee the countryside. These lies were for public consumption, of course, though team members better informed about the countryside from firsthand observation might hesitate to approach the subject, just in case Stalin actually believed his public statements. He could practice "conspiracy"—a concept and set of practices dear to the Bolsheviks—not only with respect to the broader world but even with respect to the team. It was "in the interests of conspiracy" that in 1930 he instructed his secretary Alexander Poskrebyshev to tell people he would not be back from vacation until the end of October, although in fact it was his intention to return several weeks earlier. This caused problems with Nadya, who, on the basis of information from her godfather, Avel Enukidze, thought she was the one who had been misled. Stalin had to write reassuringly to her explaining his conspiratorial strategy. "I put about the rumor through Poskrebyshev . . . Avel evidently fell victim to [it]." Some of the inner circle, however, had been trusted: "Tatka [Stalin's pet name for Nadya], Molotov and, I think, Sergo know the [real] date of my return."[12]

There were moments of affection and trust between Stalin and his wife, but they were increasingly few. Their relationship had long been rocky because of his preoccupation with work and her jealousy. She rarely accompanied him on his annual trips to the South, and their correspondence when he was away was sparse and, on Nadya's part, cold and hostile. Pregnant with a second child in 1926, she made it clear in a letter to her sister-in-law that the last thing she wanted at this time was another child tying her to Stalin and domestic duties. After Svetlana was born, Nadya apparently tried to leave Stalin, taking the two small children with her to Leningrad (where her parents still lived) and "hoping to find a job there and make a new life for herself," but was persuaded to return, partly through the good offices of Tomsky's wife Maria on Stalin's behalf. In the last years of her life, Nadya was in poor health, mental as well as physical. Her studies at the Industrial Academy should have opened new opportunities for the future. But they may also have increased the psychological strain, as these were the years of agricultural crisis, and the academy was full of Rightists who disapproved of Stalin's policies. What she learned from her fellow students about opposition within the party, arrests, and the situation in the countryside, along with the hounding of Bukharin, who had been a friend, no doubt increased her critical attitude to her husband, although she kept her own counsel and hard evidence of her political views is difficult to find. Her daughter, Svetlana, later remembered her nanny telling her that Nadya was irritated by visits from her mother and sister, Anna, "because these good-hearted, open women demanded openness from her."[13]

The last straw came at an evening party at the Voroshilovs' apartment in the Kremlin. Stalin was flirting with someone—the glamorous wife of General Egorov, Galina, according to Molotov's recollections—and Nadya stamped out in a rage. Polina Zhemchuzhina followed, walking her around the Kremlin until she seemed to calm down and went home to bed. But once at home, alone, her distress evidently returned, and she shot herself with a little pistol her brother Pavel had brought back as a souvenir from Berlin. The date was 9 November 1932. Her motives, and even the fact that it was suicide, are uncorroborated; no note is known to have been left. Although rumors that Stalin had murdered her started immediately, there is no evidence of this, and the behavior of family and associates after her body was discovered the next morning suggests that they all believed it to be suicide. Six-year-old Svetlana didn't know what had happened, but remembered Uncle Klim (Voroshilov) taking her and Vasya out to play that morning, when everything at home was so strangely out of kilter, and everyone was weeping.

Stalin's reactions are variously reported, but grief, guilt, and a sense of betrayal were evidently all present. Long after the event, Molotov reported hearing Stalin mutter at the graveside, "I didn't keep her safe"—an uncharacteristically sentimental statement from Stalin, but by the same token uncharacteristic of Molotov, so it may be true. Svetlana remembered that for a long time her father was "thrown out of equilibrium," wouldn't talk about her mother, and seemed to take her death as a hostile act (the last is perhaps hindsight, as she was almost grown-up before she learned that it had been a suicide). His personal life was hard since Nadya's death, Stalin acknowledged, but "a brave man must always be brave." Since he wrote this more than a year after the event, however, to a mother whom he kept at more than arm's length, it tells us little about his inner feelings.

In a political culture that avoided public comment on the leaders' private lives, there were no precedents about how to announce such a death, but it was handled with surprising openness. The Central Committee's notice of her death in *Pravda* described Nadezhda Alliluyeva as "an active and devoted party member" and student at the Industrial Academy, who had died "unexpectedly." That implied sudden illness, accident, or suicide, but top party officials, at least in Moscow, were officially informed that it was suicide. Rumors flew around regardless: in the Industrial Academy, Nadya's fellow students were saying that Stalin had shot her, either out of jealousy or because of political disagreements. The funeral, at 11:00 AM on 11 November at Novodevichy Cemetery, was open to the public, and documentary film footage shows an expressionless Stalin and twitchy Voroshilov standing by the open coffin as ordinary people, mainly young women, file past. Nadya's godfather Enukidze headed the funeral commission, which included Dora Khazan, the Politburo wife who was her friend and fellow student; Kaganovich spoke. In an unprecedented move, never to be repeated, the main tribute to the deceased was signed by Politburo members *and their wives*, though as not all of the wives used their

1. Sergei Kirov and Sergo
Ordzhonikidze, 1920. ITAR-TASS.

2. Kaganovich (center) with Ukrainian party secretary A.V.Medvedev (left) and Postyshev (right),
1927. RGAKFD.

3. Stalin, his wife Nadya, Voroshilov and his wife, and Enukidze in Sochi, 1932. RIA Novosti.

4. Stalin and colleague (This is the archival title: the "colleague" is probably Bukharin, and the time, late 1920s). RGASPI.

5. Sketch of Stalin by Bukharin, 20 February 1928. RGASPI.

6. Sketch of Rudzutak by Valery Mezhlauk, no date (late 1920s?). Inscription by the artist: Caption: "Missing person! Reward offered." RGASPI.

7. Leaders on Mausoleum, 1933–34. Front row from left: Valery Mezhlauk (Gosplan), Molotov, Kaganovich, Stalin, Voroshilov, Kalinin, Andreev, Chubar. RGAKFD.

8. Leaders at the XVII Party Congress, 1934. Back row from left, Enukidze, Voroshilov, Kaganovich, and Kuibyshev; front row, Ordzhonikidze, Stalin, Molotov, Kirov. RGAKFD.

9. Stalin's fifty-fifth birthday at Kuntsevo , 1934 (photo taken by Stalin's bodyguard, General Vlasik): (back row from left) Anna Alliluyeva Redens, Dora Khazan, Zinaida Ordzhonikidze; (middle row) Maria Svanidze, Maria Kaganovich, Sashiko Svanidze, Stalin, Polina Zhemchuzhina (Molotova Voroshilov); (front row) unidentified woman, Zhenya Alliluyeva, Bronislava Poskrebysheva and an unidentified man. RGASPI.

10. Group photo, 1934: Kirov, Stalin, Kuibyshev, Ordzhonikidze in front row, with Kaganovich and Kalinin and Mikoyan (obscured) behind. RGASPI.

11. Stalin and Voroshilov at Kremlin reception, 1936. RGASPI.

12. Team meeting with Comintern leader Georgy Dimitrov, hero of the Reichstag fire, 1934.
Ordzhonikidze in front at left, Dimitrov and Stalin seated on sofa, Molotov and Kuibyshev perched
on sofa at left, Voroshilov at right. RGASPI.

13. Stalin, Voroshilov, Mikoyan, and Molotov on Mausoleum on the day of the eighteenth anniversary of the revolution, 7 November 1935. RIA Novosti.

14. Beria with Svetlana Stalina (mid-1930s). RIA Novosti.

15. Mikoyan family (mid-1930s). Back row: Stepan and Vladimir; middle row, Alexei, Anastas Mikoyan, Ashkhen; front row Ivan and Sergo. RGASPI.

16. Stalin, in Eastern robes (probably a present from Central Asian delegates), at meeting with peasants, 1935. RGASPI.

husbands' names, they were not necessarily identifiable as such to the public. The wives who signed were Ekaterina Voroshilova, Polina Zhemchuzhina (Molotova), Zinaida Ordzhonikidze, Dora Khazan (Andreeva), Maria Kaganovich, Ashkhen Mikoyan, and Tatyana Postysheva—the last something of an anomaly, as her husband Pavel (also a signatory) was a Central Committee secretary but not a Politburo member. Their tribute was the only one to identify Nadya as "wife, close friend and faithful helper of comrade Stalin."[14]

Nadya's death marked the end of Voroshilova's "wonderful times" for the team. The year that followed was a terrible one for the party and the country. The annual battle with the peasantry about grain deliveries, which had been running since collectivization, was particularly tense in the autumn of 1932. Mass arrests and deportations, incompetence on part of newly formed collective farms, and foot-dragging on the part of angry peasants, meant that the harvest, which in weather terms should have been good, was going to be mediocre. Traveling through the Northern Caucasus and Ukraine in July, Voroshilov was appalled to see the fields full of weeds, and peasants approaching their work "listlessly." "Why won't people work properly, in a socialist way?" he wrote to Stalin sadly, admitting that his "soul aches" from what he had seen.

Stalin had his own version of what was happening. The peasants were staging a go-slow strike, issuing a political challenge to the regime that was no less dangerous because it avoided open revolt. After Nadya's death, a heightened note of paranoia is evident in his comments in the weeks on the situation in the countryside. As far as Ukraine was concerned, the failure of peasants to deliver grain, the alleged famine, and the flight of starving peasants from the stricken countryside were the work of Polish spies infiltrating across the border. Stalin was beside himself at the failure of Communists in Ukraine to see things his way (though in fact few were brave enough to express their disagreements openly), and furious at Ukrainian bosses Kosior and Chubar.

"Things in the Ukraine are terrible," he wrote to Kaganovich, but he didn't have starving peasants in mind. They were "terrible in the party," with district committees saying grain collection targets were unrealistic (obviously a self-serving lie), "*terrible* in the soviet organs," "*terrible* in the GPU." Polish agents had infiltrated the Ukrainian party, as well as sending their agents into the Ukrainian countryside: "If we don't make an ef-

fort now to improve the situation in the Ukraine, we may lose the
Ukraine. Keep in mind that [Polish dictator] Pilsudski is not daydream-
ing, and his agents in the Ukraine are many times stronger than [Stan-
islav] Redens [police chief in Ukraine] or Kosior think." New leadership
was called for, Stalin told Kaganovich and Molotov in the summer of 1932.
As usual, however, he went at this gingerly in practice, perhaps fearful of
antagonizing the half-million-strong Ukrainian party. Chubar was called
to Moscow to be one of Molotov's deputies at the head of the government
in 1934, but, although a similar honorific exile to the capital was contemplated for Kosior, he in fact stayed on as first secretary of the Ukrainian
party until the Great Purges (which is not to say that Stalin had forgotten
his disappointment with him). To whip the republic into line, Stalin sent
out Pavel Postyshev to serve as his eyes and ears in Ukraine. Formally,
Postyshev was Kosior's subordinate as second secretary of the Ukrainian
party, but increasingly he functioned there as top man.[15]

There was equally bad news from Kazakhstan, another major agricultural region, where attempts to forcibly settle the nomadic Kazakhs on
collective farms had led to starvation of men and cattle, and mass flight
into neighboring regions and across the border into China. The dire situation there was known to the team, as most of them had received a long,
detailed report from a brave local colleague, but it made little impact on
them. Kazakhstan was far away. Its closest neighbor, chaotic and decen-
tralized China, did not represent the same kind of threat that Poland, as
spearhead of the Western capitalists, did. Fleeing and starving Kazakhs
were not visible from the Kremlin, whereas those from Ukraine sometimes even made it to Moscow, despite transport minister Andreev's order
that nobody from the Ukrainian countryside without special authoriza-
tion should be sold train tickets, and that the OGPU should inspect all
trains from Ukraine at the Russian border for stowaways.

Officials in Ukraine and other affected areas tried to get the message
to Moscow that the peasants couldn't be made to deliver more grain because they had no more to bring and were already digging into their own
winter foodstocks and the grain set aside for spring planting. But Stalin
would have none of it. He was proud of his shrewdness and the way he
never let local officials get away with exaggerating problems so that Moscow would lower its demands. They're all pretending, he insisted; they
still have grain hidden away and are intentionally concealing it so as to

starve the Soviet cities and demoralize the army. This notion of pretending was taken up by the press, which ran some extraordinary stories about peasants "staging a 'famine,'" acting the part of victims, even starving their families "to make propaganda." If the peasants' hunger was just acting, in Stalin's opinion, their anti-Soviet intentions were for real. It's a "war of starvation" that the peasantry was waging against the regime, he told the writer Mikhail Sholokhov, who had written to inform him about the terrible situation in his homeland in the Cossack region of the Don; these peasants were not the innocent, suffering victims he supposed. In other words, it wasn't Stalin waging war against the peasants but the other way around.

Collectivization had rescued poor peasants from exploitation, given them tractors and combine harvesters, created the collective farms as a "solid foundation" for their lives, and rescued them from the ever-present threat of ruin, Stalin told the Central Committee in January 1933, the height of the famine. There was no mention of hunger in his speech. Indeed, the term "famine" was taboo in the Soviet press and evidently within the team as well. The rosy picture wasn't how it looked to officials on the spot, of course, not to mention peasants, who deluged the party leaders with letters about their plight. One Ukrainian regional party organization, not yet under good Stalinist control, issued a desperate order in February 1933 ordering local party committees "to eliminate rapidly extreme exhaustion among collective and individual farmers resulting from severe malnutrition" and put "all who have become completely disabled because of emaciation . . . back on their feet" by March 5. This miracle was to be achieved by feeding them, although with all cities on strict rationing by this time, no hint was given as to where the extra food was to be obtained.[16]

The team was not ignorant of the situation in the countryside, though the degree of their information varied. Like Stalin, Molotov and Kaganovich presumably read the situation as a fight to break the anti-Soviet spirit of the peasantry and miscalculated how tough they could be without causing the economically undesirable outcome of mass death. Molotov and Kaganovich were sent out to troublespots time after time to get out the grain, which led to their posthumous conviction by a Kiev court in post-Soviet times, along with Stalin, of the crime of genocide in Ukraine famine (Holodomor). Decades later Molotov was still denying the severity of the famine. He had twice visited Ukraine at the height of the problems, he told an interviewer, and had seen "nothing of the kind." But others on the team probably wavered. Kalinin, known as the peasants' friend, was a prime recipient in his own right of desperate letters from peasants, and as head of the Supreme Soviet, he and his deputy Enukidze were flooded with information about and petitions from the social casualties of the Great Break; in May 1932, he voted against yet another kulak deportation, thus anticipating Stalin's change of policy by a few weeks. After his annual trip South in August 1933, Voroshilov reiterated his distress at the sight of the empty, ravaged steppe, writing to Enukidze that it looked as it had after Genghis Khan or the White general Kolchak swept through in the Civil War.

Of all the great and terrible events the team was involved in over thirty years, the famine is the one on which the team said least, either at the time or later. None of them appear to have gone out on a limb for aid to starving peasants. Even in the 1970s, the subject was so touchy for Molotov that, when a sympathetic interviewer cited critical opinions on Moscow's handling of the famine, he burst out that these were the petty bourgeois ideas of Communists who came along to an easy life when the hard stuff had already been done. In a later conversation, he added, more moderately, "I understand the ... writers [who bemoan the suffering of the peasantry]: they are sorry for the peasant. But what can you do? There was no way of getting through it without sacrifices." Khrushchev, who wrote at some length about the 1946–47 famine in Ukraine, which he had to deal with firsthand, said little about 1933–34 when he was far away in Moscow. There was "hunger in the land," he knew, but as the man in charge of the city of Moscow, his preoccupations were local; he was "looking for ways to feed the working class."

Stalin didn't go out on regional inspection tours after the famous one of 1930, but he did make annual vacation trips to the South, which took him through famine territory in the North Caucasus. He could, like Voroshilov, have seen the devastation out the train window, but if he did, he chose not to comment. For several years, his stance was that the problem was basically disobedience and hostility to the regime, so massive repression was the answer. In addition to the huge number of peasants arrested and deported in 1930–31, an infamous law of 7 August 1932, said to be Stalin's own work, declared collective farm property to be the "sacred and

untouchable" property of the state and introduced the death penalty for
any peasant, starving or not, who tried to steal grain from the fields. Large
numbers of party and state officials, and collective farm chairmen in the
countryside, were also arrested for failing to deal with the peasants and
get the grain in—so many, in fact, that it left the countryside denuded of
cadres and forced the authorities to issue a general annulment of such
convictions in 1935. Stalin and Molotov, typically, had already done a
volte-face (Stalin's tactic with "Dizzy with Success" in 1930, to be repeated
many times in the future), repudiating past policies without acknowledgment or apology and putting the blame for "excesses" on local officials: a
secret instruction of 8 May 1933, not discussed beforehand in the Politburo, abruptly called off the "mass repressions" and deportations in the
countryside. Although Molotov, as head of the government, had his signature on the instruction, along with Stalin's, it has the ring of Stalin's characteristic chutzpah.[17]

As Stalin's maximalist policies had led to famine in the countryside
and a tense situation in the towns, now overcrowded and on rationing, it
is scarcely surprising that subterranean criticism of the leaders started to
circulate. Kalinin came in for some special odium, as the "peasants'
friend" who had let them down, but Stalin was the major target of scath-
ing comments and satirical songs about him that circulated widely in the
countryside. Stalin was held personally responsible for the harshness of
collectivization, and his rule was often compared unfavorably to Lenin's.
According to one popular anti-Stalin song, "When Lenin lived they fed
us, / When Stalin came, they tormented us with hunger." "Things would
have been otherwise had Lenin lived, a man with higher education and
much experience of life, but Stalin unfortunately does not have that," was
one of the comments the OGPU, snooping in the villages, picked up. If
that one ever got to Stalin, it would have been peculiarly irritating: backward peasants were not meant to call the great socialist modernizer
uncultured.

Anti-Stalin sentiments were being expressed in party circles as well.
The most notorious instance was an underground manifesto written by
Martemyan Ryutin, a second-tier Communist official who had been expelled from the party for Rightism in 1930. The thrust of Ryutin's criticism
was that Stalin had carried out a Bonapartist coup and made himself dictator. His policies had put the regime on a collision course with the peas-

ants, and it was time to get rid of him. Stalin was clearly very irked by this criticism, though the rumor that Stalin demanded the death sentence for Ryutin (who got ten years in prison) but was voted down in the Politburo has not been confirmed by archival research. His touchiness was already evident at the end of 1930, when criticisms of the leadership by former Stalin protégé Sergei Syrtsov and Beso Lominadze, an old friend of Ordzhonikidze's, were under discussion. Stalin complained bitterly that Syrtsov and Lominadze found it "necessary to abuse and defame me. Well, that's their business, let them abuse me. I'm used to it," he concluded, but clearly the claim was bravado; he minded. He was annoyed with Ordzhonikidze, too. When Postyshev remarked in passing that Syrtsov should have told Ordzhonikidze of his concerns, since Ordzhonikidze was known to be approachable, Stalin interjected, "That's all he [Ordzhonikidze] does, talk to people," a barb he later removed from the minutes.[18]

The issue of Rightist criticism was raised again a month later, when the Politburo and party Control Commission met to deal with the "counterrevolutionary group" of Alexander Smirnov, an Old Bolshevik of peasant origins and former agriculture minister of the Russian republic who had been demoted, presumably for Rightism, to a lesser job in forestry in 1930; and Nikolai Eismont, who had worked in trade and supply under Mikoyan. Though the OGPU claimed there was a conspiracy, this seemed dubious on the basis of the evidence presented. But evidently Smirnov, Eismont, and others close to them, had expressed dissatisfaction of a kind that was becoming familiar: a mixture of moderate Rightist critiques of policy and hostility to Stalin and his leadership. Stalin again complained that Oppositionists were dumping everything on him, but he said they wouldn't get away with it, as they were really criticizing the party line. Andreev supported him: "the aim of this group, like the others, is to get rid of comrade Stalin," and that was completely unacceptable.

The team naturally stood behind Stalin. It was clear, nevertheless, that many of them were uneasy about the counterrevolution accusations, and it may well be that their lack of enthusiasm had the effect of putting the brakes on Stalin's punitive urges, at least temporarily. Several showed signs of distress and human sympathy toward Smirnov, an old comrade, which was unusual on such occasions. Kuibyshev referred to Smirnov by his nickname, Foma, and said he knew him as a devoted Communist from way back in Narym exile before the revolution: evidently something extraordinary had happened that made the old Foma "completely unrecognizable." Rudzutak, using the familiar form in addressing Smirnov, said it was "very hard to listen" to his speech. Both these formulations were deeply ambiguous as criticisms. Mikoyan, Eismont's former boss and therefore potentially at risk of attack himself, stayed out of the discussion until late and then failed to come up with a clear indictment or repudiation; in a short exchange with Smirnov, he too used the familiar form of address. No personal sympathy came from Stalin, though he had shared the experience of Narym exile with Smirnov: he heckled him (though later removing this from the minutes), using the formal mode of address. The former Rightist leaders Rykov and Tomsky were present at the meeting, not exactly in the dock themselves but on the defensive. (Bukharin had gone off hunting in the Pamirs, his absence prompting some malicious sallies.) Tomsky took most of the heat, but the team seemed divided on whether to treat him as a wayward friend or an emerging enemy. Tomsky was still on familiar (*ty*) terms with Ordzhonikidze, Kuibyshev, and Kirov, whose criticism of him was notably friendly and almost jocular in tone, but not with Molotov and Kaganovich. At a Central Committee meeting not long after, Voroshilov spoke of his friendship with Tomsky in the past tense, and seemed to feel that he and Rykov were hopeless cases. He was much more optimistic about Bukharin, however, saying that he had been doing "good honest work" recently, and he even hoped that Smirnov would ultimately return to the fold.

Rudzutak made a ringing endorsement of Stalin's leadership at the January (1933) plenum. "We as members of the Central Committee vote for Stalin because he is ours," he said. "You won't find a single instance where Stalin was not in the front rank during the period of the most active, most fierce battle for socialism and against the class enemy. You won't find a single instance where Comrade Stalin has hesitated or retreated. That is why we are with him. Yes, he vigorously chops off that which is rotten . . . He is the leader of the most revolutionary, most militant party in the world . . . And he would not be the leader of the party if he didn't know how to chop off and destroy that which is slated for destruction." An even more eloquent tribute came from Voroshilov, who praised Stalin's magnanimity of spirit, as demonstrated by his personal concern for Rudzutak's health. The odd thing about Voroshilov's tribute was that it was written in a private letter to Enukidze, and in such fulsome terms that one wonders if it was really Enukidze he was addressing or (via OGPU perlustration) Stalin. As his wife would later bemoan, the team had had wonderful times together, until "life in the Party became more complicated, and our mutual relations too." Voroshilov's letter obliquely demonstrated the change in team relations with Stalin while trying to pretend he hadn't noticed them. "A remarkable man, our Koba," he assured Enukidze, an even older friend of Stalin's than he was, who on the face of it didn't need to be told about his virtues. "It's simply unfathomable how he can combine in himself both the great intelligence of a proletarian strategist and equally great state and revolutionary leader and the soul of a quite ordinary, simple, good comrade, understanding every detail, being concerned about everything which relates to the people whom he knows, loves, and values. It's good that we have Koba!"[19]

FOUR

THE TEAM
ON VIEW

THE XVII PARTY CONGRESS, BILLED AS "THE CONGRESS OF VICTORS," met in Moscow at the end of January 1934. The atmosphere was one of confident solidarity, with Stalin rapturously welcomed by the delegates and the rest of the team prominently on display, sometimes engaging in friendly and jocular cross talk. It was a message of celebration, addressed both to the home public and to watchers outside the Soviet Union, to whose reactions, hostile or sympathetic as the case might be, Stalin was particularly sensitive. Stalin gave the political report on behalf of the Central Committee, a statesmanlike presentation contrasting the growth of Soviet industrial might under the First Five-Year Plan with the Depression in the rest of the world. Molotov, Kuibyshev, Kaganovich, and Rudzutak also made reports. Kalinin was there, making the occasional folksy intervention. Mikoyan, Andreev, Voroshilov, Ordzhonikidze, and Kirov joined in the discussion of Stalin's report from the standpoint of their own bailiwicks (supply, transport, defense, heavy industry, and Leningrad), as was expected of them. Some future members of the team did the same, with Beria contributing on Georgia, Khrushchev on Moscow, and Zhdanov on Gorky (formerly Nizhny Novgorod, recently renamed in honor of the writer Maxim Gorky). No factional quarreling marred the serenity of the proceedings. As befitted a congress of victors, reconciliation with old opponents was the order of the day: Zinoviev and Kamenev, recently readmitted to the party though not to high office, spoke as repentant converts to the Stalinist program, as did the former Rightists. Bukharin was even allowed a comeback of a sort and offered an analysis of the international situation, in addition to endorsing Stalin's leadership.

There really were achievements to celebrate. Perhaps the best that could honestly be claimed for collectivization was that they did it and made it stick, with the hope that now that the famine was over, morale and collective farm productivity would improve. But as far as heavy industry was concerned, facts had sprung up on the ground all over the Soviet Union: new steel mills, tractor plants, blast furnaces, and power plants, symbolized by the giant metallurgical complex at Magnitogorsk, the "socialist city" that had risen out of nowhere on the Urals steppe. For all this spirit of celebration, nobody was likely to forget in a hurry how hard the battle for collectivization and industrialization had been. The very fact that this national party congress had been so long delayed, almost four years after the last one, was testimony to that. Despite the effusive public praise of Stalin's bold and wise leadership, the costs of the past four years of domestic war had been so high that some of the delegates, carefully chosen though they were, surely had private reservations.[1]

Some votes were votes cast against Stalin in the election of the new Central Committee at the end of the congress, and it appears that some of these dissident ballots were thrown out under Kaganovich's direction. The numbers involved were not large, and neither of these things was particularly remarkable: even the party's leaders often had votes cast against them, and according to Kaganovich, who as party secretary in charge of organization ought to know, votes were habitually added to make team members look more popular in the party than they actually were. But this particular case has aroused a lot of interest because it is linked with the story—unconfirmed but firmly embedded in Soviet myth—that a move was afoot in the corridors of the congress to get Stalin out of the office of general secretary and put Kirov in his place.

From the welter of conflicting testimony and confused memories, it looks as if some critical opinions were expressed in the corridors about Stalin's leadership, though these may initially have been flushed out by an inquiry among delegations initiated by Stalin himself. Certainly there was a move to bring Kirov in from Leningrad to Moscow as a party secretary, but it was originally suggested by Stalin and strongly resisted by Kirov, who was now as determined to remain in Leningrad as he had earlier been to stay in Baku. Ordzhonikidze supported Kirov, arguing that his presence in Leningrad, one of the country's industrial powerhouses, remained essential to the success of the industrialization drive. This resulted in the compromise decision that Kirov should become one of the central party secretaries but not, for the time being, give up his Leningrad position and residence. Those who criticized Stalin's leadership may have looked to Kirov as a possible replacement, although there is no suggestion that Kirov himself countenanced this. Molotov later poured scorn on the idea that Kirov could have been regarded as a possible replacement for Stalin—he just wasn't in that league, Molotov claimed, and "wouldn't have been accepted as top man, particularly by the senior cadres."

Kirov was indeed elected as one of the party secretaries, but he retained his Leningrad position and Leningrad residence. His fellow secretaries were Kaganovich and a new appointee, rising star Andrei Zhdanov, who was to be brought in from the Volga to Moscow, presumably to take on part of the workload that would have fallen to Kirov if he had been willing to move. As for Stalin, he quietly stopped using the title of "general secretary," signing himself simply as "secretary of the Central Committee."[2]

By now, perhaps, the title was irrelevant, for Stalin's status as leader (*vozhd'*) was well established. Now, no one could dismiss him as a backroom operator with a knack for dealing with personnel questions. The beginnings of the Stalin cult, which Stalin publicly disclaimed but probably privately enjoyed, date back to Stalin's fiftieth birthday in December 1929. On 21 December, *Pravda* devoted almost its entire eight-page issue to an unprecedented celebration of his achievements ("Stalin and industrialization," "Stalin and the Red Army") and birthday greetings. Reading "ecstatic articles" by Kalinin, Kuibyshev, Kaganovich, Voroshilov, Ordzhonikidze, Mikoyan, and others, a young Moscow Communist commented critically in his diary, "Of course comrade Stalin is a great man. But aren't these praises excessive?" Such mutterings continued in party circles for a few years, but an up-and-coming young Communist economist, Nikolai Voznesensky (who would rise into the Politburo in the 1940s before a spectacular fall) thought that the critics were just hidebound conservatives who didn't recognize Stalin's genius as a mass communicator.

Mikoyan retrospectively attached special blame to Kaganovich for fueling the cult by filling his speeches as Moscow party secretary with exaggerated praise of Stalin, but others thought Mikoyan himself, with his

Armenian blarney, contributed. A huge portrait of Stalin in a military greatcoat, flanked by smaller portraits of the other Politburo members, hung in front of the Lenin Mausoleum during the big physical culture parade in 1933, the first time such a thing had happened. When the real-life Stalin and his team stood reviewing the parade on top of these massive representations of themselves, they seemed puny by comparison. He stood "surrounded by his closest comrades-in-arms—Molotov, Kaganovich, Voroshilov, Kalinin and Ordzhonikidze," wrote Karl Radek, a repentant Oppositionist, who was probably consciously laying it on thick. "His calm eyes gazed reflectively at the hundreds of thousands of proletarians marching past Lenin's tomb with the firm step of a shock troop of future conquerors of the capitalist world. He knew that he had fulfilled the oath taken ten years earlier over Lenin's coffin." On the anniversary of Lenin's death a few weeks later, *Pravda* proudly proclaimed that Leninism had had "a great world-historic victory... Under Stalin's leadership the Bolsheviks have brought it about that SOCIALISM IN OUR COUNTRY HAS WON."

The new rituals of applause, with their reported gradations (from "Applause" to "Thundering, continuing applause. All rise") were now part of all kinds of celebratory meetings, not only party congresses. A Soviet reporter, fascinated by the sight, published an almost anthropological account of a meeting celebrating the achievements of Stakhanovites (outstanding workers) at which Stalin, Ordzhonikidze, and other leaders were present. "Applause burst forth, now dying down, now rising with new force, in honor of the leader of the people, comrade Stalin. When everything had quieted down, an excited voice from the depths of the hall suddenly shouted out a welcoming greeting in honor of Stalin in Kazakh. The Stakhanovites rose to their feet; Stalin, together with the party and government leaders, rose too; and for a long time, wordlessly, they passionately applauded each other."

Stalin was the centerpiece of these new rituals of celebration, but he didn't stand alone. *Vozhd'*, the term for a special type of top or charismatic leader, was used in the 1930s not only in the singular, for Stalin, but in the plural (*vozhdi*) for the team. Celebration of the *vozhdi* was particularly adulatory at the big national meetings of wives of senior managers in industry and commanders in the army attended by Stalin and the team in the mid-1930s. There was no sign of the team's own wives here (they were generally completely invisible in the Soviet media); it was all a matter of ec-static interaction between wives of second-tier bosses and the team, with Voroshilov, Ordzhonikidze, and Kaganovich, along with Stalin, particularly feted by "their" women, that is, the wives of commanders in their fields of the military, heavy industry and transport, respectively. Valentina Shtange, the wife of a senior railway official, seeing Kaganovich up close for the first time, recorded that "He is rather handsome, and his eyes are simply wonderful, so expressive! Above all, enormous serenity and intelligence, then firmness of purpose and an unyielding will, but when he smiles, his basic goodness shows through."[3]

The new genre of Soviet folklore—songs and poems by bards from the people, traditional in form, contemporary in content—not only celebrated Stalin in effusive terms but had a new name for Stalin's closest associates: they were the "knights" in his band. Among the knights, Voroshilov—"Klim-Our-Light Efremovich," as the folk bard Maria Kriukova liked to refer to him—was by far the popular favorite, no doubt thanks to his frequent appearance in dramatic roles in public, for example, at the Revolution Day parade in 1935, when he "reviewed the parade on a marvelous horse in a new marshal's uniform." It was the time of the return of army uniforms and decorations, which had been abolished in the first puritan years after the revolution; the troops reviewed by Voroshilov were also in new uniforms with epaulettes, not seen since tsarist times. In "Poem about Voroshilov" by the Kazakh folk bard Dzhambul, Voroshilov's experience in "smoke and fire" in the Civil War was celebrated, as well as his contemporary role at the head of the army ("Father Voroshilov on a chestnut horse / Gallops about the square bolder than the wind"). Voroshilov's special status with the public is indicated by the fact that his extensive popular correspondence included a genre that was his alone: letters from people claiming to be his relatives.

Ordzhonikidze was another knight, a sidekick to Stalin in a Civil War folk epic in which "the strong and mighty lad Stalin rises to his swift feet, walks about, strokes his black locks, twirls his moustache, and lights his pipe. He knows what must be done ... His plan is approved and Lenin tells him to take the heroes [cavalry leader Semen] Budenny and Ordzhonikidze to fight against the Whites." Kalinin's image was not knightly; he figured in the folklore as a peasant elder raised to national scale, welcoming visitors to the Kremlin and giving them food and drink.

Huge numbers of people wrote to Kalinin or came to see him in his office at the Supreme Soviet. You are "my only joy," one correspondent told him. Kirov, though locally popular in Leningrad, was not a subject of particular national attention during his lifetime, and even picked up a bit of unfavorable comment ("spell his name backward and you get *vorik*, petty thief"). But after his untimely death, he became a common subject of folk lament.[4]

To be sure, the folk had other modes of expression in which their comments on the leadership had a different tone. Anonymous letters to the leaders were a popular outlet, though the NKVD did their best to track down the authors. Some complained that the party was run by Jews, and that the non-Jews like Stalin and Kirov had sold out to them. Given that the team was, in fact, less Jewish than its former factional rivals, this might seem simply mindless reiteration of a timeworn grievance against revolutionaries, but it seems to have been known that Molotov had a Jewish wife, as well as falsely rumored that Stalin had married a daughter or sister of the Jewish Kaganovich. Some anonymous denouncers focused on another aspect of the team's non-Russianness: the prevalence of men from the Caucasus. "The supreme lord Caucasian prince Stalin and his true executant, peasant elder Kalinin" were the target of sarcasm from one anonymous writer, who wondered why they forgot to include the building of prisons in the Five-Year Plan.

The uncharismatic Molotov failed to catch the imagination of folk bards, but by the end of the 1930s his public recognition had risen substantially. His fiftieth birthday in 1940 produced a number of celebratory publications, and in the period 1939–41, he led the whole team (including Stalin) in the bestowal of his name on towns, collective farms, factories, and institutes, not to mention the city of Perm in the Urals, named after him in 1940. To be sure, he was a relative latecomer in the naming game. Stalin's name had been given to the Volga city of Tsaritsyn (Stalingrad), where he was based during the Civil War, as well as to the Ukrainian industrial town of Yuzovka (Stalino) in the mid-1920s. Tver, an old city north of Moscow, took Kalinin's name in 1931. Vyatka in the Urals and Samara on the Volga were renamed for Kirov and Kuibyshev after their deaths in the mid-1930s, and Voroshilov got Lugansk and Stavropol soon after. The North Caucasus city of Vladikavkaz took Ordzhonikidze's name in 1931, and four years later the industrial Ukrainian city of Enakievo was named for him as well. But there was a lesson here on the fleeting quality of fame, as for the previous six years Enakievo's name had been Rykovo, after the Rightist Alexei Rykov.[5]

If in domestic imagination Stalin stood with his knights around him, for foreign publicity consumption he usually stood alone. This was not because the rest of the team were excluded from foreign policy matters: on the contrary, it's quite surprising how energetically Stalin sought to involve them, both in formal Politburo settings and outside them. This applies not only to Molotov, who was Stalin's main confidant on international affairs, but to the others as well. There was, however, a constraint on team members talking to foreign journalists, which is one reason why they are so often invisible in prewar foreign accounts. Stalin himself rarely talked to foreigners either, but when he did, it was a big event—and, unlike his other business meetings, he did these interviews alone except for interpreters, without team members in attendance. In conversation with *New York Times* correspondent Walter Duranty, the writers H. G. Wells and Lion Feuchtwanger, and US ambassador Joseph Davies, among others, he presented himself with remarkable success as a straight-talking, sensible, and modest man, deploring the popular adulation of his person but accepting it as a necessary concession to a backward public; more of a realpolitiker than a wild revolutionary.

"I never met a man more sincere, decent and honest," H. G. Wells gushed (he had expected "a sort of Bluebeard"). Until Stalin warmed up, he seemed to Wells almost shy. "There is nothing dark and sinister about him. I had thought before I saw him that he might be where he was because men were afraid of him, but I realize that he owes his position to the fact that no one is afraid of him and everyone trusts him ... He is completely lacking in the cunning and craftiness of Georgians." Astonishingly, this was accounted as only a partial public relations triumph, since Wells remained critical of Soviet use of violence and restriction on freedom of speech: "We didn't manage to seduce the girl," commented the cynical Radek when he translated Wells's comments into Russian for Stalin. But there could have been no doubt about Stalin's complete success with Ambassador Davies—backed up, in this case, by a charm offensive on the part of Polina Zhemchuzhina, directed at the ambassador's wife, the extremely wealthy Marjorie Merriweather Post. Stalin was "sharp, shrewd, and, above all things else, wise," with "a sly humour," Davies wrote to his daughter. "A child would like to sit in his lap and a dog would sidle up to him."[6]

This success was all the more remarkable considering the handicap and sense of inferiority that Stalin and the rest of the team had felt in the early years when dealing with foreigners. Talking to the German writer Emil Ludwig in 1931, Stalin put the best face on it, conceding that while "those of us who did not live long abroad [before the revolution] lost something," but on the other hand, they "had the chance to do more for the revolution than those who were émigrés abroad." Privately, however, the lack of European exposure rankled. Compared to their cosmopolitan political opponents in the 1920s, the Stalin team were hicks who had never lived in Europe and didn't know foreign languages. Stalin had made brief trips to Stockholm and London for the party congresses in 1906 and 1907 (held abroad because of the underground nature of the party in Russia), adding a week in Paris to the latter trip; and in 1912 he had spent ten days in Krakow with Lenin and Krupskaya, as well as briefly visiting Vienna and staying with the Troyanovskys. He had tried, with only limited success, to learn German, French, and English, not to mention Esperanto, while in prison and exile before 1917, but his German, like Molotov's, was not good enough to speak or understand without an interpreter. Molotov had never been abroad before the revolution, and his only visit to Europe until the late 1930s was a short visit to Italy when his wife was undergoing medical treatment. He was appalled when, in the late 1920s, Stalin insisted that he take over leadership of the Comintern, previously held by cosmopolitans Zinoviev and Bukharin. He never lost the feeling of disadvantage, even after many years as Soviet foreign minister in the 1940s and 1950s. "What kind of diplomat am I?" he said to his interviewer Felix Chuev in the 1970s. "I don't know a single language. I could read German and French and understand something in conversation, but it was hard for me to reply. It was my chief disadvantage in diplomacy."

Kaganovich, similarly, had no experience abroad and knew no foreign languages, except perhaps a smattering of Polish from his youth in the multiethnic Pale. Mikoyan had never been abroad, as of the late 1920s, and spoke no foreign languages. The same was true of Voroshilov, Kirov, and Kuibyshev, though Kuibyshev may have had some German from school. Ordzhonikidze had spent a couple of months in Paris in 1912, but spoke no French, though he did perhaps know some Persian from a year of making revolution in Iran in 1909–10. The working-class Rudzutak, with no direct experience of Europe, was the exception among the team, as he had worked so hard on his self-study of French in prison that he was willing to try to translate it at sight (but the multilingual Trotsky scoffed at his mistakes).[7]

In the team's attitude to the West in the 1920s, fear and suspicion were the dominant motifs. This was based on the experience of foreign intervention in the Civil War, consciousness of "capitalist encirclement," and the renewed fears of foreign military attack of the late 1920s. Spy fears were a constant, perhaps understandably in view of the ubiquitous presence of foreign spies in Petrograd and Moscow in the early years after the revolution, even though this had been much reduced by the end of the decade. The spy fears rose to fever pitch—as with the panic about Polish spying in Ukraine during the famine—whenever political tensions were high. The series of show trials of "bourgeois specialists" in the late 1920s and 1930s dramatized the presumption of capitalist hostility, pointing the finger specifically at Britain (always suspected of being at the center of a web of international conspiracy against the Soviet Union) and France. Fears of imminent foreign attack may have been overhyped for domestic consumption in the late 1920s, but when the Japanese invaded Manchuria in 1931 and Hitler came to power in Germany in 1933, they acquired real substance.

The Soviet Union closed its borders under Stalin, trying to keep the spies out as well as the natives in. Dealing with and traveling to the West became the prerogative of a diplomatic caste, which, until the Great Purges at the end of the 1930s, consisted largely of Old Bolshevik émigré revolutionaries (many of them also former Oppositionists) with foreign languages. Travel to the German or Swiss spas for medical treatment became a cherished privilege of the political and cultural elite, but such trips had to be approved by a special Central Committee commission. Interestingly, the Politburo members themselves, though often ailing, rarely went abroad for medical treatment or for any other reason, although their wives (including Stalin's, incognito) sometimes did. Mikoyan was the sole Politburo member to make an extended foreign business trip in the 1930s.[8]

Europe's dangers included an émigré Russian community whose socialist wing continued to be infuriatingly well supplied by high-level Soviet gossip. The Menshevik Boris Nicolaevsky, related by marriage to

Rykov and editor of the Berlin-based journal *Sotsialisticheskii vestnik*, was an egregious offender. In 1936 he published "Letter of an Old Bolshevik," his own work but drawing freely on indiscreet conversations with Bukharin among others. The exiled Trotsky and his followers were another tremendous threat in the eyes of Stalin, the team, and the security agencies. While Trotsky himself had been packed off to Istanbul rather than his preferred destination of Western Europe, he had a small but noisy following in all the major European countries that was a constant irritant for all national Communist parties, and he infuriated Stalin and the Comintern by setting up a rival institution, the Fourth International.

When the team thought about European politics, including cultural politics, the Trotsky factor was never far from their minds. "Could be Trotskyites involved," Kaganovich wrote apprehensively to Stalin in 1934, apropos of a planned international conference against fascism and war. On this occasion Stalin was less alarmed, saying it was not a problem as long as the Trotskyites were denied access to the conference. But in general Stalin, who read all of Trotsky's émigré publications and critiques of his rule, was the most obsessed with Trotsky of them all. Since Trotsky's departure in 1929, Soviet foreign espionage had been trailing the family, including Trotsky's son Lev Sedov, who helped manage his European affairs from Paris before dying in mysterious circumstances in 1938, but it was during the Spanish Civil War, when Soviet intelligence and Trotskyists were locked in conflict on the ground, that matters came to a head. In 1939, Stalin allegedly told Beria, "Trotsky should be eliminated within a year, before war inevitably breaks out. Without the elimination of Trotsky, as the Spanish experience shows, when the imperialists attack the Soviet Union we cannot rely on our allies in the international Communist movement." Fortunately, he said, "there are no important political figures in the Trotskyite movement except Trotsky himself. If Trotsky is finished the threat will be eliminated." This death sentence was carried out the next year.[9]

Suspicion of foreigners extended to those residing in the Soviet Union, despite the fact that most of them were socialists with Soviet sympathies, including the large contingent of refugees arriving from Nazi Germany in the mid-1930s. "All bourgeois foreign specialists are or could be spies," Stalin reminded the team. His approach to Western journalists, similarly, was that, while a few could be usefully manipulated, their real function was to discredit the Soviet Union, which made them essentially spies. He was infuriated when some of the correspondents got out to the famine areas in 1933 ("These gentlemen must be forbidden to go travelling about the USSR. We've got enough spies in the USSR as it is"). He seems always to have taken a tougher line on disciplining foreign correspondents than the rest of the team, railing in 1932 about "our stupidity" in not expelling one who had written for the German press on taboo subjects like forced labor ("We are silent, like idiots, and tolerate the slander of this running dog of capitalist shopkeepers. Bol-she-viks, ha ha!"). In this case, Kaganovich agreed that "appropriate measures" would be taken, but it was a full five years before the man was expelled.

The surveillance on foreign residents, including sympathizers, increased. Among the more than a million Poles in the Soviet Union, there were mass arrests of peasant refugees in 1933, and two years later NKVD attention shifted to the political émigré community. The foreigners working at the French-language journal were arrested, despite protests from the Soviet foreign ministry and attempted intercession by the genial patron Voroshilov, no doubt alerted by one of his artist clients. German and Hungarian political émigrés in Hungarian Communist Eugen Varga's Institute of World Economy came under suspicion from the NKVD at the same time, despite Varga's good connections with Stalin, and Molotov's personal German tutor was arrested. A census of political émigrés began, registering a total of 811 political émigrés from Germany as of early July 1936. Compromising evidence had already been gathered against more than half of them.[10]

Although suspicious of foreigners, Stalin and the team were deeply interested in impressing them. The Paris Exhibition of 1935, where the Soviet pavilion sat challengingly opposite the German, was one such example. The team's interest in Soviet participation in competitions that their people had a good chance of winning was so strong that the Politburo agendas for the 1930s are dotted with items about sending chess players, footballers, and musicians to international competitions, with European tours for the Moscow Art Theatre and the Red Army Ensemble of Song and Dance thrown in for good measure. The Politburo took the trouble to approve the addition of child prodigy Busya Goldshtein to the list of Soviet entrants in the Brussells International Competition for Violinists in Brussels in 1937. When David Oistrakh won first prize, it was front-page news in *Pravda*.

Nor was this concern with Western opinion limited to stunning them with cultural prowess. Western reactions seem never to have been far from Soviet leaders' minds as they contemplated the country's achievements and setbacks. Kaganovich worried that the way *Pravda* was proposing to publish the trade-union budget would confuse the reader, "especially the foreign one," who might not appreciate how much money the Soviets were spending on construction of workers' housing. Reporting to Stalin on the first of the Moscow show trials of leading former Oppositionists in 1936, Kaganovich emphasized the "stunning impression" the confessions of guilt by the accused had made on the foreign correspondents in the courtroom. When the 1937 and 1939 census came in with population figures well under Soviet expectations, it immediately prompted fears that hostile Western observers would seize it as evidence of the disastrous impact of the 1932–33 famine.[11]

Stalin—who once gave his profession as "writer (publicist)"—was the team member most alert to the messages conveyed by the Soviet press, and he tried to inculcate the same attentiveness in Molotov and Kaganovich. Reminding them that, with regard to Japanese designs on China, "our military interference is, of course, ruled out, and diplomatic interference is not desirable at present, as it would only unite the imperialists, when it is advantageous to us that they quarrel," he went on to give instruction on spin. The party newspaper *Pravda* and the state newspaper *Izvestia* should take different tacks, he suggested, presumably to suggest lack of unanimity in Soviet ruling circles to foreign Kremlinologists. "Let *Pravda* abuse the interventionists and shout that the imperialist pacificists of Europe, America and Asia are dividing up and enslaving China. *Izvestia* must run the same line, but in a moderate and hyper-cautious tone. The moderate tone for *Izvestia* is absolutely necessary."

Despite the setback of his tutor's arrest, Molotov kept trying to improve his English and German in the 1930s; so did Stalin, Mikoyan, Kuibyshev, and others on the team. This might seem strange, given their ideological premise that exalted the Soviet Union as the world's first proletarian socialist nation and inevitable victor over the decadent, capitalist

West. The inevitable victory, however, was yet to come; the West, despite the Depression, had not yet collapsed under the weight of its own contradictions, and the Stalin team's condescending public superiority toward the West had an undertone of cultural cringe. Or, to put it in their terms, knowledge of the major European languages was part of being cultured, which was not only the leaders' prescription for the population but also their aspiration for themselves.

If there was some internal cringing, Stalin was keen not to let it show. By the 1930s, he already saw himself as the team's specialist on foreign affairs, coaching his closest associates, Molotov and Kaganovich, on how to handle international questions. Stalin had various maxims on dealing with the capitalist West: never trust them, recognize their cunning but be sure to outfox them, exploit their differences. Never forget that they want to destroy the Soviet Union and are just waiting for the next chance to invade. Realize that they are all likely to be spies, whether they present themselves as journalists, diplomats, or scholars, and regardless of their professed attitudes to the Soviet Union. This advice from Stalin is normally attributed to paranoia, but there was realism in it too—and it surely also reflected Stalin's wary sense that he didn't know enough about foreigners to be able to tell if they were who they claimed to be or not.

Conflict between capitalist powers should be encouraged. In the autumn of 1935, Stalin read Kaganovich and Molotov a lesson on the matter, apropos of the foreign ministry's doubts about exporting Soviet grain to Italy in light of Abyssinian conflict. It was really a conflict between two blocs, he explained, Italy and France on the one hand, and England and Germany on the other. "The stronger the quarrel between them will be, the better for the USSR. We can sell grain to both of them, so that they can quarrel. It's not in our interest that now one of them beats the other. It is in our interest that their quarrel is as long as possible, but without a quick victory for one or the other." Not being intimidated by the West was crucial, and this often meant talking tough. This applied to internal discussions ("swindlers" was one of the terms Stalin liked to apply to Western leaders) but also to public discourse. "We gave it to them right on the nose," Molotov reported with satisfaction in 1929. A few years later, Stalin congratulated Molotov on achieving just the right note in one of his speeches on the international situation: "a tone of contemptuous assurance in relation to the 'great' powers, confidence in our strength, a delicately simple spitting in the pot of the swaggering 'powers'—very good. Let them 'eat it.'"[12]

For the team, as for Stalin himself, the early 1930s were a period of intensive learning on foreign affairs. No team member was left completely free of foreign policy–related tasks in these years, with Stalin and Molotov taking the main burden and Voroshilov, Ordzhonikidze, and Mikoyan often drawn in on their area of specialization (military affairs, industry, foreign trade). Diplomats played only a limited role in the formation of Soviet diplomacy, according to later testimony from Molotov, because the issues were so immediate and challenging: "everything was squeezed into Stalin's hand, into my hand—it couldn't be otherwise at that period."

This no doubt underestimates the role of Maxim Litvinov, foreign minister from 1930 to 1939, but then Molotov, who was to succeed him in that role in 1939, was never a great admirer of his. He was a clever man and a good diplomat, experienced in foreign affairs, Molotov conceded, but "spiritually" not one of them, inwardly "not always in agreement with the decisions we took," so "of course, he couldn't enjoy our full trust." Still, Litvinov was an Old Bolshevik with long revolutionary credentials and a lack of Opposition connections quite unusual for a former émigré Jewish intellectual with good foreign languages. Molotov judged that he "had a favorable attitude to Stalin" while in office, although his later view of others on the team was highly jaundiced. (His eccentric and literary English wife, Ivy, was less restrained in her comments, even when he was foreign minister.) Throughout the 1930s, Litvinov was a regular attendee at formal Politburo meetings, as well as informal meetings with Stalin and top team members, when he was in town, but his inferior party status was indicated by the fact that he was never elected to membership of the Central Committee, let alone the Politburo, and never became part of the team's social circle.

Litvinov's name is associated with Soviet policies of entrance into the League of Nations and the search for an anti-German alliance in the 1930s. These were, of course, also Stalin's policies at the time, though no doubt Litvinov and Ivan Maisky, the Soviet ambassador to Britain, added their own flavor of positive preference for the Western democracies, whereas Stalin and Molotov were simply focused on keeping out of war and, if that proved impossible, not facing the likely aggressor (Germany)

alone. True, Stalin and others on the team made numerous snide references to Litvinov in their correspondence, often on the grounds that, mixing as he did with foreigners on a regular basis, he was likely to be conned
by them. But anti-fascism was not just the foreign ministry's line; from
the mid-1930s, it was also that of the Comintern—the only Comintern
policy that ever proved to have broad appeal to the international Left.[13]

The team didn't mix with foreigners, on the whole, and even their close
contacts with people who dealt with foreigners professionally were quite
limited. There were exceptions, of course, but many fewer than had been
the case with the cosmopolitan Oppositionists. Stalin used Eugen Varga,
a Hungarian, as advisor on the international economy, and both he and
Molotov consulted Otto Kuusinen, a Finn. Molotov had a close friend
from boyhood, Alexander Arosev, who had replaced Olga Kameneva as
head of the Society for Cultural Relations Abroad and spent much of his
time in Europe in the 1930s, taking a Czech woman as his second wife.
Two of Stalin's brothers-in-law, Alexander Svanidze and Pavel Alliluyev,
both intimates of his family circle, spent time in Berlin in the 1920s as
trade envoys. When the Bulgarian hero of the Reichstag fire, Georgy
Dimitrov, settled in Moscow in 1934 and became head of the Comintern
soon afterward, he was admitted to an outer circle of team sociability. In
this capacity he had many opportunities to see the very low regard in
which Stalin and his associates held the Comintern and European Communists. Although the West was preoccupied by the Comintern as a symbol of international conspiracy, Stalin, Molotov, and the rest were dismissive to an extent remarkable for Communists, who paid at least lip service
to the movement's internationalism.

The United States had a different and more positive resonance for the
team than old Europe. Capitalist it might be, but not decadent and class-
bound like Europe, and in terms of technological modernity, it was the
world leader. Stalin could speak with some warmth about American
know-how and entrepreneurial spirit, recommending these as qualities
the Soviets should emulate. He knew it only secondhand, of course, being
sparing even in his face-to-face meetings with American diplomats, journalists, and businessmen. But several big Soviet industrialization projects
had relied on expert American consultants.

Fittingly, therefore, it was to America that Mikoyan was sent in the
summer of 1936 for an unprecedented two-month trip to study the food

industry and its new technologies. It was Stalin's idea, apparently an off-the-cuff one, since it meant a last-minute cancellation of the Mikoyan family's planned vacation in the Crimea and the inclusion (by way of apology) of his wife Ashkhen in the group, along with assorted industrial experts. In a curious, homespun expedient, Stalin supplied the group with an interpreter in the form of a nephew of his daughter Svetlana's governess, an English-speaking German from the Caucasus, who, according to Mikoyan, did a good job, not only interpreting but also advising (on the basis of what knowledge is unclear) on local mores. The West was completely new to Anastas and Ashkhen, and they had a wonderful time; Mikoyan learned so much from the trip that he later referred to it as his "university." For Mikoyan, temperamentally not inclined to the intense suspicion and vigilance characteristic of Stalin and others on the team, Americans were welcoming, friendly, and helpful. They showed him ice-cream plants, packing materials factories, and the Chicago slaughter yards. They took him to Detroit, where he saw cars being built and met Henry Ford, who he was surprised to find was a vegetarian. Mikoyan couldn't talk to the Americans directly for lack of English, but it didn't seem to matter. He met Secretary of State Cordell Hull, at Ambassador Troyanovsky's insistence, and found him as nice as the rest of the Americans. He came back not only full of knowledge about refrigeration, American industrial processes, and department stores, but also determined to introduce the Soviet public to ice cream and frankfurters.[14]

Another foreign affairs initiative that resonated with the Soviet public was support for the republican side in the Spanish Civil War. There were no doubt strong elements of calculation in Stalin and Molotov's approach to the matter, but the Soviet public embraced the cause, responding warmly to rallies in support of the Spanish republicans and contributing funds for Spanish orphans. That emotional embrace evidently extended to some on the team, judging by Kaganovich's enthusiastic report to Ordzhonikidze, in a private letter, that while the actual war in Spain might not be going too well, "the campaign developing in the country shows what a remarkable, great people we have, and how much international feeling and consciousness they have." Kaganovich, whose adopted son Yury was reputed to be a Spanish orphan, was in awe of Stalin's diplomatic strategy on Spain (sending direct Soviet military aid while formally abiding by collective security and nonintervention): "Brother, that's really great dialectics," he wrote to Ordzhonikidze, "which our great friend and parent has mastered to the nth degree."

The Spanish campaign was an integral part of the rapprochement with foreign Leftist intellectuals, especially European, and fostered intensively from the mid-1930s as a complement to official diplomacy. Until that time, the assumption in the Comintern and Soviet agencies had been that the Soviet Union should court and support Communist and Far Left intellectuals, scorning the more middle-of the-road (and, often, better-known and more distinguished) contingent with the same vigor that the Comintern parties scorned and battled the socialists. The stimulus for a new policy—in effect, a forerunner of the Popular Front for culture—came from the writer Ilya Ehrenburg, a European cosmopolitan with broad contacts, who wrote to Stalin in 1934 suggesting a move away from the focus on a narrow sectarian public. What was needed, he wrote, was "a broad antifascist organization" that would attract non-Communist writers with high visibility and international reputations. It should have the dual purpose of "struggle with fascism" and "active defence of the USSR." Stalin endorsed this and told Zhdanov and Kaganovich to see to its implementation.

The result was the Congress for the Defense of Culture, held in Paris in June 1935 and attended by luminaries such as André Malraux, E. M. Forster, André Gide, Aldous Huxley, Bertolt Brecht, and Walter Benjamin, along with some of the Soviet Union's most distinguished writers, including Ehrenburg, Isaac Babel, and the (non-Communist) poet Boris Pasternak. On a parallel track, European intellectuals were warmly invited to the Soviet Union to see the "Soviet experiment" for themselves and make contact with artists and scholars in their fields under the auspices of Arosev's organization. Many came, including Bernard Shaw and the Webbs (Sidney and Beatrice) from Britain, André Gide from France, Lion Feuchtwanger from Germany, and Paul Robeson from the United States, and the results were generally gratifying from the Soviet standpoint. The Webbs wrote a massive tome entitled *Soviet Communism: A New Civilisation?* (removing the question mark on the second edition). Lion Feuchtwanger got an interview with Stalin and published a favorable appraisal, despite having been in Moscow during the first of the show trials of Old Bolsheviks. Only Gide proved a disappointment, publishing critical *Afterthoughts* to his memoir *Back from the USSR*, and was treated as a renegade thereafter. Feuchtwanger, like the Webbs, was impressed by

Stalin and scarcely aware of the team, with whose members he had little or no contact. This aspect of Soviet foreign relations was definitely Stalin's personal territory.[15]

At home, Stalin and the team paid the same kind of wary, half-respectful attention to the Russian intelligentsia that they did to foreigners abroad. With its long tradition of regime criticism, which was carried over from tsarist times into the 1920s, the intelligentsia, having been subjected to the stick during the Cultural Revolution and then offered the carrot of privilege in its aftermath, was only beginning to come to terms with the Communists, but the process of Sovietization proceeded apace in the 1930s. As with foreigners, Stalin and his team were initially ill at ease with the intelligentsia, daunted by the Opposition's much closer connections and cultural credentials, although the genial Voroshilov quickly made friends with artists who painted his portrait. Stalin was still reticent about his own cultural credentials in the 1920s. Someone like Trotsky, with his knowledge of languages, wide reading, and quick wit, could easily put him down as an ignoramus. This, however, was a mistake. Stalin was an indefatigable reader, with an estimated norm of five hundred pages a day, covering history, sociology, economics, and Russian literature—classical and contemporary—as well as contemporary affairs. He followed the periodical press in Russian (both local and émigré) and had important publications in European languages translated. He often went to the opera and theater. While the security services limited his theatergoing to the Bolshoi, the Maly, and the Moscow Art Theatres after Kirov's death, he had earlier been more adventurous, attending, for example, a concert of Persimfans, the first conductorless orchestra (not a good idea, he concluded: orchestras, like political teams, need a leader).

Stalin made a tentative foray into the arts in the second half of the 1920s when he started cultivating young militants from the Russian Association of Proletarian Writers (RAPP) and the Communist graduate schools in the social sciences, who were out to challenge the "bourgeois" cultural and academic establishments. This ended badly. The leader of RAPP, Leopold Averbakh, a young Jewish (nonproletarian) Communist, related by marriage to police chief Yagoda, annoyed Stalin by playing high politics and failing to develop a relationship of personal discipleship. The young Indian Cominterner M. N. Roy, whom Stalin selected as part of a personal foreign-policy brains trust that fizzled, quit Moscow, and ultimately the Comintern, amid disappointment on both sides. As for liaison with the graduate students at the Institute of Red Professors and the Communist Academy, Stalin made the unwise decision to depute the nonintellectual Kaganovich, who was no match for the competition (Bukharin).

In April 1932, RAPP and the other proletarian organizations were closed down by the Politburo, to the great relief of the rest of the cultural world, which they had mercilessly bullied. It was the beginning of a new era in the party's relationship with the intelligentsia. Attacks on the Bolshoi Theatre (always a bulwark of artistic conservatism, but also a national icon) were called off. Privileges to "specialists" were restored and expanded. A new dacha colony was built in Peredelkino outside Moscow for writers, and not just Communists either—Boris Pasternak got one.

Within the team by the mid-1930s, Stalin was justly regarded as their most erudite and cultured, as well as most intelligent, member. His special interest in cultural matters was signified by his choice of supervisory fields in the Politburo in the mid-1930s: others might keep an eye on agriculture, finance, industry, railways, and so on, but the fields Stalin took under his own supervision were state security and culture. He was still feeling his way in the cultural field, however. An attempt to assert theoretical preeminence in scholarship, orchestrated by Kaganovich in 1931, left a sour note: the young Communist intellectuals were not impressed by Stalin's "Letter to the editor of *Proletarskaia revoliutsiia*," and other scholars, forced to hold formal discussions of this (to them) meaningless document, were inclined to mock.[16]

Kaganovich, despite his unsuitability for the task, was still to the fore in Stalin's next cultural enterprise: organizing the hoopla over the return of the famous Russian writer Maxim Gorky to the Soviet Union at the end of the 1920s. Gorky, though close to Lenin and other Bolshevik leaders since the 1910s, and of lower-class origins, had been an energetic defender of the old intelligentsia under Cheka persecution in the Civil War years, and this, along with his weak health from tuberculosis, led to his departure and residence in an ambiguous, not-quite-émigré status in Capri for most of the 1920s. But he always wanted to come back, if only he could be sure of a strong enough position, and in the late 1920s Stalin managed to get him to commit. The package included enormous privileges and perks, including a townhouse in the center of Moscow (the old art nouveau Ryabushinsky mansion, picked out personally by Stalin), and dachas in the

Crimea and outside Moscow, but the most flattering offer of all was Stalin's friendship and unrestricted access to him. Stalin and the team had many things on their minds in 1932, among them oncoming famine, industrial construction problems, mass flight from the countryside, and drastic food shortages in towns. Yet at the height of all these crises, Stalin, Kaganovich, and Voroshilov spent hours and days with Gorky, getting to know one another and talking about how to organize a new inclusive Union of Writers.

With Stalin's blessing, Gorky became an international spokesman for the Soviet Union on cultural matters and, within the country, the go-to man for the intelligentsia, particularly its non-Communist part. He was the de facto defender of cultural figures in trouble with the security police, as well as maintaining contacts, to Stalin's annoyance, with old Communist friends who had ended up in Opposition. Increasingly critical of Stalin's regime and unable to travel, he began to feel like a prisoner, albeit a highly privileged one. The budding friendship with Stalin, Kaganovich, and Voroshilov doesn't seem to have lasted: as far as Stalin and Gorky were concerned, disappointment was mutual. An additional irritant, from Stalin's point of view, was that the man deputed to keep an eye on Gorky at the highest level—police chief Yagoda, who had known Gorky since youth and was almost a relative—ended up falling in love with Gorky's daughter-in-law Timosha, who along with Gorky's son and granddaughter Marfa Peshkova was a part of Gorky's extensive household. Young Marfa, as it happened, was the one in the Gorky household who became closest to Stalin by virtue of being a childhood friend of Stalin's daughter, Svetlana. Gorky was lionized and feted until his death in 1936, and canonized in the Soviet Union thereafter, but there was a gruesome postscript during the Great Purges when Yagoda, now labeled a criminal, was accused of murdering Gorky's son (and Timosha's husband) Maxim Peshkov, a dissolute type who had died in May 1934, probably after a drinking bout.

With Gorky, Stalin in a sense subcontracted out his own cultural patronage, preferring in the 1930s to remain aloof, a man of mystery whom writers literally dreamed of meeting, initiator of unpredictable telephone calls to writers of high reputation among the intelligentsia, like Mikhail Bulgakov and Boris Pasternak, which quickly became the stuff of legend. The NKVD, which monitored public reception of these telephone calls, reported that they worked beautifully: after Stalin called Bulgakov, a dramatist whose work had been under political attack and who was himself an object of suspicion to the security police, it was all around the Moscow grapevine the next day that Stalin had "given a slap in the face" to the rascals who had been persecuting Bulgakov, and in the intelligentsia they were now speaking of Stalin "warmly and with love." The call to Pasternak a few years later had similar success from Stalin's standpoint, although not from Pasternak's: when Stalin asked him if Osip Mandelstam—in trouble because of his political views, including a sharp satirical poem about Stalin—was really a great poet, Pasternak, who disliked conceding greatness to anyone else, fumbled his answer, allowing Stalin to rebuke him for failing to stand up for a friend.[17]

While it was beneath Stalin to be an ordinary patron to individual writers and artists, the rest of the team plunged into the patronage game, along with assorted military and secret police leaders from the next echelon down. The client-patron relationship, involving a personal and often social connection, brought the patron cultural prestige. For the client, it offered protection against the OGPU, censorship, or other misfortunes; help in organizing publication, exhibitions, or performances; and obtaining perks like dachas, apartments, and, in the most fortunate cases, cars with a chauffeur and foreign trips. By the mid-1930s, it would be hard to find a member of the team—Stalin excepted—who was not established as a patron to whom particular writers, artists, theater people, musicians, and scholars would turn in time of need, and equally hard to find a member of the cultural establishment (Communist and non-Communist) who lacked patronage ties at the highest level (though they might be mediated by Gorky or another cultural broker). Voroshilov, the earliest to start in the patronage business, was one of the most enthusiastic, with a stable of artists, especially painters, some of whom became friends as well as clients. He was a patron in the musical world, too, most famously for Bolshoi Theatre people but also for the up-and-coming young composer Shostakovich, who made contact with him early in his career. Molotov thought Voroshilov got too friendly with his artistic clients, and said Stalin thought so too. But Molotov himself was a patron, albeit usually without the affective ties of a Voroshilov or Rudzutak: his government mailbox was full of requests for help from writers, artists, scientists, and scholars, which he did his best to respond to.

Kalinin, Andreev, Zhdanov, Khrushchev, Kirov, Beria, and Malenkov all had their clients in the artistic, literary, and scholarly worlds. Voroshilov, Rudzutak, and Kuibyshev liked to socialize with their clients. Even Kaganovich, the least arty and most hardworking of the team, would go to the avant-garde theater director Vsevolod Meyerhold's productions with the tickets Meyerhold had sent him, and had his special intelligentsia clients; he was also a patron of the union of architects. Those two generous and approachable men from the Caucasus, Mikoyan and Ordzhonikidze, were patrons for many, Mikoyan being the obvious man for Armenians to go to, Ordzhonikidze for Georgians, as well as engineers. As young Nikolai Ezhov was beginning the steep ascent that made him head of the security police and implementer of the Great Purges in 1937, he and his literary wife launched themselves with considerable success as patrons: the writer Isaac Babel was in their stable, though the poet Mandelstam declined Evgenia Ezhova's approach in 1930, making the politically inept decision to stay as a client of Bukharin.[18]

The rapprochement of Soviet political leaders and the cream of the intelligentsia was just getting under way in the 1930s, and would develop further and faster in the 1940s as the team's children grew up and embraced intelligentsia values and, in many cases, professions. The limits were still being worked out, a test case being literary and artistic salons. The journalist Evgenia Ezhova established one, whose regular attendees included her former lover Isaac Babel and jazz king Leonid Utesov (but not her husband Nikolai Ezhov, head of the NKVD). Another was run by Olga Mikhailova, an opera singer at the Bolshoi who was the second wife of Civil War hero Marshal Semen Budenny. Olga Bubnova, wife of Old Bolshevik Andrei Bubnov, a longtime friend of Voroshilov's and Kuibyshev's, was joint hostess of a salon that met regularly on Wednesdays and Fridays in the mid-1930s, where high-ranking Communists and military men mingled with celebrities from the artistic world. Her cohostess was Galina Egorova, the film star wife of Marshal Egorov, with whom Stalin was allegedly flirting on the evening of Nadya's death. Despite this connection, it is highly unlikely that Stalin ever attended: literary salons were not his or the team's milieu. During the purges, most of the salon habitués, both political and artistic, were arrested, among them Olga Mikhailova (though not her husband, Budenny) and both the Bubnovs and Egorovs. Ezhova committed suicide in 1938, as her husband's career darkened and it became clear that she personally faced arrest.[19]

"Life has become better, comrades, life has become more joyous." That was the new slogan of the mid-1930s, indicating that the travails and hardships of the First Five-Year Plan period were in the past. Symbol of the good life to come was the Moscow Metro, whose first lines were built under the direction of Kaganovich and Khrushchev, and triumphantly opened in 1935—a rare exception to the team's determination to put all available resources into heavy industry and defense. Stalin and a bunch of family members, along with Kaganovich and Molotov, took an impromptu midnight ride a few weeks before its formal opening. New Year's trees, earlier banned as a bourgeois survival, made a comeback, thanks to an initiative from Pavel Postyshev. Polina Zhemchuzhina's growing perfume industry offered new brands to women: Red Moscow, Red Star, and New Dawn were among the favorites. Men were smartening up, too. On his return from the American trip, Mikoyan abandoned the Civil War uniform of yore and took to wearing a Western-style suit. Admittedly, Stalin was a backslider, preferring his field jacket and boots to the end of his life. Still, he joined the rest for a posed photograph that appeared on the front page of a Moscow newspaper in July 1935 in which team members sported snazzy new white summer jackets. Best of all, after years of food shortage, frankfurters, ice cream, and even champagne became available to Soviet consumers, thanks to Mikoyan and his American trip. The old specialty grocer's Eliseev reopened on Gorky Street in Moscow with a magical array of delicacies, admittedly expensive, including thirty-eight types of sausage, fifty kinds of bread, and fresh carp, bream, and pike swimming around in tanks.[20]

The new cultural shift, regarded as a sign of embourgoisement and "Soviet Thermidor" by carping critics like Trotsky in emigration, was popular with the elite and ordinary people alike. But the hope that life would really get better, with the coming of abundance and the end of terror, turned out to be a mirage. As the Soviet media were gearing up for the "joyous life" campaign with intensive publicity for the ending of bread rationing, which had been in force in the towns since the end of the 1920s, disaster struck. The date when rationing was to be lifted was 1 January 1935. Just a month earlier, on 1 December 1934, Kirov was murdered at the Leningrad party headquarters by a lone gunman, apparently with a personal grievance, and any hope of a cessation of terror in the foreseeable future disappeared.

Kirov's murder, like Kennedy's in the United States thirty years later, gave rise to endless conspiracy theories, despite the fact that the actual killer was a lone man who was immediately apprehended. Though many would like to believe that Stalin was behind it, no hard evidence of his involvement has been found, and in the nature of things, there can never be definite proof of his noninvolvement. The rumors about Stalin sprang up immediately, as they always did when a prominent person died unexpectedly. The team, judging by their later comments, gave no credence to the rumors at the time, though some thought differently in retrospect. To Stalin's daughter, Svetlana, hostile though she later became to her father, they never made sense: as both she and Molotov perceived it, Stalin was attached to Kirov, not threatened by him, and his death, following Nadia's only a few years before, was a body blow. On hearing the news, Stalin rushed to Leningrad with Molotov and Voroshilov, leaving Kaganovich to mind the shop in Moscow, and personally participated in interrogation of the killer, Leonid Nikolaev.

Whatever Stalin's initial involvement, there is no doubt that he quickly seized the opportunity to settle scores with his opponents. According to Molotov, Nikolaev admitted to being a follower of Zinoviev and was angry at having been expelled from the party, but Molotov saw him just as an "embittered man" rather than a "real Zinovievite." (In fact, anyone who had been in the Leningrad party in the mid-1920s was in some sense a Zinovievite, since Zinoviev was the Leningrad party boss.) But Stalin took the ball and ran with it, telling the local NKVD to look for coconspirators among the Zinovievites. Not particularly enthusiastic at first, within ten days the NKVD nevertheless came up with interrogation testimony that pointed the finger at a terrorist "Moscow center" headed by Zinoviev and Kamenev. Zinoviev and scores of Oppositionists who had no connection to the murderer, but were considered guilty of poisoning the atmosphere by their very existence, were arrested for terrorism. On the same principle, more than ten thousand former aristocrats and other "class enemies" were arrested or deported precipitously from Leningrad. The young Nikolai Ezhov from the Central Committee office, already sufficiently in Stalin's confidence to make the trip to Leningrad with him, organized the targeting of the Opposition on Stalin's behalf; within a month, he had compiled a list of roughly 2,500 former Zinovievites in Leningrad, 238 of whom were immediately arrested. Nikolaev pleaded guilty in a secret trial at the end of December and was executed. In Moscow, Zinoviev, Kamenev, and others associated with them were arrested, and their interrogators did their best to build up a case for direct involvement, but the two leaders would admit only that their oppositional stance might have created a climate encouraging others to act. At their trial in mid-January 1935, Zinoviev was sentenced to ten years in prison and Kamenev to six.[21]

Kirov used to stay overnight at Stalin's on his visits from Leningrad, and he had spent part of his last summer with Stalin and Svetlana in Sochi. After Nadya's death, according to his sentimental sister-in-law, Kirov had been the one who best comforted him: "he could approach him with simple affection and give him the warmth he was missing and peace of mind." After Kirov's death, talking to his brother-in-law Pavel Alliluyev, Stalin said, "I've become a complete orphan." At his birthday, celebrated a few weeks later with the team in attendance, the first toast (from Ordzhonikidze) was to Kirov, and later Stalin proposed a toast to Nadya, "his face . . . full of suffering." But after a mournful silence each time, the party resumed and even became quite noisy.

Not everyone mourned Kirov. A nasty little ditty making the rounds in the provinces had as its punchline "They've killed Kirov / We'll kill Stalin, too." Stalin had reason to be jumpy, although his suspicions were acquiring a paranoid cast. There were enemies all around, he felt, the more dangerous for being hidden. Shortly after Kirov's death, Stalin was heard to say, "Do you notice how many of them [NKVD duty officers] are around? Each time you go down a corridor you think: which of them is it? If it's that one, he will shoot you in the back, but if you go round the corner, then the next one will shoot you in the face. You go past and think about it."[22]

FIVE

THE GREAT
PURGES

THERE WAS "SOMETHING GREAT AND BOLD ABOUT THE POLITICAL idea of a general purge"; it was a "world-historic mission" beside which individual guilt and innocence was trivial. That comment came from, of all people, Bukharin, on his way to becoming one of the victims of the Great Purges. Perhaps he didn't really see it like that—he was writing one of his many appeals to Stalin, after all—but just thought Stalin and the team saw it that way, which is significant in itself. Bukharin wasn't sure, judging by his letter, whether the point (or what Stalin thought was the point) was a preemptive strike in light of the imminence of war or a "democratic" initiative to help ordinary people get rid of unworthy officeholders, no matter how eminent. Molotov opted later for the "imminence of war" argument, which has since become the favorite of historians, despite being something of a cop-out. Without the Great Purges, Molotov later said, the Soviet Union would have lost the Second World War. He knew the opposite argument, that it was just because of the savage purges of the military that the Soviet Union initially did so badly in the war, but he had something else in mind. The purges meant "that during the war we had no 'Fifth Column.'" Who constituted that potential fifth column? Molotov did not, as you might expect, point to the disaffected and injured in the Soviet population, of whom, as a result of collectivization and the purges, there were many. Instead, he focused on the apparently loyal party faithful: "After all, even among Bolsheviks there were and are people who are good and committed when everything is going well, when no danger threatens the country. But if something starts, they tremble, they desert."

We will never have a definitive answer to the question of what the Great Purges were meant to achieve. What can be said with some certainty is that to the degree that there was a firm political intention, that intention was Stalin's. The team went along, Molotov at least with some conviction, but they were executants (and potential victims), not initiators. They were frightened, like the rest of the Soviet political elite. But, as with collectivization, there was also a degree of admiration within the team for Stalin's boldness. Who else would have thought of initiating something so huge, dramatic, and risky? Only Stalin could have come up with it, Molotov rightly said, looking back.

For the team, the Great Purges were the latest episode in the party's history of struggle, starting with the revolution and Civil War and continuing with collectivization. They belonged to a revolutionary party, and fighting enemies was what revolutionaries did. This time the enemies were within the party as well as external, but that also had solid precedent: the Stalin team had spent almost a decade fighting the factions. Kaganovich made an uncharacteristic excursion in history to explain to an interviewer in the early 1990s why it had been necessary to purge the party so drastically: it was the danger of Thermidor, to which Robespierre and the Jacobins fell victim in the French Revolution. The Jacobins' factional enemy was the Girondins, and they got rid of them in the Terror, the French revolutionary equivalent of the Great Purges. But they failed to deal with the "swamp," that is, the uncommitted majority of delegates in the revolutionary convention. "The 'swamp,' which yesterday applauded Robespierre, today betrayed him. You mustn't forget the lessons of history," and how even once-true revolutionaries are "linked to the 'swamp' by many threads, both familial and non-familial." The Great Purges, in other words, were a decisive way of draining the swamp.[1]

The question of whether innocent people were likely to be caught up in the purges was uninteresting to Molotov and Kaganovich, looking back forty or fifty years later: of course they were; it could not be otherwise ("you can't make an omelette without breaking eggs"). When Molotov looked back on individual cases, like that of his former teammate Rudzutak, he would concede that while they might not have been guilty as charged, that is, not spies and saboteurs, they no longer had revolutionary fire in their belly. They had "degenerated," to use the language of the 1920s.

Svetlana Alliluyeva (Stalina) remembered that her father was in a nasty, bitter mood at home throughout this period. No doubt. Yet if you read the archival records of his activity at the office—tirelessly working through the mounting material on "enemies," keeping some cases in the "pending" category, briskly rejecting pleas, signing off on death warrants—there's a sense of excitement, even exhilaration, in his firm signature, the quick and clear decisions, the lack of any hesitation or doubt. He was at war, finally taking on the enemies in open battle. The others could not quite live up to this, though Molotov and Kaganovich did their best. Fear was a part of everyone's experience of the Great Purges, but there were different kinds of fear. Within the political elite, but below the level of the team, it was primarily fear of falling victim to the new wave of terror. As far as Stalin was concerned, the main fear must have been that the whole thing would fall apart or backfire. For the rest of the team, simultaneously perpetrators and potential victims, both kinds of fear were present.

As far as anyone has been able to establish, Kirov's murder was the trigger. It was the murder that gave Stalin the opportunity to settle scores with the old Left Opposition, and the man who carried out that task was to become the Great Executioner until he was executed himself. Nikolai Ezhov was a young man, almost boyish in appearance because of his very short stature, who had been working in the Central Committee apparatus since the late 1920s, a protégé of Kaganovich's before he became Stalin's favorite. His health was so poor—doctors diagnosed tuberculosis, myasthenia, neurasthenia, anemia, malnutrition, angina, psoriasis, and sciatica—that it's remarkable that he was able to handle his workload even before he became the Executioner. Everyone on the team liked him initially; nobody felt threatened. "Responsive, humane, gentle and tactful" was the word from former colleagues in the provinces; in Molotov's eyes, he was a good worker, though perhaps "trying too hard" because he was under such pressure for results from Stalin. Bukharin thought him "honest," and even Nadezhda Mandelstam, wife of the poet, found him "a most agreeable person."[2]

When Stalin put Ezhov in charge of finding (or creating) connections between Zinoviev and Kamenev for the Kirov murder, it was the beginning of a meteoric rise. Appointed as a secretary of the Central Committee early in 1935, he was in Stalin's office talking about security matters almost as often as Yagoda—on whose territory he was, at Stalin's behest, encroaching—long before he replaced him as head of the security police in September 1936. His mandate was to deal with the "Trotskyite-Zinovievite bloc," which Yagoda had failed to do effectively. The 1935 trial of Zinoviev and Kamenev had not produced full confessions or maximum penalties, and one of Ezhov's first tasks was to remedy this in a 1936 retrial that was the first of three big media events known as the Moscow show trials. As testament to the importance of Ezhov's work, he became a candidate member of the Politburo in 12 October 1937. For the year 1937, he was Stalin's second most frequent visitor after Molotov. The Kazakh bard Dzhambul wrote an ode to him as "a flame, burning the serpents' nests."

After the Kirov murder, the next shock was the disgrace of Avel Enukidze, an old friend and companion of many members of the team, including Stalin, whom he addressed as "Soso." At Nadya's funeral, Enukidze had comforted the six-year-old Svetlana, dandling her on his knee; a few weeks later, he was part of the group of close friends celebrating Stalin's fifty-fifth birthday. He may also have tried to defend Kamenev and Zinoviev and save them from arrest in the aftermath of Kirov's murder.

Enukidze worked directly under Kalinin in the Supreme Soviet, which was housed in the Kremlin. He was accused of laxity in allowing "class enemies" to work in his administration, often under his personal protection. He was indeed a generous patron who had quietly done what he could, with Kalinin's implicit support, to subvert the persecution of persons of aristocratic origins, which had marked the Cultural Revolution; his reputation as a soft touch was widely known. But probably this was less alarming, in the light of what had happened at Kirov's headquarters in Leningrad, than the laxness of security in the Kremlin under his watch. Stalin gave a highly colored account of the dangers in conversation with the visiting French writer Romain Rolland: female librarians, evidently of dubious social origins, had been recruited by "our enemies" to poison members of the team. Reflecting the anti-Thermidorian preoccupation he shared with Molotov and Kaganovich, he cited Enukidze as an example of "people [in the party] who believe that we can now 'take it more easily'; in view of our great victory, in view of the fact that our country is moving forward, they can now afford to rest, to take a nap." Nobody should think they could take it easy.

Conveniently, several Kamenev relatives were discovered in Enukidze's Kremlin staff, including Kamenev's brother and the brother's ex-wife. All in all, 110 employees of the Kremlin service administration (including the Kamenev relatives) were arrested in the so-called Kremlin affair; they were accused of organizing a group to assassinate government officials in the Kremlin and of receiving "terrorist instructions" from Zinoviev and Kamenev. The group was later widened to include Kamenev's first wife, Olga (who was also Trotsky's sister).[3]

Stalin seemed undecided about what to do with Enukidze, although this may well have been his famous caution: Enukidze was popular, and it was going to take time for the team to come around to the notion of complete disgrace. Months after the initial attacks, Kalinin was still trying to broker some sort of deal, and Ordzhonikidze, to Stalin's irritation, continued to treat Enukidze as a friend. Sent down to Kislovodsk as Supreme Soviet representative, Enukidze annoyed local bigwigs by playing the great man and talking about his imminent reinstatement and return to Moscow. Stalin decided he needed to be moved to somewhere less visible, and on 11 September, the Politburo sent him off to Kharkov to head the road transport office. The new appointment was clearly not to Enukidze's liking, and it took several weeks of effort to persuade him to leave Kislovodsk. Nevertheless, this was the end of Enukidze politically, despite a halfhearted proposal from Stalin and Molotov in June 1936 to restore his party membership. He was arrested a few months later, executed in 1937, and in 1938 posthumously named in the third of the Moscow show trials as a Rightist coconspirator with Bukharin and Yagoda.

In the summer of 1936, Kamenev and Zinoviev were put on trial for the second time and, in a blaze of publicity, confessed to involvement in the Kirov murder and a variety of other terrorist plans, all with detailed and dramatic scenarios. They were sentenced to death and executed. This was, of course, a Rubicon. Up to this point, the taboo against killing defeated opponents from within the party had held; now it had been broken. Indeed, within a few months it was broken again for someone who had been much closer to the team than any Oppositionist: Enukidze. Memoirs of team members are silent about their reactions, but it is hard to believe that Molotov, at least, was happy. Out of favor with Stalin for reasons that remain obscure, he suffered the indignity of *not* being named as a target of assassination in Zinoviev's and Kamenev's alleged conspiracies, although the rest of the team were all on the list. This was amended in the second Moscow trial six months later when Molotov was in his proper place as a leading target, indicating that whatever rift had existed had been healed. In fact, the estrangement cannot have lasted longer than the six-week vacations that Stalin and Molotov both took in the summer of 1936, as both before and after, Molotov was, as usual, Stalin's most frequent office visitor. But it was one of those little jolts that Stalin liked to administer to team members to keep them on their toes. When Molotov, poker-faced, was the recipient, he rarely gave Stalin the satisfaction of showing he was rattled.[4]

The Moscow show trials were extraordinary theater, outlining fantastic stories of conspiracy whose threads ultimately led to the exiled Trotsky, hand in glove with foreign intelligence agencies. The scenarios—compiled on the basis of confessions extracted under interrogation and often torture—were coordinated by Lev Sheinin, a top NKVD official in charge of the investigation branch, who was also, as it happens, a playwright: in the legitimate Soviet theater, as opposed to the political one of the show trials, his *Face to Face Confrontation* was one of the hits of 1937. Stalin enjoyed reading the interrogation transcripts regularly sent to him by Yagoda. "Did you read the confessions of Dreitser and Pikel?" he wrote to Kaganovich. "How do you like the bourgeois dogs from the camp of Trotsky-Mrachkovsky-Zinoviev-Kamenev? These shitheads, to put it mildly, wanted to 'take out' all members of the Politburo! Isn't it absurd! What people can come to."

Stalin was prudently out of Moscow on vacation for the 1936 Zinoviev-Kamenev trial, the first of the Moscow show trials (which might have turned out to be a flop), perhaps to muddy the waters about his own key role in its organization. But he conducted a running correspondence with Kaganovich and Ezhov about how best to stage it, with a particular eye to reaction in the West. "The role of the Gestapo [as the inspiration behind the plots] should be exposed in its full magnitude," state prosecutor Andrei Vyshinsky and judge Vasily Ulrich were told as the trial began. It was crucial for Trotsky to figure prominently, not just in the prosecution's case but also in the judge's summing up, so that foreign readers would know that the judge had been convinced on this point. It should be clear that the conspirators' aim was to bring down the Soviet regime. As the show trial played out in Moscow, Kaganovich kept Stalin apprised of points in the scenario that foreigners had found particularly sensational, while the NKVD regularly provided foreign reviews of the performance—not just press cuttings but also transcripts of the correspondents' intercepted telephone conversations and telegrams.

Like any good suspense story, the scenario of the first Moscow show trial hinted at future sequels. There were suggestions of links with the Right, and a promising "reserve center" of terrorist conspiracy involving former Leftists, including Karl Radek and Yury Pyatakov, was emerging in interrogation testimonies. Pyatakov was the problem: repented and re-admitted to the party, he was Ordzhonikidze's invaluable deputy at the industrial ministry, and Ordzhonikidze wasn't giving him up without a fight. Kaganovich was still unsure whether he could be publicly named in court as late as 17 August. On the last day of the trial, prosecutor Vyshinsky made the startling announcement that, as a result of compromising testimony offered in the trial just concluded, investigations would begin of Tomsky, Rykov, Bukharin, Radek—and Pyatakov.[5]

Under investigation but still in his job, thanks to Ordzhonikidze, Pyatakov thrashed around desperately, trying to save his skin during the trial by calling for the death penalty for the Zinoviev-Kamenev group ("these people ... must be destroyed like carrion"), and, bizarrely, offering personally to shoot all those sentenced to death in the Zinoviev-Kamenev case, including his own former wife. His offer was rejected with mockery by Ezhov, and Ordzhonikidze's desperate efforts also failed. Pyatakov was once again expelled from the party on 11 September and arrested the next day. He would become the chief defendant in the second of the show trials that opened in Moscow on 23 January 1937.

Ordzhonikidze was also furious and upset about the arrest of his elder brother down in the Caucasus, interpreting Stalin's refusal to intervene as a withdrawal of trust from himself. Molotov considered that it was his brother's arrest that "pushed him over the edge," but the pressures on Ordzhonikidze were multiple. His friend Enukidze was arrested on 11 February 1937, and the agenda of the upcoming plenum of the Central Committee included accusations of "wrecking" in Ordzhonikidze's industrial ministry. According to Mikoyan, Ordzhonikidze felt betrayed by Stalin ("We were such close friends! And suddenly he allows this sort of thing to be done!"), as well as threatened. He said he couldn't work with Stalin anymore and would rather kill himself—but Ordzhonikidze was a volatile man, and Mikoyan thought that he had managed to calm him down before they parted. But then, on 18 February, the eve of the Central Committee plenum, after a particularly stormy meeting with Stalin, Ordzhonikidze went home and shot himself.

His death was a blow to his numerous friends on the team, including Stalin, who surely construed it as another betrayal. Ordzhonikidze got the state funeral appropriate to his eminence; his death was not announced as a suicide, and Khrushchev claims that he only found out that it was years later. But for those who could read between the lines, there were sufficient signs that Ordzhonikidze had been in trouble when he died. The second Moscow show trial, starting a few days later, was one of them, since Pyatakov featured prominently among the defendants who received the death sentence. At the Central Committee's meeting in February, Stalin made a passing reference to Sergo's weakness of getting attached to subordinates who didn't deserve his trust, and the revelation of conspiratorial networks within Ordzhonikidze's industrial empire was the centrepiece of Molotov's report on the same occasion. This plenum, initiating a wave of accusations, denunciations, and arrests against government officials and party secretaries all over the country, is usually taken as the beginning of the Great Purges.[6]

There was worse to come. At the end of May, a group of army officials, including Marshals Mikhail Tukhachevsky, Iona Yakir, and Ieronim Uborevich, were arrested, accused of conspiracy in collaboration with Trotskyites, Rightists, and the German intelligence service. They were tortured until they confessed, with Ezhov personally supervising the interrogation, and then shot within a few days. Announcing this on 12 June, *Pravda* called them "Judases" who had been bought by the fascists.

It was another shock for the team, many of whom were close to the military leaders. Kaganovich and Khrushchev were friends with Yakir, and both were personally threatened by his arrest. Mikoyan was a friend of Uborevich, and later said he spoke out in the Politburo in June 1937 against his arrest. He was also a friend of Jan Gamarnik, another of the military group, who escaped the fate of the others only by committing suicide, possibly after being tipped off by Mikoyan. Voroshilov had served with all the accused and was on good terms with most of them (though not Tukhachevsky, a professional rival); he had to admit that "not only did I not notice these base traitors, but even when they started to unmask some of them . . . , I didn't want to believe it." To add to his unhappiness, he had been used in the process of snaring them: it was in response to Voroshilov's summons that his friend Yakir had come in to Moscow from Kiev and been arrested by the NKVD on the train.

German espionage had leaked false information to the Soviets that Tukhachevsky was planning a coup d'état, but this did not figure either in his trial or in the pretrial meeting at the beginning of June 1937, when Stalin, in an uncharacteristically wild, rambling speech, made unsubstantiated accusations against Tukhachevsky, Yakir, and the rest, in the words of one historian, "simply expressing his desire to get rid of them." The message, which must have sent chills into the hearts of all who heard it, was that it wasn't just former Oppositionists who were the danger: *anyone* might turn out to be an enemy. Particularly distressing for the team was that one of their own members had been caught in the web: Rudzutak, arrested on 24 May, who Stalin said was refusing to admit his guilt but had been shown to have given information to a beautiful German spy (who had also allegedly seduced Enukidze) in Berlin. In addition, another team member, Andreev, got a worrying passing mention as "an active Trotskyist in 1921," even though in a context of Stalin's statement that not all former Trotskyists were enemies.

Molotov conceded much later that Tukhachevsky and the rest were not actually spies, "but they were linked with intelligence people and, most important, in the decisive moment you wouldn't have been able to rely on them." This may also have been his view at the time, given his closeness to Stalin and the center of things. Khrushchev, less privileged with regard to information, says he believed the accusations, despite his friendship with Yakir. In fact, he went out of his way in his memoirs to deny that at the time he felt sympathy with Yakir and the others: on the contrary, he wrote, "I was angry and indignant with them because we were convinced then that Stalin could not be mistaken."[7]

The leaders of the Right, of course, were in the firing line too. Named as under investigation at the Zinoviev-Kamenev trial in August 1936, Tomsky shot himself, leaving a note to Stalin that protested his innocence. There was a tradition within the Russian revolutionary movement of treating suicide on a point of principle with respect, even as a heroic act, but Stalin and Molotov were having none of it. Tomsky's suicide was denounced as cowardly and anti-Soviet, and Molotov even suggested that it was part of a plot arranged by Tomsky with others to cast discredit on the regime by killing himself. Still, Bukharin would have had a more dignified end had he followed Tomsky's example, but he allowed Stalin to string him along for years, all the while writing abject letters to "Koba," still using the familiar form and protesting his devotion. He even sent Stalin a poem he had written in his honor ("With an eagle's gaze, cold and calm, / The Captain looks out from above)," and commented on the death of Zinoviev and Kamenev that "It is excellent that they shot the scoundrels. The air immediately became cleaner." Sent abroad early in 1936 to negotiate the purchase of the Marx-Engels archive in France with Menshevik broker Boris Nicolaevsky, and encouraged against all precedent to take his young, pregnant new wife, Anna Larina, with him, he turned down the implicit invitation to defect but, with his usual lack of common sense, gave Nicolaevsky a comprehensive and highly critical rundown on Soviet high politics, told another Menshevik émigré that Stalin was "not a man [but] a devil," and topped it off by informing the French Leftist writer André Malraux that Stalin "is going to kill me." These comments presumably did not long remain unknown to Stalin.

With a tempting target like Bukharin, Stalin's sadistic instincts were given full play, and the team joined in, a gang of schoolyard bullies. Tears, screams, hysterical collapses, and bouts of total depression on Bukharin's part punctuated the public bullying. At one point, Bukharin shut himself up in a small room in his Kremlin apartment, formerly Stalin's ("Nadya died here. So will I"), declaring a hunger strike and refusing to come to the February-March party plenum to respond to charges against him, only to change his mind and give Stalin and Molotov the chance to entertain delegates with cross talk like a pair of comedians:

STALIN: How many days has [Bukharin] fasted?

MOLOTOV: He said that on the first day he fasted 40 days and 40 nights, the second day 40 days and 40 nights, and then every day thereafter 40 days and 40 nights.

STALIN: Why did he begin his hunger strike at midnight?

MOLOTOV: I think because people do not eat at night; their doctors do not recommend it.

Bukharin wrote a desperate letter to his old friend Voroshilov, asking, "Do you believe all this? Really?" and ending with "I embrace you because I am pure." But Voroshilov rebuffed it, eliciting a cry of pain from Bukharin about "your *terrible* letter"—and on top of that, forwarded Bukharin's letter and his reply to Stalin, the line about purity evoking mockery as it made the rounds. Bukharin even wrote to Khrushchev, whom he didn't know well, asking pathetically to explain why "you called me a class enemy" at the banquet for Moscow Metro builders. To Molotov, an unlikely man to be swayed by emotional appeal, he wrote (rather surprisingly using the familiar form), trying to explain his torment, surrounded by "morally unbearable" suspicion, "afraid of every side glance, every unfriendly gesture." In an anguished postscript, he begged, "Couldn't this nightmare be dissipated? Couldn't I be told what doubts you have so that I could answer them calmly?" Molotov liked Bukharin, but of course, the answer was no—or, to be more exact, silence.

Bukharin was arrested on 27 February 1937, but even then the agony of waiting was not over. There was some uneasiness within the Central Committee about the death sentence that Ezhov recommended. Bukharin, ever hopeful, continued to write to Stalin from prison, suggesting on 10 December 1937 that Stalin might like to send him to America to do propaganda for the show trials and against Trotsky. "My inner conscience is pure before you now, Koba," he concluded. Not surprisingly, Stalin ignored the letter. Bukharin, along with Yagoda and others, were showcased as defendants in the last of the Moscow trials, held in March 1938.[8]

Why Bukharin or any of the other defendants in the show trials confessed has been the subject of much speculation. Torture is clearly one answer, along with threats to family (there were more confessions from those, like Bukharin and Kamenev, who had young or teenage children). But it was also a way of buying a day in court with the world's media reporting every word. Yagoda used his final statement to point out the absurdity of the charge of spying against him ("If I had been a spy, dozens of countries could have closed down their intelligence services"). Bukharin tried a similar tack, setting himself up as a counterscenarist, so to speak, to Sheinin: his plan was evidently to exaggerate to the point of absurdity, lacing his voice and text with sarcasm, confessing monstrous conspiracies to membership but then undermining the confession by noting that the conspiratorial group he had belonged to was actually nonexistent. According to Molotov, wild and implausible exaggeration (usually attributed to the NKVD) was a standard ploy of former Oppositionist defendants in the show trials. But if so, it doesn't seem to have worked very well, as the public seems to have swallowed it all anyhow—though in the case of the foreign public, not without a certain puzzlement.

As for Bukharin's self-undermining, Stalin foiled this neatly, at least as far as the published record was concerned, by simply deleting the key qualifications ("I was with Trotsky in a non-existent bloc" becoming "I was with Trotsky in a bloc"), thus leaving a relatively straightforward confession. The audience present in the hall seems to have missed Bukharin's subversive point, at least the foreigners with imperfect Russian, taking it to be a real confession but wondering why he made it. The answer, for many, was in the almost mystical revolutionary faith expressed toward the end of Bukharin's final speech, subsequently immortalized in Arthur Koestler's paraphrase in *Darkness at Noon*: in the original version, Bukharin said, "while in prison I made a revaluation of my entire past. For when you ask yourself: 'If you must die, what are you dying for?'—an absolute black vacuity suddenly rises before you with startling vividness. There was nothing to die for, if one wanted to die unrepented."

"Shoot the mad dogs!" was the cry of Andrei Vyshinsky, the state prosecutor at the show trials. Almost all the defendants were shot, and many of their colleagues, friends, and relatives were swept up into Gulag as "enemies of the people." As Molotov explained to Chuev years later, obviously the families had to be isolated; otherwise, feeling aggrieved, they would just make trouble. The wives of senior Communist victims, including the show trial defendants, were usually arrested and sent to a special camp for Wives of Enemies of the People in Kazakhstan, whose current monument outside Astana lists many illustrious names, including that of Bukharin's youngest widow, Anna Larina. Ex-wives might also be snatched up, or they might just occasionally be lucky: Bukharin's loyal first wife was arrested, but his second wife, Esfir, remained free, as did his teenage daughter with Esfir, Svetlana, an old playmate of Svetlana Stalina. Grown-up sons were often shot, while daughters and teenage sons usually just got Gulag or exile. Young children like Anna Larina's toddler Yury ended up in orphanages under another name if no family member or devoted servant stepped forward to take them.[9]

For the time being, the alleged kingpin in all this, Lev Trotsky, survived in his Mexican exile, reading the charges against him and feverishly pointing out the inconsistencies and inaccuracies in the scenarios in the hope of discrediting the show trials and clearing his name with an international audience. Soviet agents covered his every movement and that of his son, Lev Sedov, tapped their telephones, read their correspondence, and regularly sent the transcripts to Stalin. Hounded by Soviet security wherever he went, Trotsky was finally assassinated by a Soviet agent in 1940. His wife Natalia, and young grandson Seva, who were with him in Mexico, survived, but otherwise it was an almost complete swath of everyone connected with him, inside and outside the Soviet Union, including his first wife Alexandra and their nonpolitical engineer son, Sergei.

If Stalin was the man pushing the buttons in the Great Purges, the whole team, which supported his efforts and sometimes added their own initiatives, must be considered perpetrators. Any Politburo member who was available signed off along with Stalin on lists of unmasked enemies for whom the NKVD recommended the death sentence. Molotov, Kaganovich, Voroshilov, and Zhdanov were the most frequent signatories after Stalin—but this just reflects frequency of contact with Stalin in these years. Mikoyan was somewhat less frequent on both counts. This collective signature has been interpreted as a form of blackmail, ensuring the provable guilt of the whole team and not only Stalin, but it was also standard operating procedure. Stalin almost always involved the team in his enterprises, which is not the same thing as saying he let them make the big decisions. Sometimes he rubbed their noses in their complicity. When Yakir's appeal against his death sentence came before the Politburo, Stalin, refusing the appeal, allegedly wrote, "scoundrel and prostitute" next to his signature, after which Kaganovich felt bound to go one better and add, about his former friend, "For the traitor, scum and [scurrilous obscene term] one punishment—the death sentence."[10]

Stalin sat tight in Moscow throughout the purges; he didn't even make his usual summer vacation trip down South in 1937, or any subsequent year until after the war. Molotov also rarely left Moscow at this period. But most of the rest of the team were back on the road, traveling to the provinces to preside over party meetings the outcomes of which were generally the arrest of the local first secretary and those close to him. Rather unexpectedly, the reticent Andrei Andreev, generally not in the inner circle of the team, was a workhorse during this time, traveling to Voronezh, Cheliabinsk, Sverdlovsk, Kursk, Saratov, Kuibyshev (formerly Samara), Rostov, Krasnodar, Uzbekistan, Tajikistan, and the Volga German Republic in the course of the year. He was away so often that he wasn't often around to sign death warrants in the center. But "wherever he went," Khrushchev later said, "people perished." Andreev's deadpan reports to Stalin have been preserved; when he had finished purging, he sometimes had a look at how local industries were doing or (shades of the early 1930s) checked on the agricultural sowing campaign. There was a lot of train travel involved, in the special coaches the team and military leaders used, and on such trips Andreev, a music lover, liked to listen to Beethoven.

Kaganovich went to Cheliabinsk, Yaroslavl, Ivanovo, the Donbass, and Smolensk to purge the local party committees. Always a bully, he did the job with more panache and fearsome dramatic effects than Andreev, shouting and hectoring. According to an NKVD eyewitness, he rolled into Ivanovo on 7 August 1937 with an armed guard of thirty-five men on the train, immediately struck terror into the hearts of the local party bosses by refusing for security reasons to go to the dacha they had prepared for him, organized denunciations of these same bosses by their colleagues, personally supervised the arrests, and pushed the interrogators to get quick confessions, all the while checking in several times a day with Stalin in Moscow. Zhdanov did his duty in Kazan, Orenburg, and Ufa: his approach was less bullying and more high-minded than Kaganovich's—"a moral oppression has been lifted" with the purging of the old corrupt leaders, he told one local party meeting—but he got the job done. Malenkov went to Belorussia, Armenia, Yaroslavl, Tula, Saratov, Omsk, Tambov, and Kazan. Twenty years later, when he fell into final political disgrace under Khrushchev, colleagues reproached him for the deaths of the party secretaries arrested in the provincial cities he had just left, but his son had another interpretation of his trips, claiming that Malenkov was just gathering data for the report on local purging excesses that he did in fact make to the Central Committee in January 1938. Probably both versions are true. Mikoyan seems to have been sent out only once—to Armenia in September 1937, accompanied by Beria and Malenkov—and did a poor job, from Stalin's point of view. Discomforted by the presence of so many friends and clients, he kept as much as possible in the background at the party plenum and let Malenkov do the talking.[11]

Everyone was involved in the purging of the institutions they headed, otherwise they would have been accused of protecting their subordinates, a message clearly conveyed in the posthumous rebuke to Ordzhonikidze. Kaganovich, who had to purge the railways, no doubt spoke for all of the team when in old age he protested against archive-grubbing historians who pulled out "dozens of letters of Kaganovich where he agreed to or proposed an arrest" and took that as evidence of guilt. Of course there were letters like that, Kaganovich said; it was one of the conventions of the process that when there were arrests in your own bailiwick, you had to sign off on them. "Well, what could [you] do?" Voroshilov had to supervise the purging of the military, though he was not happy about it. Zhdanov, Khrushchev, and Beria, the last two not yet Politburo members, were doing the same in the regions they headed (Leningrad, Moscow and then Ukraine, and Transcaucasus, respectively), though they did it under local NKVD direction and without particular enthusiasm, since it was "their" people they were purging.

Back in the early 1930s, during collectivization, the team had gone around the provinces supervising arrests, too, but this was more than a replay. The people being arrested now were not anonymous peasants and low-level local officials. They were high-ranking officials, people the team knew personally in many cases, including trusted subordinates for whom, in normal times, they would have acted as patrons. This was true not just out in the provinces and republics but in Moscow, where NKVD purging of the entire government and party apparatus was going on at full swing. The casualty rate in the second tier of the political hierarchy, just below the team, was extraordinary: in a much-quoted figure, two-thirds of the Central Committee elected in 1934—consisting largely of top officials from government, party, military, and regional committees—perished in the Great Purges, and if we look at Stalin's office appointment book for the mid-1930s, apart from the team and some foreign visitors, it's virtually a Who's Who of future purge victims who at that point were running key sectors of the economy under the overall supervision of team (Politburo) members. Of the twenty-five ministers in the government Molotov headed, twenty were purge victims—the only survivors being team members Molotov, Mikoyan, Voroshilov, and Kaganovich, plus the minister for foreign affairs, Maxim Litvinov.[12]

Molotov, both at the time and subsequently, gave the impression of being stoically committed to the purges, but without the element of exhilaration one senses in Stalin. "[The year] 1937 was necessary," he said flatly to Felix Chuev in the 1980s. True, the Stalin team had won the battles of the 1920s and early 1930s, but it had left them with many "enemies of various shades" who "in the face of the threatening danger of fascist aggression might unite." Dismissing Chuev's concerns about individual victims, he said these were "philistine" objections, repeating stubbornly, "it was necessary." In Chuev's acute summary, "Molotov regarded repression not as an arbitrary action of the leadership, but as a continuation of the revolution in a complicated international situation." Kaganovich, who regarded Stalin almost worshipfully, seeing himself as the "pupil" of a man who had "formed him as a politician," never admitted any real regret for the Great Purges.

Khrushchev, who later revealed many of the horrors of the purge years, said in his memoirs that at the time he was just a faithful executant, but a convinced one: "I saw everything through the eyes of the Central Committee—that is, through Stalin's eyes. I also spoke with his mouth, I would repeat what I heard from him." Andreev, according to his daughter, "believed wreckers and Fifth Columnists were destroying our State and had to be destroyed," and his wife Dora was "utterly convinced" as well. On the other hand, Andreeva also says that her parents didn't discuss the arrests in front of their children, a precaution also followed by the Mikoyans and probably all the rest of the team, so the question of what husbands on the team said to their wives in private remains moot. It is reported of Chubar, one of the Politburo victims, that friends knew "how deeply indignant [he] was at the cases of illegal repression, how he refused to believe that his best friends might turn out to be spies and traitors." But it's not clear that this really differentiates him from team survivors like Mikoyan and Kalinin, except perhaps with respect to prudence.[13]

Part of the mechanism of the terror for the country as a whole was to extract confessions from those arrested under torture and publish them as proof of their guilt. A refinement of this technique, as far as the team was concerned, was to invite them to face-to-face meetings with their former colleagues, now under arrest, and participate in their questioning, either in the Politburo or Lubyanka. Ordzhonikidze—along with the semidisgraced Bukharin, himself in the most precarious of positions—had to confront a visibly battered Pyatakov in January 1937, and questioned him closely about whether the confession was coerced, but Pyatakov insisted it was not. At another confrontation, attended by Stalin and most of the Politburo, as well as Bukharin, Bukharin tried to make Radek admit that he was making up testimony incriminating him, but he got a very firm rebuff, which must have disconcerted Radek's audience as much as it does the contemporary reader: "No one forced me to say what I did. No one threatened me before I gave my testimony. I was not told that I would be shot if I refused. Besides that, I am sufficiently grown up to not believe any promises made to me in prison." Molotov was called in for a confrontation with his arrested deputy, Nikolai Antipov, who flung accusations at others working under Molotov. "I sensed that he might be making things up ...," Molotov recalled—but then the ellipse follows, implying, "What could you do?" These meetings must have been agonizing, all the more so in that you couldn't be sure the arrested person might not turn on you and say God knows what.

The arrested men didn't always take Radek's and Pyatakov's line. Rudzutak refused to admit to guilt in a confrontation with Molotov, Mikoyan, and other team members, and told them he had been tortured. Insofar as he was Molotov's deputy, the arrest was a danger signal for Molotov, though the latter claimed they were not personally close. Molotov regarded him as expendable because he wasn't pulling his weight and was mainly interested in living the good life, spending time with artists and actors: "he wasn't involved in the struggle, as a revolutionary, any more." The Moscow rumor mill had the same opinion, spreading the story that he had been arrested "at dinner with some actors—it was said that the ladies were still wearing the rags of their ball gowns in Lubyanka some weeks later." Rudzutak was still tough enough, however, to tell his colleagues of the torture (the news made no ascertainable impact on them) and, despite being tortured, refuse to admit guilt. In retrospect, at least, Molotov did not think Rudzutak was literally guilty as charged; he had just gone a bit "liberal," like the Rightists. Indeed, Molotov said that in the face-to-face confrontation with team members, he more or less believed Rudzutak's protestations of innocence but kept quiet out of caution (presumably seeing that Stalin was not going to let Rudzutak off the hook).

Rudzutak was the first of five Politburo members or candidates to be arrested. Like the others in this group—Robert Eikhe, Kosior, Chubar, and Pavel Postyshev—he was a relatively marginal member of the team by the mid-1930s (all but Kosior were candidate, not full members of the Politburo). One of the common characteristics of the group was ill health. Rudzutak and Chubar had recently been sent abroad for expensive medical treatment, a common occurrence for the political elite in general, but unusual for Politburo members. It was this trip that had allegedly exposed Rudzutak to the wiles of the beautiful female spy. Robert Eikhe, though still a relatively young man (born in 1890), had had serious health problems too. A Latvian, like Rudzutak, Eikhe can scarcely be considered a real team member because his Politburo tenure was so short, and he was far away from Moscow for most of it. The longtime party chief in Siberia, he was co-opted as a candidate member of the Politburo in 1935, but was a rare visitor to Stalin's office, and almost never attended Politburo meetings until his move to Moscow on being appointed agriculture minister in October 1937—a move that was probably itself a sign his star was waning. He was arrested in April 1938 and, despite letters to Stalin from prison pleading his innocence, shot on 4 February 1940.[14]

The other three Politburo victims were all from the Ukrainian party organization. It was more or less a total wipeout of the Ukrainian leadership, with first and second party secretaries and the head of the Ukrainian government arrested in 1938, and the republic's president—the Old Bolshevik Grigory Petrovsky, once a Bolshevik deputy at the Duma in 1912— dismissed and told by Stalin he was lucky to stay alive.

Stanislav Kosior was the eldest of four revolutionary brothers, Polish-born Ukrainians. Three of them were Bolsheviks, though one, Vladislav, had joined the Left Opposition in the 1920s and been punished by exile; Stanislav had apparently annoyed Stalin by trying to intercede for Vladislav's wife in 1936. The other brother, Kazimir, was even more discreditable, because he had briefly joined the wrong party— the Polish Socialist Party—in 1916. Although he had subsequently come over to the Soviet side, the earlier transgression was enough to get him arrested in April 1938 as a Polish spy. This time Kosior didn't try to defend his brother: he wrote a cringing letter to Stalin repudiating him ("he was never close to me"), but Stalin ignored it. Stanislav himself had not been in Stalin's good books since the early 1930s, when he angered Stalin by not being tough enough on the famine. Still, according to one story, they were on good enough terms for him to drop in on Stalin in Moscow on his way to his usual vacation in the South and be given a warm send-off —"Have a good rest, use up your whole vacation time"—only to be arrested on the train. Kaganovich, an old friend, said that he protested Kosior's arrest, but Stalin wouldn't budge. According to Petrovsky's later account, Kosior was brought in for a confrontation with Stalin, Molotov, Kaganovich, Voroshilov, and Petrovsky. Demoralized, or perhaps tired of Stalin's games, he stuck to his confession—"What can I say? You know I'm a Polish spy"— even when Petrovsky said he didn't believe him.

Chubar was called to Moscow to become one of Molotov's deputies in 1934. After his return to Moscow, he was a regular at Politburo meetings and visited Stalin's office a couple of times a month. Along with Molotov, he was one of those called in for a confrontation with the arrested Nikolai Antipov, another of Molotov's deputies (and, as it happened, a dacha neighbor of both Chubar and Molotov). At the confrontation, Antipov spewed forth accusations of treachery against Chubar, his former friend, who in return called him a provocateur and exclaimed indignantly, "What a snake I held to my bosom!" Not long after, Molotov was back for another face-to-face confrontation with a prisoner—this time Chubar. Asked late in life if he had believed in Chubar's guilt, Molotov temporized: perhaps Antipov was making things up, but he wasn't sure that Chubar was telling the whole truth either. Anyway, "Stalin couldn't rely on Chubar"—presumably a reference to their conflicts during collectivization—"none of us could."

It was Stalin's modus operandi to move prominent people to a new job before arrest, presumably to put them among strangers in an unfamiliar context. Chubar's new job, a dramatic demotion, was as head of construction of a cellulose combine out in the Urals, from which he called Stalin in tears, claiming innocence of all the accusations swirling around him. Khrushchev, who happened to be in Stalin's office at the time and liked Chubar, was heartened to hear Stalin speaking warmly and compassionately to Chubar: he must be off the hook, he thought. Chubar was arrested the next day.[15]

Stalin's most remarkable cat and mouse game was played with Pavel Postyshev, a former favorite who had been his personal emissary in Ukraine a few years earlier. Initially Postyshev's job was to crack heads in

Ukraine as an outsider, but after a while he seems to have gone native to some extent, making connections in the local political and cultural elite and cultural life, locally remembered for introducing ice-cream parlors and free open-air summer concerts to Kiev. Why Stalin had turned against Postyshev is unclear; it may be that his animus was partially directed against Postyshev's wife, Tatyana—she belonged to a category of "friends of Nadya" (including the wives of Molotov and Andreev) who all fared badly in the late 1930s. Tatyana had made herself a powerful figure in the Ukrainian cultural scene (using her own name, Postolovskaya), and, as happened with all powerful and visible figures, especially women married to even more powerful men, she was vulnerable to denunciation. One such denunciation came to Stalin's attention via Kaganovich, and he praised it publicly as an example of the salutary impact of ordinary people helping to keep high officials on the straight and narrow. Postyshev himself was criticized for insufficient vigilance against enemies in Ukraine and sent off to a new job in Kuibyshev, where he went overboard in the other direction, sanctioning the arrest of everyone in sight. But nothing helped. Early in January, Malenkov went out to Kuibyshev on an inspection tour and found that Postyshev had overdone it by disbanding thirty entire district committees after the arrest of their heads as "enemies of the people." In January 1938, not long after being assured by Stalin and Kaganovich that he was about to be brought back into favor and given a job in Moscow, he was unexpectedly pilloried by the entire team, jeering and mocking, in the schoolyard bullying technique earlier used on Bukharin. It was, of course, the prelude to arrest and, after a year in prison, execution. He was shot, along with Chubar and Kosior, on 26 February 1939.

The January 1938 Central Committee meeting at which Postyshev was pilloried was an ambiguous affair, because it also featured a report from Malenkov— Ezhov's successor as top personnel man in the Central Committee, presumably acting for Stalin—that seemed to presage a cessation of terror. Malenkov's report criticized excesses of purging at the local level, but as he took Postyshev as an example and joined in the heckling, it was a somewhat mixed message. Other team members picked up the criticism of excesses, Molotov warning against indiscriminate accusations of "wrecking" when anything went wrong, and Zhdanov criticizing groundless denunciations. Kalinin—in poor health, though still formally head of state—was now a rare attendee of meetings, but he showed up to this one,

perhaps to put in his ten cents worth on the arrest question: it was important to have *evidence* of guilt related to specific actions, he said, not just assumption of guilt by association or "looking into someone's eyes" and seeing an enemy there. But if Malenkov's report was a braking signal, it seems
to have been aborted, and in any case would accord oddly with the fact
that the third Moscow show trial, featuring Bukharin and Yagoda, was
due to open in March. There were many arrests still to come, including,
shortly after the plenum, Postyshev's, followed by Kosior's and Chubar's.[16]

There were files on everyone, including members of the team; everyone was under suspicion. "They're gathering evidence against me, too,"
Stalin told Khrushchev with a shrug, and indeed a file on him was found
in Ezhov's safe after his arrest. But a lot of this was simply routine: denunciations from the public or colleagues came in, and they were filed, not
necessarily for use. It was a different matter when interrogations of those
arrested were slanted to *produce* information, true or invented, on someone. Ekaterina Lorberg, Kalinin's wife (though they were no longer living
together) was arrested in the autumn of 1938, accused of running an anti-
Soviet salon in her apartment. It was clear from her interrogation by Beria
that what was wanted was damaging information on Kalinin. She received a fifteen-year Gulag sentence.

Lorberg's arrest was notable as the first, but not the last, arrest and
banishment of the wife of a man who remained, at least formally, on the
team. "The thing is that Kalinin was with another woman, not his wife,
that was well known," Molotov told Chuev, as if that somehow explained
her arrest. But you could live with your wife, and love her, and she might
still be arrested—as Molotov himself would find out in a few years. Kalinin, knowing appeals on behalf of family to be in vain, bided his time: it
was six years, within sight of the victorious end of the war, and on the eve
of an operation that he thought he might not survive, that he wrote a short
letter to Stalin asking, without elaboration or justification, for amnesty for
his wife.

Nobody on the team could consider himself safe. For all of them, there
were periodic reminders that they were not guaranteed immunity in the
hunt for enemies. Molotov had the jolt of being dropped from the assassination targets in the Zinoviev-Kamenev trial. Malenkov came under fire
during the purge of the Moscow party organization in May 1937, when he
was accused of contacts with the Whites during the Civil War in Oren-

burg. He also knew that Stalin had some mysterious compromising information on him "concerning personal morality" that he might dig out if he felt like it. Beria apparently came close to arrest by Ezhov in July 1938, but was warned in time and flew to Moscow to defend himself successfully before Stalin, taking over Ezhov's job a few months later. Stalin publicly reminded Andreev that he had once supported Trotsky. In casual conversation, Khrushchev said, Stalin would refer in passing, but with an implicit threat, to compromising material on him, including suggestions that he was really Polish, not Russian. Mikoyan made a similar report—in his case that he could be accused of having betrayed the other 26 Baku Commissars who were shot, allegedly by the British, back in the Civil War.[17]

The depth of their own involvement in the purges did not stop members of the team from losing people close to them. Every one of them lost work associates and friends—and many lost relatives. Whenever this happened, their own danger increased, because of what the victims might say about them under torture and interrogation. The stoic and loyal Molotov is a prime example. After his German tutor was arrested, his daughter's German nanny followed. His closest friend, Alexander Arosev, was arrested in July 1937 and executed six months later. Of his four deputies, Rudzutak and Antipov were arrested by the middle of 1937, with Valery Mezhlauk following in December, and Chubar in mid-1938. This was really bringing things home to Molotov, as such alleged perfidy on the part of one's close associates usually led to one's own arrest, all the more if (as apparently in these cases) you had not initiated the arrests yourself in the course of purging your own institution. Molotov's assistants fared no better. The head of his office, A. M. Mogilny, was arrested in August 1937 and pressured to testify against him, but "he didn't want to say anything and threw himself down the liftwell in the NKVD." Molotov knew that compromising information and denunciations were piling up in his NKVD dossier, though he wasn't shown them. When his 1970s interviewer asked naively, "But Stalin didn't accept them?" Molotov came back sharply, "How do you mean, didn't accept them? My whole office [was gone]." The fact that he remained at large didn't mean that he had been found innocent.

It was a normal prerogative of power to be able to intervene to protect subordinates, associates, and clients who fell into the hands of the NKVD, but this was suspended during the Great Purges. According to Mikoyan, "there was even a special decision of the Politburo forbidding members of the Politburo to interfere in the work of the NKVD." Molotov tried to get his tutor off the hook in 1935, though unsuccessfully, but when he tried again with the nanny the next year, it produced a warning from Ezhov not to interfere with the course of justice. By the time of Arosev's imminent arrest, he didn't even try, though he had great affection for him and never thought he was other than an honest man. "Make arrangements for the children" was all the advice he could give his friend. His wife Polina did more, helping Aroseva's first wife not only with food and clothing but also with employment in her office. Molotov followed the same pattern of non-intervention with regard to his deputies and assistants, with just one known exception. When the schoolgirl daughter of his chief secretary, who had killed himself after arrest rather than rat on him, wrote to say that when the family apartment was sealed after the arrest of her parents, she had been left without winter clothing, Molotov forwarded this to Ezhov on the same day with the note: "Lora Mogilnaya should be given warm clothing."[18]

Kaganovich was often reproached for failing to intercede on behalf of his brother Mikhail (strictly speaking, not a Great Purges victim, as it was mid-1941 by the time suspicion fell on him and he killed himself to avoid arrest) or his friend Yakir. He was defensive about this in later life, but the reproaches led him to ponder the question of why intervention was so difficult. Stalin used confessions as a shield against team intercession, he said. You would raise the question of someone's innocence, and he would come back at you with a confession, which you could only contest in the unlikely event that you had definite proof it was wrong. Stalin used the confession argument on him when he tried to save Kosior, his friend and former mentor, whose arrest had deeply upset him. Kaganovich protested Chubar's arrest as well, he claimed, saying to Stalin that "Chubar is an honest man," and even if he had made some "little 'slip,'" he didn't understand "how he could not be trusted. "'No?' said Stalin. 'Well, read this.' And he gave me a writing pad. It was written in Chubar's hand (I knew his handwriting) about how he was in Germany conducting [treasonous] negotiations and so on and so forth. I read it and thought oh my God that's torn it."

Of all the team, Mikoyan was the most active, even reckless, in trying to help the victims. Occasionally he had success getting someone out of

prison: for example, when his Armenian schoolfriend Napoleon Andreas-
ian was arrested on the accusation of being a hidden Frenchman in dis-
guise, therefore a spy. He told the story to Stalin as a joke, and Stalin
laughed and told him to phone the NKVD and tell them, in his name, to
free Napoleon. When the mother of the teenage Elena Bonner was arrested, she gave Elena a note to take to Mikoyan—an old friend of Elena's
Armenian stepfather—at his dacha. Mikoyan told her he could do nothing about her parents, not even get news about their whereabouts, but that
he and his wife would take Elena and her brother into their home. The
touchy Bonner refused this exceptionally generous offer and stormed off,
but Mikoyan didn't forget about her. In the summer of 1945, he called her
in to tell her the fate of her parents (stepfather dead, mother still alive).
Sometimes, as with the Molotovs, it was Mikoyan's wife who helped the
victims, which gave him a degree of deniability. As his son recalled, when
the widow of one of the military "plotters," Gamarnik, was sent into exile
after his suicide, Ashkhen, on Mikoyan's instructions, went to the station
with money for the journey.

It must be said for Voroshilov, who otherwise cuts a shabbier figure
than Mikoyan, that when the parents of the wife of his adopted son, Petr,
were arrested, their daughter-in-law—who, with Petr, was part of their
household—continued to live in the Voroshilov apartment, even after she
was expelled from the institute for refusing to repudiate her parents, and
regularly sent parcels to them. Moreover, when her mother was released
after a year or so for health reasons, the Voroshilovs took her in too.[19]

The mystery in all this, of course, is Stalin. His posture with the team,
when they complained or tried to intercede, was that they were all in the
same boat, at the mercy of the NKVD. When Georgy Dimitrov, head of
the Comintern, raised such cases with him, his answer was, "What can I
do for them, Georgy? All my own relatives are in prison too." In a way this
was just verbal sleight of hand: Georgy, or even team members, couldn't
get their relatives out of the hands of the NKVD, but Stalin, if he had
wanted to, could have. Still, it was true about Stalin having relatives, as
well as friends, associates, and even assistants, who had been arrested. The
scope of the carnage in his immediate environment was as high, if not
higher, than in that of other team members.

Stalin had few blood relatives, but he was close to a lot of in-laws from
both marriages. Purge victims on the Svanidze side were Mariko and Alyo-

sha, siblings of his first wife, along with Alyosha's wife, Maria (the diary-keeper with a crush on Stalin), and their son, Johnny. On the Alliluyev side, Nadya's brother-in-law, Stanislav Redens, a high NKVD official who was close to the whole Stalin family, was a purge victim, while his wife Anna remained at liberty but was evicted from her Kremlin apartment. Nadya's military brother Pavel died suddenly, perhaps a suicide, when he returned from vacation in 1938 to find mass arrests among the officers serving under him. To be sure, this was not quite a clean sweep: in-laws from both sides remained at liberty, at least for the time being, and Stalin may even have tried to enlist Pavel's widow, Zhenya, as wife/house-keeper/mother for his children. But the family circle was destroyed. The Alliluyev relatives who remained free were no longer admitted to Stalin's apartment in the Kremlin, Svetlana recalled, with the exception of her grandfather and grandmother. But relations with Sergei Alliluyev and his wife were surely strained by the arrests and the fact that Alliluyev had ad-opted the Redens' grandsons after their father was taken. (No family member emerged to take the cherished if obnoxious ten-year-old Johnny Svanidze, who was saved from an orphanage only by a former nanny.)

The loss that cut most deeply was that of Alyosha Svandize, arrested in December 1937. Alyosha and Stalin were like brothers, Mikoyan thought; he couldn't understand how Stalin could have let it happen, even if Beria (who was on bad terms with Svanidze) was plotting against him. "They were friendly up to the last days, and I didn't hear that they quarreled, that Stalin was dissatisfied with him or expressed distrust of him." And on top of that, Alyosha was the closest person that Stalin had left after Kirov died; he used to stay overnight at the dacha because Sta-lin didn't like being there alone after Nadya's death. "Later, when Sva-nidze was gone, there was nobody left to stay the night at Stalin's, and he didn't ask anyone."

When Mikoyan, with whom Alyosha had worked in foreign trade, pro-tested that he was surely not a spy, Stalin agreed that he wasn't a spy of the normal straightforward type, but said that in the course of his work he had evidently given information about goings-on in the Soviet leadership to the Germans. Untypically, Stalin later gave him a chance to avoid death by admitting guilt and seeking a pardon from the Central Committee, but Svandize spat in the face of the NKVD man who brought the message saying, "there's my answer to [Stalin]," and the sentence was carried out.

"That's aristocratic pride for you," was Stalin's grudgingly admiring comment. There are very few reported cases of Stalin intervening to rescue some personal connection or striking such names off arrest lists. An old friend from Georgia, Sergo Kavtaradze, was one exception, saved by Stalin's intercession from execution for participation in an alleged murder plot against Stalin in 1936. Svetlana records that he very unwillingly countermanded the arrest of her nanny in 1939 because she made such a terrible fuss. It was a lonely life for Stalin, as well as Svetlana, after the Great Purges had gone through the family.

Arrests in Stalin's vicinity are often assumed to be the result of Stalin's personal initiative, animus against particular persons, and so on. Perhaps, but it's also possible that he simply declined to give them special treatment. Ezhov would not, of course, have taken action against Stalin's relatives on his own initiative. But when compromising information stacked up in their files—which it undoubtedly would have, especially in the case of those who had served abroad, like Redens and Alyosha Svanidze—the prudent course would have been to send them up to Stalin and wait for a "hands-off" response. This is one of the situations that looks different when we think of Stalin as a member of a team rather than just an all-powerful dictator. To have been seen by the team to be saving his own people, while letting theirs perish, would have been a major sacrifice of moral authority. It made political sense to give a clear message that they were all in the same boat.

There are stories of Stalin's cynicism about NKVD accusations, like his teasing remark to Kavtaradze, with whom he had dinner on the night of his release from prison in 1940: "to think you wanted to kill me." Another Georgian account has Stalin, meeting up with old Georgian friends after the war, mentioning Great Purge victims of their mutual acquaintance "with the calm detachment of a historian, showing neither sorrow nor rage—but speaking without rancor, with just a touch of light humour." The insouciant note, if he really struck it, was another thing the team couldn't quite match. From their standpoint, while the Great Purges may have been partly a heroic exploit, a huge gamble that had more or less come off, they were also a very painful memory. Unlike with the Civil War, or even collectivization, they had no stomach for sitting around in later years swapping memories of what a tight place they had been in. But they *had* been in a tight place. A snowballing process like that could so easily have gone off the rails and destroyed its originators (as had happened to the Jacobins in the French Revolutionary Reign of Terror). The team had reason to give thanks, not only to fate for letting them survive, but to Stalin for having kept his nerve and managing to brake the runaway train.[20]

True to Stalin's cautious "dosage" practices, Ezhov's removal was a multistage and comparatively long-drawn-out process, although, in fact, Ezhov showed no sign of resistance but only plunged into despair, ill health, and heavy drinking as his fortunes waned. In April 1938, he was appointed minister for water transport, while retaining his position as head of the NKVD. In August, Ezhov's enemy and eventual successor, Lavrenty Beria, was brought up from Georgia to be his first deputy at NKVD, and by November the rumor mill was identifying him as the chosen successor. In November, after two tense meetings with Stalin and the team, the Politburo accepted Ezhov's resignation from his NKVD position on grounds of health and overwork. Beria was appointed to replace him, and quickly started purging Ezhov's people within the institution. Ezhov's wife Evgenia, hospitalized for depression, had killed herself ten days earlier, probably with her husband's help in supplying the poison, with team widow Zina Ordzhonikidze acting as a go-between. The frequency of Ezhov's visits to Stalin, which had held up at a high level even after Beria appeared on the scene, dropped abruptly to zero after November 23. To be sure, terror continued, even as Ezhov was on his way out. The overall rates of arrests and executions for counterrevolutionary crimes were not significantly less in 1938 than they had been in 1937. Moreover, the executions of three out of the five arrested Politburo members (Kosior, Chubar, and Postyshev) took place early in 1939, under Beria's watch. The presumption was, however, that the terror was winding down, which proved to be the case.[21]

In terror for their lives, though they had been for the past two years, the team had come through more or less intact. In fact, if you looked at Stalin's office logs in 1939, it was almost like old times as far as the team was concerned: the team was meeting there regularly, sometimes twice a day, morning and evening, with Molotov the most frequent visitor, as he had been for years, and Beria (just elected as a candidate member of the Politburo) and Malenkov (now a Central Committee secretary) as the new regulars. Compared to the pre-purge pecking order, Kaganovich was

down to sixth in frequency of visits and Mikoyan up to third. Khrushchev, a candidate member of the Politburo since 14 January 1938, and promoted to full member at the XVIII Congress, was running Ukraine and
rarely in Moscow. Zhdanov was still running Leningrad. Andreev and
Kalinin, both in poor health, were the least frequent visitors to Stalin's office and attendees at Politburo meetings, but they were still taking part in
Politburo work. What the experience meant for the future functioning of
the team, individually and collectively, remained to be seen, but as of the
first half of 1939, they were all working overtime, trying to restaff the institutions for which they were responsible and get them up and running
again.

The XVIII Congress was called in March 1939, five years after the last
one. It was a much younger group and less experienced than at the previous congress in 1934, only a fifth having joined the party during or before
the Civil War, as against four-fifths of the delegates to the previous conference. Continuity of delegates with the last congress was extraordinarily
low, with a carryover rate of only 3 percent. It was all the more reason for
the assembled Communist elite to go overboard in greeting their leaders:
"the appearance on the tribune of comrades Stalin, Molotov, Voroshilov,
Kaganovich, Kalinin, Andreev, Mikoyan, Zhdanov and Khrushchev was
met with a thunder of applause," according to the minutes. The congress
heard a report from Stalin, in which he focused magisterially on the international situation and the country's economic growth, lightly dismissing
the mistaken opinion of foreign chatterers that "if we had left the spies,
murderers and wreckers go free and not stopped them wrecking, killing
and spying, then Soviet organizations would be much firmer and more
solid." (Laughter greeted this quip.) Andreev mentioned the "deep feeling
of moral satisfaction" in the party from its recent cleansing activities.
Mikoyan, whose active participation in the Great Purges had been surprisingly minimal, nevertheless offered a medical metaphor as justification, noting that in the period since the last congress, "we managed to un-
cover and destroy hearths of counter-revolution, liquidate the infected
spots on the body of our party, as a result of which the party became still
stronger, healthier and more powerful and united around its Central
Committee, around comrade Stalin, than ever before" (this was greeted
with "stormy applause"). Of the team members who spoke, Khrushchev
was the most vehement, almost as if he were back in 1937: the Ukrainian

people "hate and curse the enemies" who can expect to be "destroyed like mad dogs" (that got "noisy applause," an unusual formulation, suggesting a certain lack of decorum). Molotov, who did not make any general comment on the party's recent history, gave the official report on the economy and unexpectedly encountered some sharp criticism for it. This was presumably a staged episode of petty humiliation, since the report—standard fare—had been approved the day before in the Politburo.

It was left to Zhdanov, as Central Committee secretary with responsibility for cadres, to make the only report on a subject surely uppermost in people's minds, the terror they had all just experienced. The event was still nameless—only later did it become "1937" in Russian discourse and "the Great Purges" in the West—so Zhdanov had to use circumlocution, but even so his approach was disconcertingly oblique. He talked not about terror but about the regular party purges involving expulsion but not arrest—we could call them small-p purges for convenience—which had been an institution in party life since the 1920s. Under Ezhov's leadership as Central Committee secretary in 1935–36, the process of regular party purging had got entangled with the process of unmasking "enemies of the people," but still, they were different things, conceptually and operationally. As the rest of the team sat silent, delegates from the provinces got up one after the other to describe local miscarriages of justice when good party people were arrested. Often this was said to be the result of "false denunciations," a neat shifting of responsibility from the party leadership to the people. The arrest of many people who were *not* in the party—social marginals, members of some non-Russian ethnic groups, and so on—was not mentioned, thanks to the formal boundaries of Zhdanov's report, and perhaps partly for this reason remained invisible to Western observers for decades.

The delegates to the XVIII Party Congress were a young group, half of them under thirty-five, and full of enthusiasm. People clapped for Stalin until their hands were sore, according to one participant, Admiral Kuznetsov. He didn't see any sign that the appalling carnage of the past few years had damaged Stalin's standing in the eyes of the party. "Strange as it may seem," he commented, the mass killing he had successfully led "created still greater authority for him."[22]

SIX

INTO WAR

ON 3 MAY 1939, LITVINOV WAS CALLED INTO THE KREMLIN AND CRITI-cized for the failure of his collective security policies to achieve results. The discussion was heated, Molotov allegedly shouting at Litvinov, "You think we are all fools." Zhdanov and Beria were also highly critical of Lit-vinov's policies. The upshot was a late-night telegram to all ambassadors informing them of Litvinov's removal from the job and replacement by Molotov, who would hold it jointly with his position as head of the gov-ernment. This signaled a very important shift in the Kremlin's interna-tional stance. Losing hope of the Anglo-French alliance against Germany that Litvinov had sought, Stalin and his team were ready to try the alternative.

The telegram to the ambassadors explained Litvinov's dismissal as the result of a "serious conflict with Molotov and the government," an unprec-edented and gratuitous introduction of the personal, which appeared de-signed to minimize Stalin's involvement. There was certainly bad blood between Molotov and Litvinov. Litvinov thought Molotov a fool and did not hide his contempt. Molotov, for his part, "chafed under Litvinov's blunt and often scorching wit" and "was as resentful of Litvinov's fluency in French, German and English as he was distrustful of Litvinov's easy manner with foreigners," according to the Belorussian-American journal-ist Maurice Hindus. "Never having lived abroad, Molotov always sus-pected that there was something impure and sinful in Litvinov's broad-mindedness and in his appreciation of Western civilization."

The handover of the foreign ministry was dramatic. NKVD troops surrounded the building, and Molotov immediately initiated a purge of ministry personnel (probably his first hands-on experience of this kind, as he had not been one of the roving emissaries of terror in 1937–38). Reportedly, Molotov was in a state of furious excitement, shouting, "Enough of Litvinov liberalism. I am going to tear out that kike's [Litvinov's] wasp's nest by the roots." This was so untypical of the usually imperturbable Molotov—who, unlike Kaganovich and some others on the team, was not given to swearing and shouting—that one might doubt the accuracy of the report if it were a totally unique occurrence. On at least one other occasion, however, Molotov turned on an apparently out-of-control shouting fit in the presence of the diplomatic corps (the date was spring of 1940 and the topic was Finnish intransigeance) and had to be removed from the hall by his assistants. His interpreter thought he must have been drunk, and was surprised the next day to find Molotov looking not abashed or hungover but rather pleased with himself. He gathered from Molotov's questions about the diplomats' reaction that the whole thing had been staged, probably on prior agreement with Stalin, to convey the message of Soviet displeasure as dramatically as possible. Assuming that this was another scripted outburst with Stalin as coauthor, anti-Semitism must have been part of the message, with Nazi Germany as the intended recipient. With Litvinov the Jew dismissed, and Molotov the Russian in charge, one obstacle to Soviet-German negotiations was gone.[1]

The foreign ministry had long been a haven for party intellectuals, former émigrés and Oppositionists, many of them Jewish. Its purge appears to be the first occasion of overt anti-Semitism on the part of Stalin and Molotov. As Molotov told the story to an interviewer (of Russian nationalist sympathies) in the 1970s, "Stalin said to me 'Purge the ministry of Jews.' Thank God for these words! Jews formed an absolute majority in the leadership [of the ministry] and among the ambassadors. It wasn't good. Latvians and Jews . . . and each one drew a crowd of his people along with him. Moreover, they regarded my arrival in office with condescension and jeered at the measures I began to implement." It was as if Molotov—not personally anti-Semitic, and with a Jewish wife—had been thrown back into the mind-set of the early 1920s, where he resented being snubbed and patronized by self-confident cosmopolitans like Trotsky and Zinoviev.

But Molotov's Jewish wife, Polina Zhemchuzhina, was one of his problems in the spring of 1939. With a major career of her own, currently as minister of fisheries, she had recently proposed a business trip to Sakhalin in the Far East to investigate the fishing industry. The local NKVD objected, presumably on security grounds, but Stalin roughly overruled them and she made the trip. Evidently this was another of Stalin's cat and mouse games, however, for while she was away, a number of her colleagues and protégés (both in the fishing ministry and the food ministry, where she had earlier worked) were arrested. Zhemchuzhina broke off her trip and hurried home, but had no success in getting her associates released. Under interrogation, some of them gave incriminating testimony against her, so she herself was in danger of arrest. In the event, however, she was simply dismissed from her position as minister for fisheries, albeit in a strangely protracted way, with the issue coming before the Politburo several times in the autumn of 1939. She was then appointed head of Russian haberdashery production, a substantial demotion. Even then, her troubles were not over but continued to bubble away in the background of Molotov's high-profile activity as foreign minister. When the Politburo voted a year or so later to drop her from the party Central Committee, Molotov annoyed Stalin by abstaining.[2]

Externally, the situation was ominous. There was tension with the Japanese over their occupation of Manchuria, where they established the puppet state of Manchukuo, and fighting broke out in 1939 on the Mongolian border at Khalkin Gol, the great tank battle where future marshal Georgy Zhukov made his name. Hitler's intention to move eastward could scarcely be doubted. Britain, France, and the Soviet Union were all deeply alarmed at the signs of the German intention to occupy Czechoslovakia in 1938, but ended up doing nothing. In the autumn of 1939, it was Poland's turn. Stalin's great hope was that he could maneuver it so that the Western powers ended up fighting Germany while the Soviet Union stood aside; the Western powers had a similar hope of an outcome with the Soviet Union and Germany at each other's throats.

At the same time, the apparent disposition of the Soviet Union throughout Litvinov's tenure had been toward an alliance with the West (Britain and France) against the German threat, and this was reinforced by the Soviet-headed Comintern, which in 1935 switched to the policy of a Popular Front against Fascism (meaning primarily Nazism in Germany). The Soviet Union had a considerable investment on the anti-German side, especially taking European public opinion into account. Nevertheless, when Britain put its negotiator on a slow boat to Leningrad in August 1939, Stalin and Molotov had had enough. Molotov was offended that the British had sent a Foreign Office official "of the second class," William Strang, to negotiate, and Strang, like other Western diplomats who encountered him in his first months as foreign minister, was struck by Molotov's lack of diplomatic technique, as well as social finesse: he had no sense of negotiation, the British ambassador later recalled, and would just "stubbornly and woodenly . . . repeat his own point of view and . . . ask innumerable questions of his interlocutors." The diplomats found him unable "to unbend and be affable on official occasions" and noted that under the new regime, the "cosmopolitan modus operandi" of the Litvinov era was being replaced with "a more truly Bolshevik" approach. Molotov would no doubt have been flattered to hear it, but his ineptness at the social aspect of his new job nevertheless caused him chagrin.[3]

Now it was a German alliance that looked the most likely. This was probably the outcome that Molotov preferred, since his hostility to England and France, as well as to their "ally" on the domestic scene, Litvinov, was acute, but Stalin seems to have felt a more or less equal hostility toward both sides, and conversely an equal willingness to work with either, if it were to Soviet advantage. The notion that he and Hitler felt a mutual affinity as fellow dictators is a myth: each regarded the other as the great enemy and ideological antithesis, and it was for both sides a marriage of convenience, Hitler being interested in neutralizing potential Soviet opposition to German moves into Eastern Europe and buying time so that he could deal with Western Europe first, Stalin buying time to rebuild his armed forces and bring them up to fighting strength. On 23 August, Molotov's German counterpart, Joachim von Ribbentrop, flew to Moscow. Discussions were held with Molotov and Stalin (neither of whom, to their disappointment, could really follow his German—alas for Molotov's arrested German tutor!), and a nonaggression pact between the two powers was signed the same day. By its terms, Germany and the Soviet Union pledged not to attack each other or support a military attack by a third party against each other.

The pact came as something of a shock to the team, given the strong Soviet commitment to a Popular Front against Fascism since the mid-1930s, and most of them had no prior warning. But they understood Stalin's explanation—he seems to have talked to them individually as well as collectively—that it was essential to buy time before the almost inevitable war. Mikoyan thought it "unavoidable, necessary and correct" in light of the English and French "refusal of serious negotations about an anti-Hitler coalition." Beria may have been privately unenthusiastic, as his son claims. Kaganovich, particularly uneasy as a Jew because of Hitler's virulent anti-Semitism, was reassured when, at a reception in Moscow after the signing of the pact, Stalin, twisting Ribbentrop's tail a little, proposed a toast to Kaganovich and walked around the table to clink glasses with him. "Stalin was giving us to understand that we had signed an agreement but ideology didn't change," Kaganovich later explained. "And as we left the hall, he said to me in the doorway: 'We have to win time.'" Molotov quoted another of Stalin's toasts that had Ribbentrop perplexed: "to Stalin, the new Anti-Cominterner!" The Germans never could understand the Marxist sense of humor, he commented.

For the Soviet public, the announcement of the pact was a sensation, but not as traumatic as it was for Communists and Popular Front supporters in the West. Many Soviet citizens were relieved, understanding it as a reprieve from the danger of war, while others remained suspicious of Germany's good faith, an attitude not alien to their leaders. The Soviet media dropped the most vehement anti-Nazi stories, but without switching to a pro-Nazi line; Khrushchev later claimed that they specially kept the play *Keys to Berlin*—set in 1760 at the end of the Seven Years' War—running in Moscow theaters as a reminder that Russians had defeated Germans and captured their capital in the past.

Unpublished secret protocols of the pact (not formally ratified by the Politburo but known at least in outline to most of the team) had recognized German and Soviet spheres of interest in Eastern Europe, the Soviet roughly corresponding to the Russian Empire's historic borders, which included Eastern Poland and the Baltic states. The real-world implications of this were quickly manifest when on 1 September Germany invaded Poland from the West, overrunning much of the country, including Warsaw, the capital, within a month. The invasion of Poland, in defiance of Allied warnings, caused Britain and France to declare war on Germany. The Soviet Union, neutral by the terms of the pact with Germany, and hoping devoutly that war in the West would occupy Hitler for a long time, followed up a few weeks later, with German encouragement, by occupying Eastern Poland. A shocking turn of events in terms of Western public opinion, it made sense to much of the Soviet public. As one foreign correspondent later noted, "there was a widespread feeling in the country that 'neutrality' paid: that, as a result of the Soviet-German Pact the Soviet Union had become bigger and, as yet without too much bloodshed, more secure."[4]

The occupation became an actual incorporation of these formerly Polish lands into the Soviet Union and hence expansion of Soviet territory; within a few months, residents of former Eastern Poland became, like it or not, Soviet citizens, specifically, citizens of the Soviet republics of Ukraine and Belorussia. Khrushchev, party boss in Ukraine, was the team member on the spot directing the process, which he did with energy and enthusiasm, along the way making some new friends from the Polish Left. One of them was the writer Wanda Wasilewska, who would shortly marry the well-known Soviet Ukrainian playwright and Communist Alexander Korneichuk; she made a great hit with Stalin when Khrushchev introduced them, and for the duration of the war became one of the very few foreign friends Stalin ever had, perhaps even his lover. These newly occupied territories created a buffer (it was hoped) against any incursions from the West. In the short term, however, they created a new set of problems: their incorporation meant that Soviet borders moved westward, thus necessitating a lengthy process of dismantling of the old fortified frontier and fortification of the new one.

The Baltic states would end up occupied and incorporated into the Soviet Union, too, but in the immediate aftermath of the pact, they were only forced to sign treaties of mutual assistance with the Soviet Union, which put them under a kind of coercive Soviet protection. In October, a similar offer was made to Finland, a small country with a strong anti-Soviet government, but the Finns refused. While the Soviet moves were intensely unpopular with all the small countries concerned, most of which had had only a few decades of independence since the 1917 collapse of the old Russian Empire, Finland was the only one to put up significant resistance. Recalling the redoubtable Baron Carl Gustaf Mannerheim, who had fought in the White armies against the Soviets in the Civil War, to head the military effort, Finland not only declared war on the Soviet Union, despite the huge disparity of forces, but, in the so-called Winter War of 1939–40, put up a brilliant performance that dramatically revealed the weaknesses of the Soviet Army.

The Soviets had miscalculated. As Khrushchev put it, they thought that "all we had to do was raise our voice a little bit, and the Finns would obey. If that didn't work, we could fire one shot and the Finns would put up their hands and surrender. Instead, they sent in their ski troops and made fools of the Russians." Stalin was furious, especially with Defense Minister Voroshilov, who was subjected to cutting criticism in the Central Committee and replaced by a real military professional, Marshal Semyon Timoshenko. Voroshilov was sufficiently provoked by Stalin's jibes to turn on him on one social occasion, according to Khrushchev's recollection, saying, "'You have yourself to blame for all this! You're the one who annihilated the Old Guard of the army; you had our best generals killed,' and then smashing a platter laden with roast suckling pig on the table." The war ended with a truce, which gave the Soviets their base on the Hanko Peninsula and an additional 15 kilometers (about 9.3 miles) between Leningrad and the border, but the Soviets had suffered up to a million casualties and a major loss of face in the international community. Stalin learned the hard way that Civil War military experience was now largely irrelevant. Voroshilov's reputation as a military leader never recovered from this fiasco, and it was the beginning of his decline in political status as well.[5]

In May 1940, Germany launched a military attack on France, which collapsed with a speed that shocked not only its ally, England, but also Germany's ally, the Soviet Union. In June 1940, citing "acts of provocation" on the part of the Baltic states, the Soviet Union sent in half a million troops to occupy the three small countries and incorporate them into the Soviet Union, a fate Finland (also, like the Baltic states, part of the Russian Empire before the Russian Revolution) had avoided by its intransigence and military valor. Zhdanov was put in charge of Sovietization in Estonia, with two of Molotov's deputies at foreign affairs, Vladimir Dekanozov and Andrei Vyshinsky (prosecutor in the Moscow trials), in charge of Lithuania and Latvia.

Hitler still had Britain to dispose of in the West. In November 1940, Molotov made a trip to Berlin, with an entourage of sixty, to discuss Ribbentrop's suggestion that the Soviet Union might care to join the Tripartite Pact recently signed by Germany, Japan, and Italy. Stalin dismissed this as a ploy to embroil the Soviets in war with Britain, the last thing he wanted, but Molotov may have been a bit more open to the idea. He was beginning to find his feet in diplomacy, or at least in his version of it: as he later described his conversations with Ribbentrop, not without satisfaction, "He stuck to his points, I to mine. He started to get nervous. I was insistent—all in all, I wore him out." One reason for Ribbentrop's nervousness may have been that they were taking shelter in a basement from a British bombing raid at the time. As the story goes, when Ribbentrop assured him that the British were already essentially defeated, Molotov asked coolly why, in that case, they were in a shelter and whose bombs were falling. Molotov had a meeting with Hitler, too, and observed with interest that he was trying to "do propaganda" on him (that is, not assuming the hardheaded realist persona that Molotov himself favored): evidently he was "very one-sided, an extreme nationalist, a chauvinist, who is blinded by his ideas." This direct contact with Hitler, and his growing aplomb at dealing with the Germans, increased his stature in the eyes of Stalin and the team, and won Stalin's respect, at least for the time being, as a foreign policy expert.[6]

As far as the West was concerned, the Second World War started in September 1939, when Britain and France declared war after the German occupation of Poland. The Soviet Union was not yet at war, but the international situation was the foremost preoccupation of its leaders. As a result of the Molotov-Ribbentrop Pact, the country had new borders to demarcate and border zones to monitor, new territories in which to introduce Soviet institutions, refugees from Western Poland to be accommodated, peasants to be resettled to strengthen border zones, industries to be switched over to military-related production, and military call-up to be organized. It no longer looked like a peacetime agenda.

One of the problem areas that preoccupied Stalin was the aviation industry, a key sector of Soviet military capacity, where production area was lagging. Mikhail Kaganovich, Lazar's elder brother, was the minister, and it was becoming clear to Stalin that he was not up to the job. He mocked Mikhail for referring to a fighter plane's "snout" instead of its "nose," saying scathingly, "What does he understand in aviation? How many years has he lived in Russia, and he hasn't learned to speak Russian properly!" Beria, a friend of Mikhail's, though he couldn't stand Lazar, claimed to have defended Mikhail in the Politburo when the aviation industry's poor performance came under fire, but that didn't stop his security police from building a case against Mikhail as a wrecker and German spy. Mikhail killed himself in mid-1941 after a meeting at which these charges were raised. (After Stalin's death in 1953, Mikhail Kaganovich was one of the first people Beria had posthumously rehabilitated—a month or so before he himself was arrested by his colleagues, including Lazar Kaganovich, and executed.)

Mikhail's fall was witnessed by a successor, aviation designer Alexander Yakovlev, one of the new post-purge cohorts filling up the empty places in the government, party, military, and diplomatic service. It was a rare occurrence (generally the old boss was purged in 1937 or 1938, before his ultimate successor was anywhere in sight), and rarer because Yakovlev left an account of it. He and his young colleagues, mainly in their thirties, shared Stalin's contempt for the fifty-year-old Mikhail Kaganovich, seeing him as a coarse, ignorant, superannuated revolutionary with a Yiddish accent who shouldn't be in charge of a technical ministry. In the short interlude between the Great Purges and the war, members of the team were all busy selecting the best of the young—often taken directly from engineering school or graduate studies—to train up as department heads and deputy ministers. Their rise could be dizzying: Alexei Kosygin was a minister in the Soviet government four years out of graduate school in engineering, at age thirty-five, and then a member of the State Defense Committee during the war; Andrei Gromyko was thirty and only three years out of graduate school in economics when he became head of the American desk in the foreign ministry; within a year or so—after he had brushed up his English a bit—he was sent off to Washington as second-in-command at the Soviet Embassy, becoming ambassador at thirty-four. The emergence of the new cohort was a source of pride, particularly to Stalin and Molotov, and Stalin, who always seemed to have time for his protégés, like Yakovlev, won their awed love and respect. He was at his best with these young men—wise, benevolent, ready with a joke and an informal remark to put them at ease, and impressively well informed about their field of activity.[7]

According to Stalin's scenario, the Soviet Union would have had several years at least to get itself back into full operational and fighting trim—but Hitler decided otherwise. Operation Barbarossa was prepared, and on 22 June 1941, breaking the pact, Germany launched a massive attack along the Soviet Union's Western border.

To say that Stalin, Molotov, and the team were caught unawares by this attack is a bit misleading, since the whole thrust of Soviet policy for the past two years had been preparation for a war from the West. But it's absolutely true that Stalin miscalculated, refusing to believe intelligence reports of the imminent attack, and desperate to avoid giving the provocation he thought the Germans were looking for as justification. Stalin and Molotov were convinced that Hitler would not risk attacking the Soviet Union before Britain had been dealt with. There is no record of dissent within the team, though in retrospect Mikoyan implied a less sanguine view of Germany's intentions on his own part. Beria, in a memo written early in June, seemed eager to stress that it was *Stalin* who had wisely determined there would be no attack that year, however frantic the many warnings Beria was receiving and passing on. Molotov and Kaganovich were in full agreement with Stalin on that, according to General Zhukov, but Zhdanov expressed doubts: "he always spoke very harshly of the Germans and stated that Hitler couldn't be trusted in anything." It was the unlucky Zhdanov who was caught out in Sochi at the start of his summer vacation with his family and had to turn around and come straight back.[8]

When Operation Barbarossa started on 22 June, Stalin's insistence on not responding to provocation completely hamstrung the Soviet response and led to the greater part of the air force being destroyed on the ground and a chaotic retreat of ground forces and population in the first weeks. New borders were not yet fully fortified, although the fortifications on the old border had been largely abandoned or dismantled. Stalin was tremendously angry at the attack, blaming everyone, even himself: "Lenin left us a great inheritance and we fucked it up." He disappeared to his dacha after the first disastrous week (29–30 June), said to be "so prostrated that he is in a state of indifference, has lost initiative ... doesn't answer the telephone." Having made a major and highly visible miscalculation, he perhaps felt it appropriate to follow Ivan the Terrible's example and go into seclusion, waiting for his nobles to invite him back and thus confirm their loyalty. This they did, but the process confirms the continuing importance of the team in Soviet governance. With Stalin absent and incommunicado, the team's core members—Molotov, Malenkov, Voroshilov, Beria, Mikoyan, and Nikolai Voznesensky (the new candidate member of the Politburo in charge of economic planning)—met in emergency session in the Kremlin. Beria proposed the formation of a new body to lead the war effort, the State Defense Committee (GKO), which Stalin would head. It was agreed that they should go as a group, uninvited, to the dacha to tell Stalin of this decision. Molotov, by common consent, was assumed to be the team leader in Stalin's absence, thus leader of the delegation.

Mikoyan's accounts say that when they arrived at the dacha, Stalin behaved as if they might have come to arrest him, but this may be a later gloss. Stalin's demeanor, in any case, was evidently team-spirited and uncharacteristically humble. He agreed to the team's suggestion of the formation of the GKO with himself as its head. But it was Molotov who, on Stalin's insistence, made the first broadcast to the nation after the German attack; Stalin said he just couldn't do it. The text was a collective team product, and Molotov's performance, in Stalin's ungrateful judgment, was lackluster; his old stammer was back. But he managed to get across the ringing conclusion: "Our cause is just. The enemy will be smashed. Victory will be ours." It was not until a week later that Stalin went on the air with a speech that riveted public attention by its opening salutation, which included the phrase: "Brothers and sisters!," a Russian Orthodox form of address. The speech made it clear that this was to be a war in defense of the Russian fatherland—it came to be called "the Great Fatherland War" in Soviet parlance—with Hitler playing the role of Napoleon a century and a half earlier as the invader from the West. But Stalin, like Molotov, sounded ill at ease and could be heard to be taking gulps of water as he spoke.[9]

Despite the June debacle, there was no subsequent diminution of Stalin's role, rather the contrary. He had taken over from Molotov as head of the government in May 1941 (something of a demotion for Molotov, who formally became one of fifteen deputy chairs, though he continued to handle much of the everyday workload, as well as foreign affairs). In July, Stalin took the position of minister of defense (formerly Voroshilov's, who had been demoted after the Finnish War debacle). On 8 August, in a risky move, Stalin put himself personally on the line by assuming the new position of supreme commander in chief of the armed forces. The State Defense Committee took over from the Politburo for the duration as the top decision-making body, its members constituting the inner core of the team. Stalin chaired, with Molotov as his deputy, along with Malenkov, Beria, Kaganovich, Mikoyan, Voroshilov, and the newcomer, Voznesensky. (Malenkov and Voznesensky had both been raised to candidate membership of the Politburo in February 1941.) From December 1943, the

GKO had an Operational Bureau consisting of Molotov, Malenkov, Beria, and Mikoyan.

The initial stages of the war were disastrous, with huge retreats, loss of territory and industrial infrastructure, hasty and disorganized evacuation of millions of people from the Western territories of the country, and German encirclement and capture of literally millions of Soviet troops, including whole armies. German troops were approaching Leningrad by the end of June and had the city blockaded by September. The Soviet retreat went on for one and a half years, with German troops advancing all the way to the Volga and the invaders occupying territory that before the war had held 85 million people (45 percent of the total Soviet population), produced 63 percent of the country's coal, and 58 percent of its steel. In this time, remarkably, there is no indication that the Soviet regime and Stalinist leadership were ever seriously challenged from within—a striking contrast to the experience of the First World War, when Russian defeats and huge casualties were the precipitating causes of the overthrow of the tsarist regime. But there were moments when military defeat must have seemed almost inevitable. Stalin's reaction was predictably harsh: in the fall, he drafted the infamous order branding all soldiers who surrendered or were taken prisoner as traitors, with punishment to be visited on their families back home. He had moments of panic in these first months of the war: one of the generals reported an almost hysterical telephone call to him on the shaky Western Front in which Stalin, speaking of himself in the third person, said, "comrade Stalin is not a betrayer, comrade Stalin is not a traitor, comrade Stalin is an honest man, . . . [he] is doing everything in his power to correct the situation."[10]

At the beginning of October, with the rapid German advance threatening Moscow, the GKO ordered the government and the diplomatic corps to evacuate to Kuibyshev on the Volga. On 16 October, with the Germans in the northern Moscow suburb of Khimki, resisted largely by civilian volunteer defense forces, Stalin told Politburo members to leave too. But all the core team members—Mikoyan, Molotov, Malenkov, and Beria—resisted this instruction and stayed in Moscow. Voznesensky went out to Kuibyshev as acting head of the government, hoping, according to a bitchy Mikoyan, to add to his power and status, but found himself out of the loop once he got there. Andreev, Kalinin, and Kaganovich went out to

Kuibyshev too, along with their own wives and children, and those of other members of the team, but Andreev and Kaganovich were soon back in Moscow. Stalin's own intentions and movements were unclear for a few days, but in fact he stayed in Moscow, though dispatching Svetlana and his household out to Kuibyshev. These were desperate days: looters were abroad in the streets and ordinary Muscovites were making last-minute decisions about whether to stay or flee. A German bomb killed the writer Alexander Afinogenov as he left the Central Committee building in the very heart of Moscow. On 7 November, in an assertion that the Soviet Union was not out of the game yet, Stalin, Beria, Kaganovich, Molotov, Malenkov, Mikoyan, and Alexander Shcherbakov (Khrushchev's replacement as first secretary of Moscow, a candidate member of the Politburo since February 1941) attended a skeleton version of the usual Revolution Day parade in Red Square, with Civil War hero Marshal Budenny reviewing the troops on a white horse, his luxuriant moustache flecked with snow. In a prerecorded address, Stalin invoked heroic figures from the Russian past, from Alexander Nevsky fighting off the Teutonic Knights in the thirteenth century to tsarist military leaders Suvorov and Mikhail Kutuzov resisting Napoleon.

Leningrad was another near disaster. Voroshilov, who was in charge of forces in the area, proved unable to cope with the German advance and was removed by GKO representatives Molotov and Malenkov in a flying visit. Zhdanov, the political leader in Leningrad, was also distraught and in bad physical and psychological shape (he had had a heart attack in September and suffered from asthma). Malenkov's son claims that his father found Zhdanov in a state of collapse, cowering "in a luxurious bunker—demoralized, unshaven, drunk," and Molotov, less colorfully, remembered him as "very upset." According to Mikoyan, Zhdanov later told Stalin that he had a panicky fear of being shot at and bombed so had had to leave much of the day-to-day work aboveground to his deputy, Alexei Kuznetsov. At first, the city's fall seemed only a matter of time, but in November 1941, the front, now commanded by Zhukov, stabilized. With less than a week's food supplies left for the Leningrad population of several million, a road across the ice of Lake Ladoga was built, and in January 1943 a narrow land corridor was added. Nevertheless, more than a million people died in besieged Leningrad, and the blockade was not lifted until 27 January 1944.[11]

Given what the team had gone through in the Great Purges, it's surprising they could perform at all in subsequent years, let alone show any initiative. Yet, for the most part, they did both during the war, working efficiently under enormous pressure and often necessarily making decisions on their own. GKO members, like most of their subordinates, went the entire war without leave. The war years showed a reversion to the pattern of the early 1930s, a "collective leadership" coexisting with Stalin's de facto dictatorship, in which various members had their own defined areas of responsibility. Within these areas, they were not just allowed but required to exercise initiative. As Mikoyan later recalled, the first years of the war were a high-water point of the team as a cohesive entity, when everyone worked at full power in a context of mutual trust, big questions were decided by telephone with minimal red tape, and the team operated in "an excellent atmosphere for comradely work." When the GKO's core Group of Five (Stalin, Molotov, Malenkov, Beria, and Mikoyan) met, as they usually did late in the evening without a precirculated agenda or minutes taken, "each of us had full possibility to speak and defend his opinion or suggestion," and Stalin's attitude was "reasonable and patient," even if he didn't like what someone said. It quite often happened that Stalin, "convinced by our arguments," changed the opinion he had had at the beginning.

Every Soviet official and military man who visited Stalin in the Kremlin at that time remembers that he was habitually flanked by Molotov and others from the team, usually Beria and Malenkov, though they rarely spoke. Some of the visitors regarded them simply as yes-men and were annoyed by their presence, but Marshal Zhukov, who had as close access as anybody outside the team, saw it differently: "Taking part many times in discussion of questions in Stalin's office in the presence of his closest entourage, I had the opportunity to see arguments and squabbles, to see stubbornness displayed on various questions, in particular by Molotov; sometimes things went so far that Stalin raised his voice and even lost his temper, but Molotov, smiling, would get up from the table remaining of his opinion. Many of Stalin's suggestions concerning strengthening of defence and arming of the army, met opposition and objections. After that, commissions were created, in which there were arguments, and some issues drowned in those discussions. It was also a form of resistance."

Molotov, despite the troubles of 1939 and his apparent demotion in May 1941, was almost permanently at Stalin's side in the Kremlin and other Moscow-area meeting places, which included the air-raid shelter in the "Kirov" Metro station. Mikoyan later unkindly claimed that this enforced attendance actually hampered Molotov's ability to be useful during the war, calling him "decoration," but this may have been inspired by jealousy. Mikoyan himself was also often in Stalin's Kremlin office, though not as often as he claimed (he was not Stalin's second most frequent visitor during the war years, after Molotov, but fourth on the list, with Beria and Malenkov ahead). Stalin and Molotov were the two members of the team who stayed firmly in Moscow, while the others dashed around from front to front. Apart from the Tehran Conference with the Allies at the end of 1943, Stalin virtually never left the capital during the war. Molotov made two or three domestic trips in the first years of the war to crack the whip on some erring senior military commander on Stalin's behalf, but otherwise his trips as foreign minister were international: an important (and dangerous) plane trip as foreign minister to Britain and the United States in 1942, and then Tehran in 1943.[12]

In the partially formalized division of labor in the GKO, Stalin was in charge of the military side and the rest were in charge of the economy (whose performance, in the opinion of historians, was remarkably good, better than the military). Malenkov, Beria, and Mikoyan, along with Molotov, formed the operational leadership of the GKO. Mikoyan, as usual, was running supply, including that of the Red Army, and later also armament production; he was also still head of the foreign trade ministry and thus superintended lend-lease deliveries from the United States and Britain. This was one of the high points of his career, both in terms of operational effectiveness and closeness to the center of power. Tank production, aviation production, and the atomic industry were at different times under the charge of Molotov, Malenkov, and Beria, with a tendency for Beria to take over more responsibilities during the course of the war. Planning was under the fast-rising Nikolai Voznesensky, Stalin's new favorite.

Nikolai Voznesensky, born in 1903 and an ethnic Russian, competent, energetic, and (to his critics) arrogant, was one of comparatively few graduates of the Institute of Red Professors who made it into high positions. An economist by training, he was distinguished within the team not just by his youth and education but by having the manners of an intellectual.

He was the team's first professional, and the front-runner in the new co-hort of young Communist professionals promoted upward, in the wake of the Great Purges, of whom Stalin and Molotov had such high hopes. A Zhdanov protégé, he had worked in state planning in Leningrad for a few years before being promoted to head Gosplan (the State Planning Com-mittee) in Moscow in 1938. After only a few years on the job, he was ap-pointed a candidate member of the Politburo in February 1941. Stalin was "captivated" by Voznesensky, Mikoyan writes, and sometime in 1942 or 1943 announced that he would now be first deputy chair of the Council of Ministers for economic questions, which made him the nominal superior of both Mikoyan and Molotov. This went to his head, in Mikoyan's view, and he became arrogant and showed his ambition, which led Beria to in-trigue against him, with some success.[13]

Beria, heading security services and working closely throughout the war with the military, was riding high during the war, though some put this down to intrigue. It is always hard to get a clear picture of Beria, since his disgrace in 1953 made him a convenient scapegoat, and reminiscences of his wartime performance by military and civilian leaders are almost uniformly hostile. Beria's wartime responsibilities were huge. In addition to internal security, foreign intelligence, Gulag deportations, and several hundred thousand NKVD border troops, he supervised the evacuation of the defense industry, labor supply, and the movement of troops and equip-ment to the front. In the GKO, he oversaw defense production, particu-larly armaments and munitions. The expanding sphere of his responsibili-ties, often described as a sign of his habit of empire-building and intrigue, also suggests an unusual degree of competence. Moreover, he didn't al-ways *want* the new responsibilities: when Stalin, dissatisfied with Kagan-ovich's running of the railways, tried to get him to take over, he declined. "Clear thinking, cold-blooded and rational" was how Stalin saw him, a close observer reports. In the context of Stalinist modus operandi, for good and ill, he was a stellar performer.

Malenkov lost ground with Stalin at the beginning of the war, but made a comeback early in 1943. There was always a competitive edge to his relationship with Zhdanov, and the promotions of two Zhdanov proté-gés (Voznesensky and Shcherbakov) must have complicated things for him. Mikoyan, not usually a great admirer, conceded that Malenkov's contacts with provincial party officials were a big help to aviation production during the war. Zhdanov, a full member of the Politburo since 1939, was out of Moscow and, as a nonmember of the GKO, out of the loop for most of the war. One might have expected that Zhdanov's fairly lamentable performance in Leningrad at the beginning of the war would have told against him, and Stalin did indeed give him a thorough dressing down in the autumn of 1941, but he seems to have been at least half forgiven during his next brief visit to the capital in June 1942. According to Mikoyan, Stalin knew Zhdanov's weaknesses—drinking and cowardice are those listed by Mikoyan—but forgave him.[14]

Khrushchev had an exciting war, bookended by the establishment of Soviet rule and institutions in the newly acquired Western Ukraine in 1939 and their reestablishment in Ukraine, old and new, as the Germans retreated in 1944. He seems to have handled this energetically and effectively. From the fall of Kiev in mid-September 1941 to his reentry to the Ukrainian capital on 21 November 1943, he was on the road and at the fronts, with his family evacuated to Kuibyshev. Like Zhdanov, he was a full Politburo member (since 1939) but not a GKO member. He had a major clash with Stalin about the failure of the disastrous Kharkov counterassault in the spring of 1942, with almost half a million soldiers lost or captured, but was not demoted and subsequently recovered status. Yakov Chadaev, whose position as manager of the Council of Ministers gave him a close-up view of the leaders, said Stalin put up with Khrushchev's rather simplistic approach to problems because he was one of the few working-class members of the team, but this is an opinion expressed after Khrushchev's fall in 1964 and probably unduly negative. Stalin was not about to have a mere "token worker" running Ukraine; he obviously appreciated Khrushchev's abilities to get things done, take the initiative, and adapt to new situations. Unlike some of the other civilians who toured the fronts, Khrushchev seems to have been a genuinely welcome presence. Evaluating his contribution in the late 1960s (*after* Khrushchev's fall from power, thus in a climate where negative assessments might be expected), Marshal Alexander Vasilevsky gave him a positive grade for his wartime performance: "Khrushchev was an energetic man, bold, out with the troops all the time, never sat in HQs and command points, tried to see and talk to people, and, it must be said, people loved him."

Kaganovich was one of the old team members whose stature declined sharply during the war. Put in charge of evacuation of industry from the

Western regions of the country immediately after the German attack, 24 June 1941, he was removed after three weeks for not coping. The same thing happened with the railways, admittedly a challenge for any administrator given the tremendous demands the war put on them. Kaganovich was always very proud of his achievement with the railways, whose budget he had defended so vehemently in the 1930s ("People would attack me: 'Give, give!' I wouldn't give up a thing"): he boasted in 1990 that the performance of the railways, along with the army, were the two miracles of the war. As railways minister in the first year of the war, he was "working eighteen-hour days, cursing and threatening everyone and sparing no one, including himself." But by the spring of 1942, the major railway lines were jammed with trains carrying soldiers and freight in a situation of virtual paralysis, and Kaganovich was contributing nothing to the situation "except hysterics," according to the highly critical account by the man who succeeded him. He was dismissed from the job in a GKO resolution of 25 March 1942 that noted that "despite his satisfactory work in . . . peacetime, he could not cope with the work in wartime circumstances." Exactly what it was that had worked in peacetime but didn't work in the war is not clear: some observers cite his old habit of shouting, swearing, and even hitting subordinates, while others refer to his disinclination to listen to specialist advice, and yet others to "a bureaucratic style that didn't fit new circumstances." Although he was back in charge of railways again in 1943–44, his political standing never really recovered. He was "out of the political game" by the end of 1942, according to one historian; after the first two years of the war, he was a rare presence in Stalin's office.[15]

Voroshilov was also out of the political game by the end of 1942, though he was still a name to conjure with in popular understanding, his stature expanded by major celebrations of his sixtieth birthday in February 1941. The Great Purges, in the opinion of Admiral Kuznetsov, had left him demoralized and unable to handle things. His leadership of the defense ministry in the Finnish War, and his failure as the leader of the Northwestern Front to prevent the Leningrad blockade, were criticized in a Politburo resolution of 1 April 1942, which sent him to "military work in the rear." After that, although remaining a member of the Politburo and, for several years, the GKO, his colleagues just wanted him out of the way; in the judgment of one historian, he lost "the moral right even to express an opinion" at their meetings. True, he still had free access to Stalin, and they continued to use the familiar form of address with each other (Molotov and probably Mikoyan being the only other team members who still did so). But his visits to Stalin became much less frequent after he was dropped from the GKO in 1944, and Mikoyan claims that he was no longer invited even to Politburo meetings, although formally he remained a member.

Andreev, who, like Kaganovich, had been one of the most active members of the team during the Great Purges, also experienced a decline in status during the war. Still a secretary of the Central Committee, his particular areas of responsibility in the first years of the war were evacuation, supplying food and uniforms to the front, and the organization of hospital places for wounded soldiers; later he was put in charge of agriculture. As in the 1930s, he made many trips to the provinces, now for the purpose of organizing procurement and dispatching food to the front. It's not exactly clear why his status declined. He was not in good health, and one source suggests he was dropped from Stalin's social circle in the late 1930s. A somewhat lackluster recollection of his activity in 1941 from a wartime minister says his contributions to the war effort were useful, but mentions a business meeting of the two of them with a general, "who knew me, but he didn't know Andreev. In general few people did know him. [Andreev] was short, dressed modestly. A subdued personality. And then he had a bad heart."

Kalinin, who was almost seventy by the end of the war and in poor health, still held the office of president, but information on his wartime activities, if any, is sketchy. He evacuated to Kuibyshev for the first couple of years but was probably back in his Kremlin apartment at least by the middle of 1943. The wartime recollections of him—in the celebratory genre, since he, unlike most of the rest of the team, remained undisgraced in the post-Stalin decades—mainly recall the pleasure of his conversation, his benevolent presence, and his wise advice. Marshal Zhukov was one who recorded a strong affection and remembered dropping by in 1945 to tell him about the Battle of Berlin. Kalinin was a rare presence in Stalin's office, but Yakov Chadaev says Stalin and other members of the team often called in to consult him about economic matters. Rather surprisingly, Kalinin's most frequent visitor from the team was young Voznesensky, head of the State Planning Commission.[16]

Stalin's hands-on involvement with the direction of the war effort is well known, though opinions vary as to the value of his contribution. After the war, Stalin once told Molotov that "none of you are interested in military affairs," and Molotov agreed that the comment had a grain of truth. It was probably true of Molotov himself, who had a desk job throughout most of the Civil War and again in the Second World War. He didn't take to wearing a military uniform and lacked the long-standing work and personal ties with Red Army leaders that Mikoyan, Kaganovich, and Khrushchev had, not to mention Voroshilov, who for many years passed as a military man himself. True, the Great Purges had removed many of the team's old military buddies, like Egorov, Yakir, Gamarnik, and Uborevich. But the war forged new ties between military leaders and the political leaders, both professionally and personally.

Stalin was in constant contact with the military leaders throughout the war; his interactions with them were as many and as important as his interactions with the team in the GKO. Stalin had his own informal military "brain trust," including Marshal Boris Shaposhnikov (chief of the general staff and Stalin's deputy at the defense ministry in 1941–42), Marshal Alexander Vasilevsky (Shaposhnikov's successor as chief of the general staff and deputy defense minister), and Marshal Georgy Zhukov (deputy commander in chief from 1942). He had particular respect for Zhukov, who was one of the few people who risked talking back to him. Stalin's contact with his military men was via telephone and meetings in the Kremlin, and his knowledge of the front and the state of the army was from reports, not firsthand. He did not consider this necessarily a disadvantage. When the Ukrainian dramatist Alexander Korneichuk (husband of Stalin's favorite Polish writer, Wanda Wasilewska, and one of Molotov's deputies at the foreign ministry in the war years) wrote a play critical of "old style" leadership in the army, Stalin considered this valuable information and was furious when Marshal Semyon Timoshenko attacked Korneichuk in the press. "You are arrogant, you military," he said. "[You think] you know everything and we civilians understand nothing."

Other team members had their own military contacts, many of whom remained friends in civilian life after the war. Khrushchev, who ended the war with the rank of lieutenant general, lived a nomadic wartime life at the front as Politburo representative, and had whole shoals of military contacts and protégés. He soon found himself as much, or more, at home with the professional soldiers than with his colleagues in Moscow, and sometimes took their side against the Kremlin. When, after two years on the road with soldiers at the front when his fiefdom of Ukraine was under German occupation, he reentered Kiev in November 1943, he recalled that he "would have loved to see something of our pursuit of the Germans into Eastern Europe" but had to stay and put the Ukrainian house in order. Khrushchev's friends included Zhukov, Vasilevsky, and Timoshenko, "a good man and a good soldier," whom he accompanied, surely in violation of the rules, in a plane "deep into Bessarabia behind Rumanian lines" in 1940 to see Timoshenko's brother and sister in their native village.

Mikoyan, in charge of Red Army supply, formed close relationships with his counterpart on the army side, General Andrei Khrulev, and General Nikolai Vatutin, commander of the Voronezh and Southwest Fronts. Beria, according to his son, was a patron and protector of a number of military leaders, including Zhukov and Vasilevsky, as well as a good friend of Timoshenko since before the war. He clashed with various military leaders during the war, which was scarcely surprising given that he had control over the NKVD support units, which were not supposed to be used in active combat. His visits to the front, like Kaganovich's, often annoyed the military leaders because he came with a big entourage and threw his weight around.

Even team members who spent most of the war in Moscow during the war acquired military friends in the 1940s. Take Malenkov, of whom Khrushchev recalled that "whenever the [military] situation was looking gravest Malenkov would fly in with... representatives from General Staff. Frankly, I was never very pleased to see them." Yet his son, like all the family memoirists, emphasizes his father's "personal friendship" after the war with Zhukov, Vasilevsky, Konstantin Rokossovsky, and Admiral Nikolai Kuznetsov, head of the navy. Andreev's daughter, similarly, notes that her father was friendly with Kuznetsov and Marshals Ivan Konev, Rokossovsky, and Timoshenko, and in the postwar years, used to enjoy getting together with them and reminiscing about the war.[17]

Meanwhile, the wives and children were living in comparative comfort, but also considerable boredom, out in Kuibyshev, mixing with celebrity writers, the Bolshoi ballet, foreign correspondents, and the diplomatic corps, and itching to get back to Moscow. Stalin's daughter, Svetlana, who turned sixteen in 1942, managed to return in June of that year, and immediately plunged into trouble. Introduced by her brother Vasily to Alexei Kapler, a famous filmmaker and writer twenty-two years her senior, she fell in love with him and they conducted a passionate but apparently unconsummated relationship, with her worried bodyguards skulking in the wings. It ended on a high romantic note, with Kapler publishing an essay in *Pravda* in which he dared to mention looking at the Kremlin from his hotel and thinking of his beloved. Svetlana got a tremendous dressing down from her father, of whom she had seen little since the outbreak of war. Predictably infuriated when she invoked love as a justification, and seeing Kapler (whose telephone conversations with Svetlana had been tapped) as a middle-aged seducer of a schoolgirl, he not only reverted to Georgian paterfamilias mode but added his own personal vein of cruelty ("Look at yourself—who would want you?"). Kapler, who was one of those privileged members of the cultural elite who had contact with foreigners, was arrested in 1943 as an English spy and sent to Gulag for five years.

The next year, Svetlana offended Stalin again by impulsively marrying a schoolfriend, Grigory Morozov, who, like Kapler, was a Jewish intellectual with extensive contacts in Moscow high society. Stalin and the NKVD came to see the young couple as a security risk, liable to be cultivated for ulterior motives by ambitious (and possibly treacherous) members of the cultural elite. This was partly because Grigory's father, a bit of a rogue, though reputedly a friend of Polina Zhemchuzhina, took to boasting about the Stalin family connection and gossiping about Stalin (he would be arrested in 1948 for "slanderous inventions about the head of the Soviet government"). The NKVD reported to Stalin that another of Polina's friends, the Yiddish theater director Solomon Mikhoels, was cultivating Morozov and Svetlana in the hope of getting a direct line to Stalin. In any event, the marriage quickly broke up—of its own internal problems, according to Svetlana. But Stalin, while allowing the marriage, would never meet her new husband ("He's too calculating, your young man," and should be at the front), and the Moscow grapevine insisted that it was Stalin who had insisted on a divorce. A son, named Joseph in his honor, was born of the marriage in 1945, but Stalin hardly ever saw him.[18]

The war did not leave the children of the team unscathed. The sons of team members were expected to volunteer for military service, and all seem to have done so. They included Stalin's sons, Yakov and Vasily, as well as his ward Artem Sergeev, who remembered him summoning the three of them and telling them, "Boys, there will soon be war, and you must join the military!" Though the team's sons no doubt received special treatment, whether or not their parents asked for it, one Mikoyan son— Vladimir, an airman—perished over Stalingrad in 1942. Timur Frunze, the Voroshilov's adopted son, was another casualty, leading Voroshilov to bitter self-reproach for having succumbed to Timur's pleas to be allowed to go to the front and not secretly given instructions to the contrary: "his parents left him in our trust," Voroshilov grieved, "and we let them down."

Yakov (the child of Stalin's first marriage, who, unlike the children of his second, used the last name Dzhugashvili) and Leonid Khrushchev also perished, but in their cases, the circumstances were more complicated. Yakov, an artillery officer, was captured on the Belorussian Front on 10 July 1941. The Germans offered to trade him, but Stalin was not willing to negotiate for his release, saying all of Russia had missing sons. Yakov refused to cooperate with the Germans and died as a POW at Sachsenhausen concentration camp in the spring of 1943, apparently shot after disobeying a guard's orders. Because of his POW status, his wife was sent into exile for several years, leaving her young daughter to be brought up until her release in Svetlana's household, on Stalin's instructions.

The death of Khrushchev's eldest son, Leonid, a fighter pilot, in 1943 was even murkier. Like Yakov, Leonid was the son of a first marriage whose relationship with his father was rocky. Shot down by German fighters and badly wounded in July 1941, he was hospitalized for months in Kuibyshev, where the evacuated Khrushchev family lived. During this time he managed to kill a sailor in a drunken shooting game and was court-martialed. Back at the front in 1943, he went missing in action, and the family was told that he "died the death of the brave," which is what Khrushchev says in his memoirs. This may well be the case, according to Khrushchev's biographer, but the gossip had it that he had been found to be a collaborator and shot, a rumor Molotov repeated in old age, after his bitter break with Khrushchev in 1957. Leonid's widow, like Yakov's, was punished, though perhaps for her own sins rather than his: she was arrested on charges of contact with foreign intelligence—evidently related to social interaction with diplomats in Kuibyshev—and released only in the 1950s, which left the elder Khrushchevs to bring up their grandchild Julia.

There were a lot of Soviet grandparents bringing up young grandchildren after the disappearance of their parents, for it was standard practice to arrest the wives of those who, like Yakov, had been taken prisoner by the enemy. It comes as a bit of a surprise, all the same, to think that these grandparents included not only one of Stalin's team (Khrushchev) but also Stalin himself. Mikoyan's turn to have an in-law arrested would come after the war, but in 1943, with two of his sons fighting at the front and a third a recent casualty, he suffered the disaster of having his two youngest sons, Vano and Sergo, fifteen and fourteen years old, arrested in the "Kremlin children's" case. This started with a murder-suicide involving the son of a government minister and the daughter of a Soviet ambassador. The gun used belonged to their friend Vano Mikoyan. It was a case of thwarted love, but as usual in a Soviet context, the investigation turned political when the boy's teenage diary was alleged to contain fantasies of a future government of which he and Vano and Sergo Mikoyan would be members. It was not the only such case (another tangentially involved Voroshilov's adopted son Petr and the daughter of Old Bolshevik Nikolai Shvernik): the NKVD was evidently rattled by the idea that the Kremlin children, exposed to who knew what influences at school and among their peers, knew everything about the layout of the Kremlin and the team's dachas outside Moscow. The two Mikoyan boys disappeared into the Lubyanka and were then sent into exile in Central Asia until after the end of the war, when they were allowed to return to Moscow. Mikoyan made no attempt to intercede on their behalf, knowing such interventions to be pointless, and did not discuss the matter with Stalin.[19]

The war's turning point was the battle of Stalingrad, the Volga city— far from the Soviet Union's Western border in normal times—that had been Stalin's base in the Civil War. The city was virtually destroyed in building-to-building fighting in the winter of 1942–43, with German general Paulus's army and the Soviets slugging it out on the Moscow side of the river. Khrushchev was there as political advisor to Marshal Eremenko, who as commander of the Southern Front was initially responsible for the defense of Stalingrad. Eremenko was later joined by Rokossovsky, commanding a new Don Front, and deputy commander in chief Marshal Zhukov, who assumed the position of overall commander of the Soviet forces in the engagement. It was not just in retrospect that the battle of Stalingrad assumed such symbolic importance; its ebbs and flow were followed in minute detail by Stalin in Moscow, who sent Malenkov and Marshal Vasilevsky as his emissaries. In Khrushchev's opinion, Malenkov's particular job was keeping an eye on him (Khrushchev) and reporting back: "he didn't know anything about military matters, but he was more than competent when it came to intriguing," Khrushchev later remarked acidly. It got quite crowded in the army's Stalingrad billets with all the celebrity observers come to be present at the victory. Zhukov turned the fight from defense to attack, Paulus's army was encircled, and, in a great coup for the Soviets, Paulus himself was captured on 31 January 1943, the day after his promotion by Hitler to field marshal.

The Germans were in retreat after Stalingrad, with the Soviet Army pushing its way through formerly occupied territory, but it took a year and a half of steady fighting to reach the Polish border and then almost another year to reach Berlin. The Allies opened a Second Front, long demanded by the Soviet Union, with the American landing in Italy in September 1943, but the Western Front, which the Soviets really wanted, was not opened until the Allied Normandy landing in June 1944. As the tides of war turned, Stalin's behavior changed—for the worse, as those around him reported. Stalin had worked well, in general, with the team and his military leaders, for the first three years or so of the war. While there were occasional outbursts, his behavior was usually "reasonable and polite," according to Admiral Kuznetsov. "He treated people better during the war than in peacetime." But by 1944, Zhukov thought he was becoming jealous of his army commanders, and Mikoyan noticed him "becoming arrogant, start[ing] to be capricious." With hunger threatening in the devastated Ukraine, Mikoyan and Andreev proposed that seed grain should be given to collective and state farms to ensure a reasonable harvest the next year, but Stalin "rudely refused [Mikoyan's] suggestion" and accused him of "behaving in an anti-state way," letting himself be taken in by the local officials (who, in Stalin's mind, always asked for more than they really needed) and "corrupting" Andreev, his weaker partner in sin.[20]

The move westward and the liberation of formerly occupied territory added a new set of tasks for Beria, already one of the team's busiest men. The security police force was divided in two in April 1943, with Beria remaining in charge of the NKVD, the Ministry of Internal Affairs (which retained responsibility for Gulag), and his former deputy, Vsevolod Merkulov, in charge of the new NKGB, the ministry of state security, but this does not seem to have significantly reduced his powers. With the introduction of military ranks for security police personnel in the summer of 1945, Beria became a marshal. Under his command, whole ethnic groups from the Caucasus were accused of wartime collaboration and collective treason, and deported in 1943–44, in operations of fearsome efficiency and cruelty. In the tiny autonomous republic of Chechnya-Ingushetia, NKVD troops swept in on 23 February 1944, read out the deportation orders, and had the entire Chechen and Ingush population (almost half a million people) loaded into trucks and trains for eastward deportation in less than a week. A total of one and a half million people—Chechens, Ingush, Karachai, Balkars, Kalmyks, Meskhetians, and Crimean Tatars—were deported to Central Asia or other points east, where the angry and aggressive Chechens, in particular, caused considerable problems as deeply unwanted and unwilling guests of the Kazakhs. Stalin was the general director of these punitive actions, but Beria seems to have been an enterprising and eager partner, as well as a brilliant executant.

The deportations were only the most dramatic of the arrests and punitive actions going on at the end of the war. Letters to an army friend criticizing Stalin in homemade code led to the arrest of young officer Alexander Solzhenitsyn, the later chronicler of Gulag. The Baltic states, reoccupied in the autumn of 1944, were subjected to mass arrests and deportations. In Lithuania, as in the Western Ukraine, fierce partisan warfare against Soviet rule continued for some years after the end of the war.[21]

The army's westward march, punctuated by fierce battles, brought Khrushchev back to Kiev in November 1943. "There was something eerie about the city," he remembered later. "It had been such a noisy, lively, youthful place before the war, and now there was no one around. As we walked along the Kreshchatik and turned onto Lenin Street, our footsteps echoed along the empty stretch of pavement around us. Soon people began to emerge from hiding. They appeared as though they had come out of the ground. As we were walking along Lenin Street in the direction of the Opera, talking and comparing impressions, we suddenly heard a hysterical scream, and a young man came running toward us. He kept shouting, 'I'm the only Jew left! I'm the last Jew in Kiev who's still alive.'" Khrushchev thought perhaps the man had gone mad.

Leningrad, and Zhdanov with it, was freed from the blockade early in 1944. The corpses that had filled the streets in the winter of 1942 were gone, but the wide gray streets seemed strangely quiet and empty. Harrison Salisbury of the *New York Times*, entering the city a few weeks later, found Zhdanov at his desk at Smolny, working day in and day out, hoarse and coughing from asthma. He had had two heart attacks during the blockade, and his health never recovered. Handing over the administration of Leningrad to his deputy, Alexei Kuznetsov, in January 1945, Zhdanov became head of the Soviet Control Commission in Finland, commuting from his Kremlin apartment to Helsinki throughout the year, learning a little Finnish, and taking part in the city's numerous diplomatic receptions while still wearing the military uniform that, like most of the team, he had donned during the war.

In Eastern Europe and the Baltics, the Soviets arrived as liberators in their own eyes but conquerors in the view of many whom they liberated. With final victory in sight, Marshal Zhukov was summoned to Moscow to plan the Berlin operation. He found Stalin in a gloomy and reflective mood, obviously utterly overworked and close to exhaustion: "What a terrible war," he said. "How many lives of our people it has carried away. There are probably very few families of us left who haven't lost someone near to them." It was a race to Berlin, with Zhukov and Marshal Konev competing on the Soviet side and British and American forces pressing in from the West, and even in the city itself the Germans put up stubborn resistance. But Berlin was finally taken in May 1945, after a tough street-by-street battle toward the city center, like Stalingrad two and a half years earlier, in which the Soviets lost hundreds of thousands of men. After the capture of the Reichstag on 30 April, two soldiers from Zhukov's army raised the Soviet flag (though the iconic image, captured by a Soviet photographer, was actually a reenactment). Early in the morning on 9 May, Zhukov and British, American, and French commanders accepted the Germans' act of capitulation.[22]

The Soviet Union had paid a tremendous price for the victory—close to eight million military dead, and perhaps another seventeen million civilian deaths (though some estimates are double that), along with massive destruction of infrastructure, industrial plants, railways, and bridges, carried out by the Germans in a "scorched earth" policy during their retreat, in the huge area that had been under German occupation. There were twelve million evacuees to return to their homes and eight million men under arms in the Soviet Army, most of whom were to be demobilized in short order. Against the odds, the Soviet regime had survived the disasters of 1941 and 1942, and so had the Communist Party. Admittedly, that party was now something of a different animal from before as a result of the destruction of old cadres in the Great Purges and the war and massive wartime recruitment at the front. Stalin—Generalissimus, as he had allowed himself to be styled, a mistake he later regretted—now headed a party that in terms of composition was something like a veterans' association. The team, with the exception of Molotov and Kalinin, were often to be seen in military uniform, and a number of them held military ranks.

May 9 became the Day of Victory, celebrated annually in the Soviet Union (and in its successor, the Russian Federation). But it was not until 24 June 1945 that the Victory Parade took place in Red Square in front of the Kremlin. Stalin had thought of greeting the troops himself on horseback, a brave act for a man not known to have any significant riding experience (his son Vasily unkindly told a story that he had practiced but fallen off and decided to give up, but we don't have to believe this). In any event, he asked Zhukov to do the honors, riding a white Arabian steed, which Zhukov duly and memorably did. When Zhukov was hailed with shouts of "Hurrah," he noticed with some apprehension that Stalin didn't like it, his muscles clenching. But the official film shows a cheerful Stalin—despite the rain that caused the flyby to be canceled and many in the crowd to put up umbrellas—jovially exchanging greetings with his colleagues, who looked very much like a team as they mounted the steps to the rostrum over Lenin's Mausoleum. Many of the team, including Stalin, were in military uniform (not, in Stalin's case, that of the Generalissimus, the title he would assume four days later), but Kalinin, with pointed beard and overcoat, wore his usual worker's cap. Though their contribution had been great, the team made a modest showing compared to the military leaders, who led their troops in full dress uniform with arrays of medals.

Marshal Zhukov was the only one to speak at the parade, but at the Kremlin reception afterward Stalin made a toast—not to the military commanders, nor to his Politburo team, nor to the party, but to the "Soviet people, above all, the Russian people." Evidently he had not forgotten his own mistakes at the beginning of the war and counted himself lucky to have survived them. Another people, he said, might have kicked out the government responsible for the reverses of 1941–42, but the Russian people stayed with them, and eventually they won. "Thank you, Russian people, for that trust."[23]

SEVEN

POSTWAR HOPES

Mikoyan was in a buoyant mood at the end of the war, or so he remembered later. He thought there had to be changes for the better. Stalin had reverted to his good side during the war; the team had worked well together. The Soviet people had grown up ("war turned out to be a great school for political education"), and army service had instilled a "comradely democratism" in millions of soldiers. Contact with Europe in the last stages of the war had widened horizons—Mikoyan was speaking of popular horizons, but he might well have had the team in mind too—and shown that a better standard of living was possible. Mikoyan couldn't imagine a repeat of the arbitrary repressions of the 1930s. He expected a return to the political system of the 1920s, before collectivization and the Great Break, when "democratic relations" prevailed in the party. In fact, he was sure of it, which filled him with "a feeling of joy." Many in the country shared Mikoyan's hopes, and probably most of the team along with them. But not Stalin. He evidently had a different idea of the normality to which the Soviet Union should be returning, one in which the prewar concepts of "struggle," "vigilance," and "enemies" remained salient.

There were two ways of seeing the Soviet Union at the end of the war. One was that it had won a glorious victory and become, for the first time, a superpower, with a new external empire covering most of Eastern Europe. The other was that it was a devastated country facing a tremendous task of postwar reconstruction. Stalin and the team had both pictures in mind, though with regard to the means of reconstruction, and the crucial questions of postwar relations with the West that it raised, there were some differences of opinion within the team.

In the course of the war, Stalin's image had become familiar to the whole world—no longer as a revolutionary wild man in a faraway country but as one of the towering leaders of the Grand Alliance, the benign, pipe-smoking "Uncle Joe." The sobriquet slightly annoyed him when President Roosevelt passed it on, as he wrongly read disrespect. He had in fact done an amazing job convincing Franklin Roosevelt and Winston Churchill, his two Alliance partners, of his greatness, however infuriating they might sometimes find him. Drawing perhaps on his 1937 practice with US ambassador Davies, he managed to turn on a sustained demonstration of personal magnetism that took him through the leaders' conferences at Tehran in 1943 and Yalta at the beginning of 1945. Of his two peers, Roosevelt was the one for whom he felt most human sympathy, for his bravery in rising above the paralysis that confined him to a wheelchair. But it was Churchill, the old interventionist nemesis from Civil War days, whom Stalin took the most trouble to charm, with surprising success. "I walk through this world with greater courage and hope when I find myself in a relation of friendship and intimacy with this great man, whose fame has gone out not only over all Russia, but the world," Churchill said in a celebratory toast. At one dinner, some slightly drunken badinage about the desirability of killing off fifty thousand officers and leaders to keep Germany in its place after the war offended Churchill, and he left the room in a huff. Stalin and Molotov followed him, in the role of rueful and remorseful friends, and persuaded him to come back. Stalin had "a very captivating manner when he chooses to use it," Churchill commented about this incident.[1]

It had taken an effort to get Stalin out of the Soviet Union, even to Tehran, which was comparatively close. The Baku-Tehran flight was his first in a plane, and he was terribly apprehensive; in any event, he hated it and never flew again. Passionate supporter of Soviet aviation development as he was, he was very jumpy about planes, even for his associates. Politburo members were strictly forbidden to fly without special permission, and Mikoyan got into quite serious trouble when he went up for a joyride in the Caucasus—it took him years to get the official rebuke off his file, and it was not until 1955 that the ban on Politburo air travel was lifted. Molotov, the stoic, had had to get used to air travel, having been subjected in his capacity as foreign minister since 1939 to a variety of trips to Germany, Britain, and the United States, including one particularly harrowing one over the Atlantic under enemy fire. Later, the writer Konstantin Simonov, reflecting on the admiration he had felt for Molotov, singled out this example of his courage.

The end of the war was a high point for Molotov, whose international visibility was second only to Stalin's. After foreign ministry personnel were issued with uniforms, resplendent with braid and epaulets, a foreign journalist who knew him saw him as a man transformed: "in his smart-fitting uniform ... unsmiling but looking very pleased, [he] carried himself with a buoyant stateliness." At a victory celebration in May 1945, Stalin's first toast was to Molotov—"To our Vyacheslav!"—with the reminder that "good foreign policy sometimes outweighs two or three armies at the front."

Previously insular, like all the Bolshevik leaders, Molotov's acquaintance with the world had widened. In the course of his job as foreign minister, he was in San Francisco, Washington, New York, Berlin, Paris, and London in the immediate postwar years. At the end of his 1946 trip to Paris, his daughter Svetlana joined him and they did some sightseeing together, he "delighting in her mastery of the French language and in her quick enjoyment of the western scene." In London, living in the Soviet Embassy, Molotov had no time for sightseeing, as he wrote to Polina, except for a single trip up to Highgate to see Marx's grave. He did manage to get to the opera in Paris (Mozart's *Marriage of Figaro*) but it was a ceremonial occasion, sitting in a box, with the "bourgeois public" eyeing him, and he felt under strain. In general, negotiations with the capitalists were not only a "great responsibility" for him but a kind of exam: with all three of the other powers against you and trying to catch you out, you have to be "on the alert the whole time, tense, for fear of overlooking something, making a mistake," he wrote to Polina. Still, it was gratifying to be taken seriously and deferred to as the representative of a great power.[2]

Some other team members managed to see a bit of the world in the immediate postwar years. Beria was at Tehran, Yalta, and Potsdam, albeit in his capacity as security chief rather than as a Soviet leader, and later he was in and out of Berlin, keeping an eye on the Soviet occupation forces. Voroshilov—rather surprisingly, given his fall from grace as a military leader, but no doubt in token of his old friendship with Stalin—was at

Tehran with Stalin and Molotov, mingling with the Allied leaders, though he was not invited to Yalta or Potsdam. Chairman of the Soviet Control Commission in Budapest for the first two years after the war, Voroshilov made many Hungarian friends, not just political leaders like Mátyás Rákosi but also artists, some of whom he continued to patronize after his return to Moscow. Khrushchev, still based in Ukraine, had close contact with Poland; in the waning days of the war, he made trips to Lublin and Warsaw, and he and Bulganin saw the gas chambers at Majdanek. Later he would become an indefatigable and enthusiastic traveler, but his first trip farther West, to Austria, Hungary, and East Germany in 1946, was incognito with a group of experts negotiating reparations.

Mikoyan's wartime work had brought him into contact and negotiations with the Allies, especially the Americans, over lend-lease and other economic issues. Within the team, he was the man most committed to closer economic relations with the West. Even before the war's end, he and American ambassador Averell Harriman had talked about possible reconstruction credits from the United States, and he urged Stalin to raise this issue at Yalta (he didn't). Mikoyan was probably miffed at not being included in the Yalta delegation, and the fact that he had no foreign trips in the immediate postwar years until 1949, when he was sent to China to negotiate with Mao Tse-tung, may indicate that Stalin and Molotov thought his enthusiasm for Western contacts should be curbed. Foreigners came to Moscow, however, and in the course of extensive negotiations with the young British politician Harold Wilson, Mikoyan not only achieved a deal setting grain exports against wartime credits but also made a lifelong personal friend of the man who was to become British prime minister in the 1960s.[3]

If some of the team still lacked languages and cosmopolitan polish, all were eager for their children to acquire them. It was not just the gifted Svetlana Molotova who made her father proud with her knowledge of French. Beria's son had been learning German from age four and English from age five, giving him "complete command of those languages." Malenkov's two boys studied at a special English school. The Zhdanovs, priding themselves on their German culture, were put out to find that their Yury's German was not as good as Sergo Beria's. Sergei Khrushchev topped his class in English, thanks to the intensive coaching his mother had organized, while Stepan Mikoyan not only studied German at school but shared a German tutor with his father; after the war, he took private lessons in English as well. Svetlana Stalina's language was English, though her father was dubious about her translation and speaking abilities, and when he brought Churchill home during the war, she was too shy to converse with him.

The team children who came of age in the 1940s belonged to a Soviet elite generation that fell in love with America. It was possible for the first time to learn about the outside world from Russian-language magazines distributed in Moscow by the Allies—*Amerika*, modeled on *Life* magazine and brought in by the US Information Agency, and *Britanskii soiuznik*, published in Moscow by the British Embassy—and the younger generation took full advantage of it. In wartime Kuibyshev, elite evacuees even managed to get hold of *Life*, *Fortune*, and the *Illustrated London News*, presumably from Western diplomats; it was by reading them to improve her English that Svetlana Stalina found out that her mother had committed suicide. Probably that was not the only eye-opening information that the team's children absorbed from foreign sources. When Svetlana went to Moscow University, she chose to study the history of the United States, "prompted by the general enthusiasm and interest in America": all her university friends and her first husband gravitated toward US history, economics, and foreign policy, because "everyone strove to learn more about that great democracy beyond the ocean." Among the rising young men working in the Central Committee, the same cohort as many of the leaders' children, cultural Anglo- and Americaphilia was in vogue.[4]

One could have imagined a postwar future in which Stalin, his suspicious nature appeased by international fame and victory, and his companions, with some of the insularity rubbed off by foreign contacts and their minds broadened by their increasingly cosmopolitan grown-up children, would have lost their suspicion of the West and let the closed frontier—necessarily opened, as far as the Allies were concerned, during the war—remain ajar. It didn't happen. As far as the team was concerned, the first warning signal came in 1945, a few months after the end of the war, when Stalin savagely turned on Molotov for allegedly currying favor with the West.

Stalin's health was bad in these months. He may have had heart problems at Potsdam—that, at any rate, was what *Newsweek* reported, and it was part-owned by the US ambassador to Moscow, Averell Harriman, who had his ear to the ground—and he had some kind of heart attack in October 1945, though it was kept secret. In his first vacation since 1937, he was in the South recuperating for two and a half months in the autumn of 1945. As had been his wont in the 1930s, he kept a close watch even on vacation on what the team left in charge in Moscow was doing. That meant the "Group of Four" that was currently at the center of things: Molotov, Mikoyan, Beria, and Malenkov. Reading extensive daily summaries of the foreign press, Stalin discovered, to his fury, that it was full of rumors about his ill health and imminent retirement—and speculation about his heir. Molotov, well known in the West because of his travels as foreign minister, was the front-runner for succession in many of these stories, which portrayed him as representing "a new, strong Soviet Union, demanding an equal position among the great powers of the world," implicitly in contrast to the old, weak, and internationally marginalized country that Stalin had led for the past two decades. Molotov, the "second citizen of the Soviet Union after Stalin," was said to be very popular in the USSR and to have "won great authority for himself" (Stalin underlined this passage in blue pencil).

Stalin himself had started to talk about aging and the inevitability of a succession sometime soon, but his colleagues were understandably unwilling to take him at his word. In 1946, according to Molotov, Stalin actually "gave in his resignation," saying that it was time for someone younger to take over, adding, more concretely, "Let Vyacheslav have a go." People took this suggestion different ways, as Molotov remembered, but presumably no one, including himself, embraced the idea with enthusiasm (Kaganovich, always jealous of Molotov, allegedly wept). But this didn't mean that Stalin enjoyed being second-guessed in the Western press. Not surprisingly, he found it extremely irksome, and picked a fight with Molotov about the latter's alleged "liberality" with foreign correspondents in Moscow, apropos of a recent easing of censorship regulations approved by the foreign ministry, which he attributed to Molotov's sneaky desire to get himself a good press. Having blasted Molotov by telephone from Sochi, he then upped the ante by directing his complaint to the Group of Four with the implicit request that they discipline their errant member. This they did, though not without some awkwardness and hesitation, which produced the extraordinary event of tears from Molotov and a stiff-necked apology, after which the issue was dropped. But this

17. Molotov, Khrushchev, and Stalin, in summer suits, watching an athletic parade from the Mausoleum in 1936. Sovfoto.

18. Voroshilov, Molotov, Stalin, and Ezhov on Moscow-Volga canal, 1937. RGAKFD.

19. Stalin with children Vasily (on left), Svetlana (standing)
and Yakov (on right), with Zhdanov next to Vasily, 1 July 1938.
RGASPI.

20. Party leaders at People's Meeting of Western Ukraine, 4 October 1939. Front row from left:
unknown, Shvernik, Andreev, Molotov, Voroshilov, Stalin, Kalinin, academician Tsitsinov,
unknown, Kaganovich, Zhdanov, Malenkov, Khrushchev. RGASPI.

21. Churchill and Stalin, Kremlin, 1942. RGASPI.

22. Molotov signing Soviet-Czech agreement, 1 December 1943. Voroshilov, Kalinin, and Stalin in background. RGASPI.

23. Zhukov on white horse at Victory Parade in Red Square, Moscow, 24 June 1945. Sovfoto.

24. Stalin at Potsdam conference, 1945. RIA Novosti.

25. Team at Kalinin's funeral, 1946: Beria, Malenkov, Stalin, and Molotov (in front), Voznesensky (next row, between Malenkov and Stalin), Kuznetsov (visible behind Voznesensky's shoulder), Kaganovich (behind, between Stalin and Molotov), Zhdanov (behind, far right).

26. At Kuntsevo dacha, 1 October 1947. (Front row, left to right) Kaganovich, Malenkov, Stalin, and Zhdanov; (back row) Stalin's children Vasily and Svetlana, with Poskrebyshev next to Svetlana. RIA Novosti.

27. Stalin's coffin, March 1953. Molotov, Voroshilov, Beria, and Malenkov at left, Bulganin, Khrushchev, Kaganovich, Mikoyan at right. RGASPI.

28. Pall-bearers at Stalin's funeral, March 1953. In front, Malenkov at left, Beria at right, with Voroshilov just behind him, Mikoyan and Khrushchev visible behind at right. RGASPI.

29. Molotov family, 20 April 1953. (Standing) son-in-law Alexei Nikonov, Polina Zhemchuzhina (photo must have been taken within weeks of her return from exile in Kazakhstan); (seated) daughter Svetlana and her three-year-old daughter Larisa, Molotov. RGAKFD.

30. Members of "collective leadership" in China, 1954. Front row: Mikoyan, Ekaterina Furtseva (first secretary of Moscow party), Khrushchev, Bulganin, Shvernik. RIA Novosti.

surely laid the foundation for Stalin's intensifying suspicions, not only of Molotov but also of the team, whose response to Stalin's barrage had clearly implied a sense of team solidarity.[5]

The Group of Four all had reason to worry about falling out of favor with Stalin. Mikoyan had got the rough side of Stalin's tongue in 1944, then again in 1946 when Stalin claimed that "thanks to his weak character," he had "allowed thieves to gather" in his trade ministry. His two youngest sons had only recently returned to Moscow after their wartime arrest and exile for involvement in an alleged plot against the state. Still fourth or fifth in frequency of visits to Stalin's office, he was not quite as prominent in the leadership as he had been during the war.

Beria overtook Molotov as the most frequent visitor to Stalin's office in the fourth quarter of 1945 and retained that position through 1946 and 1947. A full member of the Politburo from March 1946, he was in charge of the crucially important nuclear program, which produced the successful atomic bomb test on 29 August 1949, far quicker than the Americans—who had pioneered the weapon at Hiroshima in 1945—had expected. However, his career suffered an apparent setback at the end of 1945 when the security ministry was divided into two, the Ministry for State Security (MGB) and the Ministry of Internal Affairs (MVD), the first headed by a close associate but the second not. His official position thereafter was simply deputy chairman of the Council of Ministers, with overall supervisory responsibility over the security agencies for that body (though not for the Politburo), but it is clear that this fails to reflect either his closeness to Stalin or his continuing connections with the world of security, the exact nature of which remains hard to penetrate. His son said that Beria, even when no longer directly in charge of the security organs, had "his own intelligence network, which was not dependent on any existing structure," the function of which was to serve as an additional information channel for Stalin.

Malenkov, the faithful executant, was appointed full member of the Politburo in March 1946, along with Beria, but two months later was dropped from his position as secretary of the Central Committee in May 1946 and had to wait more than two years before being reinstated in July 1948. The cause of Stalin's dissatisfaction was apparently defects in aviation production, which Malenkov supervised: he came "very close to the wire" for several months in mid-1946, with close associates arrested and his own name mentioned in their confessions. His son recalls that "for a while [he] found himself under house arrest" before being dispatched to help with grain procurements in Siberia, and he slipped to last place among Politburo members in the protocol rankings in the press. However, in 1947, even before his restoration as Central Committee secretary, he was back as the third most frequent visitor (after Beria and Molotov) to Stalin's office. Andrei Zhdanov, who tended to be up when Malenkov was down, had survived his poor wartime performance (Stalin liked him more than anyone else on the team except Kirov, according to Molotov) but spent most of 1945 away from the center as head of the Soviet Control Commission in Finland, from which he was recalled in December because of a "complex situation," not further explained, related to Stalin's illness. Back in Moscow as a Central Committee secretary, he worked closely with Stalin for several years in disciplining the intelligentsia, but despite this ongoing contact, he was not one of the most frequent visitors to Stalin's office (fifth in 1946, down to sixth the next year).[6]

Nikolai Voznesensky, Alexei Kosygin, and Alexei Kuznetsov, all three with Leningrad backgrounds and reputedly protégés of Zhdanov, were rising fast in the early postwar period. Voznesensky became a full Politburo member in February 1947, having been a candidate since 1941. Khrushchev remembered Voznesensky from these years as "bright, self-assured, tough-minded." He reportedly became arrogant after his rapid rise and could be rude to team colleagues, even senior ones like Molotov, but Stalin was said to value him for giving him straight answers on economic questions. Kosygin, a young economic administrator who had chaired the Leningrad Soviet before coming to Moscow in 1939 as an industrial minister, became a candidate member of the Politburo in March 1946. Alexei Kuznetsov, a tough, good-looking young man who had been Zhdanov's highly valued deputy in Leningrad, was one of the working-class cohort that rose in the wake of the purges, although unlike many of them, he never left Komsomol and party work to get a postsecondary education. He moved in 1946 to become a secretary of the Central Committee whose responsibilities included party oversight on the security police. It was rumored that Stalin was preparing the three of them as future leaders—Voznesensky as head of government, Kuznetsov in charge of the party—to replace the Old Guard. Not surprisingly, Malenkov and Beria viewed their rise warily.

Kalinin, gravely ill by the end of the war, died in March 1946. The letter he had written to Stalin asking for the release of his wife, Ekaterina
Lorberg, didn't reach Stalin's office until after his death, but she was released anyway in a 1945 amnesty, although not allowed to return to her
former apartment in the Kremlin. She was thus able to attend her husband's funeral, which was with full state honors. Kalinin was replaced as
head of the Supreme Soviet by Nikolai Shvernik, an Old Bolshevik Russian ex-trade unionist of working-class origins, contemporary of Molotov and Voroshilov, and a Central Committee secretary with Stalin back
in the mid-1920s. A candidate member of the Politburo since 1939, Shvernik was not a member of the innermost circle, but he was a familiar
face to the team who had performed creditably on the economic front
during the war.

Nikolai Bulganin, who became a candidate member of the Politburo
in March 1946, was another newcomer. Ethnically Russian, like the other
recent recruits to the team, he was appointed Stalin's deputy as defense
minister in 1944 and was a fairly frequent visitor to Stalin's office thereafter. His background was not military: after an early start with the Cheka
during the Civil War, he had become an industrial manager and then
headed the Moscow Soviet, working closely with Khrushchev in the
1930s. Khrushchev, though a friend of Bulganin's, never claimed he was a
great intellect or military genius; others called him a "braggard" and
lightweight. He was an educated person by the standards of the team; his
wife Elena was an English teacher. But his great characteristic seems to
have been high-level sociability. His family already had multiple social
connections with the team: his wife was a friend of Khrushchev's wife;
his daughter Vera, later to marry the son of Admiral Kuznetsov, was in
school with Svetlana Stalina and Svetlana Molotova and a friend of Rada
Khruscheva and Valentina Malenkova; his son Lev was a friend of Vasily
Stalin's.[7]

As for the rest, Khrushchev was off in Kiev, rarely in Moscow, and thus
out of the inner circle. The year 1946 to 1947 was a tough year for him, first
because famine struck again in Ukraine, and second because Stalin sent
out Kaganovich to "help" him cope; his former patron took over for ten
months in 1947 as first secretary of the Ukrainian party, with Khrushchev
humiliatingly forced to stay on as second secretary. Little wonder that
Khrushchev, who had been almost continuously on the road for most of

the war, fell seriously ill with pneumonia. By the time he got back to work, Kaganovich had become "simply unbearable," as Khrushchev remembered, pursuing not just the usual suspects (Ukrainian nationalists) but Jews as well. With the exception of this uptick in 1947, Kaganovich's status did not improve markedly in the first postwar years from their low point during the war: before the Ukrainian foray, he headed for the Ministry of Industrial Construction Materials and then the State Supply Agency.

Andreev, who had become almost totally deaf and was in very poor health, had also fallen further out of favor. He was not reappointed as Central Committee secretary in March 1946 and disappeared almost entirely from Stalin's office visiting list, although he continued to work, now in the field of agriculture. Voroshilov remained out of favor too. Stalin often treated him with contempt—"like a dog," one foreign observer said—twisting the screw by refusing to confirm his invocations of old friendship. Around this time, Stalin started hinting that Voroshilov might be a British spy, but with Stalin you never knew how to take such remarks. Voroshilov remained, in any case, a full member of the Politburo, and on his return from Hungary was given a job in cultural administration—not such a stretch as it might seem, given his long history of friendship with and patronage of artists and theater people, but a long way from his previous specialty of military affairs.

The upshot of all this playing around on Stalin's part was, in a sense, very small. There were some new faces on the team (though most of them turned out to be temporary), but the old team members stayed in place—with a reminder, sometimes quite a humiliating and frightening one, that tenure wasn't guaranteed. That was on the political side. On the military side, Marshal Zhukov wasn't so lucky. It was almost overdetermined that the immensely popular victor of Berlin, the man on a white horse in the 1945 Victory Parade, should arouse Stalin's suspicion and get his comeuppance in the postwar years, and that is what happened. Head of the Soviet military administration in Germany immediately after the war, Zhukov was recalled to Moscow early in 1946 to become commander in chief of Soviet ground forces, then within months abruptly dismissed from this position, accused of "losing all sense of humility and claiming credit for all major operations in the war," and demoted to head of the Odessa military district. In 1948, there was a scandal about "trophy" goods he had brought back from Germany, his apartment was subjected to a house search, and he was demoted again, this time to the command of the Urals military district. Although he was well remembered by the people (and the team as well), his name started to disappear from histories of the Second World War, and he even vanished from paintings of the Victory Parade. Taking his banishment like a good soldier, he found a new wife in the Urals, to the fury of his old one, and by 1952 he was edging back into favor again, though he didn't get back to Moscow until after Stalin's death.[8]

The wartime honeymoon with the Allies was already souring by the time of the Potsdam Conference, held in the summer of 1945; no sooner was it over than the United States, without prior consultation, dropped its fearsome new weapon, the atomic bomb, on Hiroshima. The Western powers were unhappy about the degree of Soviet control in the East European states, which had been assigned at Yalta to the Soviet sphere of influence but were now moving toward Communist one-party regimes under Soviet tutelage and looking increasingly like satellites. Churchill was still saying nice things about Stalin—"I personally cannot feel anything but the greatest admiration for that genuinely great man, father of his country," he told the House of Commons in November 1945—but Stalin was unimpressed: Churchill was just trying "to calm his unquiet conscience" for organizing an "Anglo-American-French bloc against the USSR," he wrote to the team from Sochi, adding, in what was probably a sideswipe at Molotov and Mikoyan, "we have quite a few senior figures who go into calf-like ecstasy at praises from Churchill, Truman, Byrnes." Presaging things to come on the domestic front, Stalin declared such attitudes to be demeaning and dangerous. "We must conduct fierce struggle against servility ... and bowing and scraping before foreigners."

Churchill's famous speech at Fulton, Missouri, a few months later dramatized the rift between the erstwhile allies: "A shadow has fallen upon the scenes so lately lighted by the Allied victory ... From Stettin in the Baltic to Trieste in the Adriatic, an iron curtain has descended across the Continent." All of Eastern Europe was in the Soviet sphere, with police states under Moscow control emerging; no one knew "what are the limits, if any, to [Soviet] expansive and proselytising tendencies ... This is certainly not the Liberated Europe we fought to build up. Nor is it one which contains the essentials of permanent peace." Stalin's response was that Churchill's speech must be interpreted as a "dangerous act"; he had now essentially gone over to the side of the warmongers in Britain and the United States, a group "strikingly reminiscent... of Hitler and his friends." The Fulton speech was "a call to war against the Soviet Union."

What we identify in retrospect as the Cold War had begun. At the time, however, it was not yet clear whether it was going to stay cold or burst into flames in a Third World War. Stalin was not alone in the Soviet leadership in his anger and alarm. For Marshal Zhukov, Churchill's and Truman's behavior at Potsdam "more than ever demonstrated their desire to capitalize on the defeat of Nazi Germany to strengthen their position and dominate the world." For another Soviet marshal, the American use of the bomb was meant to intimidate the Soviet Union and show that "the US elite was already considering the establishment of its world domination." From Washington, the Soviet ambassador to the United States, by no means a hawk in Soviet terms, sent back reports about the alarmingly anti-Soviet mood developing in the United States.[9]

With the United States in possession of the bomb, it became top priority for the Soviet Union to acquire one too. Beria was the man in charge, both of the clandestine activity that obtained information on the American atomic program and of the all-out Soviet scientific effort headed by nuclear physicist Igor Kurchatov to build a bomb. He and the Soviet scientists did a brilliant job, successfully testing their own bomb in Kazakhstan at the end of August 1949. This seems to have been Beria's chief preoccupation in the first prewar years, and—in contrast to the general rule of negativity on all sides in assessing Beria after his fall and execution in mid-1953—a number of his scientists on the program later spoke very highly of his intelligence, willpower, energy, and administrative efficiency. You had to give him "a very high rating" as a manager, a high official outside Beria's direct sphere of activity conceded, even if fear was part of the mixture: he took his specialists' advice and then backed them to the hilt in the Kremlin.

The Marshall Plan was put forward by the United States as a European recovery program in mid-1947. Leaving aside the question of whether the US Congress would have approved the inclusion of the Soviet Union had the Soviet Union opted for this, the proposal raised complex issues for Stalin and the team. On the one hand, Soviet postwar economic reconstruction was a huge task, straining Soviet resources to the utmost. On the other hand, the Soviet Union had a long-standing, Marxist-based suspicion of foreign money and its political implications. As the economist Eugen Varga put it in his expert advice to the Politburo, the Marshall Plan was not just economic imperialism but cultural imperialism as well, aimed at opening the Soviet Union to American ideas as well as Western goods. Stalin supported this position, insisting on rejection of the Marshall Plan both by the Soviet Union and by the Eastern European countries in its orbit, including Poland and Czechoslovakia, whose Moscow-approved regimes showed signs of wanting to accept it. He rejected it "without even trying to negotiate," thinking that the less contact the Soviet Union had with Westerners, the better. "As he saw it, this plan aimed at American control of Europe." Molotov supported him, saying later that "the imperialists were out to turn all of Europe into something like dependent colonies." But some of the team, notably Mikoyan and Beria, were much more favorably inclined to Soviet contact with the West. Mikoyan wanted to negotiate on the Marshall Plan and was still pushing this line into 1948. Beria, according to his son, was against categorical refusal of American aid, as was Voznesensky and others involved in organizing German reparations.

The Soviet answer to the Marshall Plan and the creation of a Western sphere in Europe came in the form of a provocative resurrection of the Comintern (closed down in 1943 to assuage the Allies) in the watered-down form of the Cominform, founded in September 1947 at a meeting of European Communist parties in Sklarska Poreba in Southwest Poland. Zhdanov and Malenkov were the two team members in attendance, and Zhdanov set a tone of sharply anti-Western rhetoric, declaring the world to be divided into "two camps," criticizing "the ruling clique of the American imperialists" that had embarked upon the "enslavement of the weakened capitalist countries of Europe," and calling on European Communist parties to resist the US presence in Europe by any means necessary, including sabotage. Like Stalin in his comments on Churchill's "iron curtain" speech, the Soviet report treated the current anti-Soviet imperialist aims of the Western powers as a continuation of Hitler's drive to the East.[10]

Malenkov's presence, effectively with a watching brief on Zhdanov (and vice versa), can scarcely have been welcome to either. They were political competitors who cordially disliked each other: in the Zhdanov household, Malenkov was always referred to by the woman's name of

Malanya in reference to his chubby, nonmacho appearance. This mutual hostility was neither an unusual state of affairs within the team nor, from Stalin's standpoint, an undesirable one. When Zhdanov died in 1948, as his son remembered bitterly, Beria walked along Gorky Street behind the coffin, not even bothering to feign sadness, talking to Malenkov and laughing all the way. Beria, for his part, "never concealed his antipathy to Zhdanov," Beria's son recalled, "and made fun of his artistic pretensions." Time was, as Ekaterina Voroshilova sadly remembered, when a spirit of comradeship and friendship prevailed, but now the team's two best-liked members—Ordzhonikidze and Kirov—were long dead, and the prevailing spirit was one of distrust, spiteful competition, and mutual intrigue. Stalin encouraged this, on the principle of "divide and rule." It was still a team, as developments in the last years of Stalin's life clearly demonstrate, but it was, much more clearly than before the Great Purges, a team of rivals. The antagonism between Malenkov and Zhdanov, and their respective men in the Central Committee office, was the prime example. But there were also tensions between cohorts—the old-timers Molotov and Mikoyan, along with the partially sidelined Voroshilov, Andreev, and Kaganovich, whose sense of team identity was strong; a middle group of Malenkov, Zhdanov, Khrushchev, Bulganin, and Beria, who for the most part had never formed the bonds with one another that the older cohort had done; and, finally, the new men, Voznesensky and Kuznetsov, who were perceived, particularly by the middle cohort, as a threat.

Beria, "a great intriguer," in Molotov's later characterization, allegedly played a general troublemaking role. In addition, he was the one—apart from Stalin—who was closest to the security agencies, which by this point were routinely keeping tabs on team members, or so, at least, it was believed. "I think I was listened in on my whole life," Molotov said in answer to Chuev's question about telephone bugging. "The Chekists told me, I didn't check. So you try not to chatter about things." After the war, "the Beria mafia surrounded every member of the Politburo, the Central Committee and the government, including Malenkov, with a tight ring," Andrei Malenkov reports. "All telephones were tapped all the time, and a security guard was on constant duty at the apartment." Team members were accompanied everywhere by bodyguards, and so were their children, though Svetlana was able to persuade Stalin to lift this requirement when she went to university. Beria's mysterious private information service was ostensibly running for Stalin's benefit, although people—including Stalin—came to suspect it was for his own benefit as well. But Soviet security was not monolithic. Malenkov allegedly had fifty-eight volumes of transcripts of telephone taps on Voroshilov, Zhukov, and others in his office in Stalin's last years. Beria's handsome townhouse on Kachalov Street (he was the only team member to have one) was bugged, too.[11]

According to the prevailing mores of the postwar period, team members had become more wary than before about expressing opinions that might conflict with Stalin's. Molotov was the most willing to stick to his guns, according to reports, and Voznesensky and Zhdanov are also mentioned as occasional objectors. Mikoyan later described a number of disagreements with Stalin in the postwar period, though possibly one-on-one rather than in more public forums, and the same is true for Beria, as reported by his son. But on the whole, according to outside reports, the convention was to agree dutifully with what Stalin suggested. It was time wasted, in Admiral Kuznetsov's opinion, to talk to Stalin with members of the team, especially Beria, around: "it was enough for Stalin to express something that was still only a suggestion for the whole chorus to repeat it, thinking thus to flatter the 'Leader' and 'teacher.'" Stalin sometimes snapped at them: "What's the point of talking to you? Whatever I say, you reply: 'Yes, Comrade Stalin, of course, Comrade Stalin, you have taken a wise decision, Comrade Stalin.'"

But Stalin's own interpretation of the team's apparent servility was different from Kuznetsov's. He saw them as depriving him of valuable knowledge of their internal disagreements: it was one of his strategies to "pay attention to disagreements, to objections ... analyze why they arose, what is going on. But they hide it from me." As Stalin realized, this concealment was actually a *team* strategy of getting business done without too much interference from the old man. "If there are disagreements [within the team]," Stalin once complained "they try first to come to agreement among themselves, and then bring what they have previously agreed on to my attention. Even if they remain in disagreement with each other, all the same they make an agreement on paper and bring [to me] the thing they have agreed on."[12]

It had become the unwritten rule of Soviet high politics that members of the inner circle did not form special alliances or meet each other socially except under Stalin's eye and at his place. Life was different in Moscow than in Kiev, as young Sergei Khrushchev found when the family moved there at the beginning of 1950. "No more guests . . . Here friends and friendship were dangerous." Alexei Adzhubei, husband of Khrushchev's daughter Rada, recalled that when the Khrushchev family summered in the Crimea in 1949, Svetlana Stalina and her new husband Yury Zhdanov were staying there too, both families in the old tsarist palace in Livadia, but "there was no social contact between us. Family acquaintanceships were not encouraged." There were a few exceptions, to be sure. Beria, who was the most likely to be able to break the rules, often shared a ride with Malenkov in the same car out to the dacha. Khrushchev, perhaps out of touch with the change in mores, tried a bit of socializing at the dacha with other team members after this family's return from Ukraine at the beginning of 1950, but it wasn't very successful. In Moscow, the Khrushchevs and the Malenkovs lived on adjacent floors at No. 3 Granovsky Street, and for a while Khrushchev organized joint family walks around the nearby streets in the evening: he and Georgy in the lead, followed by their wives and children, the whole stately perambulation accompanied by security men; strangely, few people appeared to recognize them and there were no untoward incidents.

According to the memoirs of the Beria and Malenkov sons, their respective families much preferred to socialize with members of the intelligentsia than with other team members. Malenkov, evidently forgetting the Granovsky Street walks of his childhood, and certainly informed by a post-1957 animus against Khrushchev, wrote that "our family circle was a world in which father and mother remained highly cultivated people," and for this reason found the older members of the leadership, with their swearing and lack of polished manners, crass. "Not once did any of the oligarchs of the first Stalinist rank come to us as guests, nor any of their households." Indeed, the parents had such refined taste that it was hard even to imagine "the boring Molotov" or the crude Kaganovich, "swearing like a coachman," at the family table, not to mention the vulgar Khrushchevs. The Berias had similarly discriminating tastes, according to their son. "Thinking, talented, energetic men" were the type that Beria and his cultured wife Nina (a scientific researcher at the Timiryazev Agricultural Academy) liked to have around, and their dinner guests included physicists, historians, distinguished medical men, and architects (harking back to Beria's own first choice of profession), along with Georgian writers, artists, and philosophers.

Bulganin was known for his contacts with artistic circles, though these were not of the "family friendship" type but followed an alternative model of male romances with ballerinas and singers. His dogged pursuit of the opera singer Galina Vishnevskaya, heedless of her recent marriage to the young cellist Mstislav Rostropovich, gets an ironic telling in her memoirs (though she appreciated his activity on her behalf as a patron) and seems to have made a laughingstock of him. Voroshilov, too, had many social contacts with the intelligentsia, mainly (male) painters and sculptors whom, to his wife's slight irritation, he brought home. As for Molotov, nobody on the team or off it seems to remember socializing with him in the postwar period: when describing their relationship with him in retrospect, team members usually spoke in terms of cool and wary respect. His wife, Polina, was another story: she had many contacts in the intelligentsia, of which we will hear more later, but evidently socialized with them mainly without the hardworking Molotov's participation. The Andreevs also had intelligentsia friends, according to their daughter, as well as military ones in the postwar period. Indeed, it is likely that most of the team emerged from the one with a new set of friends from the professional military.[13]

It may well be that the team children who later wrote memoirs exaggerated the depth of their parents' contacts with the intelligentsia, since for the most part they felt themselves to be of that group. In particular, they are likely to have exaggerated its frequency as far as their fathers were concerned, since the team's extremely demanding work lives left little room for socializing except occasionally at the dacha. But the children themselves, now mainly grown, and probably the only nonpoliticians with whom most of the team were in regular contact, were themselves proving to be agents of intelligentsia socialization for their parents. A highly educated bunch, the Kremlin children included arts graduates (Svetlana Stalina, Svetlana Molotova, Eteri Ordzhonikidze, Rada Khrushcheva, and Sergo Mikoyan), scientists and mathematicians (Julia Khrushcheva, Vladimir Andreev, Sergo Beria, Voroshilov's ward Tatyana Frunze, Stepan Mikoyan, Natalia Andreeva, Egor Malenkov, Andrei Malenkov, and Yury Zhdanov), and architects (Maya Kaganovich, Galina Kuibysheva, and

Valentina Malenkova). Many of them subsequently took higher degrees, and several ultimately became professors in their fields. Yury Zhdanov, who followed his science degree with graduate work in philosophy, was the only one to follow his father into politics, but he soon returned to academia and ended up as rector of Rostov State University. Sergo Beria became a distinguished physicist, and Andrei Malenkov achieved similar stature as a biologist.

These were young people who "tried never to miss good concerts at the Conservatory," as Svetlana Stalina later recalled, and taught their parents, in later life, to do the same. "The young people determined the whole mode of life [in their families] . . . To a certain degree their elders must have lent an ear, adapted themselves to the views and tastes of their children."

Svetlana was no doubt thinking more of the Zhdanovs, Mikoyans, Malenkovs, Berias, and Molotovs, whose warm home lives she envied, than of her own family. Even the busy Molotov made time for his Svetlana, who to her parents' joy won a gold medal in her university entrance exams in 1946 and went on to study history at Moscow State University. This meant that he met her university friends. Surprising as it may seem, postwar student life at Moscow University was by all accounts exceptionally lively, intellectually serious, and imbued with a sense of optimism about the future, which had not yet abandoned its socialist roots and drifted into dissidence. Molotov was favorably impressed, especially by the healthy political mood. "A new generation is coming up," he wrote to Polina, and, judging by Svetlana and her friends, they had received a solid education and "moreover are devoted to the Soviet state and look ahead with confidence."[14]

Stalin and his Svetlana had grown apart since the beginning of the war, when the teenager was evacuated to Kuibyshev. Having married and moved out of the Kremlin during the war, she was no longer his default dining companion. Stalin had been lonely since the breakup of his prewar social circle, first through his wife's death and then through the arrest of various relatives during the Great Purges, and he grew lonelier after the war, with a total estrangement from the old network of in-laws and no new friends or partner to fill the gaps. This threw him back on the team for companionship. A wartime habit of team meetings late in the day, ending in a shared supper, was continued in less spartan form. Since Stalin hated to be alone, the team was drafted with increasing frequency for dinners at Stalin's dacha that started late, often after a film showing at the Kremlin; were marked by heavy (compulsory) drinking, as well as a certain amount of actual work discussion; and went on until the not-very-early hours of the morning (4:00 or 5:00 AM).

In 1944, the visiting Yugoslav Communist Milovan Djilas had found these dinners relatively congenial occasions: consumption of food and drink was not immoderate, and members of the team "were at their closest, most intimate with one another. Everyone would tell the news from his departments, whom he had met that day, and what plans he was making." The atmosphere was cordial and informal, and "an uninstructed visitor might hardly have detected any difference between Stalin and the rest. Yet it existed. His opinion was carefully noted. No one opposed him very hard. It all rather resembled a patriarchal family with a crotchety head whose foibles always made his kinsfolk somewhat apprehensive." But when Djilas came back in January 1948, admittedly at a time when Yugoslav-Soviet relations were deteriorating sharply on the way to the explosive break with Tito that occurred in June, he found the atmosphere much more constrained. Stalin was forcing his companions to drink to excess, so that they sometimes passed out and had to be carried home. In order to avoid the heavy drinking, Khrushchev reports, Beria, Malenkov, and Mikoyan at one point made an agreement with the waitresses to serve them colored water instead of wine—but then Alexander Shcherbakov, Zhdanov's unpopular brother-in-law, gave them away. (Stalin was very angry at their deceit.) Wives were no longer invited, and there was lots of horseplay and practical jokes, like tomatoes slipped on chairs, reportedly initiated particularly by Beria. Stalin enjoyed humiliation, so he would force Molotov to waltz with Polish leader Yakub Berman, or Khrushchev to dance the Gopak, squatting down on his haunches and kicking out his heels, "which frankly wasn't very easy" for the chunky Khrushchev.

Stalin had become a night owl, and it was part of the strangeness of the period that not only the team but also the entire government had had to move onto his schedule. Even when a team member was not invited to dine with Stalin on a particular night, he had to remain in the office, often long past midnight, in case he was summoned at the last minute. When, for medical reasons, Voroshilov wanted to depart from Stalin's late-night regimen, he had to ask special permission from him. This regime took a toll on their health; they were all chronically tired. Zhdanov's heart condition had worsened, and he was also, according to Khrushchev, an alcoholic—which meant that, in contrast to his practice with the others, Stalin forced him *not* to drink at the dinners. As one colleague described Zhdanov at this time, "his face would be very pale and incredibly weary, his eyes inflamed by lack of sleep. He would gasp for air with his mouth open. For Zhdanov, with his heart disease, those nightlong vigils at the 'nearby dacha' were catastrophic." Andreev was in bad physical shape too, though not because of the dinners, to which he was no longer invited. Voroshilov was suffering from headaches, insomnia, and dizziness. Bad health was endemic among the Soviet political elite, which doctors associated with the unnatural working hours. A memo of March 1948 stated that twenty-two ministers were suffering from severe fatigue, three from ulcers, and one from nervous exhaustion. Molotov, Mikoyan, Beria, and Khrushchev appear to have had iron constitutions—though Khrushchev and Molotov kept themselves going by naps in the daytime, and Mikoyan admitted to the subterfuge of taking rest breaks during the endless dinners on the pretext of going to the bathroom.

While Stalin's personal lifestyle remained ascetic, luxurious living was gaining ground, in the team as well as in the political elite in general. Some of the wives—Zinaida Zhdanova, Nina Beria, and Polina Zhemchuzhina—were described as living it up in their periodic visits to the Carlsbad spa in Czechoslovakia (one of the bonuses of the East European empire), and Polina's cherished daughter Svetlana was said to be "a real Bolshevik princess," chauffeured daily to the university and "wearing a new outfit every day." Molotov's wife was "always the best-dressed of all the government ladies," but poor Ekaterina Voroshilova, once a revolutionary, "had grown into a fat Soviet lady," as had Zinaida Zhdanova. The Molotov apartment and dacha were distinguished by "good taste and luxurious furniture (by Soviet standards, of course)," while the Voroshilovs' dacha was "sumptuous," crammed with "fine rugs, gold and silver Caucasian weapons, [and] valuable porcelain," some of it gifts from countries in the socialist bloc. The dachas now had hothouses, film rooms, and even stables (Voroshilov and Mikoyan still liked to ride, though Voroshilov's wife thought he was getting too old). The Kaganoviches showed their lowly origins by having "the home of a rich parvenu, full of ugly expensive objects and palm trees in buckets standing in various corners." The Berias, on the other hand, had a dacha even more sumptuous than the Voroshilovs, with architect-designed furniture, wallpaper and lamps, and English and German books and magazines scattered around.

"Trophy goods" brought back from Europe after the war contributed to the growing luxury of elite apartments and the new prevalence of grand pianos. In Svetlana Stalina's view, it was the older cohort that had embraced luxury most thoroughly (though she exempted the modest Ashkhen Mikoyan from these strictures). The Malenkovs, Zhdanovs, and Andreevs lived less extravagant and more "democratic" lives, but even there, Svetlana pointed out, the state—which owned all these apartments, dachas, and fine furniture (little of it was private property)—was supporting them at a level unknown to ordinary Soviet citizens.[15]

The Zhdanovs were perhaps the most demonstratively cultured of the team families. Nonetheless, Zhdanov's name was soon to be forever linked with cultural disciplinary policies that were deeply offensive to the Russian intelligentsia—and, by the same token, an embarrassment, if not worse, to the team children who identified with that group. "Zhdanovshchina" was the term given to the campaign launched in 1946 to tighten up discipline in the cultural field and combat decadent modernism and Western influence. An allied "anticosmopolitan" campaign attacked "servility and bowing and scraping" to the West in all its manifestations.

The first strike in the cultural campaign was an attack on two Leningrad literary journals and the Leningrad writers Mikhail Zoshchenko and Anna Akhmatova. Zhdanov, whose responsibility as Central Committee secretary included ideology and culture, was the executant, and no doubt a supporter of restoring cultural controls, which had relaxed somewhat during the war. But the initiative evidently came from Stalin, who acted as prompter throughout, and it seems unlikely that Zhdanov would have chosen to attack his own former bailiwick, Leningrad, or identified for special odium writers whom he had earlier protected. Stalin personally edited Zhdanov's speech to the Leningrad writers and was uncharacteristically warm in his praise of the text, a document of interest, among other things, for its thoughtful inclusion of staging instructions ("stormy applause" at appropriate moments). The security services also did their part, supplying damaging materials on Zoshchenko and Akhmatova. The burden of Zhdanov's speech, and the Orgburo resolution of 9 August 1946 on which it was based, was that writers who satirized Soviet life, like Zoshchenko, or tried to ignore it in a kind of internal emigration, like Akhmatova, should not be published in Soviet journals. Stalin, who took the lead role in cross-examining the Leningraders at the Orgburo meeting, added his own glosses: Leningrad was going too much its own way in culture, influenced by the local intelligentsia as much as by the party, and its cultural climate showed the tendency to bow and scrape before foreigners, which he had already deplored in connection with the Churchill speech the previous year.

The next strike was against cancer researchers (Professors Nina Klyueva and Grigory Roskin) who, with the encouragement of the minister of health, had given information about their research findings to American scientists via the US Embassy. A spy motif was introduced into the story, of course, but the main point was a warning to the Soviet intelligentsia and bureaucracy that they should be very cautious indeed in their dealings with foreigners, always mindful of the sanctity of Soviet "state secrets," an ever-expanding category. This prompted a "Closed Letter of the Central Committee," which attacked servile bowing and scraping before foreigners as "unworthy of our people"; it pointed the finger particularly at the intelligentsia. Once again, Zhdanov was the front man but Stalin the reported initiator, and, as before, Stalin carefully corrected the text of Zhdanov's speech. This speech was delivered to a "court of honor" on the Klyueva-Roskin affair, a new weapon in the Soviet ideological armory that was one of Zhdanov's pet projects. The distinctive characteristic of courts of honor was that they humiliated and censured those who came before them but did not usually result in arrests and spells in Gulag. Zhdanov probably saw them as a progressive, even democratic, measure, instilling discipline without the drastic punitive measures of the 1930s, and moreover involving judgment by one's professional peers. The trouble was that, in the wake of the Great Purges, this didn't work: the peers simply looked for instructions from above (which were freely supplied) and outdid themselves in vilification, a practice known in the Soviet Union as "taking out insurance."

The "anticosmopolitan campaign" was initially firmly attached to the *foreign* danger, though by the late 1940s—after Zhdanov's death—it transmuted into a euphemism for anti-Semitism. Foreign contacts were a particular danger to the intelligentsia, but not only to them: the "Closed Letter" recommended closer surveillance of foreign visitors, and the objects of its strictures in different parts of the country ranged from listening to the Voice of America radio broadcasts in Krasnodar to being overimpressed by German culture during the German occupation in Velikie

Luki. In the port city of Riga, sailors on oceangoing steamers had to be cured of their admiration for American "freedom" and living standards.[16]

During the war and immediately after it, many members of the Soviet elite had had contact with foreign journalists or diplomats, going to receptions and film showings at the embassies. But then came the tightening up. Marriage between foreigners and Soviet citizens was forbidden in 1947, which ruined the personal lives of a number of resident Westerners, including a future Stalin biographer, Robert C. Tucker, then a junior diplomat at the US Embassy. Those who spent too much time at foreign embassies or became friendly with diplomats risked being accused of consorting with spies, as the composer Sergei Prokofiev's former wife Lina found to her cost—she ended up in Gulag until after Stalin's death. Boris Suchkov, a rising young cultural official with excellent Central Committee connections, trained in Anglo-American literature, was director of the State Publishing House for Foreign Literature when he was arrested as an American spy, along with his wife, essentially because they had socialized with American diplomats. The two foreign Russian-language publications in circulation in the Soviet Union, *Britanskii soiuznik* and *Amerika* were criticized for "tendentious" content and had their print runs and distribution reduced until they could be bought almost nowhere but at the Metropol and National Hotels in Moscow.

Zhdanov's last significant cultural intervention took place in January 1948, eight months before his death. This time it was about music, a passion with Zhdanov. He slammed all the top Soviet composers, including Shostakovich, Prokofiev, and Aram Khachaturian, for modernism, catering to an elite audience, ignoring tunefulness and harmony, succumbing to Western bourgeois degeneracy, and falling out of touch with popular taste. The sophisticated intelligentsia of the capitals was outraged, and Shostakovich later wrote a satire on the occasion. But, in line with the general Zhdanov approach, the composers' punishment was mild by Soviet standards (problems getting work published and performed, with consequent drop in income, but not loss of privileges and status, let alone arrest). While Zhdanov genuinely believed that the composers would do better to return to a more melodic and less dissonant idiom, he seems to have been in a strangely jolly mood during the proceedings. When Prokofiev, a returned émigré not yet fully socialized in Soviet mores, snubbed the head of the party Control Commission, who objected to his chatting to a neighbor, several witnesses assert that Zhdanov, observing this exchange from the podium, started laughing. Whether he was enjoying the Control Commission man's discomfort or the clashing of two different systems of value and hierarchy is not recorded. He even wrote his own satirical sketch (words only, no music), featuring a government minister dragged to a concert by his culture-loving wife. He goes to sleep, as usual, and when his wife wakes him, he tells her with conscious virtue that she must not have read the Central Committee resolution condemning all this degenerate modernist rubbish. But it turns out that that the music being performed was by the revered nineteenth-century Russian classic composer Mikhail Glinka.[17]

Zhdanov's son Yury was the person who resurrected this little spoof in his memoirs, in line with his general presentation of his father as both a man of culture and a genial, likable person. The Zhdanovs seem to have been a happy family, whose life "centred around its only son, the son's friends, the son's interests. They used to have amusing, gay young parties." That testimony comes from Svetlana Stalina, who was drawn to the family because of the contrast with her own lonely life in the Kremlin. Svetlana's marriage to Morozov had broken up, and she was back living in Stalin's apartment with her son Oska (diminutive for Joseph) and his nanny, with Stalin spending most of his time at the dacha. She was desperate to get out, and Yury was moved to rescue her from her Kremlin isolation.

The question of marriage had been on Stalin's mind as well as Svetlana's, and evidently they both concluded that the best thing would be for her to marry a son of one of the team and avoid further disasters. After her divorce, Mikoyan related, Stalin mentioned to "us" (evidently the inner circle) that he had been talking to Svetlana about whom she should marry. "She said that she would marry either Stepan Mikoyan or Beria's son Sergo. I told her: 'Neither the one nor the other. You ought to marry Zhdanov's son.'" Mikoyan and Beria were intensely relieved, though Mikoyan at least was fond of Svetlana. "If the choice had fallen on my son," Mikoyan wrote later, "Stalin would have started interfering in the life of our family." "It would have been terrible," Beria agreed. Whether Svetlana and Yury knew of this conversation is unclear, but Svetlana later wrote that Stalin, who had loved Andrei Zhdanov and respected his son, "always hoped that the families would 'become related,'" so no doubt she had a wistful idea of pleasing him again. But the moment had passed. When Svetlana told Stalin she planned to marry Yury and move into the

Zhdanov apartment in the Kremlin, he was annoyed: he was building a second story on the Kuntsevo dacha and hoped she and her son would come and live with him there. But she knew Yury wouldn't agree to live with her father, so that was out. They married in the spring of 1949.

In fact, it was Beria's son that Svetlana had really had her eye on; they had even had a brief romance during the war. But Sergo's mother discouraged the affair, not because she disliked Svetlana (the two had always been close, and continued to be so) but on prudential grounds: "Stalin would have interpreted the marriage as an attempt to worm your way into his family," she told her son. In any event, Sergo married the beautiful Marfa Peshkova, the writer Maxim Gorky's granddaughter, in 1947. Stalin, who had known Marfa from childhood as Svetlana's best friend, nevertheless had reservations about the marriage, viewing it as a move to "establish links with the oppositionist Russian intelligentsia," or perhaps a ploy by Sergo's father "to infiltrate the Russian intelligentsia." In the copy of his favorite Georgian epic, which he gave Sergo as a wedding present, he wrote, "You would do better to form bonds with the Georgian intelligentsia!" The young couple lived in their own quarters in Beria's townhouse—visited on Sundays by Marfa's grandmother, Gorky's first wife, Ekaterina Peshkova, a longtime maverick defender of political prisoners, the nearest thing Stalinist Russia had to a civil rights activist, who was no doubt the "oppositionist intelligentsia" Stalin had in mind.[18]

The intelligentsia milieu was attractive to Svetlana and Yury Zhdanov, too; but Yury, alone of the team's children, had just made the switch from a professional life—he was teaching chemistry and studying philosophy at Moscow State University—into a political one. Yury had been a favorite of Stalin's as a boy, and it was Stalin who had the idea of drafting him to work in the Central Committee. His father was probably dismayed that he was going into the dangerous political world, and Stalin too, oddly enough, had warned him against it back in 1940, when he advised the then twenty-one-year-old Yury not to get too involved in Komsomol work at the university: "Politics is a dirty business. We need chemists." Dirty business or not, Yury plunged in headfirst when he was appointed head of the Central Committee's Science Department in December 1947, thus abruptly becoming, without experience at lower levels, one of the party's top cultural officials.

Yury was of a postwar generation of young, educated Communists who valued professional norms and international standards in science. For them, the scientific dominance of Trofim Lysenko, a self-taught agronomist whose optimistic prescriptions for increased crop yield had won him the admiration of Stalin and other Soviet leaders before the war, was the epitome of everything that needed to change in the postwar period. For Yury and his somewhat older peers, like Dmitry Shepilov, deputy head of the Central Committee's agitprop department when Yury was appointed to the Science Department, the prewar machinations that had led to the virtual outlawing of genetics had created an "absolutely abnormal situation" that needed to be rectified. "With all my being, I longed for the collapse of Lysenkoism, which discredited both our science and my fatherland," Shepilov wrote in his memoirs. But it was Yury, fired up with enthusiasm for what he no doubt saw as a cause whose time had come, who jumped in just a few months after his appointment, with a public attack on Lysenko's theories in a lecture to party propagandists.

The anti-Lysenko position had some support in the team. Beria probably sympathized: his wife had been very upset when he was unable to save the biologist Nikolai Vavilov, a colleague at the Agricultural Academy and scientific opponent of Lysenko's, before the war, and she had criticized some of Lysenko's theories in her PhD thesis. Yury's father Andrei was no fan of Lysenko's and had warned his son not to tangle with him: "he'll make mincemeat of you." Andrei was right. Lysenko counterattacked, apparently with the support of Zhdanov's rival Malenkov, and Stalin took his side, rebuking Yury in his father's presence at a Politburo meeting ("Don't you know that our entire agriculture depends on Lysenko?"). The consequences for Yury were relatively mild, since Stalin judged him to be young and inexperienced, and he blamed his seniors (Shepilov and Yury's father) for not steering him in the right direction. Yury even kept his job in the Central Committee. But his optimism about reform must have taken a beating. He had misread the zeitgeist, or perhaps just anticipated it by a decade. The old obscurantists, in the person of Lysenko, had showed their continuing strength. The reform-minded, educated young were not going to carry the day as long as Stalin was in charge. And, as Yury and everyone else were soon to be reminded, politics was a dirty business.[19]

EIGHT

AGING LEADER

STALIN WAS A SICK AND AGING MAN AFTER THE WAR, HIS WORK ABIL-
ity diminishing with each passing year. He spent more and more time in
the South: an average of almost three months a year from 1945 to 1948, almost five months in 1950, and finally no less than seven months from August 1951 to February 1952. Even when he was in Moscow, his working day
contracted sharply. He stopped chairing the Council of Ministers, handing it over to Voznesensky and then to Malenkov. He complained ever
more often of age. Even the loyal Molotov noted that his work capacity
was diminishing as time went on. Others not in daily contact with him
were shocked by the decline between 1945 and 1948. When Ambassador
Novikov came back from the United States in the spring of 1947, having
not seen Stalin up close since 1941, he discovered "an elderly, very elderly,
tired person who was evidently straining to bear the heavy burden of his
great responsibilities," in place of the powerful, energetic figure he had
met during the war. Stalin made mistakes that nobody dared correct; he
forgot names (Bulganin's, on one occasion; admittedly, Bulganin was for-
gettable). He spent more and more time at the dacha and not at his Kremlin office. "You would be lost without me," Stalin liked to say to the team.
Once, they would have agreed; now, probably not. A future without Stalin
was becoming imaginable.

Beria, who had always had a sharp tongue despite his deferential face-
to-face manner, was increasingly open in his acid remarks about the
leader; the others, fearing it was an incitement to subversive comments on
their part, reacted warily. Khrushchev, who retained an attachment to
Stalin, was beginning to find dealing with him something like dealing

with an elderly relative with time on his hands. "He suffered terribly from loneliness," he remembered, so "he needed people around him all the time. When he woke up in the morning, he would immediately summon us, either inviting us to the movies [at the Kremlin in the evening] or starting some conversation which could have been finished in two minutes but was stretched out so that we would stay with him longer." It was a waste of time for the team, busy running the government, but going on vacations with him, which he also demanded, was "sheer torture." "I had to spend all my time with him, sitting over endless meals. Whenever I was offered up in sacrifice, Beria used to cheer me up by saying: 'Look at it this way: someone has to suffer; it might as well be you.' "[1]

Stalin's loneliness was exacerbated by a near-total breakdown of relations with his two surviving children, Svetlana and Vasily, and the arrest of more of his in-laws, including people he had been close to. Svetlana's marriage to Yury Zhdanov was not going well: Yury was always busy at the office, among other things being instructed by Stalin, with evident relish, on how to apply the faction-fighting skills Stalin had honed in the 1920s to science. Svetlana was left at home in the Zhdanov apartment—making a bibliography of Marx and Lenin's dicta on science for Yury—surrounded by older women giving her good advice. Life became "intolerably, unbearably boring," and complications in a second pregnancy plunged her into depression. In the hospital for six weeks before Katya's premature birth, she found herself in a maternity ward with Svetlana Molotova, and was bitterly envious, because Molotov, like any normal father, came every second day to see his daughter and newborn grandchild. Stalin never came. After she wrote him an anguished, reproachful letter, he finally wrote back affectionately to "my Svetochka," promising that she would see her *papochka* soon, but he still didn't come. When her marriage fell apart early in 1950, Stalin was unsympathetic ("What a fool! Finally she found a decent man, and couldn't keep him").

The in-laws who fell victim in the late 1940s included Stalin's sister-in-law Zhenya Alliluyeva (whom Stalin had once admired and perhaps thought of marrying), who was sentenced to ten years for "anti-Soviet agitation," in other words, careless talk; Anna Redens, another sister-in-law; Fedor Allilyuev, a brother-in-law; and twenty-one-year-old Dzhonik (John-Reed) Svanidze, whose father (a great crony of Stalin's until his arrest in 1937) and mother had been Great Purge victims. The arrests were, of course, among the causes of Stalin's estrangement from Svetlana, whose remaining family members were vanishing before her eyes. When she asked what they had done wrong, Stalin just said they talked too much, which was a help to the enemy. Paranoia is a term often loosely used of Stalin, but in the last five years of his life, it certainly seems to apply. This time, in contrast to the late 1930s, his suspicions were particularly acute with regard to the people closest to him. He was becoming afraid of being poisoned, Khrushchev said, but didn't want to admit to the fear; he just waited at the almost nightly dinners with the team to take a particular dish until somebody else had tried it first. Once, when Khrushchev and Mikoyan were on leader-sitting duty in the South, Stalin muttered to nobody in particular, "I'm finished. I trust no one, not even myself."

As Stalin's energy and competence declined, he handed over more and more business to other members of the team, just signing off on whatever they decided when it was sent to him at the dacha for signature. His judgment grew erratic: Mikoyan describes a meeting of the team when Stalin suddenly suggested abolishing state farms, a basic component of Soviet agriculture. Mikoyan objected, or so he later claimed, while the rest, even Malenkov and Kaganovich, sat silently, looking at their hands. "Nobody supported him. He dropped it." Some people complained that Stalin's abdication of responsibility created logjams and procrastination. But the other consequence, perhaps of more significance for the future, was a revival of "semi-collective decision-making" on the team's part. A Group of Four (Beria, Malenkov, Khrushchev, Bulganin) was running the Politburo; in the perhaps exaggerated judgment of one well-placed observer, "even Stalin could do nothing against them." But a broader Group of Seven, including Molotov, Mikoyan, and Kaganovich, was also part of the informal structure of power. Judging by the government's archival records, things were flowing along smoothly and in an organized manner, a great improvement technically on the prewar period. But it's also true that all sorts of big issues were being shelved—tensions with the West, living standards, peasants, Gulag, nationalities—because the team knew that Stalin wasn't going to go along with any changes. The team appears to have been in unspoken agreement on what changes were needed; they were, in effect, shelving the issues until Stalin died.[2]

As long as he was alive, however, Stalin was anything but out of the picture. He still had the key power to kill, although with respect to the team, anything of that sort needed to be approached with caution. He could still launch bold initiatives that nobody on the team dared stand against. One of them was a policy turn against Jews, which was very much his idea, against the silent disapproval of most of the team. The background was a *pro*-Jewish initiative from the war period, when the Jewish Anti-Fascist Committee (JAC) was set up, primarily to publicize the Soviet cause abroad and incidentally to collect money from American Jews. The team member most actively involved in its creation seems to have been Beria, a philo-Semite, according to his son, with enthusiastic support from prominent Jews in the Moscow intelligentsia and strong backing from Molotov, Kaganovich, and Voroshilov. The committee was an anomaly in Soviet terms, since the Stalinist system did not usually accommodate associations representing special interests. But in the special circumstances of wartime, it was not unique: a Pan-Slavic Union aimed at Slavs in Eastern Europe and Russian émigrés, and sponsored by Russophile Alexander Shcherbakov, had been set up at the beginning of the war for similar purposes of financial and emotional appeal to members of a particular international constituency, as were anti-fascist committees for women, youth, and scientists. The Jewish Anti-Fascist Committee came on the scene in 1942, headed by longtime director of the Moscow Jewish Theater, Solomon Mikhoels, under the supervision of Solomon Lozovsky, Molotov's deputy at the foreign ministry and an important governmental figure in his own right. It proved to be by far the most successful in rallying both international and domestic support.

The first tricky issue for the JAC was the proposal to create a Jewish autonomous region in the Crimea. This was not so wild a scheme as it sounds in retrospect. Autonomous national regions were part of the Soviet way of doing things; indeed, there already was a Jewish one in Birobidzhan out in the Far East, but it hadn't taken, partly due to the lack of a long-settled Jewish population. The idea of a Crimean autonomous region for Jews had already been raised in the late 1920s, with lots of enthusiasm in the Soviet Jewish population, though it was ultimately rejected in favor of Birobidzhan. The JAC, whose leaders had for some years anticipated that the Soviet Union must become a haven for Jewish refugees from Nazism, revived the Crimean proposal, pointing out that American Jewish financial support would be readily forthcoming. Their proposal was sent to Stalin via Lozovsky and Molotov in 1944, but he responded negatively and the proposal was dropped. Evidently it remained in his mind, however, as evidence of the ambitious aspirations, suspicious foreign connections (though it was the committee's brief to raise money for the Soviet war effort from American Jews!), and potential untrustworthiness of what he no doubt already saw as the domestic Jewish lobby.

The plight of Europe's surviving Jews in the wake of the Holocaust was one of the thorniest international issues as the war came to an end. Although the Bolsheviks were long-standing opponents of Zionism, the Soviet Union was an early supporter of the creation of the state of Israel and was looking for a beachhead in the Middle East, as well as playing Stalin's favorite divide-and-rule game with capitalist powers (the United States supported the creation, while Britain, as the colonial power in the region, dragged its feet). In addition to realpolitik considerations, Molotov also had personal sympathy for the creation of a Jewish state, though whether Stalin ever shared this is unclear. According to Beria's son, Stalin and Beria had the more Machiavellian idea that "by helping the state of Israel to come into being they would ensure the support of international finance for the Soviet Union. They saw in this state a base from which to influence the world of Jewry, with all its financial resources, in the interests of the USSR."[3]

The Soviet Union was the first country to give Israel de jure recognition as a state on 17 May 1947. In the autumn of 1948, future prime minister Golda Meir arrived in Moscow as the first Israeli plenipotentiary. She received a rapturous welcome from Moscow Jews, including Polina Zhemchuzhina, who embraced her at a diplomatic reception, announcing herself in Yiddish as "a daughter of the Jewish people." This enthusiasm was itself something of a warning signal from Stalin's standpoint. Problems in relations between the two states were surfacing as early as the summer of 1948, exacerbated by a flood of American money to Israel in its first year of existence, which the Soviet Union couldn't match. In the United States, aid to Israel was already being recommended in Cold War terms as a way of blocking Communist expansion. Emigration of Jews to Israel was another problem, since the Soviet Union, which in general made legal emigration almost impossible for its citizens, was not inclined to make an exception for the Jews. "No financial support, no population," was how a disappointed Meir summed up Soviet prospects on her departure from Moscow in March 1949.

The JAC was remarkably successful in its international endeavors, especially with the socially conscious American Jewish community, many of whose families had roots in the Russian Empire and left-wing sympathies. But of course, given Cold War tensions and Stalin's tendency to see potential espionage in every foreign contact, there was danger attached. This was increased because of the fact that JAC had acquired an overenthusiastic domestic constituency that was eager to find an institutional protector in the Soviet system. It was turning into something like a ministry of Jewish affairs, one security report noted disapprovingly. This was all the more dangerous in a context in which popular resentment against Jews as a privileged elite "sitting out the war in Tashkent" had gained wide currency in the Soviet Union.

The proposal to dissolve the JAC seems to have been first mooted by Central Committee ideological officials in the winter of 1946–47. Conceding that it had at first played a positive role, they argued that its anti-fascist mission was now outdated, that it had become too cozy with American Jews, and that it had started trying to act as a Jewish lobby within the Soviet Union. Moreover, there was the worrying aspect that Zionism was growing in the Soviet Jewish population, especially among the intelligentsia. The Politburo discussed the issue three times but came to no decision, no doubt because of JAC's strong support within the team.[4]

Then came a shocking event: the murder of Solomon Mikhoels, the JAC chairman and director of the Moscow Yiddish Theater, in January 1948. His death was allegedly the result of a car accident in Minsk, but rumors that there was something fishy about it flew around immediately. The security services put it about that it was the work of Polish nationalists, or, alternatively, of Zionists seeking to hide nefarious deals associated with the creation of the state of Israel. The popular rumor mill added a third version: that Stalin was behind it. This, as we now know, was actually the case. It must have been extremely alarming for the team, especially for Molotov, whose wife was not only a supporter of JAC but also a personal friend of Mikhoels. Others with Jewish connections—Kaganovich, as a Jew; Voroshilov and Andreev, with Jewish wives; Beria, supporter of JAC and good relations with Israel—also had reason to worry. Voroshilov's wife Ekaterina, née Golda Gorbman, an Old Bolshevik (and thus an opponent of the Zionists) who had stopped going to synagogue in her youth, had nevertheless been deeply moved by the creation of the state of

Israel: "Now we have a homeland," she is reported to have said. She was not arrested—though after Zhemchuzhina's arrest, the apocryphal story going around was that when the secret police came to arrest his wife, the old cavalryman Voroshilov had refused them entry, flourishing his saber. There was another casualty among the wives at this time—Andreev's Jewish wife Dora Khazan, who was dismissed as deputy minister of the textile industry, downgraded to director of a scientific research institute, and then driven out of that position in a virulently anti-Semitic campaign.

It seems likely that the team half knew or at least strongly suspected that the security services, acting on Stalin's instructions, were responsible for Mikhoels's killing. Polina Zhemchuzhina was later charged with having contributed to "anti-Soviet provocational rumours about Mikhoels' death" at his funeral; and her sister, under interrogation, said Polina had told her "they killed Mikhoels," but wouldn't say who. Kaganovich sent word to the Mikhoels family, privately through a relative, that, for their own safety, they should not ask questions about his death. The team's alarm must have been all the greater in that political assassination was not a standard weapon in Stalin's armory, or at least the team did not recognize it as such. Perhaps, as rumor has it, Stalin was behind Kirov's assassination, but the team didn't think so at the time. The covert political assassination they all knew about was the murder of Trotsky by Soviet secret agents—under Beria's direction, on Stalin's orders—in 1940. But as that was in another country, and Trotsky was the archenemy, it could scarcely be seen as a precedent.

The savagery and brutality of this way of disposing of Mikhoels needs explanation beyond the MGB-fueled suspicion that he was a Zionist who had dealings with American intelligence, all the more since it occurred at the height of Soviet support for the Israeli cause and hopes that Israel would prove a Soviet beachhead in the Middle East. "Anti-Semitism" is often given as the answer, but even if that is an accurate characterization of Stalin in later years, it does not explain a sudden lurch into personal involvement in murder. The most plausible explanation is that Stalin regarded it as a personal vendetta involving slighted honor, even though the personal connection was rather tenuous. It started with newly adult Svetlana and her marriage to Grigory Morozov, well connected both directly and through his father, Joseph Morozov, with the Jewish intelligentsia of Moscow. MGB sources disclosed that Mikhoels, seeking channels of access and influence to the highest authority, decided that Svetlana and Morozov were promising conduits. Both Mikhoels and Joseph Morozov, according to the MGB, displayed a keen interest in learning anything they could about Stalin's personal life, and cultivated other family members as well as (apparently unsuccessfully) the newlyweds. Arrests were made, and one of the suspects confessed under torture that Mikhoels had been commissioned by American intelligence to collect information on Stalin through his relatives. The Mikhoels murder followed, as did arrests of Stalin's in-laws (already described earlier) and also Morozov's father. "They sicced a Zionist on you to get information on me," Stalin told Svetlana.[5]

Finally, in November 1948, the decision was made to dissolve the JAC as "a center of anti-Soviet propaganda . . . regularly providing anti-Soviet information to organs of foreign intelligence." The Politburo's resolution stipulated that "for the time being nobody is to be arrested," but that didn't last long. By the end of January 1949, the remaining JAC members, including their patron, Lozovsky, were in prison. Zhemchuzhina had already been expelled from the party by Politburo decision for having ties with "Jewish bourgeois nationalists," attending Mikhoels's funeral and encouraging rumors about his death, and participating in a religious ceremony in the Moscow synagogue back in 1945. Her arrest followed, on Stalin's instructions, on 21 January 1949.

Molotov later remembered that when Stalin raised the issue of Zhemchuzhina in the Politburo, his knees started to tremble. "But the case had been made against her. You just could not fault them [the Chekists]." In the vote on expelling his wife from the party, he initially abstained, but then retracted his abstention the next day, as "an act that I now see to have been politically mistaken," citing "my heavy sense of remorse for not having prevented Zhemchuzhina, a person very dear to me, from making her mistakes and from forming ties with anti-Soviet Jewish nationalists, such as Mikhoels." Beria's son says Beria abstained too, but there is no confirmation for this. In fact, the allegations about Zhemchuzhina were not wild fantasies: she *had* been strongly pro-Israel and swept up in the Jewish cause, more so than was acceptable in a normal party context. The interrogations of her arrested relatives and colleagues in 1949 contain many plausible reports of critical comments made by her on Soviet postwar policies toward Jews, including purging them from ministries. There are reports that as early as the summer of 1946, she had told JAC people that there was no point in going to Politburo members on Jewish policy: it was Stalin's bag, and he had a "negative" attitude to Jews. She reportedly embarrassed Nina Beria by the passion with which she spoke of the Jewish question and her distress at Stalin's attitude: "How can he not understand that the Jewish people deserved help after all they had done for the revolution? Ought not the proletarian state show its gratitude?" (The Berias, to whom she had allegedly introduced Golda Meir, were sympathetic, according to their son, but nobody wanted to listen to heresy—you could be in trouble yourself for not reporting it. As for Meir, her 1975 memoirs suggest that she had no further contact with Zhemchuzhina after their initial meeting, but this may have been just a diplomatic omission.)[6]

Shortly before Zhemchuzhina's arrest, Stalin had insisted that the Molotovs divorce. Polina's stoical response was "If it's necessary for the party, we will get divorced," and she moved out to her sister's. It wasn't the only such divorce in team circles. Malenkov's daughter was married to a Jew, Vladimir Shamberg, who was a grandson of Solomon Lozovsky. Shamberg was a friend of Malenkov's, as well as working in his office, and the couple lived with the Malenkovs. In January 1949, the day before Lozovsky's expulsion from the Central Committee, Malenkov arranged his daughter's divorce from Shamberg. He wasn't personally anti-Semitic, a puzzled Khrushchev concluded; he must just have been acting out of "a lackey's servility to his master." It was probably Malenkov's intervention, however, that spared Shamberg and his parents from the exile later imposed on most relatives of disgraced JAC members.

In March 1949, a couple of months after Zhemchuzhina's arrest, Molotov was removed from his job as minister of foreign affairs and replaced by Andrei Vyshinsky, one of his former deputies. The decision seems to have been made at a meeting at Stalin's dacha at which the only team members present were Malenkov, Beria, and Bulganin. This suggests a certain wariness on Stalin's part as to the team's reaction, but in fact all the absent members of the Politburo subsequently canvassed endorsed the decision (though Voroshilov added the qualification that he was in favor "if everyone else is"). Mikoyan was replaced as minister of foreign trade by his deputy at the same time. The significance of such changes is difficult to read, in that team members were sometimes moved into or out of direct leadership of sectors for which they had supervisory responsibility in the Politburo, depending on whether their hands-on involvement was considered necessary. In this case, Molotov's removal, in particular, looked like a censure, given both Zhemchuzhina's arrest and the crisis over the future of Germany, which led to the 1948 Berlin Blockade, understood as a failure of Soviet diplomacy. In his memoirs, Mikoyan denied that anything derogatory was involved in his case. Both Molotov and Mikoyan appear to have had good working relationships with their replacements, who continued to respect their seniority, and over the next few years, most of their former responsibilities in foreign affairs and foreign trade, respectively, were quietly restored.[7]

A bigger shock in high politics in early 1949 was the Leningrad Affair, an alleged conspiracy of "Leningraders" in the party hierarchy, which also brought down a Politburo member, Nikolai Voznesensky. Nobody has uncovered any real plot (except on Stalin's part, to destroy some subordinates and potential challengers), and even the story line—in the absence of public trials—lacks the comparative clarity of that of the Great Purges. The victims were high officials in the Leningrad party committee, along with Voznesensky and Central Committee secretary Alexei Kuznetsov. Khrushchev thought that Malenkov, Zhdanov's old opponent, and Beria, hostile to Voznesenky, were fanning the flames, but Malenkov's son claims, on the contrary, that his father was the only one to vote *against* condemnation of Kuznetsov and Voznesensky in the Politburo. Zhdanov's son thought it was intended as retrospective discrediting of Zhdanov. Beria's son said it wasn't Beria who was gunning for the Leningraders, and Malenkov's son said it wasn't Malenkov. The whole issue of internal rivalries is so confused that it is hard to make any sense of it, other than that everyone was maneuvering and hoping that the ax would not fall on them but on someone else and his patronage network. (Mutual accusations of guilt were revived when the team split in 1957, but no real light was cast.) According to Malenkov, the organizer was Stalin. None of the team seems to have believed anything untoward was going on in Leningrad, and Khrushchev and Molotov both later claimed that they just didn't know what was at the root of Stalin's suspicions of the Leningraders.

The net result of the Leningrad Affair was to remove two rising stars in Voznesensky and Kuznetsov, both ethnic Russians in their forties, whom Stalin had reportedly spoken of as possible successors. Thus, apart from any goals Stalin may have been pursuing with the Leningrad Affair, one can't help suspecting that the main beneficiaries, Malenkov and Beria, had a hand in discrediting the two, if not in their actual destruction. Khrushchev's analysis—based on deduction and hints dropped by Malenkov and Beria later, since he said Stalin never discussed the affair with him—was that Stalin was preparing Voznesensky and Kuznetsov as "successors to the Kremlin Old Guard which meant that Beria first and foremost, then Malenkov, Molotov, and Mikoyan, no longer enjoyed Stalin's confidence." He assumed that the Old Guard had got rid of the competition by undermining Stalin's confidence in the young challengers, though he didn't know exactly how.

Intrigue apart, the Leningrad Affair was a shock to the team, as they had hoped that bloodletting at the top was a thing of the past. For Mikoyan, there was personal trauma as well. His youngest son Sergo was due to marry Kuznetsov's daughter Alla just at the time the affair broke in March 1949. Mikoyan showed "unheard of effrontery," his biographer writes, not only in going ahead with the wedding at his house and failing to disinvite the father of the bride but even sending his own official car to pick him up. Alla became a cherished part of the Mikoyan family until her premature death in 1957, and the Mikoyans also looked after her younger siblings after their mother's arrest (according to Stepan Mikoyan, they were saved from an orphanage by Mikoyan's intercession with Stalin). Voznesensky and Kuznetsov were arrested in the autumn, six months after their removal from all offices; in Kuznetsov's case, the arrest took place as he left Malenkov's office after a visit. The investigation was reportedly conducted personally by Beria, with Malenkov, Beria, and Bulganin taking part in interrogations, reviving a practice of the Great Purges. The two were shot in the autumn of 1950.[8]

Meanwhile, offstage from the standpoint of the team, interrogation of Zhemchuzhina and the many relatives and colleagues arrested along with her was in progress, the reports of which had been routinely sent to Stalin (but not the other leaders) by the MGB. The initial intention was evidently to make a case against her as a Jewish "bourgeois nationalist," linking her up with JAC members in some kind of spying-for-the-United States case, but surprisingly (given that the Jewish material is quite rich) that line was abandoned and the interrogation started to focus on her sex life. This material also turned out to be rich, especially after one lover (I. I.

Shteinberg, husband of her niece Rosa), broke down and provided an almost pornographic description of their lovemaking. (Beria later attested that these witnesses were subjected to beatings and other physical abuse, and several of them died in prison.) When the report on the sexual relationship with Shteinberg came through in August 1949, Stalin departed from past practice and circulated it to the entire Politburo, which of course included Molotov. In later life, Molotov never mentioned this peculiar humiliation. Khrushchev related it in somewhat bowdlerized form in his memoirs, still wincing. In December, the MGB decided for whatever reason to drop the case—Beria's later claim that it was because of absence of proof is scarcely convincing, since that had never stopped such cases before—and Zhemchuzhina was sent off to Kustanai in Kazakhstan with a five-year sentence of exile.

According to a high security official, the real point of arresting Zhemchuzhina was to get compromising material on Molotov. If so, it was a total failure. She provided no damaging testimony on her husband (indeed, she appears not to have made a confession at all), and in the confessions of her relatives and colleagues, Molotov went completely unmentioned, as did her daughters. It was as if they didn't exist, and her entire world consisted of ne'er-do-well relatives, colleagues, and assorted lovers. This would scarcely have been the case if the MGB had been trying to concoct a case with these witnesses against Molotov. But that doesn't mean that the MGB was not working on a possible Molotov case. One favored scenario involved treasonous contact on Molotov's part with the British, but there was also an American variant. Stalin became obsessed with the idea that when Molotov traveled between cities in the United States, he must have had his own private railway car, and since the Soviets didn't pay for it, it must have been the Americans, rewarding him for services rendered. Both these scenarios remained on the drafting board, testimony to Stalin's and the MGB's diligence in preparing for every contingency.[9]

By the spring of 1949, there was no team member except the bland Bulganin, who had not received some kind of a slapdown since the war. This time, however, two departures were permanent. Combined with Molotov's and Mikoyan's semidisgrace, it gave the team a lot to think about. Yet in a way it was still plus ça change: Voznesensky had been a relatively recent acquisition to the Politburo, while Kuznetsov had not even made

Politburo membership despite being gossiped about as an heir apparent, and the status indicator based on access to Stalin was not significantly altered. Malenkov, Beria, and Molotov were among the top five most frequent office visitors, sometimes switching positions, every year from 1949 to 1952 (Molotov nose-dived briefly in the second half of 1949, only to return to second place in 1950). Mikoyan was in the top five in 1949–50, and a few notches down in 1951–52. Kaganovich was back among regular visitors from 1948, though not in the top five. Voroshilov's visits were few, and Andreev was not in Stalin's office at all after 1948.

Khrushchev, returning from Kiev at the beginning of 1950 to take up the position of Central Committee secretary in Moscow, was a new factor in the Kremlin equation: earlier, he had been a team member, but his non-resident status kept him remote from much of the intrigue. The new appointment, which came up quite suddenly, was probably motivated by Stalin's desire for a counterweight to Malenkov and Beria, both made more powerful by the outcome of the Leningrad Affair. It made him a member of the inner circle from mid-1950. The other rising man was Nikolai Bulganin, who in 1947 took over from Stalin as defense minister (having previously been his deputy), becoming a full member of the Politburo in February 1948 and Stalin's top deputy chairman (replacing Molotov) at the Council of Ministers in April 1950. Molotov saw him as a political lightweight: "whichever way the wind blows, Bulganin will be sure to follow."

Between August 1950 and February 1952, Stalin was out of Moscow vacationing/recuperating for a total of close to twelve months, with a mere seven months on the job in the middle of two long periods of absence. Even when he was in Moscow, his workweek was much shorter than it had been (in March 1951, about half as long as it had been two years earlier) and he was seeing fewer people apart from the team. This set the stage for an important development: a new kind of "collective leadership" *without* Stalin.

As Beria's son tells it, "in 1951 the members of the Politburo, Bulganin, Malenkov, Khrushchev and my father, began to appreciate that they were all in the same boat and it mattered little whether one of them was thrown overboard a few days before the others. They felt a sense of solidarity once they had faced the fact that none of them would be Stalin's successor—he intended to choose an heir from among the younger generation. They therefore agreed among themselves not to allow Stalin to set one against another, and that they would immediately inform each other of anything Stalin said about them, so as to frustrate his manipulations. They recalled their former intrigues and buried their old grievances." This is the kind of self-serving account that immediately raises questions and alarm bells. Who were these younger potential heirs, now that Voznesensky and Kuznetsov were gone? How come a group that was so internally fractious that they had just disposed of two unwanted members could suddenly bury the hatchet and unite?

By other accounts, the current favorite in the succession stakes was Malenkov, with Beria in an increasingly precarious position. This may explain Beria's new interest in team solidarity, but not Malenkov's. Yet the evidence is that something like the alliance that Beria described *did* come into being in Stalin's last years, and that it included Malenkov. The only plausible explanation is that, in the first place, the team feared for their own lives (presumably not having intended that the intrigues against Voznesensky and Kuznetsov should end in execution), and, in the second, that they thought Stalin sufficiently weakened or abstracted to take the risk.[10]

The innermost circle of Stalin's last years consisted of Beria, Malenkov, Khrushchev, and Bulganin. But Molotov and Mikoyan were still players. Molotov's status had waned since the 1940s, when he was viewed by the team, according to Khrushchev, as "the future leader of the country, who might replace Stalin when he died," but he still ranked second to Stalin in the media (which conventionally indicated hierarchy by listing Politburo members nonalphabetically) and was regarded by the public as the no. 2 man. "I respected Molotov," wrote the Communist writer Konstantin Simonov (a member of the party Central Committee). "He was the man standing closest to Stalin, the most visible and weighty in our eyes, sharing governing responsibilities with Stalin." Other leaders came and went, but Molotov remained, at least until 1948, "a constant . . . in the milieu of my generation, earning the firmest and constant respect and priority." Evidently the Four thought they needed him for legitimacy in any future transition.

Someone from the Four, probably Malenkov or Khrushchev, was delegated to tell Mikoyan about their solidarity pact. This was all very risky: such behavior would undoubtedly have been viewed by Stalin (not without reason) as a plot. Beria—evidently functioning as primus inter pares—

had told the others that "one must defend Molotov. Stalin is settling scores with him, but he is needed by the party." This surprised Mikoyan, though he was glad to hear it. It was Mikoyan's job, evidently, to pass the news of the Four's support on to Molotov, perhaps because Mikoyan was personally closer to them. Molotov's reaction is not recorded, but he later conceded that Beria seemed at this point to be defending him. As to his motives, Molotov surmised that "when he [Beria] saw that even Molotov can be dismissed, [he thought] now you take care, Beria! If Stalin doesn't even trust Molotov, he could get rid of us in a minute!"

Although Molotov and Mikoyan remained regulars in the team meetings in Stalin's office and at Politburo meetings, and Mikoyan was still personally close enough to Stalin to be meeting him on holiday in the South in the summer of 1951, their political situation was precarious. As Molotov put it, "a black cat had run between me and Stalin." He could see that Stalin had become very distrustful of him but wasn't sure what the grounds of his distrust were—perhaps his wife's arrest, which was carried out on Stalin's instructions? But that seemed more likely a product of Stalin's suspicions of Molotov than a cause. Stalin had started to drop remarks about Molotov and Mikoyan plotting against him and being English or American spies, the kind of table chat that reminds one of how unusual this particular milieu was. One such vignette comes from Mikoyan's description of an incident at Stalin's dacha in December 1948, and the accusing remark—surely a setup by Stalin—came from Stalin's secretary, Alexander Poskrebyshev, not one of the usual dinner guests, who suddenly announced, "Comrade Stalin, while you were in the South, Molotov and Mikoyan were preparing a plot against you in Moscow." With Caucasian fervor, Mikoyan "would have hurled himself at Poskrebyshev" and demanded satisfaction, but Beria restrained him. Molotov sat "silent like a statue," and so did the others. After a while, "Stalin led the conversation to a new topic."

A second vignette is in its way even more striking. In conversation with Mikoyan, Malenkov or Khrushchev remarked that Stalin had been calling him and Molotov English spies. At first, Mikoyan didn't pay too much attention (a remarkable reaction in itself). Then he remembered Stalin using this gambit before, when, two or three years after Ordzhonikidze's suicide, a broodingly angry Stalin wanted to announce him retrospectively as an English spy. "But nothing came of it because nobody supported him." With such things, in Stalin's mind, the team generally needed to come on board, or at least have time to get used to the idea; his handling of the Molotov/Mikoyan exclusion in 1952 suggests that his strategy hadn't changed. But there were rare times, notably the Great Purges, when the rules changed pro tem. The team hoped they were not heading for another suspension of normal rules.[11]

Stalin failed to take his usual vacation in the autumn of 1952, such a marked departure from the pattern of previous years as to suggest that he had some plans brewing. Things came to a head at the plenary meeting of the Central Committee summoned in October 1952, when Stalin, acting alone and apparently without consultation with the rest of the team, launched a remarkable public attack on Molotov and Mikoyan. No minutes were taken, so we have to rely on people's memories. According to one witness, Stalin's demeanor at the plenum was surly and sinister: when delegates greeted his entrance with the usual "stormy applause," he asked unpleasantly why they were all clapping. He immediately announced that within the party and the Politburo, there was a "deep schism" (he used the word *raskol*, normally reserved for the long-ago split between Bolsheviks and Mensheviks). Molotov was a "capitulationist" taking an "anti-Leninist position," and Mikoyan was behaving like a Trotskyite. Molotov and Mikoyan had fallen under the spell of America when they visited and appeared to have become its agents. According to Konstantin Simonov, Stalin attacked Molotov with particular viciousness, shocking the audience. He brought up the old charges of currying favor with Western journalists in 1945; he also raised the question of why Molotov wanted "to give Crimea to the Jews" and why he had told his wife about secret Politburo decisions. As for Mikoyan, Stalin said he had probably been plotting with Lozovsky—who had just been sentenced to death in the JAC case—to sell out Soviet interests to the Americans.

"The faces of Molotov and Mikoyan were white and dead," according to Simonov; their colleagues looked panicky. Khrushchev found Stalin's accusations against Molotov and Mikoyan "very surprising and confusing." Mikoyan remembers shock, and that he attempted to defend himself point by point, whereas Molotov spoke briefly, saying nothing more than that he had always been in agreement with the party line in both foreign and domestic policy. At some point in this terrible meeting, Stalin asked to be relieved of his position as party secretary because he was too old and sick to carry out his duties. Malenkov, in the chair, was in agony; when the hall resounded with cries of "No! You can't! We beg you to stay," he had the look of a man who had stared death in the face before being reprieved.

Stalin then made an extraordinary suggestion, apropos of the new institution of the Central Committee—the Presidium—which was replacing the Politburo. They should "deceive" the enemies of the people by creating a big Presidium and publishing its composition in the papers, but then elect a little Presidium and not tell anybody who was on it. This absurd suggestion was accepted. A big Presidium of twenty-five people was elected, including Molotov and Mikoyan, along with other members of the former Politburo (but not Andreev, about whose incapacity Stalin had made a slighting remark in passing); and also a little one (the "Bureau") of nine members, including Voroshilov (a late addition, written by hand) and Kaganovich, along with the rest of the team and a couple of new faces, but *not* including Molotov, Mikoyan, and Andreev. The enemies of the people must have been duly baffled and frustrated, but so was the team. Khrushchev, who "very much regretted" the exclusion of Molotov and Mikoyan, and regarded the gratuitous swipe at Andreev as outrageous, exchanged "knowing glances" with Beria and Malenkov because what Stalin proposed was crazy. He wondered who had helped Stalin make up the list (which the Four all swore they hadn't), since he obviously couldn't have come up with it on his own—he didn't even know most of the new people. Khrushchev surmised that it was perhaps Kaganovich, now back in comparative favor with Stalin, who had suggested the names, since they came mainly from his field of industry.[12]

The nine-member Bureau of the Presidium turned out, as so often with Stalin, to be more or less a fiction; he operated instead with an inner circle of five, usually himself, Malenkov, Beria, Bulganin, and Khrushchev—which, as it happens, was exactly the same group he had been most closely working with for the last several years, the Group of Four plus one. Molotov and Mikoyan had been cast into outer darkness—or had they? They certainly ceased to visit Stalin in his office after the October plenum, but Mikoyan later claimed that they regularly attended meetings of the bureau, for all Stalin's efforts to keep them out. This is not how it looks in the officially recorded attendance lists (though these could have been edited), but in any case, the bureau met relatively infrequently, not weekly as it was meant to, and it appears that the most important business in the last months of 1952 was discussed at the December meetings of the *full* Presidium. Both Molotov and Mikoyan are recorded as present, Mikoyan participating in a discussion of agricultural policy (Stalin seemed interested in what he had to say on lack of incentives for peasants) and being appointed to the commission set up to work on the question.

In the past, Stalin had always kept a firm hold on the power of exclusion, with his invited Groups of Five, Seven, and so on regularly substituting for the formal Politburo. Now, in an extraordinary development, he seemed close to losing it. It had never happened that someone excluded by Stalin started turning up on his own initiative, or on the invitation of others in the team. But that was the situation in the last months of 1952 with respect to the evening film showings in the Kremlin, followed by late-night suppers at Stalin's dacha, which had become the heart of the team's collective life. Here, even according to the normal conventions of social life, one might have expected Stalin to have sole power to invite or not, and he had made it clear that Molotov and Mikoyan were in disgrace. Nevertheless, they continued to attend. "They wouldn't bother to call Stalin and ask permission," Khrushchev remembered. "They would find out whether Stalin was at the Kremlin or at his dacha and then simply appear. They were always allowed in, but it was obvious Stalin wasn't very glad to see them."

After a while, Stalin "got fed up and told his staff not to tell Molotov and Mikoyan where he was." But this didn't work, as the rest of the members of the team were quietly subverting his instructions. Molotov and Mikoyan "had a talk with Beria, Malenkov, and me," Khrushchev reports. "We agreed to try to soften Stalin's attitude toward them. We also agreed to notify them when Stalin was going out to the Nearby Dacha or coming in to the Kremlin movie theatre so that they could meet us there. For a while, whenever we went to the movies with Stalin, Molotov and Mikoyan showed up too." Then there was a big blowup: Stalin "had figured out that we were acting as Molotov and Mikoyan's agents," and started shouting, "Stop this! Stop telling them where I am! I won't tolerate it!" So they stopped, but then came Stalin's birthday on 21 December, when it was traditional for the team to meet at Stalin's dacha for a celebratory dinner. Molotov and Mikoyan took counsel with Malenkov, Khrushchev, and Beria (more plotting!), and decided to go. "Stalin greeted everyone pleasantly, including us," Mikoyan recalled, "and there was an impression that nothing had happened and old relations had been restored." But then, a few days later, came the message delivered by Malenkov or Khrushchev that Stalin had been very angry about them coming to his birthday party: "he is no longer your comrade and doesn't want you to go and see him."

The team's behavior sounds, on the one hand, like the way you would deal with a father with dementia who has developed an irrational hatred of particular family members, which the rest of the family hope to train him out of. On the other hand, it can be read—and surely must have been read by Stalin—as a quiet, collective defiance on the part of the team, implying a belief that one way or the other Stalin was on his way out. After Stalin's blowup about the invitations to Molotov and Mikoyan, Khrushchev wrote that he, Malenkov, and Beria "saw that it was useless to persist ... Without bringing the subject up again among ourselves, we decided to wait for the natural outcome of this situation," presumably Stalin's death or incapacity. With the team in this new mood, no wonder Stalin didn't go on vacation that year.[13]

There were other things on Stalin's mind as well, notably, his anti-Semitic campaign. He had decided that Viktor Abakumov, head of the MGB, was not giving it his best shot and had him dismissed and arrested on 12 July 1951. One of Abakumov's projects, now taken over by chief investigator Mikhail Ryumin, was the preparation of a trial of JAC members. In its long gestation, the nature of the planned trial had changed, notably by the dropping of Zhemchuzhina from the list of the accused. It finally took place in a closed military court within the Lubyanka from 8 May to 18 July 1952. At first it looked as if the defendants were going to act in the normal way and produce abject confessions of treason and espionage, written with the help of their MGB interrogators. But then, in the third week of the trial, Solomon Lozovsky, the biggest political fish in the group, took the stand and immediately retracted his earlier confessions, making a trenchant autobiographical statement that stressed his long revolutionary credentials and his Jewish heritage. This was an extraordinary moment: in a long history of staged trials since the 1930s, nobody had done this before.

It was even worse the next day, when Lozovsky lit into the absurdity of the accusations ("It's like some kind of fairy tale—there was no Central Committee, no government, just Lozovsky and a couple of Jews who did everything," he said, adding, apropos of his work in the Soviet Information Bureau during the war, "if the word 'information' implies 'espionage,' then all of the activity of Sovinformburo was espionage activity"). His manner, judging by the transcript, was confident and detached, sometimes with an ironic tinge; listening, the other defendants took heart, and in subsequent testimony started to retract their confessions too. In other words, the whole thing started to fall apart. Worst of all, from the point of view of the stagers, the military judge presiding over the proceedings, General Alexander Cheptsov, found that he was not convinced by the evidence and suggested to Malenkov, whom he must have known from earlier work in the Central Committee office, that an acquittal was in order. How he had the nerve to do this remains obscure, but surely it was not unrelated to uneasiness in the political elite, including within the team, about the anti-Semitic campaign. Malenkov did not support him, and, after a month's holdup to deal with Cheptsov's objections and the defendants' appeals, things reverted to the standard Stalinist pattern. The convicted defendants, including Lozovsky, were shot on 12 August 1952.[14]

In these last months, Stalin's paranoia seemed to know no bounds. His suspicion of the security services was almost as intense as his suspicion of Jews. During the preparation of the Doctors' Plot case, Stalin "ordered the arrest of all Jewish colonels and generals in the MGB," some fifteen people, but the purges within the security services in his last months went much wider. Within his immediate entourage, five people were arrested on suspicion of spying in January 1953. He got rid of his longtime secretary, Poskrebyshev, who was not only a key executant and intermediary but a personal confidant, if not a friend. The same fate befell the head of his bodyguards, Nikolai Vlasik, head of Kremlin security, as well as Stalin's personal bodyguard, who was dismissed from those positions and then, in December 1952, arrested. Among the accusations against Vlasik and Poskrebyshev was a failure to pull their weight on the Jewish doctors' case.

Toward the end of 1952, in what was essentially Stalin's last political gambit, the anti-Semitic campaign went into high gear with preparations of the Doctors' Plot case, which targeted a group of Kremlin physicians, mainly Jewish, on charges of spying and terrorism. They were accused of causing the untimely deaths of Zhdanov and Shcherbakov and even, for good measure, poor Andreev's deafness. The first arrests of prominent

Jewish doctors had taken place in the winter of 1950–51, but November 1952 saw a new wave, including the arrest of Stalin's own personal physician, Dr. Vladimir Vinogradov. Khrushchev claims to have heard Stalin, "crazy with rage," berating his new MGB head (Semyon Ignatiev) on the telephone, "demanding that he throw the doctors in chains, beat them to a pulp, and grind them into powder." A less highly colored report has him telling his associates that "any Jewish nationalist is an agent of American intelligence. Jewish nationalists consider that the USA saved their nation (there one can get rich, become a bourgeois, and so on). They consider themselves in debt to the Americans." According to Khrushchev's son Sergei, Stalin was not just supervising the Doctors' Plot investigation— "he directed it."

Whether Stalin was a lifelong anti-Semite or became one in his final decline is a matter of debate. Khrushchev said he was, but other members of the team denied it. What seems clear is that until close to the end, he was careful in public to follow the Bolshevik party line, which had always been strongly condemnatory of anti-Semitism. There was never any hint of anti-Semitism in his public statements, and as Khrushchev commented, "God forbid that anyone should quote publicly from any private conversations in which he made . . . anti-Semitic remarks." That prohibition remained in force even in Stalin's last years, when, with de facto state-supported anti-Semitism rampant, the press continued not only to avoid overt anti-Semitism, even in coverage of the Doctors' Plot, but also from time to time to report punishment of specific officials guilty of it. For the benefit of the philo-Semitic Russian intelligentsia, Stalin took the trouble in the early 1950s to stage a little scene in front of intelligentsia leaders, where he expressed outrage at reports of anti-Semitism and ordered that it be stopped. They believed him at the time (until the Doctors' Plot opened their eyes) and duly spread the word on the grapevine that the current anti-Semitism had nothing to do with Stalin.[15]

The team, who had internalized the same set of Bolshevik values against racial discrimination—perhaps more successfully than Stalin— were uneasy in varying degrees about the rampant anti-Semitism of Stalin's last months. When the team was shown the interrogation transcripts with the doctors' confessions, Stalin said to them, "You are blind like young kittens: what will happen without me? The country will perish because you do not know how to recognize enemies." But the team was not convinced—as indeed Stalin's remark suggests that he knew. Molotov and Kaganovich later emphasized that they were out of the loop on the Doctors' Plot and had nothing to do with it (a slightly suspect claim on Kaganovich's part, as he was the author of a long anti-Semitic article around this time). The others, or their sons, did their best to dissociate themselves (difficult in the case of Malenkov, who was clearly involved, if only in an executive capacity) and indicate their disapproval, and the swiftness of their collective repudiation of the anti-Semitic campaign after Stalin's death suggests that this was largely genuine. Among themselves, Bulganin said later, the team had concluded that the Doctors' Plot was a put-up job, even while Stalin was alive, and Khrushchev said the same. It wasn't just the anti-Semitic aspect that gave them pause. As Khrushchev pointed out, "We knew some of these people personally because we had . . . been treated by them." For the Berias and the Andreevs, and no doubt other team members as well, Dr. Vinogradov, Dr. Vovsi, and some of the other defendants were family friends.[16]

The Doctors' Plot leaped into public consciousness on 13 January 1953, with the publication in *Pravda* of a communiqué reporting the arrests, accompanied by a lead article entitled "Spies and murderers in the guise of doctors." Both had gone through Stalin's prepublication editing. The fact that most of the doctors were Jewish was not explicitly stated, but this was evident to Soviet readers from their names and patronymics; moreover, it stated that the core group (members' Jewish names listed) was "linked with the international Jewish bourgeois-nationalist organization 'Joint'" and that one of them, Dr. Miron Vovsi, had admitted ties with "the well-known Jewish bourgeois nationalist Mikhoels." A big orchestrated campaign of condemnation of the "doctor-murderers" followed, including a letter condemning them signed by leading Jewish figures in the world of culture and government. Kaganovich was asked to sign this and hotly refused—not because he was against its content but because it was an insult for a Politburo member to be downgraded to the category of "Jewish public figure." (Kaganovich was never keen on being publicly associated with Jewish causes; because of this, he had refused to serve on the Jewish Anti-Fascist Committee back in the early 1940s, according to Beria's son, despite Beria's urgings.)

International outrage followed the announcement, and confusion on the part of the international Left, with its many Jewish supporters. The domestic reaction was mixed, with distress among the intelligentsia and what appears to be enthusiasm in the broader population. There was some uneasiness among party functionaries, uncertain how openly anti-Semitic the new policy shift required them to be, and whether it was now acceptable to refer to Jews pejoratively as "Yids." The popular backlash was directed not only against Jews but also doctors, regardless of ethnicity. Some loyal citizens started worrying about Stalin's health and whether he was in danger from the ministrations of his doctors. Others remembered that Molotov's wife was Jewish and wondered if she was involved in the plot. Rumors swept Moscow about the impending deportation of Jews, on analogy with the 1940s deportations of "traitor" nations from the North Caucasus to Central Asia and Siberia, though nobody has ever been able to prove that such an official plan existed. From the reactions around the country reported by local party committees, there was a lot of popular support for this policy, mainly on the grounds that Jews were privileged, elite members, strangers to manual labor and shirkers of military service, who should be banished from urban centers and forced to give up their good jobs, spacious apartments, and dachas to honest "toilers."[17]

With this apocalyptic popular mood in the background, the team's level of alarm rose sharply. At a Presidium meeting in December, Stalin attacked Molotov and Mikoyan again, calling them hirelings of American imperialism. Mikoyan started to suspect that Stalin had some big bloodletting of the leadership in mind, as in 1937–38; "one of the comrades" told him a few weeks before Stalin's death that he was preparing to summon a Central Committee plenum that would "settle scores with us" once and for all, "a matter not just of political but of physical annihilation." Molotov's and Mikoyan's days were probably numbered, Khrushchev concluded; "their lives were in danger." Archival documents reportedly show that the MGB had been preparing cases against them since the middle of the year. In the opinion of historians who have had access to them, a new wave of party purges and show trials was imminent, perhaps as soon as March 1953, with Molotov and Mikoyan cast in the role of Rightists. A special prison had been set up, on Stalin's orders, under direct control of the Central Committee (in effect, Malenkov) and not the security services, to handle party political cases.

Beria's situation was looking increasingly precarious. Although he had survived the murky Mingrelian Affair in 1951, in which he was accused of being a patron for Mingrelian nationalists in the Caucasus, Stalin was still looking for dirt on him in Georgia—perhaps annoyed, among other things, by the Beria cult that had developed there. One line of attack from within the MGB was that Beria was fomenting conspiracy against Stalin in Georgia; it was also rumored that he was a Jew who was hiding his true identity. In these last months of Stalin's life, Beria had warned his wife and son that his and their survival was a risk; in the independent estimation of a highly placed security official, he "was next on the list for elimination by Stalin."[18]

Then, in the midst of it all—incredibly convenient for the rest of them—Stalin was felled by a stroke. Stalin's health had been markedly deteriorating from the beginning of 1952, according to his personal physician, Dr. Vinogradov. Although angry with Vinogradov for pointing this out, Stalin did give up smoking and cut down on working time. But "his physical condition came to be a source of concern to those around him, as the leader suffered from sudden memory losses, reduced stamina, and very sharp mood swings." His seven-minute speech at the party congress in October was cited by Khrushchev as a token of his reduced powers, evidence that he really wasn't fit enough to go on working. On the other hand, just two days after this speech, Stalin spoke without notes to the Central Committee, denouncing Molotov and Mikoyan, for more than an hour and a half. You couldn't count on him not, once again, bouncing back.

His stroke happened on 1 March, the night after the usual film at the Kremlin followed by supper at the dacha with the Group of Four (Malenkov, Beria, Khrushchev, and Bulganin), when Stalin had seemed cheerful and in normal health. He was not discovered until the evening, since he was generally a late riser and the dacha staff was unwilling to take the risk of disturbing him. When they found him unconscious on the floor, having evidently had a stroke, they called the Four, who hurried out to the dacha. Voroshilov was summoned too, early on the morning of the next day; the old soldier was transformed, as he always was at critical moments in the Civil War and the Great Patriotic War, his loyal wife noted admiringly, becoming "still more braced and resolute." Observing state secrecy, Voroshilov told his wife nothing, but she guessed what had happened and wept. Beria doesn't seem to have observed the state secrecy rules. He told his wife, an old favorite of Stalin's, and she, like Voroshilova, wept. When her son asked why, given that Stalin had seemed likely to destroy them all, she agreed that it was irrational, but said she was sorry for Stalin: "He was such a lonely man."

When the team arrived at the dacha, their reaction was lethargic. It took them some time even to call a doctor, no doubt partly because of the complication that Stalin's personal physician, Dr. Vinogradov, was under arrest. The replacement seemed almost paralyzed with fear and hesitant to take any action. For the next few days, the team kept vigil in pairs, waiting for Stalin to die (but with a tinge of fear that he would suddenly wake up). Molotov and Mikoyan were not invited to the bedside but were otherwise fully readmitted to team status—the others asked them to keep the government running on their behalf, according to Mikoyan. In this hour of crisis, Malenkov might have been the natural one to take command, but it was Beria who stepped forward. "Beria was in charge," Molotov noted laconically, and Voroshilov remembered that as Stalin lay unconscious, Beria "took the lead in everything all the time, was the one who made suggestions and anticipated every contingency, the one who knew everything and took charge."

Clearly this provoked resentment in other team members, though no open resistance. Sharing vigil for a few hours with Bulganin, Khrushchev took the opportunity to have a conversation with his old friend about the future, specifically the danger that Beria might represent for the rest of the team. The retrospective comments on Beria's behavior by others at the deathbed are uniformly critical; Khrushchev and Svetlana (who had been summoned to the dacha by the Four on 2 March) both described Beria as excited, hyperalert, and making effusive speeches of devotion to Stalin whenever it looked as if he might be coming round, but otherwise speaking of him with such mockery and hatred that Khrushchev found it "unbearable to listen to him." The rest of them were subdued, grief for Stalin being one of their emotions. Svetlana and Vasily (drunk, as usual) had been sent for, too. When Svetlana arrived, Khrushchev and Bulganin embraced her and they wept together. Voroshilov, Kaganovich, and Malenkov had tears in their eyes as well.[19]

Long afterward, with Beria himself disgraced and dead, some of the surviving team members speculated that Beria might have had a hand in dispatching Stalin. Molotov told Chuev in the 1970s that, standing on the Mausoleum at Stalin's funeral, Beria had told him, "I got rid of him . . . I saved you all"—but that could just have been Beria boasting or currying favor, and Molotov certainly didn't know how it could have been done. Malenkov told his son that Beria had a plan to get rid of Stalin, including the removal of loyal servants like Poskrebyshev and Vlasik, but he didn't know whether he in fact carried it out. Pavel Sudoplatov, a member of the intelligence services, said he couldn't have done it, because he didn't have control over the staff at the dacha. In general, the lack of specificity in the later accusations (especially in the wake of detailed investigations of Beria's actions during his trial in mid-1953), and the fact that there is no evidence that the team saw him as a murderer at the time, argues against the theory, at least of Beria's sole responsibility. If Stalin was killed by his associates (for which there is no evidence), it would have to have been a joint action by the Group of Four, which none of them ever disclosed. All in all, it doesn't seem likely that Stalin was murdered by the team, though once he had been stricken, they certainly didn't knock themselves out trying to keep him alive. But it's a wonder, considering the provocation he had been offering them.

The popular rumor mill didn't suspect Beria or the team of murder. Logically enough, given the current climate, it pointed the finger at the usual suspects: Jews and doctors. "What a pity he is so ill! I wonder if the Jews have anything to do with it," was one reaction reported by the MGB. And "those 'killer doctors' are responsible for comrade Stalin's grave illness. They must have given him poisonous medications that release their poison over time."[20]

The Bureau of the Presidium of the Central Committee, chaired by Malenkov, met twice on 2 March, at noon and 8:00 PM, in the usual place, Stalin's office in the Kremlin. Stalin's health was the only item on the agenda. On 3 March they met twice again, this time discussing press releases and the summoning of a Central Committee plenum. Molotov and Mikoyan, along with Voroshilov and Kaganovich (but not Andreev) were firmly back on the team, present at every meeting. By the night of 4–5 March, the group had moved on to the really important stuff: who would staff the new government (without Stalin) and how it would be constituted. The proposals were presented by Beria and Malenkov, Molotov remembered, and it was all very well worked-out and procedurally correct.

A few hours later, they—or rather Malenkov, Beria, and Khrushchev—were called back to the dacha: Stalin was finally dying. They watched him die, Khrushchev with distress, Beria probably not. The end came at 9:50 PM on 5 March. The moment it was over, Beria called for his car—his voice rang out in the silence with "a note of triumph," Svetlana remembered—and rushed back to Moscow. Stalin was dead. The team, his heirs, had survived him and were now ready—none more than Beria—to claim their inheritance.[21]

NINE

WITHOUT STALIN

EVEN BEFORE STALIN WAS DEAD, THE TEAM HAD THE NEW GOVERN-ment up and running. Malenkov was chairman of the Council of Ministers "while comrade Stalin is absent," as Beria delicately put it in proposing his appointment, with Molotov, Bulganin, and Kaganovich as his first deputies. Molotov was in his old position as minister of foreign affairs and the same went for Mikoyan at the Ministry of Internal and Foreign Trade. The two security ministries were reunited as the Ministry of Internal Affairs (MVD), with Beria in charge. Bulganin was minister of defense, with two World War II military leaders, Marshals Vasilevsky and Zhukov, as his deputies. Voroshilov was given Kalinin's old, mainly honorific, job of president of the Supreme Soviet. Khrushchev was secretary of the party Central Committee (after a few months, this was raised to first secretary). The party's Presidium (formerly Politburo) was cut back to fifteen members—including team members Beria, Bulganin, Kaganovich, Khrushchev, Malenkov, Mikoyan, Molotov, and Voroshilov—and its bureau abolished. But it was the new government, not the new Presidium, that got top billing in the press. Described as a "collective leadership," the pecking order indicated by contemporary newspaper reports was Malenkov, Beria, and Molotov. Evidently the new leadership meant to break with Stalinist tradition and emphasize the government, rather than the party, as the main locus of power.

The team—Malenkov, Beria, Molotov, Voroshilov, Khrushchev, Bulganin, Kaganovich, and Mikoyan—carried Stalin's coffin at the funeral a few days later. As Shepilov remembered, "Molotov [was] expressionless as ever ... Voroshilov, cast down and bewildered ... Malenkov, pale and weary but composed. Behind his thick pince-nez, Beria's face kept twitching spasmodically. Khrushchev stood near me, his eyes red and in-flamed, tears coursing down his cheeks." (Shepilov noted, however, that in the first meeting of the Presidium after Stalin's death, where a gener-ally low-key tone prevailed, Khrushchev and Beria were the two who seemed excited rather than grief-stricken.) Eulogies were delivered by Malenkov, Beria, and Molotov, but, in a portent of things to come, "only Molotov showed the slightest emotion at the loss of his old leader." Beria, in his short speech, introduced an unexpected theme: the freedoms guaranteed to all Soviet citizens by the Constitution. Malenkov also struck an un-Stalinist note when he spoke of peace and international cooperation.

Behind the coffin trudged Stalin's two surviving children, Vasily's face "puffy with tears," Svetlana "dignified and reserved." Svetlana sat for hours at Stalin's lying-in-state, flanked by Stepan Mikoyan's wife, Elya, on one side and Mikhail Shvernik's daughter Lyusya on the other. At this point, the team children were still idealistic believers for whom Stalin's loss seemed "a cosmic tragedy"—even those like Sergo Mikoyan (married to Alla Kuznetsova) who had suffered under his rule. Sergo's elder brother Stepan attended all three days of the viewing out of respect, and men-tioned this to his father, evidently expecting approval. "You were wasting your time," was his father's curt response. For thirty-year-old Stepan, "it was the first signal that there could be a critical attitude to Stalin, and that my father had that attitude."

The day of the funeral was Molotov's sixty-third birthday, and two days later Beria gave him a birthday present. With the flair of a magician pulling a rabbit out of a hat, he presented his gift—Polina, flown in from Kazakhstan exile that day on Beria's orders. The Molotovs were both stunned. Molotov's recollection was that as he stepped forward to take her in his arms, Beria got in first, embracing her with a theatrical cry of "Heroine!" Polina didn't even know Stalin was dead, and her first ques-tion was about him. Molotov later cited this as evidence of her unswerv-ing loyalty to Stalin and the cause, but of course it was also a key piece of political information. Within ten days, Polina was exonerated of any wrongdoing on Beria's initiative and her Communist Party membership

restored. The Molotovs resumed their life together, as devoted, by all accounts, as they had been before Stalin had divided them.[1]

On Stalin's death, the poet Evgeny Evtushenko later wrote, "the whole
of Russia wept. So did I. We wept sincerely with grief and perhaps also
with fear for the future . . . Trained to believe that Stalin was taking care
of everyone, people were lost and bewildered without him." Huge crowds
gathered in Moscow, trying to get to the Hall of Columns where Stalin
was laid out, causing bottlenecks and panic in which hundreds were tram-
pled to death. The new leaders seemed at first to be tensely anticipating
disaster, virtually pleading with the Soviet people to resist "panic and disarray"—but actually the Moscow tragedy, which was not a political demonstration but a failure in crowd control, was the worst of it. The team's
confidence grew, and the mood changed. The American journalist Harrison Salisbury noted that "the most astonishing [thing] that happened
after Stalin died was the quickness with which symptoms of a thaw appeared." Within months if not weeks the team had started to show a kind
of euphoria, behaving in public not with the old stiffness required in the
Stalin days but, in Crankshaw's words, "like children let out of school."
"The new masters of Russia [were] positively unfolding," he wrote, "blos-
soming like leathery cacti."

They might well have been euphoric. Who would have thought that
the Soviet Union could achieve a *peaceful* transition after Stalin's death? A
real collective leadership, at least for the time being; moreover, one
launching on a coherent, wide-ranging reform program with Stalin
scarcely cold in his grave? The magnitude and surprising nature of the
team's achievement has often been overlooked, partly because in the end,
the team was to fall apart with bitter mutual recriminations. It owed a
great deal, paradoxically, to the team's defensive closing of ranks against
Stalin's capricious finger-pointing in his last years, as well as to the unspoken consensus that had developed in those years about the policy changes
that were desirable, if only the old man would agree, which he wouldn't.
There was a tacit consensus that Gulag was too big and too expensive, and
needed to be sharply reduced. Urban living standards should be raised,
and the burden on the peasantry reduced. Police repression must be
eased, relations with the West improved. The anti-Semitic campaign must
be called off and excessive Russification of government in the non-
Russian republics reversed. All this seems to have become common wis-

dom within the team, although it was something they didn't talk about while Stalin was alive.

Common to the group, too, was the revived sense of themselves as a team, demonstrated in their passive resistance to Stalin's outcasting of Molotov and Mikoyan. Their embrace, on Stalin's death, of the old principle of collective leadership might be regarded simply as a prudent agreement to put the inevitable succession struggle on hold in the first dangerous months of transition, but, as we shall see, it was more than that. Collective leadership was the opposite of something for which the team, at the time of Stalin's death, felt something like revulsion, namely, the arbitrary power of one man. Overt attacks on Stalin were still in the future, but in the spring of 1953, Soviet citizens still mourning the lost leader were disconcerted to find that Stalin's name, formerly ubiquitous, had vanished from the press—only one mention in *Pravda* in June 1953!—and his familiar words of wisdom were no longer quoted in editorials. The adjective "Stalinist," formerly applied freely to all Soviet achievements and projects, suddenly disappeared from the lexicon. At the Central Committee meeting in July 1953, Stalin's "incorrect, mistaken" attacks on the loyalty of Molotov and Mikoyan were repudiated, to "stormy applause." For those who followed such things, the publication of Stalin's collected works stopped abruptly at volume 13, even though volumes 14 and 15 were set in type at the time of his death. Then, shockingly, in a media culture where anniversaries were meticulously celebrated, Soviet newspapers failed to mark the first anniversary of his death in March 1954.[2]

This wasn't the only sign that a new era had begun. Within three weeks of Stalin's death, an amnesty for nonpolitical prisoners led to the release of more than a million prisoners. Two months later, the convicted defendants in the Doctors' Plot were announced to be innocent and released, with leading security officials taking their place in prison. The Supreme Court rehabilitated victims of the Leningrad Affair in April. Feelers were put out to the West, beginning in the eulogies at Stalin's funeral, and by midyear a truce was signed ending the Korean War. In August, Malenkov started talking of "détente" in the Cold War. Diplomatic relations with Israel and Yugoslavia were restored. The 1947 law forbidding marriages of Soviet citizens and foreigners was quietly dropped, allowing seven hundred Russian wives to leave the Soviet Union with their foreign husbands. Rapid de-Russification of government in the non-Russian republics, along with encouragement of the use of indigenous languages in place of Russian, was under way by June, leading to remarkable shake-ups in administration in Belorussia, Ukraine, the Baltics, the Caucasus, and Central Asia. Government offices throughout the Soviet Union went back to a normal workday, no longer constrained to follow Stalin's nocturnal habits. In the late summer and autumn of 1953, taxes on peasants were lowered and procurement prices on agricultural goods raised. For the urban population, the government announced a major expansion in the consumer goods sector, with production of radios tripled, furniture doubled, and all types of clothing significantly increased, not to mention promise of the first domestic refrigerators.

Many of these measures were popular in the country, but not all of them. The Gulag amnesty terrified ordinary citizens in Siberia and the Urals, who were now faced with an influx of penniless, desperate characters without jobs or housing into their towns. Street crime rose, generating a law-and-order panic that spread throughout the Soviet Union and lingered on for many months as the prisoners slowly made their way back home. The release of the Doctors' Plot defendants was equally unpopular, though a minority (mainly from the intelligentsia) applauded. Many members of the public had seen the anti-Semitic campaign as a long-overdue attack on a serious social problem, and Stalin's death semed to them simply confirmation of the charges that enemies had been systematically killing off their leaders. An anonymous writer warned Khrushchev later in the month that "90 percent of our people don't believe that Stalin died a natural death"; Jewish involvement was suspected. "Get the Jews out of the government, the people don't trust them. They are parasites on the neck of the people." "If war came, they would be a Fifth Column."

"What does it mean to free those enemies, the professor-murderers?" a correspondent from Kazan asked Molotov rhetorically when the Doctors' Plot victims were freed. "It means, in the first place, blackening Comrade STALIN, showing the whole world that it was he who sanctioned the arrest of 'innocent' people; it means that comrade STALIN taught the organs of [the] MGB to behave arbitrarily and use force." Molotov was often the recipient of such letters, since their writers wrongly expected him, as a Russian and an old Stalinist, to sympathize. Except for Voroshilov, other team members were not well known to the Soviet public. It was rumored that

Beria was a Jew, and perhaps Malenkov also. "The people are dubious about . . . Malenkov and Beria," wrote Molotov's Kazan correspondent. "They call them drunken, over-hasty, incompetent leaders 'dreaming of being Napoleons.' You Old Bolsheviks should get rid of them."[3]

Molotov was the man looked to by the team as their senior member, just as he had been in 1941. "According to popular and general party opinion," an insider later wrote, he was "the single worthy successor" of Stalin. Certainly he received many letters in the weeks after Stalin's death calling on him to step forward. "In a hard moment, the people puts its hopes for the proper leadership of the country on YOU" (from a self-styled "Group of Old Bolsheviks"). "We are convinced that you as a true Russian man will lead our state" (no identification, but evidently a Russian patriot). "Why don't you become our Leader?!" (from a group of Tambov housewives); "We ordinary people all wanted to see you in the place of Joseph Vissarionovich!" (from a "simple, elderly, non-party woman," who wept as she wrote). The women among Molotov's correspondents made no overt comparative judgments, but the men often spelled it out: Molotov was their man, and "Malenkov and Beria should go."

Molotov, however, showed no signs of challenging the collective leadership. The experience of decades had made him as much a team player as a Stalin acolyte. In the first weeks of the transition, he seemed not even to be trying to define his role, but rather waiting, "with his consummate self-discipline and cultivation," for the "collective intelligence" of the team to do it for him. The others were equally keen on team solidarity, fearing, as Mikoyan remembered, that the public would pick up on any signs of factionalism within the team and anarchy would result. Still, within the team in these first months, a core group quickly emerged. It consisted of Malenkov, Molotov, Beria, and Khrushchev. It was noticed by the others (Mikoyan, Voroshilov, Kaganovich, and Bulganin) that the Four were holding preliminary meetings *before* business was discussed at the Presidium. They would walk around the Kremlin together in lively conversation; after work, the three living in town would leave in one car, with Beria dropping Malenkov and Khrushchev off at their apartments in Granovsky Street before going home to his townhouse on Kachalov Street.

Mikoyan might be irritated by this, but he still felt that the important policy decisions were being made at meetings of the Presidium and were truly collective, an impression confirmed by Dmitry Shepilov, editor of

Pravda, who attended Presidium meetings ex officio as a nonvoting member. Shepilov noted that Molotov routinely brought issues for decision of the Presidium that would earlier have been decided in consultation with Stalin: it was not a difficult switch for him. Malenkov, who as head of the government presided—according to a custom dating back to Lenin—at Presidium meetings, made a point of conducting business democratically, doing his best to obtain consensus and refraining from pushing his own status. Although Malenkov was seen abroad as the likely emergent leader, Shepilov emphasizes how "naturally and sincerely" he played the role of team coordinator: "I don't think he had any thoughts about strengthening the role of his own person." This, of course, makes sense in terms of Malenkov's own past work experience: he had always been a dutiful executant and facilitator for Stalin, never one to strike out on his own or to challenge consensus, and now he was transferring these skills to a new playing field.[4]

There were, however, exceptions to this remarkable display of team-mindedness. Beria was the most glaring. Even as Stalin died, and Beria rushed off abruptly back to town, Mikoyan remembered thinking that he had "gone to take power." He "seemed to have been lent wings," said another observer, and the speed of the reform legislation in the next few months owed a great deal to Beria's frenzied pace. Within six weeks, as head of the security police, he had released the Jewish doctors, investigated Mikhoels's death and informed the team of Stalin's involvement, forbidden the use of torture in interrogations, transferred much of the MVD's industrial empire to civilian ministries, and set in motion the release of more than a million prisoners from Gulag.

Moving on to nationalities policy, Beria pushed for an astonishing tempo of de-Russification in the republics, starting with the MVD. The Latvian MVD was ordered to replace all Russians in senior positions with Latvians *within one day*, and when the locals objected that they couldn't find that many Latvians with clean security records, the instruction was to go ahead regardless. In response, the (Latvian) first secretary of the republican party was brazen enough to give his speech at the party plenum in Latvian, without translation, so that the Russians couldn't understand it—and moreover used the occasion to report that since Latvia's wartime incorporation into the Soviet Union, the secret police had killed almost 20,000 Latvians and exiled another 60,000 to distant parts of the country.

In Lithuania, jubilant shopkeepers demonstrated their hostility to Russians by refusing to serve anyone who didn't speak Lithuanian.

De-Russification was the team's policy, not just Beria's, and others were working on it too in the spring of 1953. But the reactive upsurge of nationalism in the republics was alarming, as was Beria's arrogant behavior. He had always been known for his sharp tongue, but now he was sometimes shouting at other team members in the presence of subordinates, and taking unilateral actions, such as signing an instruction for testing the hydrogen bomb on his own authority, without even telling his nominal boss, Malenkov. Khrushchev was angry when Beria started to interfere in party matters, trying to put "his" men at the head of the Ukrainian and Belorussian Communist Parties. Even Beria's initiatives that the team really approved, like the release of the Jewish doctors, somehow grated, Kaganovich remembered: he was talking as if the rest of them were irrelevant—"I am the authority, I am the liberal, after Stalin I give the amnesties, I make the exposés, I do everything."

Never one to emphasize the sanctity of the party, Beria was now openly contemptuous. "What is the Central Committee?" he said when Khrushchev, as party secretary, objected. "Let the Council of Ministers decide everything, and the Central Committee can spend its time on cadres and propaganda." To be sure, the team as a whole was in favor of increasing the authority of the Council of Ministers, but this kind of disrespect was hard for them to stomach. What made it worse was that Beria was not only self-confident but also the smartest, best-informed, and most quick-witted of the team. News of the flowering of Beria's own personality cult in Georgia, despite his opposition to such things in Moscow, was another annoyance.[5]

Beria was throwing his weight around even in foreign affairs, an area where he had no particular track record in which Molotov was the recognized authority. On one occasion, when Molotov presented a draft of a policy statement for publication that was met with "friendly approval" by the rest of the team, Beria jumped up with many objections and then dictated what was essentially a new text. In one observer's description, Molotov "sat motionless, with an unreadable expression on his face, only rhythmically scrunching up the table cloth with three fingers, an old habit of his." He had responded to Stalin's bullying with the same passive resistance. After a long, embarrassed silence, Malenkov, in the chair, finally

proposed the acceptance of "Molotov's text with Beria's corrections"—
that is, Beria's text.

The disagreements were sharper about Germany, a particularly thorny
issue. In the wake of the Berlin Blockade of 1948, Germany's de facto division was formalized by the creation of two German states: the Federal Republic of Germany, in the Western sphere, and the German Democratic
Republic (GDR), in the Soviet. The GDR's leaders were pursuing policies
of rapid socialization modeled on Soviet policies of the collectivization
era. As in Eastern Europe, this aroused substantial popular objections,
but Germany's situation was unique in that its citizens could—until the
construction of the Berlin Wall in 1961—vote with their feet and go over
into West Germany, and were doing so in large numbers. In addition,
strikes and street demonstrations had broken out in Berlin and elsewhere.
This very much alarmed the Soviet leadership, and they summoned the
East German leaders to Moscow and read the riot act to them, urging
them to back off their policies of "forced construction of socialism" in
order to avoid catastrophe.

The team was in agreement on this, even Molotov and Kaganovich,
but Beria would have gone even further, dropping the "forced" and telling
the Germans to abandon their policies of building socialism tout court.
Socialism in East Germany was maintained only by Soviet troops, he said,
and what the Soviet Union needed was not necessarily a socialist Germany but a peaceful one. Within the Presidium, Beria had spoken so con-
temptuously of the GDR leaders that Shepilov was moved to protest that
this was the government that would be building socialism in the new Germany. "Socialism?" Beria shouted at him. "What socialism? We should
stop chattering mindlessly about socialism in Germany!" He spoke, as
Shepilov recalled later, "with such disgust that it seemed as if the very
word 'socialism' and the journalists who used it were intolerable to him."
Beria's dismissive attitude to socialism was, of course, anathema to Molotov and disconcerting to most of the team. Khrushchev was particularly
strong on the Molotov side, seeing the GDR leader Walter Ulbricht as "a
bona fide Communist in a tough struggle for fulfilment of the old Bolshevik dream, that there would be a German proletarian state in the heart of
Europe," and fearing the West Germans as possible heirs to Hitler's Reich.
Molotov was so moved that he made an uncharacteristically personal
overture, proposing to Khrushchev that they switch to the intimate form

of address instead of the respectful, formal one that Khrushchev, as junior and younger colleague, had always used with him.[6]

In addition to feeling bullied by Beria, the team was frightened of him. As the man in charge of the secret police, he was presumed to have the dirt on every one of them in his files. It was Khrushchev—perhaps the team member least cowed by decades of intimidation by Stalin, by virtue of his long absence and comparative independence in Ukraine—who took the initiative. It was a very tricky matter, since if Beria got wind of any planned action against him, he had the resources to reverse the plot and arrest the plotters. The first person Khrushchev spoke to about the need to remove Beria from his posts was Molotov, who understood him immediately and indicated his full encouragement with the laconic question "Just remove him?," implying that harsher measures might be appropriate. Malenkov was a more doubtful quantity, as he and Beria were old allies. It turned out, however, that Malenkov had had enough of Beria's high-handedness, as he was frustrated in his efforts to keep up collegial unity in the Presidium by Beria's refusal to go along. He joined the plot, as did Kaganovich, who brought Voroshilov on board. Khrushchev was worried about Mikoyan, who was keeping up good relations with Beria, so didn't tell him in advance of his plans to arrest Beria, suggesting only that there might be a proposal to move him out of the MVD and put him in charge of oil production, to which Mikoyan agreed.

Beria was in Germany, supervising the suppression of a revolt in Berlin in early June 1953, while the plot was being hatched. Summoned back from Germany, he apparently had no suspicions about what was going on. Afterward, Khrushchev liked to tell the story of how he conned Beria the night before, "kidding around and making jokes," and complimenting him shamelessly about his leadership since Stalin's death. Flattered, Beria told him it was only the beginning, and laid out his plans for a luxurious lifestyle for the team, with townhouses and dachas that would be their own property, to be left to their heirs. This made two bad mistakes—strange for a man who was renowned for his cunning: the first was to trust Khrushchev and be taken in by his "simple peasant" facade, the second to think that Khrushchev could be won over through cupidity. As the GDR discussions should have told him, Khrushchev actually believed in socialism; he was outraged by the idea that a Soviet leader might want to acquire heritable private property. Nevertheless, being a better actor than

Beria, he shook his hand long and warmly, all the while thinking (as he would tell the story later), "All right, you bastard, I'm shaking your hand for the last time."[7]

Beria duly showed up, still unsuspecting, at the Presidium meeting the next day, 26 June. At first, he thought it was some kind of joke when the others turned on him; indeed, his reaction suggests that not only did he think Khrushchev and Malenkov were his friends, but also that, to the degree that friendship exists in politics, they probably had been. After Beria's disgrace, when he could be blamed for everything that was wrong with the Soviet Union, it was convenient for everyone to pretend they had hated him all along, but this has to be taken with many grains of salt. The most honest of them all was the realpolitiker Molotov, who had never pretended any great love for Beria, and may well have thought in June 1953 that Beria was too dangerous to be left alive and was an enemy of socialism to boot. Yet in his 1970s conversations with Chuev, he didn't claim to have disliked him.

When Beria understood what was going on, he seemed astonished, but put up no resistance to his arrest by Marshal Zhukov (brought back from the provinces after Stalin's death to be deputy minister of defense) and the military team that Khrushchev had organized, which had been waiting outside the meeting-room. He was then taken to a military prison, from whence he sent hopeful appeals to Malenkov, Khrushchev, Molotov, and Voroshilov, reminding them of shared battles and past camaraderie. "We were always good friends," he wrote to Khrushchev and Malenkov, using the familiar form of address. Interrogated for some months (without torture, abolished from MVD practice on his instructions a few months earlier), he spoke fairly freely but confessed no significant guilt. Many other people, both associates and victims, gave testimony as well, and the scenario that emerged, as in the Zhemchuzhina case back in 1949, came to focus on his sex life, with lurid allegations of multiple rapes, forcible abduction of young women from the street, and so on. Although this subsequently entered into Soviet folklore, the story of Beria as a sexual predator seems, though not wholly unfounded, to have been wildly exaggerated. His own account under interrogation of how he conducted his relations with the women he had affairs with, including a young one picked out on the street for him by a subordinate, is basically supported by that of a singer claiming to have been his mistress, after catching his eye during a performance, who described seduction (admittedly under intimidating circumstances) rather than rape.

In December, a closed military court, to which Beria's former colleagues were listening in on a specially installed link to the Kremlin, brought in its verdict: guilty of treason, anti-Soviet conspiracy, terrorism, and spying for a foreign power (working for the Muslim Musavat Party's counterintelligence in Baku during the Civil War, hence, by extension, for the British). It was clearly a verdict in the spirit of the old Stalinist trials rather than one dictated by the weight of the evidence, and the death sentence was carried out immediately. Most of the team had evidently come to see Beria's execution as "necessary"—that great catchall category of Marxist thinking—although Mikoyan, who had told Khrushchev that Beria could "still be useful," probably remained unconvinced. We may guess, however, at a degree of uneasiness in the team at reverting to Stalinist methods from the fate of Beria's wife and son, who were arrested, as was standard procedure in such cases, but subsequently released. Sergo Beria said it was the atomic scientists who, out of respect for his father, "practically saved my life . . . got me out of prison, then supported me morally and offered me material help." But the politicians must have had something to do with it too: Molotov evidently intervened on Sergo's and his mother's behalf, supported by Mikoyan, and Khrushchev is said to have been "touched" by their appeals, and his wife to have been "glad that [Nina Beria] and her son were allowed to live."

As far as public opinion was concerned, Beria's execution and subsequent damnation turned out to be a masterstroke. It wasn't that Beria's reputation in the country was wholly bad. They liked him down in the Caucasus, and he was also well regarded by prisoners, ex-prisoners, and their families—a not insignificant segment of public opinion—because of the amnesties and mass releases from Gulag. To be sure, another section of the public associated him with the release of the Jewish doctors and hated him as a crypto-Jew who was possibly responsible for Stalin's death, but for most Soviet citizens, he was not sharply differentiated initially from the rest of Stalin's associates. A more negative reaction to him set in after the propaganda machine started to publicize his alleged crimes, including sexual depravity ("Could he be hung?" one anonymous writer asked hopefully). The public relations coup, facilitated by the decision to destroy regional secret police archives from the Stalin period, was when

luded that once the head of the security police, evidently a
over, had been executed, it was a signal that the new leaders
repudiated Stalinist repression. An added bonus, from the team's
point of view, was that henceforth *all* past acts of repression—including
the Great Purges, in which he was essentially the cleanup man rather than
the executor—could be laid at Beria's door.[8]

"We were drunk with joy," Shepilov remembers of the period after the
removal of Beria, confident that "Leninist norms" could be reestablished
and "the marvelous building of socialist society" completed without the
shameful deformations imposed upon it by the Ezhovs and Berias. For
Shepilov and Khrushchev, along with the old gang of Molotov, Kaganovich, Voroshilov, and (with less dogmatism) Mikoyan, the marvelous society that was finally to come into being was by definition and essence socialist (Beria had been more open-minded about that, and the same was
probably true of Malenkov). Part of their euphoria, no doubt, was just relief at a threat lifted and a tricky maneuver brought off. Khrushchev
couldn't stop boasting of his brilliance in the Beria operation; he was a
changed man afterward, "more self-assured, more dynamic," and with a
new confidence that, having initiated the action, he had shown himself to
be the most energetic and decisive in the team. Before the Beria affair, he
had ranked fifth in the leadership, with very little name recognition outside Moscow and Ukraine; now he moved up into third place, after
Malenkov and Molotov, no doubt with aspirations to move higher.

A new freedom to travel was part of the team's liberation. For Khrushchev and Bulganin, the trip to the Geneva Summit in 1955 was exhilarating, despite the mockery in the European press of their identical "baggy
pale-mauve summer suits with flapping trousers." Malenkov's three-week
trip to England in the spring of 1956 was a similar personal milestone: the
first time he was "let out" abroad. Their children, of the generation falling
in love with Hemingway, were even more fascinated by the outside world.
Sergo Mikoyan, who managed to secure a place on a delegation to Ceylon,
and Rada Khrushcheva's husband Alexei Adzhubei, who went with six
other journalists on a trip to the United States in 1955, were the envy of
their contemporaries.

"We looked to the future with optimism," remembered Rada Khrushcheva, a journalist like her husband. "We believed that we could do everything, that in our country everything would turn out all right." It was the

beginning of a decade—later to be called the Thaw—when reform-minded journals would dedicate themselves to "truth-telling" about past and present, and poets like Evgeny Evtushenko could fill football stadiums for their readings. Sergo and Stepan Mikoyan undoubtedly knew Evtushenko's name in 1955, but it was still new to their father when he found his government limousine blocked by a crowd in central Moscow. Asking what was going on, he was told laconically, "Evtushenko." "When he inquired who that was, the answer was 'A poet.' Mikoyan later admitted: 'I saw people queuing up for poetry, not for food. I realized that a new era had begun.'"

Picasso was the subject of passionate debate at Petr Voroshilov's birthday party in July 1954, attended by the sons and daughters of Mikoyan, Kaganovich, and Shvernik, and Ekaterina Voroshilova's heart swelled with pride as she listened to them ("Many of them have PhDs!"). According to her diary, even the Picasso devotees still accepted the official tenets of socialist realism, but Stepan Mikoyan told a slightly different story. The Kremlin children, along with the rest of the intelligentsia, were becoming more political- and reform-minded, and as a result, some of them started disagreeing with their parents. Stepan remembered family visits to the Voroshilovs' dacha, where the Mikoyan sons, Petr Voroshilov, the Voroshilovs' adopted daughter, Tanya Frunze, and their respective spouses got into such passionate debates with their parents that Mikoyan asked Stepan "not to argue with him in the evening because 'I can't get to sleep.'" Mikoyan was one of the fathers who responded quickly to the changing times and his children's perception of them. Others, like Khrushchev, were slower off the mark. For all his public bonhomie, Khrushchev was a less-approachable father than a number of his colleagues, and when his youngest son Sergei—a belated convert to the anti-Lysenko orthodoxy of the reform-minded intelligentsia—tried to enlighten him about Lysenko and genetics, Khrushchev simply brushed him off. Nevertheless, it was Khrushchev whose son-in-law, Adzhubei, was to become one of the molders of Thaw opinion in his capacity as editor of the youth newspaper *Komsomol'skaia Pravda*, and later—appointed by Khrushchev—of the government newspaper *Izvestia*.[9]

As a sign of the times, the Kremlin was thrown open to the public in 1955, so Molotov, Voroshilov, and Mikoyan had to move out of their Kremlin apartments. The more junior Malenkovs, Khrushchevs, and Bulganins, who had never lived there, had apartments on Granovsky Street a few blocks away; they were joined in the spring of 1953 by Marshal Zhukov, back from his Urals banishment. Team socializing was one of the watchwords of these years, and Malenkov's plan was that the team should all move into villas to be built for them in Lenin Hills, near the new university wedding-cake building. The younger contingent did in fact move out there. Molotov and Voroshilov, however, declined and settled into apartments on Granovsky Street. The Molotovs were still socially aloof from the rest of the team, though Sergei Khrushchev, then a young adult, remembered a rare family visit to their apartment at which he was surprised to find Molotov, a legendary figure for him, to be "a small, bald old man" who was happy to show off his library.

The Malenkovs were family friends of the Khrushchevs at this period, as were the Mikoyans. Khrushchev did his best to establish similar relations with the Bulganins and Zhukovs, but in both cases the family relationship foundered because Nina Khrushcheva disapproved of Bulganin's and Zhukov's abandonment of their old wives, so Khrushchev took to meeting Zhukov on his own. The gregarious Khrushchev was the initiator of team socializing during vacations down in the Crimea, too, starting in 1953, when the Khrushchevs, Voroshilovs, and Kaganoviches made "quite a big and interesting company," though not without undercurrents, as Ekaterina Voroshilova noted in her diary. The Mikoyans often vacationed in the Crimea too, and they, as well as the Voroshilovs and others, were roped in for various social events at the Khrushchevs' in subsequent years, often involving the entertainment of East European Communists or friendly foreigners like Paul Robeson.

Andreev had not been readmitted to the working team after Stalin's death; he was the only team member still alive who was left out of both the government and the Presidium in March 1953. "Why was [he] not on the new [party] Presidium?" a concerned citizen from Penza inquired, and the answer is not wholly clear. Perhaps it was his deafness, but he may also have been perceived as too much of an old-style Stalinist by the new leadership. In 1955, the Voroshilovs, Kaganoviches, and Bulganins attended a celebration of Andreev's sixtieth birthday that, as Ekaterina Voroshilova noted in her diary, was "particularly touching because for reasons of health, and perhaps also for some other reasons, Andrei Andreevich had been obliged to cut down somewhat on his work activity." He did get a final honorary appearance when he was added, apparently as an afterthought, to the list of leading figures at the XX Party Congress the next year.[10]

Malenkov, perceived by many in the outside world as Stalin's potential successor, seems in fact to have been quite happy working within the collective framework. Khrushchev's son Sergei later formulated this as a negative: Malenkov had "never in his life led anything, he had always served under someone," deferring first to Stalin, then to Beria, and then to Khrushchev, not to mention his strong-minded wife, Valeria, at home. The man who, by contrast, instinctively felt that he had the leadership gene was Sergei's father, Khrushchev. Khrushchev was not pleased by Malenkov's growing popularity as one who had lifted the economic burden on the peasantry and pushed for more consumer goods for the towns. By the second year after Stalin's death, tensions between the two men were rising. Personal relations, formerly good, deteriorated because of the hectoring, condescending tone that Khrushchev now adopted in talking to Malenkov, to the embarrassment even of his own wife and son. The sniping between them, mainly initiated by Khrushchev, was not only felt in the Presidium but could be guessed by attentive newspaper readers, since Khrushchev had started to contradict Malenkov in public on issues like nuclear war (unthinkable, in Malenkov's opinion; survivable by socialists in Khrushchev's), though without mentioning his name. Molotov and Kaganovich—who disliked Malenkov, suspected him of lacking deep socialist commitments, and saw Khrushchev as the better socialist, however unpolished—abetted the conflicts, with a tendency to favor Khrushchev's side.

Malenkov was finally pressured into resigning the premiership in January 1955. His close relationship with Beria was cited against him, as was his "cheap" pursuit of popularity by promising more consumer goods. "I do not doubt the integrity of comrade Malenkov," Khrushchev told the Central Committee plenum, "but I doubt very much his abilities in pursuing the [party] line: he lacks character and backbone." What if he had to negotiate with a cunning capitalist like the British prime minister Winston Churchill (who had several times angled for an invitation to Moscow to meet the new premier)? Malenkov, with his amenable character, might just hand over the store. Molotov and Kaganovich agreed that Malenkov had turned out not to be up to the job. However, the fact that his replacement was Bulganin, who would surely have been even less of a match for the wily Churchill than Malenkov, suggests that this was not the real issue. Malenkov was not dropped from the Presidium, and his new job as minister of electric power stations was at least in Moscow (and in his old engineering specialty). Still, according to his son, this was one of the worst periods of his life.[11]

Khrushchev, like Beria before him, had taken the bit between his teeth and launched a whole series of initiatives at home and abroad. The year 1955 was notable for Khrushchev's emergence as a figure in the West, as he made highly publicized trips—to Belgrade, Geneva, and London, and then India, Burma, and Afghanistan—in which he took visible delight. The world press hailed this as a huge breakthrough in relations, as well as an indication of Khrushchev's new top-dog status, but at home, there was a subterranean muttering about gallivanting around the world spending the people's money. As Khrushchev moved into foreign policy, with the evident intent of establishing closer relations with the West, Molotov became increasingly critical, and their relations, never really close, frayed. For all his intelligence, Khrushchev reflected later, Molotov was so narrow-minded and dogmatic that you had to feel sorry for him. Khrushchev was pushing reconciliation with Yugoslavia's Josip Broz Tito, cast out of the socialist fold by Stalin and Molotov in the late 1940s; Molotov (and, it seems, a goodly segment of the public) was highly dubious: for him, Tito remained a renegade and a traitor. There were tensions about domestic policy, too. Molotov thought Khrushchev's ambitious and expensive Virgin Lands scheme, intended to turn Kazakhstan into a major grain-growing area, "absurd," or so he said later. As for Khrushchev's impulsive transfer of the Crimea from the Russian to the Ukrainian Republic early in 1954, it was a mistake, of course, Molotov muttered at the Presidium when it was discussed, but "evidently we have to accept it."

There were major clashes on foreign and domestic policy between Khrushchev and Molotov at the Central Committee plenum in July 1955, Khrushchev accusing Molotov of "aspiring to the role of grandee in the Presidium" and being stuck in a mind-set of the past in international relations. "Why don't you retire, we'll give you a good pension," Khrushchev burst out at one point. Personal relations definitively collapsed when Khrushchev turned his fire on Molotov's wife for meeting US ambassador

Charles Bohlen and his wife. There was nothing new about this, as Polina, alone of the wives, had socialized with ambassadors and their wives since the 1930s, when she entertained Ambassador Joseph Davies's wife for lunch at the Molotov dacha. But Khrushchev chose to take offense: "Here a minister's wife opens a private diplomatic shop and receives anyone who strikes her fancy. You're the minister of foreign affairs, but your wife isn't your deputy . . . I have to tell you, Vyacheslav Mikhailovich, that she does you a disservice, your wife." Although the rest of the members of the team were also critical of Molotov's lack of flexibility in foreign relations, Molotov survived this round and remained foreign minister for another year. He was finally forced out of the job in June 1956, although, like Malenkov, he remained a member of the Presidium. His new job, allocated only after some months of nonassignment, was the relatively insignificant post of minister of state control.[12]

Stalin's legacy was an issue that remained to be publicly addressed. Although Beria's 1953 amnesty had not covered political prisoners, they started to be released from Gulag on an individual basis in 1954. Victims—or, more often, wives and children of highly placed victims—were beginning to make their way back, petitioning individual team members to help their political rehabilitation and to get apartments in Moscow. Rykov's daughter Natalia, exiled after her father's arrest when she had just graduated from university, was one of them, returning to Moscow in 1956. Her mother had died in prison. Voroshilov and Molotov ignored her pleas for help, but Mikoyan got her a room in a communal apartment. When she ran into Molotov and Polina on the Metro a few years later, she greeted Polina but wouldn't give Molotov the time of day. Johnny (John-Reed) Svanidze, Svetlana Alliluyeva's cousin, was back too, now going by the plain Russian name Ivan or the Georgian Vano; Khrushchev helped to get him an apartment.

Mikoyan, always generous, was deluged with petitioners and helped many of them; from 1954 he headed the official Commission on Rehabilitation. But there was nobody on the team, however stonyhearted, who was exempt from contact with the victims and the painful and guilty memories they aroused. The daughter of Molotov's friend Arosev showed up in 1955, to be greeted warmly by Polina and coolly by Molotov (at supper, Polina reproached him for not doing more for the Arosevs, but then, when he quietly left the table, felt remorseful and told Olga Aroseva, "there was nothing he could do"). Jewish prisoners began to write to Kaganovich after Stalin's death, hoping to find a protector in him, and in one untypical instance, he took action. This was for Lev A. Sheinin, someone he had known way back in the prerevolutionary underground, who had been arrested in connection with the JAC affair. The MGB duly released a Lev Sheinin, but it turned out to be the more famous Lev R. Sheinin, chief investigator in the Moscow show trials of the 1930s and successful playwright, who had been arrested in connection with the Zhemchuzhina case. Then, when Kaganovich pointed out the mistake, "they released the right one."

The former exiles and prisoners brought back shocking stories of their experiences. Some came back as crusaders, with indictments of Stalinist repression that they wanted to make public. The two who had the most impact on the team were Olga Shatunovskaya and Alexei Snegov—both Old Bolsheviks with long-standing connections to a number of team members—who had been arrested in the Great Purges and released after almost twenty years in Gulag.

Snegov was still a prisoner at the time of Beria's arrest in 1953, but from camp he managed to get a letter denouncing Beria's crimes out to Mikoyan, who passed it on to Khrushchev. The result was that he was brought in to Moscow to testify at Beria's trial in December 1953 (Beria reportedly recognized him and called out, "Are you still alive?," to which Snegov, also using the familiar form of address, responded, "Lousy work on the part of your police"). Later, he briefly held a job in the MVD, appointed by Khrushchev (who consulted him extensively in preparing his 1956 indictment of Stalin) to keep the new MVD leaders honest. Mikoyan said that Snegov and Shatunovskaya "opened my eyes to many things, talking of their arrests and the tortures they were subject to, of the fate of dozens of common acquaintances and hundreds of people I didn't know . . . They played an enormous role in our 'enlightenment' in 1954–55."[13]

How much the team needed to be "enlightened," and how much they already knew, as Stalin's associates and coperpetrators, was a tricky question. If victims were to be rehabilitated, that is, declared innocent, at whose door was the blame for the victimization of innocent men to be laid? Stalin was the obvious target, and it was and remained to the team's advantage to stress his single responsibility and their own comparative

noninvolvement (this is a major reason for the widespread lack of understanding that the team actually mattered under Stalin). Beria, being dead,
could also be safely blamed for inciting Stalin to evil deeds. But people
like Snegov were not happy to see other accomplices go free. Charges of
responsibility for inciting him to evil deeds had been made in the Beria affair, and Khrushchev was starting to see political advantages in spreading
the blame. Questions about Malenkov's role were raised in the tussle that
led to his replacement as head of the government in 1955, and Molotov and
Kaganovich, as Stalin's chief henchmen in the 1930s, were also obvious
targets.

According to his son, Khrushchev had been thinking about the problem of confronting Stalin's crimes as far back as the summer of 1953, when
he asked new Soviet general prosecutor, Roman Rudenko, if the show trials of the 1930s were to be believed, and was told no. But there were great
risks in pursuing this. The team, collectively and individually, was com-
plicit in Stalinist repression. This applied even to Khrushchev, who would
later make his outsider status and innocence of goings-on a key point in
his autobiographical tapes, though he was less vulnerable than most of the
others. The rising tension concerning the issue within the team is indicated by the shouting match that erupted at the end of 1955 when Mikoyan
reported to the Presidium on Olga Shatunovskaya's charge that the Leningrad NKVD—hence, by implication, Stalin—was responsible for
Kirov's death. Even without any hard evidence to support it, the charge
was politically explosive. Voroshilov shouted out that it was a lie, and Molotov offered a calmer refutation, but Khrushchev said it smelled bad and
ought to be investigated. A commission of investigation into Stalinist repression was set up under Petr Pospelov, a Central Committee secretary
who had edited *Pravda* in the 1940s.

After a month's intensive work in the archives, Pospelov, though
known as a diehard Stalinist, produced a devastating seventy-page report
that laid the blame for unleashing the Great Purges and sanctioning torture during interrogations squarely at Stalin's door, but also made it clear
that other Politburo members besides Stalin had seen copies of interrogation protocols and knew about the torture. Between 1935 and 1940, the report said, almost two million people had been arrested for anti-Soviet activity, and 688,503 had been shot. Khrushchev "was appalled" when the
report came in, his son wrote. "He expected disclosures, but something

[*sic*] like this" "The facts were so horrifying," Mikoyan later recalled, "that in certain very difficult passages Pospelov's voice shook, and once he broke down and sobbed."

The revelations of the Pospelov report came "as a complete surprise to some of us," Khrushchev said in his memoirs. Now came the question, political rather than historical: Who was the *most* surprised, that is, the least guilty? In Khrushchev's analysis, Malenkov, having been in charge of personnel during the Great Purges, was in it up to his neck, though as an executant rather than as an initiator, while Molotov and Voroshilov were "the best informed about the true dimensions and causes of the Stalinist repressions." That was convenient, as Malenkov and Molotov were his two significant political opponents. But, to make sure Khrushchev himself stayed on track with the exposure of Stalin's crimes, there was a hint of blackmail in Snegov's warning that "either you tell them at the upcoming congress, or you'll find yourself under investigation." "Telling them"—the question of publicity—was the other big issue, made more acute by the imminence of the XX Party Congress, scheduled for February 1956. If terrible things were disclosed by Pospelov's research (as of course everyone knew they would be), how much should be told to the party, the country, and the world?[14]

The Presidium held a tense discussion of the Pospelov report on 9 February 1956. In Khrushchev's version, he alone was the rapporteur (the official protocol lists Mikoyan as well), arguing passionately that it was impossible to ignore the evils of the past and keep innocent people in the camps and exile. Voroshilov, in Khrushchev's version, furiously attacked him, supported by Kaganovich, who said that making the Pospelov report known to the congress would have a terrible effect on the party's and country's prestige. "You won't be able to keep what you say secret. Word will get out about what happened under Stalin, and then the finger will be pointed straight at us." Khrushchev, in a noble vein, responded that when crimes have been committed, people have to be prepared to take responsibility, and he personally was ready to do so—if necessary, by making the speech to the congress on his own behalf, in effect getting himself off the hook but leaving the others dangling. After that, everyone reluctantly agreed that a speech should be made to the congress, and Khrushchev allowed himself to be drafted (though with a show of unwillingness) to be the speaker.

The official protocol glosses over objections to telling the congress, for which all present eventually voted, but indicates that team members had different ideas about the story that ought to be told. Molotov wanted Stalin's achievements to be included, as well as his crimes. Mikoyan thought the narrative should be that "up to 1934 [Stalin] behaved like a hero, after 1934 he did terrible things," but wondered "whether one could forgive him agriculture" (that is, the excesses of collectivization). Malenkov was against the 1934 break (which would have put his entire work with Stalin in the "bad" period) and recommended focusing on the cult of personality, which would allow them "really to reinstate Lenin." It was the cult of personality—glossed as "the concentration of power in one man's hands. In unclean hands"—that won out.

Mikoyan later felt aggrieved, not without reason, at Khrushchev's appropriating all the credit for the decision to come clean. In fact, Mikoyan was the first to touch on sensitive issues at the congress with his acknowledgment that "after a long break, collective leadership has been created in our party." But it was Khrushchev's speech on the final day of the congress that stunned the delegates and the world. Freely based on Pospelov's report, almost sixty pages long in its English translation, delivered in Khrushchev's inimitable folksy way on behalf of the whole Presidium, it was a bombshell. In Khrushchev's version, the Presidium had just become aware, through the researches of the Pospelov Commission, that terrible abuses had been committed, with Stalin acting in the name of the Central Committee but in fact not consulting it or the Politburo. There was shock in the hall when he announced that 70 percent of the Central Committee members and candidates elected at the party congress in 1934 had been arrested and shot by the time the next congress met five years later. He singled out the five Politburo victims—Rudzutak, Eikhe, Postyshev, Kosior, and Chubar—for particular notice, along with the military leaders, and spoke of the Leningrad Affair and failures in Stalin's wartime leadership. Even more alarming was his reference to the lack of clarity concerning Kirov's murder and the need for further investigation. By the end of the Stalin era, Khrushchev said, the lives of the whole team were at stake: indeed, "had Stalin remained at the helm for another several months, Comrades Molotov and Mikoyan would probably have not delivered any speeches at this congress." The audience took that in stunned silence.[15]

It has gone down in history as "the Secret Speech," and indeed, it was not reported in the Soviet press, this being the compromise between Khrushchev and the more conservative members of the team. But even leaving aside the fact that the CIA got hold of the text and gave it world-wide distribution, it was scarcely a secret, even in the Soviet Union, since it was read out to meetings throughout the country in subsequent weeks. The popular response was strong but contradictory. A minority, in which students and intelligentsia were particularly well represented, was appalled by the revelations but welcomed Khrushchev's initiative in breaking the taboos of the past. Many more (at least of those who publicly expressed an opinion) were outraged or confused, particularly by the criticism of Stalin's war leadership. Party loyalists wrote indignantly to Molotov, reproaching him for allowing Khrushchev and Mikoyan to slander Stalin: "Khrushchev and his friends will destroy the cause of communism ... It is necessary as soon as possible that Khrushchev and his friends resign. Leaders should be those who worked with Lenin and Stalin [underlined in red]. We await your taking the leadership of the party into your hands, comrade Molotov." In Georgia, dethronement of a native son caused outrage. Tanks had to be called in to disperse angry crowds, and demonstrators on the streets of Tbilisi carried placards calling for Molotov to take over the country's leadership.

Georgia was an isolated case; in general, the Soviet population did not react to Khrushchev's speech by going into the streets. It was different in the Soviet bloc countries of Eastern Europe, where the legitimacy of Soviet-backed regimes was shaky. Khrushchev's de-Stalinization was particularly destabilizing in Poland and Hungary. In Poland, leader Bolesław Bierut, in hospital in Moscow with pneumonia, read Khrushchev's speech, had a heart attack, and died, leaving a succession crisis that was not resolved for months. In Hungary, a long rivalry between Mátyás Rákosi and Imre Nagy had culminated in the ouster of Nagy, the less hard-line, but the situation remained unstable. News of Khrushchev's Secret Speech opened rifts among Communists and emboldened those who disliked the pro-Soviet regimes in their countries. The Soviet leaders watched uneasily for several months as the situation deteriorated. The Polish situation was the first to reach crisis point from the team's point of view, when the Polish party decided on Władysław Gomułka, Bierut's longtime opponent—only recently released from prison—as his succes-

sor and at the same time proposed to drop Marshal Konstantin Rokossovsky (a Soviet appointee, though a Pole by birth) as defense minister.
"Anti-Soviet . . . forces are seizing power," the Soviet ambassador in Warsaw reported in alarm.

So worried were the Soviet leaders, and so unsure of how to handle the
crisis, that virtually the whole team—Khrushchev, Bulganin, Molotov,
Mikoyan, and Kaganovich, along with Marshals Zhukov and Konev
(Warsaw Pact commander)—flew together, without invitation, to Warsaw. It had only been a year since restrictions on travel by Presidium
members had been lifted, and the trip was certainly a demonstration that
Soviet leadership remained collective; lucky their plane didn't go down,
since that would have left Malenkov and Voroshilov as the team's only
survivors. By decision of the Presidium, Soviet troops had already started
to move toward Warsaw, but at the last minute, the crisis was averted
when Khrushchev was persuaded by Gomułka (who from that day he
considered a friend) to give the order to stop them. This he did on his own
authority, causing Molotov and Kaganovich, who were very suspicious of
Gomułka, to criticize him for exceeding his authority and violating
collective-leadership norms.[16]

Hungary went into free fall the next week, with police overwhelmed
by rebels in Budapest and the West making gestures of warm encouragement. On 23 October, Zhukov reported to the Presidium that there was a
demonstration of a hundred thousand in Budapest and the radio station
was on fire. "With Nagy left on his own, Hungary is coming apart," Molotov said. Except for Mikoyan, the whole team plus Marshal Zhukov
agreed that this time Soviet troops must be sent, but Mikoyan would not
back down, even in a minority of one. With the Hungarian government in
meltdown, Soviet troops and tanks entered Budapest on 24 October, evidently with the hope that their mere presence would stabilize the situation, for Mikoyan and Central Committee secretary Mikhail Suslov were
simultaneously sent to negotiate. The next week was one of collective vac-
illation in the team: "I don't know how many times we changed our minds
back and forth," Khrushchev later said. Mikoyan never wavered in his position of objection to the use of Soviet troops, and at one point, the whole
group, including Molotov and Kaganovich, decided the troops should be
pulled out, evidently out of uneasiness at imposing Soviet power so bra-
zenly in the face of popular hostility in Eastern Europe. But then news

came from Mikoyan and Suslov in Budapest that Nagy was talking about the need to take Hungary out of the Warsaw Pact, and opinion swung round again. Voroshilov, an old friend of ousted Hungarian leader Rákosi (Nagy's predecessor), was furious with Mikoyan for opposing the use of force: the American Secret Service was doing a better job in Budapest than he was, he raged. Khrushchev, Bulganin, Malenkov, and even Kaganovich objected to his noncollegial comments, but their attitudes on the use of force were hardening.

On 28 October, Kaganovich used the term "counterrevolution" in the Presidium for the first time. Khrushchev echoed this in his memoirs, claiming in a throwback to his Bolshevik past that the Hungarian working class refused to support the counterrevolution, but his language at the time was more pragmatic. What he was afraid of, along with the rest of the team, was that the Nagy government would fall, leading to a bloodbath that ended with Hungary moving into the Western sphere, and that the contagion would spread throughout the Soviet bloc. The decision for decisive military action was made on 31 October, with Mikoyan still in a dissenting minority of one, and so angry that he thought of resigning from the Presidium. (He never spoke in public about his dissent, and it remained unknown until the 1970s, when Khrushchev's memoirs were published in the West.) Once Soviet troops and tanks were given the green light, it took them less than a week to crush the Hungarian Revolution, at a cost of thousands of Hungarian lives and hundreds of Soviet ones. Two hundred thousand Hungarians, known in the West as "freedom fighters," fled over the border, and "Hungary 1956" became a milestone in the Cold War that the team had been trying to de-escalate.

The team had kept up a reasonable approximation of team spirit during the crisis but emerged from it with tempers frayed. Molotov and Khrushchev were going hammer and tongs about Hungary in the Presidium in November, Khrushchev and his supporters calling Molotov a dogmatic Stalinist whose ideas were "pernicious" and accusing Kaganovich of "toadying" to him; the two of them of were "screeching and face-slapping," which provoked the usually phlegmatic Molotov to tell Khrushchev that he "should keep quiet and stop being so overbearing." Khrushchev was badly rattled by Hungary, since Soviet intervention there conveyed a completely contradictory message to the reform promises of the XX Party Congress, and moreover stimulated worker unrest and intelligentsia alienation within the Soviet Union. But instead of making him more cautious and conciliatory with his colleagues, it seemed to have the opposite effect. Increasingly recognized abroad as the real leader of the Soviet Union, he started thinking of himself as the new boss, granting interviews to the foreign media and sounding off on foreign policy without clearing what he said in advance with the team. He pushed ahead with a radical bureaucratic reform that his colleagues distrusted, and made extravagant promises about catching up with the United States in consumer goods, which his colleagues and economic advisors thought were unrealistic. Relations with China were deteriorating, and the Virgin Lands scheme, which had started so well, seemed headed for disaster. In Kaganovich's view, "the last remnants of Khrushchev's former humility disappeared" after the XX Party Congress.[17]

Increasingly, the team felt Khrushchev had become a loose cannon. The list of his impulsive, uncensored outbursts lengthened. In May 1957, in an attempt to mend fences with the intelligentsia, Khrushchev had the idea of inviting about three hundred luminaries from the Moscow literary and artistic world, Communists and non-Communists, along with the team, to a lavish picnic at Stalin's old dacha at Semenovskoe, a hundred kilometers (about 62 miles) outside Moscow. It turned into a disaster, with Khrushchev ranting at the writers and breaking all the rules by telling them about his disagreements with Molotov in the Presidium. The final straw was a sharp altercation with two elderly women writers whom he threatened to "grind to dust" (one of them had "thrust the horn of her hearing aid under his nose[,] shouting, as all deaf people do, 'Tell me, why is there no butter in Armenia?'"). A thunderstorm interrupted the festivities, heavy rain almost bringing down the tent, but Khrushchev raged on. "Not for nothing do they say 'What the sober man has on his mind is on the drunk's lips,'" was Kaganovich's acid comment.

After this, Mikoyan remembered, tension in the Presidium "became simply unbearable"; even he, a Khrushchev supporter in the main, was critical of his behavior at the picnic. Molotov and Kaganovich were outraged at Khrushchev talking about their disagreements in front of non-party people, and the next day Molotov, Kaganovich, Bulganin, and Malenkov met in Bulganin's office to discuss how to rein in, perhaps even get rid of, Khrushchev. It's unbearable, Voroshilov told former Khrushchev protégé Shepilov in mid-June, that Khrushchev "insults everyone, puts everyone down, doesn't take any account of anyone." On 16 June, the team congregated at the Khrushchevs for the wedding of their son Sergei, but the atmosphere was strained. The usually mild Bulganin exploded with anger when Khrushchev jokingly interrupted his toast. The Malenkovs came late, looking gloomy; and "as soon as supper had finished," Molotov, Malenkov, Kaganovich, and Bulganin demonstratively left the wedding and went off to Malenkov's dacha next door. At a Presidium meeting on 18 June, Molotov and others heaped reproaches on Khrushchev, Molotov canceling out the last three years of friendship by switching back to the formal mode of address. It ended in a shouting match.[18]

What happened next has variously been described as a conspiracy and a preemptive strike. It was the anti-Khrushchev group—Malenkov, Voroshilov, Kaganovich, Molotov, and Bulganin, with Molotov as the dominant member—that took the initiative; Malenkov was later quoted as saying that Khrushchev would get them if they didn't get him first. Initially, they had a majority in the Presidium. Khrushchev had to listen to a litany of complaints about errors of judgment, erratic behavior, and failure to consult as collective leadership demanded, and his first reaction was apologetic. The question of removing Khrushchev from his position as first secretary of the party was mooted, and there was a definite sentiment in favor of dismissing Khrushchev's security chief, Ivan Serov, whom the team saw as working for him personally, not for them (Bulganin and others complained that he was tapping their phones). But it was unclear exactly what the aims of the anti-Khrushchev group were. Perhaps, as Dmitry Shepilov, a member of the Central Committee, later wrote, it was more "a kind of explosion" of collective discontent than a well-formulated political action.

While the majority of the old team was on the anti-Khrushchev side, and Khrushchev's fate "hung by a hair," in Mikoyan's judgment, the balance of forces in the broader party leadership was less clear. Khrushchev had the support of Central Committee secretaries and candidate members of the Presidium who had not been at the first meeting, and the presumption was that a majority of the full Central Committee—consisting in large part of regional party secretaries appointed by Khrushchev—would support him. Equally important was that Mikoyan was on Khrushchev's side, while recognizing his defects, because he thought that a victory for the Molotovites would mean an end to de-Stalinization. It was

Mikoyan who saved him. His clever delaying tactics gave Khrushchev time to rally and launch his counterattack, a brilliant improvisation that, like his coup against Beria in 1953, broke all the rules.

Once again Marshal Zhukov was a key player (though he had wavered early on, critical like everyone else of some of Khrushchev's excesses), as was the loyal Serov, who knew the critics were out for his blood. Khrushchev regretted having to turn to the police and military for help against his colleagues, his son Sergei later reported, but what could he do? They were plotting against him. Khrushchev's response was to get supporters in the Central Committee to request an urgent plenary meeting of the Central Committee to resolve the disputes in the Presidium. Then he had the KGB and the military provide planes for an emergency airlift to bring Central Committee members to Moscow from whatever distant parts of the country they found themselves in. The Central Asian party leader Nuriddin Mukhitdinov was inspecting sheep in the Fergana Valley when he was summoned. In they flew, and by 22 June, when the Central Committee plenum convened, the Khrushchev critics—for whom a new and sinister name, the "Anti-Party Group," had been coined—were on the retreat.[19]

The Central Committee meeting that followed was a spectacular slanging match that lasted for eight days. Khrushchev seized control of the agenda and, in a brilliant move, turned it from a fest of criticism of his mistakes to an excited and often vicious discussion of responsibility for Stalin-period crimes, in which he pointed the finger at Molotov, Malenkov, and Kaganovich. On the Leningrad Affair, Khrushchev attacked Malenkov savagely: "Your hands are covered with blood, Malenkov; your conscience isn't clean; you're a vile person." Molotov and Kaganovich came under heavy fire, accused of special responsibility for the terror because they had been Stalin's closest associates. Zhukov said Molotov had turned into a party "lord"; another Khrushchev supporter objected to his air of superiority, reading moral lessons to everyone, as if he alone had access to truth ("the kind of role you find, for example, in Korneichuk's plays," he added unexpectedly, showing that reverence for the literary word had not disappeared with Stalin). Khrushchev said Molotov's disastrous foreign policy had united the capitalist world against them.

Voroshilov—who, like Molotov and the others, was driven wild by the "Anti-Party" label—was the only one of the team critics to get off rela-

tively lightly. He hadn't seen any harm in comradely criticism of Khrushchev, he said apologetically; he had known Molotov and Kaganovich for a
long time, and didn't think such clever people could possibly be plotting
against the party—they must have been seized by some kind of temporary madness. His feeble jokes won laughter, and Zhukov and others in
the Khrushchev camp made friendly gestures and described him as (unlike the others) a man of principle. It wasn't that Khrushchev had any particular personal affection for the old man. "What is important is Voroshilov's name; it carries weight, so he had to be dragged out of it," he
explained later. Bulganin backed off quickly under relentless criticism at
the plenum, and his hide, along with Voroshilov's, was saved, at least to
the extent that, although subsequently sidelined, they were spared public
humiliation and kept their Presidium membership. There was, of course, a
good political reason for this: if Voroshilov and Bulganin (together with
their junior Presidium colleagues Pervukhin and Saburov) had been labeled as members of the Anti-Party Group, it would have been obvious
that Khrushchev had in fact had a majority of full Presidium members
against him.

In the end, Kaganovich and Malenkov unwillingly admitted to being
part of a "plot," Kaganovich asking for forgiveness, while Malenkov continued to assert the right to criticism. Molotov, projecting "toughness
and aplomb" in the face of heavy attack, was the most defiant, repeating
his criticism of Khrushchev's violation of collective leadership in his
final statement, while conceding that his earlier criticism had been in-
temperate. He was an "honest communist," he asserted, whose actions
could possibly be considered *gruppovshchina*—a shade better than factionalism—but certainly not a plot. He was the only one of the alleged
conspirators to abstain from voting for the resolution that condemned
them. The defeat of the Anti-Party Group, consisting for public consumption of Malenkov, Kaganovich, and Molotov, along with *Pravda* editor Dmitry Shepilov, was reported in the Soviet press early in July. The
announcement stated that the group had used factional methods and opposed the party line on important issues and were to be dropped from
the Central Committee and Presidium. In the edited public version, the
issue of guilt for repression, which had been central to the actual discussion, was not even mentioned.[20]

Signs of fighting at the top always produced disapproving comments at the grassroots level, and, in addition, Khrushchev was not particularly popular in the country. The intelligentsia found him crude; there was widespread popular resentment at his well-reported foreign trips and receptions for foreign visitors ("organizing banquets on the people's money"), and some even worried that he was striving for a dictatorship. So there was little in the way of enthusiastic endorsement of the ouster of the Anti-Party Group. A rare accolade came from an anonymous writer to *Pravda*, who hailed it as a long overdue comeuppance for Jew-lovers (it must have given some satisfaction to Shepilov, in one of his last actions as editor, to forward this to Presidium members with a note drawing attention to the regrettably anti-Semitic tone). But in general, the kind of people who wrote letters to *Pravda* and the Central Committee—usually solid citizens remaining with the conventions of Soviet discourse—were uneasy at this summary dismissal of Old Bolsheviks with many services to their country, and moreover saw it as a retreat from the move toward greater political openness and democracy since Stalin's death. "Why aren't Molotov, Kaganovich, and Malenkov given the chance to express their opinions in the press?," some correspondents asked. Others criticized the rituals of unanimous condemnation in the party: "Today they drove out Molotov—we approve. Tomorrow they will drive out Khrushchev—and will we also approve?" In one citizen's opinion, the Central Committee voted unanimously against Molotov because its members have been bought off: "they get [salaries of] 20–30,000 rubles, and I have lived forty-three years and been hungry for forty of them."

In the subterranean world of popular opinion, expressed illegally in leaflets and graffiti, reaction was particularly negative and often linked with a sharpening resentment of elite privileges, which reflected the disappointment that the promised economic improvement seemed to have stalled. Now that they had joined the fellowship of victims, the disgraced leaders—not necessarily popular in themselves—had acquired an aura of martyrdom among the disaffected. "Molotov and Malenkov are old Party men; they have done a lot for the people; now they have been crushed like bugs." "Malenkov wanted to let people have a decent life." "It looks as though Molotov and others were dismissed because they cared for the people." Even Kaganovich, usually as a Jew the butt of hostile popular comments, was now an object of sympathy.

It was not yet clear, either to the public or to the party elite, how definitive this political victory was. After all, the losers kept their party membership and government jobs (as Malenkov had done in 1955) and might yet live to fight another day. In retrospect, however, it looks like the end of an era. It was a radically new Presidium that met on 8 July 1957, with only four out of the eleven from the previous (pre-plenum) meeting surviving, swamped by seven new faces of Khrushchev supporters, Leonid Brezhnev among them. Of the old team, only Khrushchev and Mikoyan remained key players, although the tarnished Bulganin and Voroshilov were still members. But it was Khrushchev's time now, perhaps still residually a collective leadership but no longer a collective leadership of the team. The team had outlived Stalin by more than four years and accomplished a successful transition that few would have dared to hope for in the awful winter of 1952–53. But now, after an astonishing run of almost thirty years, its day was done.[21]

TEN

END OF THE ROAD

Khrushchev "was extraordinarily proud" of the fact that in 1957, "for the first time in Russian history," a political coup was not followed by repression of the defeated. It was indeed a fortunate precedent from his point of view. Seven years later, he too would be toppled—bloodlessly, and this time fully legally—to be succeeded by a new self-consciously collective leadership headed by Leonid Brezhnev and Alexei Kosygin. Khrushchev was not quite the last of the team to leave the political stage. That honor went to Anastas Mikoyan, the great survivor of Soviet politics. Persuaded by Khrushchev to take on the challenge of trying to turn the Supreme Soviet into something more democratic, like a European parliament, he chaired that body until the end of 1965, more than a year after Khrushchev's ouster in October 1964, retiring with the appropriate honors at the age of seventy. When he left the Presidium a few months later, it was after almost forty years of continuous tenure.

The fate of the Anti-Party Group after their political defeat and expulsion from the Presidium was at first rather mild. All three lost their Presidium and Central Committee membership, and the city of Molotov in the Urals reverted to its old name of Perm. But they kept their party membership and all were given jobs, although Molotov and Kaganovich, aged sixty-seven and sixty-five, respectively, might well have been simply retired. Admittedly, the jobs were not stellar, and all were out of Moscow. Molotov got the ambassadorship to Mongolia, and buckled down to the job with his usual conscientiousness; he was liked by the embassy staff and feted by the Mongolians, who were proud to have such a famous man among them. He did too well, in short, so after some months in Ulan Bator, various humiliations were arranged to remind the locals that he was a man in semidisgrace. He was then (1960) shipped off to Vienna as Soviet cochairman on the Atomic Energy Commission, where he again worked hard and earned the respect of his staff.

Kaganovich was sent off to the Urals to head a chemical factory in the industrial town of Azbest, where he did badly, bullying subordinates. Whenever there was an accident at the plant, Kaganovich, in true Stalinist style, started a hunt for wreckers. Malenkov, in his early fifties, got a similar posting in Kazakhstan, heading a hydroelectric plant (he had originally trained as an electrical engineer). Like Molotov, he worked hard and did well, establishing himself as a "liberal" director, making friends, and settling so fully into local life that he was elected as a delegate to the regional party conference. This very much annoyed Khrushchev and earned Malenkov an official rebuke for "seeking cheap popularity." He was then moved from Ust-Kamenogorsk to Ekibastuz, as a director of another smaller power plant, where for ten years he and his wife had a lonely time, under blatant KGB supervision and afraid that if they made friends, they would get them into trouble.

Bulganin, though not officially disgraced, was nevertheless on his way out, being replaced as chair of the Council of Ministers by Khrushchev (who thus became top man in the government as well as the party) in March 1958 and dropped from the Presidium six months later. He retired in 1960, just before his sixty-fifth birthday. Voroshilov, at almost eighty, retired from the Presidium and the chairmanship of the Supreme Soviet in the same year. For Bulganin, who was linked unfavorably in the public mind with Khrushchev's junketing and foreign travel, there were few regrets. Voroshilov, as a legendary military man and the leader people liked to imagine as their uncle or grandfather, kept a place in the popular imagination.[1]

While Khrushchev had originally intended to treat his former colleagues with respect, it didn't work out that way. In a second wave of de-Stalinization in 1961, when the decision was taken to remove Stalin's body from the Lenin Mausoleum, the Anti-Party Group came under renewed attack, Voroshilov along with them. "Certain stars, which are very far removed from earth, seem to shine on although they have been extinct for a long time," Khrushchev said snidely, accusing them of trying to put a lid on exposure of Stalin's crimes in order to conceal their own guilt. The outcome was that all three members of the Anti-Party Group (but not Voroshilov) were expelled from the party, about which they were understandably bitter. As Kaganovich complained, since 1957 they had "honestly and zealously toiled in the positions offered to them, as communists should," and no new criticisms had been offered. It was a shabby end to a lifetime in the party—but then again, they weren't the first whose careers ended like that.

With the end of his Vienna posting, Molotov and Polina were allowed to return to the old Granovsky Street apartment in Moscow, and were also given use of a dacha. People didn't usually recognize Molotov on the street, but he was occasionally sighted in the First Hall of the Lenin Library (reserved for members of the Soviet Academy of Sciences, professors, and foreign scholars), working away on his memoirs, according to rumor, though it turned out to be a treatise on socialist economics. For the other two, banishment from Moscow lasted longer—until 1965 in Kaganovich's case and 1968 in Malenkov's. According to urban legend, Kaganovich was sometimes recognized and abused on the street after his return (nobody ever forgot that he was the Jew on the Stalin team), and occasionally got into fights with people who called him a murderer. He lived in straitened circumstances, as did the Malenkovs, who for some time had to share their daughter's apartment, until Valeria's successor as director of the Power Institute took pity and got them a two-bedroom one of their own. Nobody recognized Malenkov on the street, perhaps because he had lost so much weight.

By the time all three members of the Anti-Party Group were back in Moscow, Khrushchev had joined them in unwilling retirement. After 1957, by all accounts, Khrushchev became even more bumptious, impetuous, and prone to unilateral action. Hampered by a lagging economy and tarnished by a series of policy setbacks, the most notorious being the Cuban Missile Crisis, he was ousted in October 1964 by a unanimous vote of the Central Committee after his fellow Presidium members took advantage of his absence on holiday in the Crimea to plot his removal. Their complaints against him were essentially the same as those raised in 1957—rudeness, impatience with colleagues, nonconsultation—but this time it was not the Old Guard against him, with all their Stalinist baggage, but a new one, headed by his former protégé, an active supporter in the fight with the Anti-Party Group in 1957: Leonid Brezhnev. The only person on the Presidium who spoke up for him was Mikoyan, who—as he had done for Beria in 1953—argued that for all his faults, he could still be useful in a reduced position, but his suggestion was angrily rejected by the others. Khrushchev didn't put up a fight, agreeing to resign his positions and go into retirement. The notices in the press linked his retirement with "his advanced age and state of health," but nevertheless printed his colleagues' criticisms about violating "the Leninist principle of collective leadership," so that it was clear he had been pushed out. He was allowed to stay in Moscow and keep his apartment and dacha, and given a reasonable pension.[2]

Sharing a common fate of nonhonorable retirement did not bring the old team members back together. On the contrary, the antagonisms and bitterness between them after 1964 exceeded even the worst periods of the past. There were too many resentments, too many betrayals. Malenkov, Molotov, and Kaganovich could never forgive Khrushchev for what he had said about them in 1957, and saw his own disgrace in 1964 as well deserved. For Molotov, Khrushchev was now a Rightist; for Kaganovich, a Trotskyist. Even Mikoyan, naturally inclined to maintain relations with all and sundry, and an ally of Khrushchev's up to the end, kept his distance after being rebuked by Brezhnev and the KGB for telephoning the disgraced Khrushchev with New Year's greetings. As for the Anti-Party Group, who had never been close friends or even a real political faction, they kept aloof from each other. Malenkov appears to have had no contact with either of the others after 1957. Kaganovich occasionally telephoned Molotov in the 1970s, even claiming to Chuev that they were friends. But Molotov did not reciprocate and kept him at arm's length.

The arguments about responsibility for the crimes of the Stalin period continued through retirement up to the team members' deaths and even beyond, through the medium of surviving family members, supporters, and advocates. The politicians themselves, with the exception of Malenkov, either took up the pen or gave extensive interviews in self-justification. In Khrushchev's case, it was the tape recorder, on which after his disgrace in 1964 he dictated memoirs that were smuggled out to the West by younger family members and published in many languages in the 1970s. Kaganovich tried his hand at a memoir in the 1990s (*Notes of a Worker, Communist-Bolshevik, Trade-Union, Party and Soviet-State Functionary* was its wonderfully leaden title). Mikoyan's memoirs were published posthumously around the same time, edited by his son Sergo. The Stalinist/Russian nationalist writer Felix Chuev published two thick volumes of interviews with Molotov and Kaganovich conducted in the 1970s and 1980s.

As they looked back at the past, what could they still be proud of? There was general agreement that in fighting the factions in the 1920s, the team had been on the right path, paving the way for the industrialization drive, which made the Soviet Union modern, and victory in the Second World War, which made the Soviet Union a great nation. When it came to collectivization, there was less certainty, not just because of the famine but also because of the poor performance thereafter of Soviet agriculture, which the team had agreed needed reform in first order after Stalin died. Still, the consensus was that the basic principle of collectivization was good, an important step forward toward socialism, although there had been "excesses," for which both overenthusiastic local officials and Stalin were to blame. Molotov and Kaganovich, who had been deeply involved with Stalin in the direction of such "excesses," were much less inclined to emphasize them than Khrushchev and Mikoyan.

Soviet achievements had been gained through struggle, and in struggle, the team assumed, there are bound to be casualties. The question raised by the 1956 de-Stalinization, which remained contested for decades, was which casualties were unjustified to the point that rehabilitation was called for? In his Secret Speech, Khrushchev had put Politburo and Central Committee members and top military leaders—purged in 1937–38—and victims of the postwar Leningrad Affair in this category, and the rehabilitation commissions of the second half of the 1950s broadened this to include most Communist officials and other elite members who were arrested as "enemies of the people" during the Great Purges.

But what about the various Oppositions? The demonized Trotsky was quite out of the question, nor was there strong pressure for rehabilitation of others from the old Left Opposition, but the Right was a different matter. Mikoyan and even Molotov remembered Bukharin with some personal affection, as probably did Voroshilov, though mixed with guilt. Khrushchev, on the other hand, hadn't really known Bukharin and had launched his political career in the fight against the Right. The question of rehabilitating Bukharin and Rykov was raised at a Presidium meeting in 1957, and Mikoyan supported it. Khrushchev, while agreeing that the show trials were "rubbish, all made up," thought he had had enough on his plate dealing with Stalin, and Bukharin would have to wait. Later, after his fall, he regretted this. After he was gone, the new Brezhnev-Kosygin leadership came under renewed pressure, including from economic reformers who were advocating return to a partial market system on the lines of the Soviet NEP in the 1920s, but they too held the line. It was not until November 1987, under Gorbachev, that Bukharin was officially rehabilitated, along with other victims of the Moscow show trials, including Zinoviev and Kamenev (but not Yagoda or Trotsky) following the next year.[3]

Retrospective appraisal of Stalin and the Great Purges was the great issue for all the team members and a bone of contention between them. The team was pulled several ways on this, and all undoubtedly were internally conflicted. On the one hand, their lifetime achievements were also Stalin's; if all Stalin's achievements were discounted, they had nothing to claim except (in Khrushchev's and Mikoyan's case) recognition of their role in condemning him in 1956. On the other hand, since the question of responsibility for the Great Purges was inescapable, it was in every team member's interest to pile as much as possible on Stalin, either alone or as incited by Beria. The aim of all but the staunch Molotov was to suggest that other team members were more culpable than themselves. Yet, on the still more painful question of responsibility for failure to prevent the death of friends, even Molotov may sometimes have wavered. When Olga Aroseva, daughter of the friend he didn't save, visited the Molotovs in the mid-1950s, he was still doggedly resisting any notion of guilt. But when she saw him again a few years later, after his fall from power, she found him quite different, penitent and regretful: "the daughter of Sasha Arosev may not want to shake my hand . . . I am guilty before Sasha."

Molotov never ceased to insist in later life that, while Stalin had done some things wrong, he was basically a great and irreplaceable leader, responsible for industrialization, keeping the party together, winning the Second World War, and making the Soviet Union a great power. "Not one man after Lenin, not only I but not Kalinin, Dzerzhinsky or others, did even a tenth of what Stalin did. . . . As a political figure he played a role that nobody could take on their shoulders." He had not done it alone—he needed the team, and Molotov in particular had been an important support. The Soviet Union had real enemies, at home and abroad, and its leaders had to be tough. Even the Great Purges were basically justified in Molotov's account, and he admitted personal responsibility, while pointing out that it was shared by all the other members of the team. By all accounts, both Molotov and his wife remained loyal Stalinists. Polina—who, unlike her husband, had not lost her party membership in 1961—was "full of energy and militant spirit" and regularly attended meetings of her primary party organization in a candy factory. When Svetlana Alliluyeva visited the Molotovs in the 1960s, Polina told her, "Your father was a genius. He destroyed the fifth column in our country, and when the war began, the party and people were united." Molotov was quieter, but nodded assent to Polina's statements. The Molotovs' daughter and her husband were embarrassed, "looking down at their plates," and to Svetlana Alliluyeva, now mixing with quasi-dissident intellectuals like the writer Andrei Sinyavsky, they seemed like "dinosaurs."

Kaganovich took a similar stand, though a bit more defensively. Accusations about his failure to save his brother Mikhail always upset him, and he emphasized more than Molotov how Stalin manipulated his associates to make them accomplices in the death of their colleagues. Voroshilov was uneasy about Khrushchev's de-Stalinization initiative and wrote of Stalin in 1968 that for all his mistakes, "I cannot speak of him without respect." When speaking privately to Vasily Stalin in 1960, he qualified his endorsement of "the good that your father did" with the comment that "in the last years your father got very strange, he was surrounded by scoundrels like Beria . . . It is all the bad influence of Beria."

Even the team's strongest de-Stalinizers, Khrushchev and Mikoyan, were not without ambivalence about Stalin. He wasn't overall an "enemy of the party and the working class," Khrushchev told Polish Communists in 1956, "and that's where the tragedy is, comrades." He wanted to "serve society," and it was in that context that his crimes were committed. Clearly, he developed a "persecution mania." "But, comrades, Stalin—I wish I could describe the warm side, his concern for people."[4]

Reputation was a delicate bloom in the Soviet Union. The team, even when riding high in the Stalin period, were subject to sudden changes of fortune, and in the post-Stalin period, all the more. Beria came crashing down first, then Molotov, Kaganovich, and Malenkov, then their destroyer, Khrushchev. It was more or less de rigueur for at least one family member of anyone prominent in politics or the arts to devote a large part of their life to keeping the flame, lobbying whomever they had access to in the political leadership, sponsoring favorable journalist publications and academic research, rebutting criticism, holding memorial evenings, and doing everything they could to burnish their man's reputation. Just as supporters and family members of Great Purge victims did their best to get them rehabilitated in the 1950s, so in the decades that followed did sons, daughters, widows, and sometimes personal assistants of the Stalin team.

First into the field of celebration was Sergo Ordzhonikidze's widow, Zinaida, with her biography *The Path of a Bolshevik* (1938). Ordzhonikidze's reputation, though not overtly attacked in the years after his death, was at least tarnished and in need of a polishing (the Caucasus city named after him, formerly Vladikavkaz, had its name changed in 1944; when Zinaida protested, Stalin reassured her that he would get another, better city named after him, but it never happened). Zinaida's initiative made Ekaterina Voroshilova uneasy (should one be acting as publicist for one's husband?), but nevertheless the fashion took hold. In the 1960s Galina Kuibysheva published her book on her brother Valerian. In the 1980s, Natalia Andreeva rather tentatively took up the cudgels on behalf of her father, Andrei Andreev. The sons of Beria, Malenkov, and Khrushchev all entered the lists in the 1990s, the first two with memoirs of their fathers, the third with hybrid volumes of memoir-history written for a Western audience. In 2005, Molotov's son-in-law published the first volume of a biography.

The big loser in the family memoir stakes was Stalin. His surviving son Vasily was ready enough to defend him ("I have never repudiated my father and never will"), but he was in such bad shape after Stalin's death that the best he could do was make dark references to his father's enemies, who had probably murdered him, in long, incoherent sessions with drinking companions. After his arrest in April 1953 for loose talk to foreigners and trading on his position as son of a famous man, he was in and out of prison and hospitals, with relatives and party leaders (the "uncles" of his childhood) trying unavailingly to help. Khrushchev called him in and received him "like a real father," begging him to change his ways; Voroshilov did the same; they all embraced and wept, and Vasily promised amendment, but it never lasted. He died of drink in 1962, at the age of forty.[5]

In Voroshilov's conversations with Vasily, Svetlana was held up as an example to him, as had been the case for most of his life. But Svetlana, for so long the good child in the Stalin family, was also going off the rails. The "uncles" had seen and sympathized with her suffering in her first affair (with Kapler) and two short failed marriages (to Grigory Morozov and Yury Zhdanov). They hovered uneasily during de-Stalinization in 1956, Mikoyan inviting her over to read Khrushchev's speech in advance and being immensely relieved at her calm reaction ("the worst thing is, guys, that it's true," she told the Mikoyan sons). Her attitude angered Vasily, who told Voroshilov he felt she was repudiating their father. After she became a researcher at the Institute of Literature in 1956, she did her best to forget the milieu she came from, legally changing her last name to Alliluyeva and seeking rebirth both in the intelligentsia and the Orthodox Church. She sought out former "Kremlin children" who had returned from Gulag and exile, and in quick succession had an affair with Yury Tomsky (Mikhail's son) and then married her cousin Vano (formerly Johnny) Svanidze, both bitter, nervy, and at best ambivalent about Stalin's daughter.

Struggling to keep her head above water after Svanidze divorced her in 1959, she met an Indian Communist, Brajesh Singh, who was substantially older and in bad health, and they decided to marry. This was, of course, endlessly complicated: he was a foreigner and had to leave the country upon expiration of his visa; when he finally got back and they tried to register their marriage (a special procedure when a foreigner was involved), permission was refused. Mikoyan, to whom Svetlana turned for support in the summer of 1964, had been encouraging and checked it out with Khrushchev, who made no objections—but by the time they actually got to the registry office, Khrushchev was out of power, and the new leadership, fearful of the publicity fallout outside the Soviet Union, for some time refused permission for her to marry "this old sick Hindu." Mikoyan tried in vain to convince her that marriage was a formality—look at him and Ashkhen, who were never formally married, but it hadn't hurt them or their five children. Then, in October 1966, Singh died. Svetlana was given permission to take the body back to India on condition that she avoided contact with the press. Once in India, however, she ended up—

not, she later insisted, according to a prior plan—going to the American Embassy in Delhi and asking for asylum. It was an international and domestic sensation: Stalin's daughter defects! The official Soviet reaction was outrage, though Khrushchev and Mikoyan (now both in retirement) were not without sympathy for Svetlana. "It was an unforgivable thing for a Soviet citizen to do," Khrushchev said in his memoirs (probably dictated shortly after her defection, in 1967–68). "Nevertheless, I still feel very sorry for her ... The very thought of Svetlanka brings tears to my eyes." He hoped that one day she would change her mind and come back.

She had left two children behind in Moscow: twenty-year-old Osya (Joseph) and sixteen-year-old Katya, who reportedly never forgave her mother for leaving. (The Mikoyan family swung into action yet again to help them, as did Katya's father Yury Zhdanov.) But what Svetlana took with her was an autobiographical manuscript, published in the West to fresh sensation in 1967 as *Twenty Letters to a Friend*. A touching document, it contained Svetlana's effort to imagine her mother (who died when she was only six) in idealized terms, and her attempt to come to terms with Stalin, both as a father—loving and beloved when she was a child, later increasingly estranged and, on both sides, critical—and a national leader. It was clearly Svetlana's own work, though the Soviet press thundered about the hand of the CIA, and it was not a hatchet job. But it didn't show the kind of unquestioning loyalty that other Kremlin children displayed when writing about their parents, or that her brother Vasya would have considered appropriate. Moreover, Svetlana's public comments after her arrival in the United States were on the standard "I chose freedom" model, hence, extremely offensive in Soviet terms. "She betrayed her father," Sergo Beria said flatly. "Morally, humanly. As a daughter." Poor Svetlana, after a bumpy fifteen years in the United States, was to redefect in the mid-1980s, briefly denouncing the United States and the CIA in terms not dissimilar from her earlier denunciations of the Soviet Union and the KGB, but her children were unwelcoming, and some of her old friends were too. Yury Zhdanov would meet her from time to time in Moscow, at the apartment of some old friend, but Sergo Beria and his mother cut her. She left again after a few years, this time without fanfare, and died in obscurity in the United States in 2011.[6]

The team had started to die long before. As always in the Soviet Union, great emphasis was put on the type of funeral and who went to it. When

Ekaterina Voroshilova died in 1959, both Khrushchev and Mikoyan attended, as well as Andreev, an old family friend. Ten years later, Voroshilov was buried with full honors in the Kremlin Wall. Molotov and Kaganovich attended the funeral, along with the entire current Politburo, but not the now-disgraced Khrushchev. When Polina Zhemchuzhina died in 1970, she was buried as a Communist by the factory party cell in which she was registered. Mikoyan and Bulganin were in attendance, as well as the only grandson of Stalin's to bear his name, Colonel Evgeny Yakovlevich Dzhugashvili, and Molotov made the last public speech of his life, praising both her life's work as a Communist and the era in which she had lived. He did not mention the interlude of arrest and exile.

Khrushchev died the next year, in September 1971, but there was no state funeral or Kremlin Wall burial for him. It was a private funeral attended only by family, some old Communist colleagues from the Donbass, and a few members of the liberal intelligentsia who, for all the fights during his leadership, had come to have a soft spot for the man who presided over de-Stalinization. Khrushchev had also had second thoughts about the intelligentsia in the years of his retirement, when artists and professors were the only ones to risk official opprobrium by calling on him. Among them were the Thaw poet Evgeny Evtushenko and the avant-garde artist Ernst Neizvestny, whom Khrushchev had blasted in his time for departing from realism. It was Neizvestny who sculpted the head of Khrushchev that now adorns his grave in Novodevichy Cemetery. None of the team came to Khrushchev's funeral, but there was a moment of high drama at the last moment, as the mourners were already leaving the graveside, when a messenger came dashing in with a wreath from Mikoyan.

When Mikoyan himself died in 1978, age eighty-two, the Soviet Politburo (the old title was restored in the mid-1960s) came to pay their last respects, and the government of the Soviet Union's Armenian Republic provided an official guard of honor. He was buried, like Khrushchev and Stalin's wife Nadya, in Novodevichy Cemetery. For all the respect, however, the current rulers were anxious to discourage any kind of political demonstration, and publicity and attendance was limited. It appears that none of the team's survivors, the three Anti-Party Group members, showed up. Some of Khrushchev's children were present—Khrushchev's son Sergei had, in the years of estrangement, been a conduit to the Mikoyans through his friendship with Sergo—though his widow stayed home because of a heart condition (later regretting that she had done so).[7]

The triumphant survivors, in terms of longevity, were the Anti-Party Group, Molotov, Malenkov, and Kaganovich. Having lived lives that should have driven them into early graves, the three of them managed to live not only through the long Brezhnev period but into the reforming era of Gorbachev. Malenkov, the youngest, died in 1988 at the age of eighty-six, twenty years after his return to Moscow. He thought of himself as a reformer in later life, and in conversations with his son tended to avoid discussion of Stalin. He did not write memoirs or put much emotional effort into getting readmitted to the party. An omnivorous reader, especially of science and the theory of history, Malenkov developed a passionate interest in his son's field of biology, and with the support of Yury Andropov (Brezhnev's longtime KGB head and briefly his successor in the 1980s), the two of them set up a research project on the defensive powers of the human organism. The coauthored scientific monograph that resulted argued that resistance to the force of gravity, demonstrated constantly by all living organisms, including humans, is as basic to life on Earth as the force of gravity itself. Recognition of this, in the authors' view, provided a new underpinning to the idea of progress in human affairs. Thus, Malenkov died an optimist, to whom the world of politics was remote. His death went unremarked in the Soviet press.

The other two survivors stayed closer to the preoccupations of their working lives. For Molotov and Kaganovich, recovering the status of party member was enormously important. They both applied repeatedly for readmission to the party, starting with the change of regime in the autumn of 1964. During the long Brezhnev reign, they had no success, but in 1984, in the brief successor regime of Konstantin Chernenko, Molotov was finally readmitted. The party card he was issued dated his membership back to 1906, making him the oldest living party member. In describing the event to his faithful Boswell, Molotov, true to form, played down the emotional side. But Chernenko, who personally handed over the card, described the ninety-four-year-old Molotov as saying it was "like being born again." Despite this rapprochement, Molotov was not given a state funeral when he died in 1986 at the age of ninety-six, but the government newspaper *Izvestia* (though not *Pravda*) noted his passing on the front page. (He was identified as a "personal pensioner of all-Union significance," a peculiarly Soviet status statement, the "personal" connoting some kind of special achievement or contribution, the "all-Union" meaning that his contribution was on a national rather than local level.) Around two hundred mourners attended, and he was buried with Polina in Novodevichy, not far from Stalin's wife Nadya.[8]

The last to go was Kaganovich. Long widowed, lonely, and underoccupied, he grew bitter in old age. His daughter, Maya, was devoted but wrote no exculpatory memoir; Felix Chuev's interviews with him took place so late in life that much had been forgotten, and Kaganovich was inclined to burst out with "It's a lie" on the slightest provocation. He had hoped desperately for readmission to the party, and it was galling to be rejected again when Molotov finally succeeded. There would be strong objections from sections of the public to Kaganovich's readmission, the KGB advised, mentioning specifically Great Purges victims rehabilitated in the 1950s, and not mentioning the anti-Semites whose objections would have been equally vehement.

All things being equal, the Chernenko Politburo would have been amenable to readmitting Kaganovich and Malenkov, as well as Molotov, to the party. Brezhnev, who had been an active supporter of Khrushchev's move against them in 1957, was gone. There was recognition that they would never have been expelled in the first place if Khrushchev had not wanted to settle scores with political rivals, and in the 1970s and 1980s, Khrushchev's name was mud, as the man whose impulsive actions had "soiled and stained us and our policies in the eyes of the world." Much of the Chernenko Politburo, like Andrei Gromyko (Molotov's successor as foreign minister and an important supporter of his rehabilitation bid) and defense minister Dmitry Ustinov, belonged to the generation that had first risen to high positions in the late 1930s, in the wake of the Great Purges, when Molotov, and to a lesser extent the rest of the team, were names to conjure with.

Stalin, of course, was even more a part of their past, and the question of Stalin's standing was much on their minds in 1984 because of the upcoming celebration of the fortieth anniversary of Soviet victory in the Second World War. It had been proposed, as part of the celebrations, to restore the Stalinist name to the city of Volgograd, site of the battle of Stalingrad. There were powerful arguments pro and con, as the youngest Politburo member, Mikhail Gorbachev—future leader, reformer, and involuntary destroyer of the Soviet Union—noted. In the end, they decided against, for the time being. But it was not unreasonable to expect that in due course Stalin, and with him the team (shorn of Beria and Khrushchev), would be back in the history books as builders of the Soviet Union, whose mistakes were outweighed by their contribution.

It turned out otherwise. Kaganovich lived on to his ninety-sixth year. When he died, still outside the party, during Gorbachev's perestroika, his death was noted in the papers, and hundreds of people turned out, mainly photographers, local and foreign journalists, and sensation-seekers, for the cremation at Donskoi Monastery, which preceded burial at Novodevichy. The date of Kaganovich's death was 25 July 1991. He had been the last survivor of Stalin's team. Just five months remained until the collapse of the Soviet Union would turn their life's work into dust.[9]

CONCLUSION

THIS BOOK HAS BEEN WRITTEN TO INTEREST A BROAD AUDIENCE, NOT just scholars and specialists in the field, so it includes only a minimum of historiography. But I am, after all, a scholar myself, aware of what other scholars have written on the topic, so my account is bound to be either implicitly in agreement or disagreement with other accounts on particular issues, or sometimes just setting off in a direction of my own. The point of this final chapter is, on the one hand, to alert the interested general reader as to what debates are going on behind the scenes, and, on the other, to flag new findings and conclusions for scholars to argue about.

The easiest way to write about politics is in terms of formal structures and policy decisions. But that doesn't work well for Stalinist politics, since the formal structures were often misleading and the most important policy decisions often went unannounced and sometimes simply unarticulated. Things become even harder for the researcher when, after the 1920s, political factions—and, along with them, public policy debates—disappear. My approach in this study has been to ignore formal structures and pronouncements as far as possible and try to find out how high politics worked by looking at practices, in other words, what the actors in my story *do*, and deducing from that what the informal rules of the game are. This doesn't mean that I don't pay attention to what they say as well, but my assumption is that what people say is often a smokescreen. This applies particularly to tricky characters like Stalin. In addition, political language under Stalin became quite formulaic, thus easy to invoke as boilerplate and comparatively inexpressive of individual intention. It's quite legitimate to write books examining the use and subtle misuse of formulas as a way of working out what is really going on, but I haven't taken that tack. Being accustomed to focusing on everyday practices in my work as a social historian, I tried to apply the same approach in this book to writing about high politics. This meant looking at the Stalin team in terms of the implicit rules of the game that prevail within it (changing over time, of course), the way the team captain maintained his authority and exercised control over the other players, the tactics of survival, cooperation, and competition, and the furthering of interests those players followed.

To say that Stalin's and the team's deeds are better clues to the historian than their words is not to deny the salience of ideology or to suggest that core beliefs were irrelevant in determining action. (This is one of the set-piece arguments in Soviet history: the "ideology" people say that beliefs matter, and accuse the "everyday" social historians of ignoring them, while the "everyday" people think the "ideologists" fall in love with their texts and ignore the situation on the ground.) Core beliefs were highly relevant, in my opinion—why, except for ideological reasons, would Stalin and the team have embarked on collectivization at the beginning of the 1930s?—but all too often not deducible from formal statements of ideology and policy pronouncements.

Again and again in the Stalin period, important things happened and only later (if at all) received any articulate policy statement. All-out collectivization was announced as policy at the beginning of the 1930s only in the most general terms, although the message that party officials should get cracking in the villages, including breaking some peasant heads, was clear. The antireligious drive that accompanied it was never announced as policy nor even identified as such at the Politburo level, and the same goes for the anti-Semitic campaign thirty years later, which, in addition, was accompanied by a low-level press campaign of disinformation that suggested that anti-Semitism on the part of officials might still be punished. Patronage, a key process in Soviet life and politics, was never regulated or formally recognized, except for occasional condemnations from the Kremlin of "family circles" in the provinces. Yet a highly significant (albeit temporary) change in the informal rules of the game occurred when Politburo (team) members were forbidden to intercede with the security agencies on behalf of subordinates, clients, and relatives for the duration of the Great Purges. Of course, policy statements and resolutions were made, sometimes even before the fact, but in order to understand the politics of the time, you often have to reverse their surface meaning. Looking just at Lenin's "Ban on Factions," duly approved by the Tenth Congress of the Communist Party in 1921, for example, you might conclude—as some scholars have incautiously done—that factions disappeared from Soviet politics at that moment. In fact, factions remained the underpinning of Soviet politics for a decade until, without formally banning them, Stalin finally succeeded in getting rid of them.[1]

Historians are less fond than political scientists of systemic models, preferring metaphors or (in the past twenty years) references to cultural theory. They do, however, invoke models on occasion. The totalitarian model, popular during the long Cold War in which Western Soviet studies developed from the 1950s onward, was a case in point. Based on observation of similarities between mid-twentieth-century fascist regimes and the Soviet regime under Stalin, the totalitarian model posited a regime headed by a charismatic leader, ruling through a mobilizing party aspiration and a secret police force, and aspiring to total control over society. Much ink has been spilled, including by me, on the applicability of this model to Soviet history. As far as the present study is concerned, however, the model's relevance is quite limited, as it never focused on Stalin's relationship with his closest advisors or attached particular importance to it.

Stalin's rule is often described as a personal dictatorship. For practical purposes, the term fits well enough, despite some theoretical complications, but it tells us comparatively little about how Stalin actually exercised his power. A metaphor that has probably had more relevance for historians' thinking about Stalinist high politics, though not generating much theoretical debate, is "court politics." The implied comparison is, of course, with the ancien régime, in Russia and elsewhere, where relations between the monarch and his courtiers were an important part of the political process, and the implication is that this traditional reality reasserted itself behind the facade of new revolutionary institutions like the Politburo. Simon Sebag Montefiore invokes court politics in the subtitle of his *Stalin: The Court of the Red Tsar*. As befits a popular history, he puts the metaphor out there for readers' guidance without further explication, and scholars have sometimes used it in much the same way. From Montefiore's use of the term "magnates" (evidently an English version of boyars) to describe Stalin's associates, it looks as if the court he had in mind was a Muscovite one, back in the early modern period, when the relevant players at court were landed nobles with regional bases, sometimes plausible competitors for the tsar's throne. But Stalin-era "magnates" didn't have land or regional power bases; their bases were specialized government and party bureaucracies. If I were to use the "court politics" metaphor, it would probably be with reference to the late tsarist version, when the players were ministers, appointed by the tsar and competing for influence with him, while running the most important of the various government bureaucracies (finance, trade and industry, interior/police) generated by modern states. Yet this analogy falls short too, for the tsars of the late imperial period preferred to deal with their ministers separately and strongly resisted anything resembling a cabinet or ministerial team, and were certainly not inclined to socialize with them or embrace the fiction of being just first among equals. Stalin's team, in my view, was a quite different animal from anything Nicholas II worked with.[2]

For a long time, studies of Stalin focused on the man alone, emphasizing his charisma, cult, and omnipotence, and keen to expose as fallacious claims that institutions like the party Central Committee or the Council of Ministers had any real power. When the archives opened in the 1990s, however, previously invisible aspects of the political process came into sight, and scholars' interests started to shift to the relationships of Stalin and the men around him, variously referred to as his "entourage" or the "inner circle." In scholarly terms, the pioneer was the Russian historian Oleg Khlevniuk, starting with his archive-based study of the Politburo of the 1930s, published in the 1990s. In that first pass at the topic, Khlevniuk thought the inner circle/Politburo was important up to the Great Purges but not thereafter. Approvingly quoting Moshe Lewin, he characterized the dependence of the inner circle on Stalin thereafter as "slavish," concluding that "the Politburo was in fact liquidated as a regularly functioning organ of political leadership, turning into, at best, a consultative instance under Stalin." This was sharply criticized by Arch Getty, who rejected the "slavish" characterization, pointing out that the inner circle members were powerful politicians in their own right, and that in Stalin's long absences—without even telephonic communication with the South until 1935—they collectively ran the country, with Stalin intervening by letter and telegram only on a minority of issues. By 2005, after extending his intensive research from the 1930s into the late Stalin period, Khlevniuk himself was seeing things differently and added an oligarchical paradigm to the paradigm of personal dictatorship. "We can identify the formation of quasi-collective mechanisms of decision-making as evidence of the emerging oligarchisation of power in the last years of Stalin's life," he wrote. "Oligarchy" has a long pedigree as a pejorative characterization of Soviet leadership, starting with "democratic centralist" Bolshevik critics of Lenin and his team back in 1920. In effect, Khlevniuk is saying that, while Stalin, the personal dictator, remained supreme, his closest associates were important too, as would become more evident when they took over after his death, using "some of the procedures of collective leadership."

This cautious formulation leaves it unclear whether Khlevniuk thinks that the "oligarchs" (Stalin's associates) constituted a team or were simply individual players. But Stephen Wheatcroft definitely sees them as a team and offers a statistical analysis of Stalin's appointments data in a 2004 article to show the regularity of the team's meetings from the 1920s to the early 1950s; he notes that Stalin's "working style was as part of a working collective or editorial team, rather than as a 'loner.'" This is my perspective, too, though I arrived at it independently and by a less quantitative route. It is also consonant with Arch Getty's recent work, which explores the analogy between Stalin's modus operandi in dealing with his team and that of modern Western prime ministers in dealing with their cabinets.[3]

I and many others have written extensively about the Great Purges, but looking through the lens of Stalin's closest associates, who were both coperpetrators and potential victims, is something new. In this case, as in others, the team perspective makes familiar processes look subtly different. Take, for example, the casualty rate in Stalin's own family and intimate circle during the Great Purges, as high or higher than that of other team members, which compounded the personal isolation begun with his wife's suicide some years earlier and left him lonely and needing companionship (generally provided by the team) for the rest of his life. If noticed at all, this has generally gone unexplained except by vague references to paranoia. But it seems at least equally plausible that in this instance (as in his later refusal to do a deal with the Germans when his son Yakov was taken prisoner of war), Stalin was following a precept of the unwritten revolutionary code of honor that had always been dear to him, namely, subjugating personal interests to the interests of the revolution; and, moreover, that he felt that his moral authority with the team required him not to intervene on behalf of his own intimates once the team were unable to do so for theirs.

Similarly, Stalin's famous principle of "dosage"—slow, incremental destruction of political figures he had decided to get rid of—is frequently remarked upon in the scholarship but never explained except in general terms as an illustration of his craftiness. No doubt that is part of it, but the political victims (Enukidze or Bukharin, for example) often had friends on the team, and with the incremental approach, Stalin could always back off if the friends' unhappiness became too pronounced. Moreover, as experience showed, after a couple of years of dosage, during which the victim appeared increasingly desperate to his friends on the team, irritating and frightening them, the friends often got used to the idea that the chosen victim was doomed and were almost persuaded that he deserved it.

The Great Purges might have flattened the team for good, but, as T. H. Rigby pointed out in a challenge to conventional wisdom in the 1980s, Stalin proved loyal to his closest associates ("gang," in Rigby's terminology), even as the echelons immediately below were decimated. Individual survival does not, of course, necessarily imply the survival of the team as a significant collective entity. It was the Second World War that achieved that effect (something not noted in the scholarship before the present study), since the team's confidence and sense of itself as a collective was dramatically revived when Stalin lost his gamble that the Germans would not attack in June 1941. Whether or not Stalin expected the team to throw him out in the legendary June visit to the dacha, as Mikoyan later claimed, it was the core members of the team, meeting initially without Stalin, who proposed and subsequently constituted the State Defense Committee that ran the war on the home front. The war constituted the second high point of team activity (the first occurred in the early 1930s during the Sturm und Drang of the industrialization drive), featuring both regular collective meetings and a clear division of responsibilities for different sectors of government and economy. In this book, and originally in an article published in the 1980s, I have shown how institutional interest contributed to Politburo dynamics in the early 1930s. A similar argument could be applied to the functioning of the State Defense Committee in wartime.[4]

The team perspective makes the postwar period look different, too. The remarkable story of Stalin's attempts to prevent Molotov and Mikoyan, team members who were in disgrace in his eyes, from turning up to gatherings at Stalin's dacha and the Kremlin has been told before, notably by Khrushchev in his memoirs, but nobody seems to have noticed how extremely strange it was that Stalin, allegedly all-powerful, was for so long unable to banish them. They were able to come to the gatherings, as Khrushchev makes clear, because other members of the team were tipping them off. In other words, Stalin was using the dosage principle to get the team used to parting with some more political victims—but the team was balking, and he didn't bring it off. Perhaps he would have in the end, of course, but death intervened.

Like Wheatcroft and Getty, I am deeply impressed by Stalin's long absences from Moscow and hands-on government in his last years: a full seven months' absence between August 1951 and February 1952, during which the team was running the country. But I am also impressed by the fact that after his return from the South in February 1952, he didn't leave again, surely a sign that he was planning something big. The anti-Semitic campaign was undoubtedly a part of that project. We will probably never know its exact nature, but the indications are that, as far as the team was concerned, this was entirely Stalin's project: the rest of the team appear to have been unanimous in their silent uneasiness, and unceremoniously ditched it within days of Stalin's death.

The scholarly literature on the 1953 transition after Stalin's death is so slight that any detailed analysis would have to be innovative. In general, the years of collective leadership, 1953–57, tend to disappear altogether in general histories, with the story jumping from Stalin's death to Khrushchev's assumption to power. For the sake of simplicity, book titles often imply that, once Stalin was gone, Khrushchev, the sole reformer, immediately started running the show. But the reforming impulse came from the post-Stalin collective leadership, in whose policy making Khrushchev was at first far from the dominant figure. In the present study, I conclude that the transition was brilliantly handled by the team, aka "collective leadership," which managed not only to maintain stability but even to launch, in remarkably short order, a whole raft of reforms. These achievements of the transition are worth emphasizing, not only because of their intrinsic importance but also because they provide indirect confirmation of the team's significance and resilience, even in Stalin's last years. It is hard to believe that such rapid and coherent action would have been possible had the new ruling group not had prior experience of working together as a team. Indeed, the speed and range of the reform effort also suggests that an unspoken consensus on such matters existed within the team even before Stalin's death.[5]

As a historian of everyday Soviet life in the 1930s, I was accustomed to using the 1930s equivalents of public opinion data—citizens' letters to the authorities to get some idea, however fallible, of what my subjects were thinking about the world. Since ordinary people knew little of any member of the leadership circle except Stalin, they tended to express opinions (surprisingly often negative) about him rather than about his associates. This changed after Stalin's death, when much more information about high politics was available to the general public, and the inhibitions on expressing negative opinions were weaker. Suddenly, individual members of the team came to life in the public "conversation," and, at the same time, the leaders, anxious about legitimacy, became much more attentive to what was being said about them than they had been since the 1920s. One of the innovations of this study has been to incorporate public reactions to the leadership's actions and policies, insofar as they were known to the team, with a more conventional analysis of the processes of high politics of the early post-Stalin era. I was particularly interested to see what a strong following Molotov had in 1953–54, particularly, but not solely, among party members, making his acceptance of collective leadership and failure to bid for the top job all the more striking. Equally striking is Khrushchev's *lack* of popularity, initially because people didn't know him, and then, in the later 1950s, because many of them didn't like what they knew.

Another surprising finding was that, in terms of domestic opinion, the team's biggest problem appeared to be the Jewish one. Their abrupt reversal of the anti-Semitic drive of Stalin's last years upset and disappointed much of the (non-Jewish) public, and the fact that Stalin died straight after pointing the finger at (Jewish) doctors as possible spies and assassins made many suspect that doctors had murdered him. For the next several years, the Jewish issue got mixed up with everything; the popular approach to Kremlinology at this period, including the interpretation of foreign relations, consisted largely in speculating on which of the leaders was actually Jewish, or acting on behalf of Jews. There is nothing like this popular obsession with Jews in the opinion data ("mood reports" and citizens' letters) of the 1930s, so evidently something happened during the 1940s that changed things in a fundamental way. Whether one sees the root cause as wartime bitterness about privileged Jews "sitting out the war in Tashkent" or late Stalinist anti-Semitic policies, the consequences were fateful in the long term as well as the short term, as Yuri Slezkine has argued, not only for Soviet Jews but also for the regime and its legitimacy with the Soviet educated public.[6]

My reading of the collective leadership that took the reins after Stalin's death (or, to be strictly accurate, a day *before* that event) is that it was a more or less genuine team enterprise, at least for a number of key players, such as Molotov, Malenkov, and Mikoyan, not to mention team members—now of lesser political importance—like Voroshilov and Kaganovich. But there were exceptions. Beria, who quickly emerged as the boldest and most radical of the reformers, is a case in point; hence, not surprisingly, he became the first casualty of the post-Stalin leadership when the others collectively arrested him in July 1953, which led to his execution at the end of the year. Beria's removal turned out to be a brilliant public relations move: it meant that now Beria could be blamed for everything, leaving the rest of the team to take credit for the post-Stalin repudiation of mass terror (which actually had been Beria's initiative as much as anybody's). Khrushchev was the other member of the collective leadership who privately preferred another model, with himself in the leading role. The fact that in mid-1957 he prevailed over the majority of the team, led by Molotov, was a mixture of luck and timely help from the military and security leaders.

The general view has been that with Khrushchev's rise to personal power, the Soviet system settled back into the position that was most natural to it: personal dictatorship via the party. This is the way I probably saw it too, but research for this book changed my mind. Not only did Khrushchev's critics initially win the argument when they reproached him for departing from collective leadership norms, but their criticisms were exactly the same ones as would be made by Brezhnev and his colleagues seven years later, when Khrushchev was ousted from power in his turn. Brezhnev restored what he claimed to be a collective leadership, a description greeted skeptically in the West. But the most recent scholarship suggests that the form of rule under Brezhnev was, in fact, something not too far from collective leadership, or at least the traditional Soviet version by which one man, understood to be the top leader, operated in regular consultation with a team whose agreement he normally wanted to obtain, and within which the convention prevailed that he was just first among equals. This was the way Lenin, for whose rule "personal dictatorship" never seemed an adequate characterization, had operated. Stalin sometimes operated this way, too, and sometimes only pretended to do so, but even the pretense allowed space for the continued existence of a team. Khrushchev became increasingly impatient with teamwork, but the convention was too strong for him wholly to dispense with it, even when he had removed almost everyone of roughly equivalent status from the team.[7]

Western Sovietologists were always very wary of acknowledging any kind of diffusion of power away from the *vozhd'* or top leader. This was partly because the Soviet claims about such diffusion, couched in terms of "democracy" and focused on institutions like the party Central Committee and the Supreme Soviet, were self-serving and unconvincing. But, as this book has tried to show, formal institutions are not necessarily the place to look when you want to understand everyday operating procedures. If we look, instead, at informal practices of the Soviet leadership over seven decades, we find that top leaders almost invariably worked with a group of associates with major governmental responsibilities of their own who acknowledged the top leader's special status but saw themselves as working with him as a team. Teams are collectives, but they don't have to be democratic, and their captains may turn into dictators. As we have seen, Stalin could treat his team brutally, as well as in a comradely manner. He could drop players from his team, and he could even kill them. But he never dispensed with the team, whatever his (unrealized) intentions may have been to some of its core members in his last years. "You would be lost without me," he used to tell the team. *But, come March 1953, they weren't.* That's the big surprise at the end of this book, and I hope scholars will take note and reexamine their assumptions about late Stalinism accordingly.

ACKNOWLEDGMENTS

IN ITS PRESENT FORM, THE OUTLINE OF THIS BOOK WAS CONCEIVED IN 2009, when I was a Fellow at the Wissenschaftskolleg zu Berlin, on leave from the University of Chicago. The book was largely researched in Moscow and Chicago, but written after I moved to Australia in 2012. The writing took place in my office at the University of Sydney, far from the natural terrain of Sovietologists. I am grateful to Graeme Gill, who read the whole manuscript; to Ann Curthoys and Kay Dreyfus, who read chapters; and to the University of Sydney, which provided a welcoming and congenial new home. In thinking how to approach the project, I profited from discussions with Bernard Wasserstein and Mark McKenna. Andrea Graziosi, Arch Getty, Stephen F. Cohen, Michael David-Fox, Oleg Khlevniuk, John Besemeres, Yoram Gorlizki, Mark Edele, Stephen Fortescue, and Stephen Wheatcroft were kind enough to answer queries. Leonid Weintraub copied some archival documents for me in Moscow, and June Farris, Slavic librarian at the University of Chicago, provided unstinting support by email.

I benefited greatly from my collaboration with Stephen Wheatcroft on a Discovery Project grant on Stalinism funded by the the Australian Research Council. A particular debt of gratitude is owed to Katja Heath, whose photo-researching skills were invaluable, as well as to Brigitta van Rheinberg, Quinn Fusting, and the fine editorial team at Princeton University Press, and Sally Heath at Melbourne University Press.

The Research Group of the History Department of the University of Sydney made helpful comments on chapter 1. I had useful feedback from papers on the project delivered at Carleton College, Kenyon College, and the University of Madison at Wisconsin (2010); the University of Pittsburgh and the University of Melbourne (2011); the University of California at Berkeley (2012); the University of New South Wales and Nazarbayev University, Kazakhstan (2013); and the Europe Centre, Australian National University (2014). Particularly important during the final revision of the manuscript in autumn 2014 were the comments and suggestions on my presentation of conclusions at the University of Bremen, the École des hautes études en sciences sociales (EHESS) in Paris, the Humboldt University in Berlin, the University of Manchester, the London School of Economics and Political Science, and a joint meeting of the Deutsches Historisches Institut and Centre Franco-Russe (with Oleg Khlevniuk as commentator) in Moscow.

The middle section of chapter 3 is a revised version of "The Boss and His Team: Stalin and the Inner Circle, 1925–1933," published in Stephen Fortescue, ed., *Russian Politics from Lenin to Putin* (London: Palgrave Macmillan, 2010), a Festschrift for T. H. Rigby.

I owe a large general debt to the good friends and colleagues who have worked longer and dug deeper than I on Soviet political history—among them, Oleg Khlevniuk, Yoram Gorlizki, Arch Getty, Jörg Baberowski, Jerry Hough, and Bill Taubman—whose pioneering works served both as inspiration and reference.

Igor Alexandrovich Sats first sparked my interest in the human aspect of Stalin's team back in the 1960s, while in the 1970s Jerry Hough encouraged me (at the time, vainly) to use the knowledge I had acquired from Sats to write a political history. I would like to end with a respectful acknowledgment of political scientists of a senior generation who were my mentors long ago, and in some cases later became friends: E. H. Carr, Leonard Schapiro, Robert C. Tucker, Robert W. (Bill) Daniels, and T. H. (Harry) Rigby. I think the last two would have liked this book—and perhaps Carr as well, despite the sternness with which, in his *History of Soviet Russia*, he concealed his own keen interest in human drama and personality.

NOTES

INTRODUCTION

1. **Getting it past the Politburo**, Adam B. Ulam, *Stalin* (New York: Viking Press, 1973), 572, 607; *Foreign Relations of the United States: The Conferences at Malta and Yalta* (Washington, DC: Department of State, 1955), 666; **use of "team,"** Stephen G. Wheatcroft, "From Team-Stalin to Degenerate Tyranny," in E. A. Rees, ed., *The Nature of Stalin's Dictatorship* (Houndsmill: Palgrave Macmillan, 2004); **use of "gang,"** T. H. Rigby, "Was Stalin a Disloyal Patron?," *Soviet Studies* 38:3 (July 1986), 324.

2. **Stalin as loyal patron**, Rigby, "Was Stalin a Disloyal Patron?," 311–24.

3. **Ordzhonikidze project**, Sheila Fitzpatrick, "Ordzhonikidze's Takeover of Vesenkha," *Soviet Studies* 37:2 (1985); **Igor Sats**, Sheila Fitzpatrick, *A Spy in the Archives* (London: I. B. Tauris, 2014), 142–63.

4. **Stalin**, Simon Sebag Montefiore, *Stalin: The Court of the Red Tsar* (New York: Knopf, 2004); Oleg Khlevniuk, *Master of the House: Stalin and His Inner Circle* (New Haven: Yale University Press, 2009); Yoram Gorlizki and Oleg Khlevniuk, *Cold Peace: Stalin and the Soviet Ruling Circle, 1945–1953* (Oxford: Oxford University Press, 2004); Wheatcroft, "From Team-Stalin to Degenerate Tyranny."

5. **Evil**, Hannah Arendt, *Eichmann in Jerusalem: A Report on the Banality of Evil* (London: Faber & Faber, 1963); **objectivity problem**, Sheila Fitzpatrick, "Demoyte's Grey Suit: Writing Memoirs, Writing History," *Australian Book Review*, June–July 2014; Thomas Nagel, *The View from Nowhere* (New York: Oxford University Press, 1986).

6. **Institutional interest**, see note 3 above (Ordzhonikidze project); **patronage**, Sheila Fitzpatrick, "Intelligentsia and Power: Client-Patron Relations in Stalin's Russia," in Manfred Hildermeier, ed., *Stalinismus vor dem zweiten Weltkrieg* (Munich: Oldenbourg, 1998), republished in Sheila Fitzpatrick, *Tear Off the Masks! Identity and Imposture in Twentieth-Century Russia* (Princeton: Princeton University Press, 2005); **everyday interactions**, Sheila Fitzpatrick, *Stalin's Peasants: Resistance and Survival in the Russian Village after Collectivization* (New York: Oxford University Press, 1994); Sheila Fitzpatrick, *Everyday Stalinism: Ordinary Life in Extraordinary Times; Soviet Russia in the 1930s* (New York: Oxford University Press, 1999); Fitzpatrick, *Tear Off the Masks!*

7. **Name changes,** E. M. Pospelov, *Imena gorodov: Vchera i segodnia (1917–1992)* (Moscow: Russkie slovari, 1993).

CHAPTER 1. THE TEAM EMERGES

1. **Central Committee membership,** lists for 1912–57 in Robert V. Daniels, *The Conscience of the Revolution* (New York: Simon and Schuster, 1960), 422–33.

2. **Ban on factions,** Feliks Chuev, *Sto sorok besed s Molotovym* (Moscow: Terra, 1991), 181; A. I. Mikoian, *Mysli i vospominaniia o Lenine* (Moscow, 1970), 139; **provinces,** Chuev, *Sto sorok besed,* 227; Lazar Kaganovich, *Pamiatnye zapiski* (Moscow: Vagrius, 1996), 236 and 242–47; Mikoian, *Mysli o Lenine,* 156; and A. I. Mikoian, *Tak bylo: Razmyshleniia o minuvshem* (Moscow: Vagrius, 1999), 169–77.

3. **Stalin,** Leon Trotsky, *Stalin: An Appraisal of the Man and His Influence* (New York: Grosset & Dunlap, 1941), 392–93; N. N. Sukhanov, *The Russian Revolution, 1917: Eyewitness Account* (Oxford: Oxford University Press, 1955), 229–30; Victor Serge, *Memoirs of a Revolutionary* (New York: New York Review of Books, 2012), 98 (quotation); Boris Bazhanov, *Bazhanov and the Damnation of Stalin* (Athens: Ohio University Press, 1990), 104–6; Robert Service, *Stalin: A Biography* (Cambridge, MA: Belknap Press, 2005), 196 (quotation).

4. **"Testament,"** ("Letter to the Congress"), V. I. Lenin, *Polnoe sobranie sochinenii v 55-i tomakh,* 5th ed. (Moscow: Gosudarstvennoe izdatel'stvo politicheskoi literatury, 1958–70), 45:343–48.

5. **Lenin's conflict with Stalin,** Moshe Lewin, *Lenin's Last Struggle* (Ann Arbor: University of Michigan Press, 2005) (esp. Caucasus question, 43–64); Service, *Stalin,* 211 ("loved with all his heart"); Feliks Chuev, *Molotov* (Moscow: OLMA-PRESS, 2000), 272 ("same toilet").

6. **"Thin stratum,"** Chuev, *Sto sorok besed,* 37.

7. **Faction-fighting, 1923–24,** I. V. Stalin, *Sochineniia* (Moscow: Gosudarstvennoe izdatel'stvo politicheskoi literatury, 1952), 5:354–55, 5:370 ("On the tasks of the party," 2 December 1923); Daniels, *Conscience,* 221 (Zinoviev quotation), 233; Stalin, *Sochineniia,* vol. 6 (1952), 14 (quotation), 29; *XIII s"ezd RKP(b), Mai 1924 g. Stenograficheskii otchet* (Moscow: Gosudarstvennoe izdatel'stvo polititicheskoi literatury, 1962), 158 (Trotsky), 224 (Krupskaya).

8. **Runs away,** Mikhail Tomskii, *Vospominaniia* (Moscow: RGGU, 2001), 158, 275–76; **letter from "brother,"** "Protiv prisvoenii familii Stalina vozvrazhenii ne imeiu," *Istochnik,* 1996, no. 2, 156–60; **Turukhansk quotation,** Service, *Stalin,* 224.

9. **Ego bruising,** Feliks Chuev, *Tak govoril Kaganovich* (Moscow: Otechestvo, 1992), 35; **proletarians,** *XV konferentsiia Vsesoiuznoi Kommunisticheskoi Partii (b), 25 oktiabria-3 noiabria 1926 g. Stenograficheskii otchet* (Moscow-Leningrad: Gosudarstvennoe izdatatel'stvo, 1927), 669 (Molotov quotation); Stalin to Molotov, 25 September 1926, RGASPI 558/11/70, ll. 56–57; **ambiance quotation,** Service, *Stalin,* 225.

10. **Molotov,** Olga Aroseva, *Bez grima* (Moscow, 2000), 30 (parents' disapproval); Chuev, *Sto sorok besed,* 180–81 ("not shrewd enough"); RGASPI (Rossiiskii gosudarstvennyi arkhiv sotsial'no-politicheskoi istorii), 558/11/767, ll. 15, 26–29, 31–32 (Marxist theory); Chuev, *Molotov,* 268 (youngest member) Bazhanov, *Bazhanov and the Damnation of Stalin,* 53 ("stone-bottom"); **Voroshilov,** Isaac Deutscher,

The Prophet Armed (London: Oxford University Press, 1970), 423–25 (Tsaritsyn); Larissa Vasilieva, *Kremlin Wives*, ed. and trans. Cathy Porter (London: Weidenfeld & Nicolson, 1994), 80–81 (marriage).

11. **Kaganovich**, Chuev, *Tak govoril Kaganovich*, 78, 129 (*Ty*: like French and German, Russian has a familiar form for "you" and a more formal one, *vy*, which is also the plural); Bazhanov, *Bazhanov and Damnation*, 16; Chuev, *Molotov*, 384, 385 ("200 percent" quotation). **Kuibyshev**, G. V. Kuibysheva, *Valerian Vladimirovich Kuibyshev* (Moscow: Izdatel'stvo politicheskoi literatuury, 1966); Chuev, *Sto sorok besed*, 192–93; N. Zenkovich, *Samye sekretnye rodstvenniki: Entsiklopediia biografii* (Moscow: OLMA-PRESS, 2005), 206–10.

12. **Rudzutak**, RGASPI 558/11/70, ll. 56–57 ("proletarian" quotation, Stalin to Molotov, 25 September 1926); G. A.Trukan, *Ian Rudzutak* (Moscow: Gosudarstvennoe izdatel'stvo politicheskoi literatury, 1963), 58, 144–45; Chuev, *Sto sorok besed*, 412; A. I. Mikoian, *Tak bylo*, 268; *Pis'ma I. V. Stalina V. M. Molotovu, 1925–1936 gg.* (New Haven: Yale University Press), 103 ("playing politics" quotation, Stalin to Molotov, 24 June 1927); **Andreev**, A. A. Andreev, *Vospominaniia, pis'ma* (Moscow: Politizdat, 1985), 225, 286, 289; Chuev, *Molotov*, 252; *Kak lomali NEP: Stenogrammy plenumov TsK VKP(b), 1928–9 v piati tomakh* (Moscow: Mezhdunarodnyi fond "Demokratiia," 2000), 1:190 (Voroshilov); N. S. Patolichev, *Measures of Maturity* (Oxford: Pergamon Press, 1983), 97.

13. **Kalinin**, 1926 defense of peasant interests in K. M. Anderson et al., eds., *Stenogrammy zasedanii Politbiuro TsK RKP(b)-VKP9(b), 1923–1938 v trekh tomakh* (Moscow: ROSSPEN, 2007), vol. 1 (1923–26), 616, 626 ("as a peasant"); Zenkovich, *Samye sekretnye*, 170–71; Trotsky, *Stalin*, 388–89 (quotation); **Ordzhonikidze**, Chuev, *Molotov*, 250 (quotation); Trotsky, *Stalin*, 348 (quotation).

14. **Mikoyan**, A. I. Mikoian, *Dorogoi bor'by* (Moscow: Izdatel'stvo politicheskoi literatury, 1971), 560–61; A. I. Mikoian, *V nachale dvatsatykh…* (Moscow: Izdatel'stvo politicheskoi literatury, 1975), 204, 208; A. I. Mikoian, *Tak bylo*, 272–73, 352; RGASPI 74/1/429, l. 104 (Ekaterina Voroshilova, "Something like a diary," entry for 2 September 1957); Stepan Anastasevich Mikoian, *Vospominaniia voennogo letchika-ispytatelia* (Moscow: "Tekhnika molodezhi," 2002), 25; **Kirov**, *O Sergee Kirove* (Moscow: Izdatel'stvo politicheskoi literatury, 1985), 202; Matthew E. Lenoe, *The Kirov Murder and Soviet History* (New Haven: Yale University Press, 2010), 33; *Nash Mironych* (Leningrad: Lenizdat, 1968), 257–58; Mikoian, *Dorogoi bor'by*, 534; RGASPI, 80/26/55, ll. 1–2, RGASPI, 80/26/56, l. 1, and *Bol'shevistkoe rukovodstvo* (Moscow: ROSSPEN, 1996), 314–15 (1926 letters to wife); Sergo Beria, *Beria, My Father* (London: Duckworth, 2001), 15S; RGASPI, 558/11/746 (correspondence with Stalin); Chuev, *Sto sorok besed*, 311.

15. **Stalin**, Chuev, *Sto sorok besed*, 261; Chuev, *Molotov*, 294; Chuev, *Tak govoril Kaganovich*, 154–55; **party bureaucrats**, *XV konferentsiia Vsesoiuznoi Kommunisticheskoi Partii (b), 25 oktiabria–3 noiabria 1926 g. Stenograficheskii otchet* (Moscow-Leningrad: Gosudarstvennoe izdatel'stvo, 1927), 756; **Bukharin**, RGASPI, 558/11/69; Stephen F. Cohen, *Bukharin and the Bolshevik Revolution* (New York: Alfred A. Knopf, 1972), 241 (quotation).

16. **Zinoviev**, *Pis'ma I. V. Stalina*, 71 (Stalin to Molotov, 15 June 1926); Chuev, *Molotov*, 224; Chuev, *Molotov*, 241; **Kamenev**, A. I. Mikoian, *Tak bylo*, 352; Daniels,

Conscience, 268; **preoccupation with factions**, *Pis'ma I. V. Stalina* (Stalin to Molotov), RGASPI 558/11/766–69 (Molotov to Stalin).

17. **Stalin's style**, Robert Service, "The Way They Talked Then: The Discourse of Politics in the Soviet Party Politburo in the late 1920s," in Paul R. Gregory and Norman Naimark, eds., *The Lost Politburo Transcripts* (New Haven: Yale University Press, 2008), 127; Nikita Khrushchev, *Khrushchev Remembers* (Boston: Little, Brown, 1970), 27; A. I. Mikoian, *Tak bylo*, 287; **Leningrad conflict**, Daniels, *Conscience*, 269–70; *Bol'shevistskoe rukovodstvo*, 314–15, 320–21 (Voroshilov to Ordzhonikidze, 6 February 1926), 322; RGASPI, 558/11/766, l. 86 (Molotov to Stalin, 11 January 1926); RGASPI, 80/26/55, ll. 1–2, RGASPI, 80/26/56, l. 1; *Bol'shevistkoe rukovodstvo*, 314–15 (Kirov's letters to wife).

18. **Ordzhonikidze**, RGASPI, 74/2/43, l. 12 ("defeat for our party"); A. I. Mikoian, *Tak bylo*, 266–67; RGASPI, 74/2/43, l. 15 (letters to Voroshilov, 1926); **Mikoyan**, A. I. Mikoian, *Tak bylo*, 268; Michal Reiman, *The Birth of Stalinism* (Bloomington: Indiana University Press, 1987), 136–37 (Kuibyshev quotation).

19. **Hit separately**, *Pis'ma I. V. Stalina*, 74 (Stalin to Molotov, letter of 25 June 1926); **dosage**, Leon Trotsky, *Stalin* (New York: Universal Library, 1941), 416; **Kalinin case**, see p. XX; **outcasting**, RGASPI, 558/11/766, ll. 75, 144–47 (Molotov to Stalin, September 1926); *Pis'ma I. V. Stalina*, 71 (Stalin to Molotov, 15 June 1926).

20. **Trotsky's account**, Trotsky, *Stalin*, 413–14; **"insinuator,"** letters of Tovstukha and Molotov to Stalin, both 28 May 1926, RGASPI, 558/11/69, ll. 2–3 and 558/11/766; Voroshilov, October 1926, Anderson, *Stenogrammy zasedanii Politbiuro*, 2:399; Rudzutak, September 1927, in Anderson, *Stenogrammy*, 2:573–74; **Stalin-Trotsky exchange**, Anderson, *Stenogrammy*, 2:586, 2:593; **high road**, *XV konferentsiia Vsesoiuznoi Kommunisticheskoi Partii (b)*, 544–55, 577–604, 756.

21. **Sarajevo**, RGASPI, 558/11/767, l. 33 (Stalin to Molotov, 8 June 1927); **London's agents**, RGASPI, 558/11/71, l. 29 (Stalin to Menzhinsky, 23 June 1927); **strengthen OGPU**, RGASPI, 558/11/767, ll. 35–39 (Molotov to Stalin, 10 June 1927); **Voroshilov's jitters**, quoted in Gregory, *Lost Politburo Transcripts*, 24; **German archives**, Reiman, *Birth of Stalinism*, xi–xii; **leaks**, Gregory *Lost Politburo Transcripts*, 20–22; Reiman, *Birth of Stalinism*, 127.

22. Menzhinsky's report, Reiman, *Birth of Stalinism*, 124–26, 132–33; **high treason**, Reiman, *Birth of Stalinism*, 127; **war and guillotine**, Deutscher, *Prophet Unarmed*, 343–44, 349–51.

23. **Inkpots**, quotation in Deutscher, *Prophet Unarmed*, 366–67; Yaroslavsky in letter to Ordzhonikidze, 29 October 1927, in *Bol'shevistskoe rukovodstvo*, 352; **unhappiness in team**, Reiman, *Birth of Stalinism*, 34 and 161; **Ordzhonikidze**, *Bol'shevistskoe rukovodstvo*, 347–52 (letters to him from Stalin, Yaroslavsky, and Shkiriatov, *XV konferentsiia Vsesoiuznoi Kommunisticheskoi Partii (b), 25 oktiabria–3 noiabria 1926 g. Stenograficheskii otchet*; Yaroslavsky quotation, 352).

24. **Trotsky's expulsion from party**, Reiman, *Birth of Stalinism*, 133 (Menzhinsky memo); **Zinoviev's and Kamenev's capitulation**, *XV s"ezd VKP(b): Dekabr' 1927 goda; Stenograficheskii otchet* (Moscow: Gosudarstvennoe izdatel'stvo polititicheskoi literatury, 1961), 2:1596–99; **heckling**, *XV s"ezd VKP(b)*, 1:279–85; **criticism**, *XV s"ezd VKP(b)*, 1:215–21 (Rudzutak), 154–55 (Kaganovich), 291 (Rykov), 421 (Stalin).

25. **OGPU materials**, RGASPI, 329/2/26 (Bukharin archive); **waverings**, *Kak lomali NEP*, 4:316, 4:405 (vote of 7 January 1929); **Trotsky's expulsion from the country**, Robert Service, *Trotsky* (London: Macmillan, 2009), 373–75; Isaac Deutscher, *The Prophet Outcast* (London: Oxford University Press, 1970), 468–71; **"stain,"** Chuev, *Sto sorok besed*, 419.

CHAPTER 2. THE GREAT BREAK

1. **Great Break** (*velikii perelom*), I. V. Stalin, *Sochineniia* (Moscow, 1952), 12:125–39 ("The year of the great break. For the 12th anniversary of October," 7 November 1929); **class enemies**, Stalin, *Sochineniia* (1948), 9:126–27; **Lenin**, quoted in E. H. Carr, *Socialism in One Country* (London, Macmillan, 1959), 2:41; **Stalin on retreats**, *Kak lomali NEP*, 2:517.

2. **Uprooted Peasants**, O. V. Khlevniuk, *Politbiuro: Mekhanizmy politicheskoi vlasti v 1930-e gody* (Moscow: ROSSPEN, 1996), 54; **collectivization process**, Sheila Fitzpatrick, *Stalin's Peasants* (Oxford: Oxford University Press, 1994); **peasant disturbances**, Lynne Viola, *Peasant Rebels under Stalin* (New York: Oxford University Press, 1996); **Stalin's comment**, Winston Churchill, *The Second World War*, vol. 4: *The Hinge of Fate* (Boston: Houghton-Mifflin, 1950), 447–48; **Molotov's comment**, Chuev, *Sto sorok besed*, 383; **Molotov in Ukraine**, Chuev, *Sto sorok besed*, 377.

3. **Stalin and OGPU leaders**, J. Arch Getty, *Practicing Stalinism* (New Haven: Yale University Press, 2013), 170–81; **Menzhinsky and Yagoda**, Donald Rayfield, *Stalin and His Hangmen* (London: Viking, 2004), 105–14, 204–13.

4. **Economic debates**, Alexander Erlich, *The Soviet Industrialization Debate, 1924–1928* (Cambridge, MA: Harvard University Press, 1960); **drafting First Five-Year Plan**, E. H. Carr and R. W. Davies, *Foundations of a Planned Economy, 1926–29*, vol. 1, pt. 2 (London: Macmillan, 1969), 843–97 (Kuibyshev quotation, 868); **Voroshilov**, Carr and Davies, *Foundations*, vol. 1, pt. 2, 873; **war and the Five-Year Plan**, Carr and Davies, *Foundations*, vol. 1, pt. 2, 869n1, 873; **Stalin quotation**, Stalin, *Sochineniia* (1951), 13:38–39 ("On the tasks of the industrialists," 4 February 1931).

5. **Cultural Revolution and Shakhty Affair**, Sheila Fitzpatrick, "Cultural Revolution in Russia," in Sheila Fitzpatrick, *The Cultural Front* (Ithaca, NY: Cornell University Press, 1992); **Molotov's comment**, RGASPI, 558/11/767, ll. 85–88 (Molotov to Stalin, 13 June 1928); **Stalin and OGPU scenarios**, Diane P. Koenker and Ronald D. Bachman, eds., *Revelations from the Russian Archives* (Washington, DC: Library of Congress, 1997), 243 (Stalin to Menzhinsky, 1930).

6. **Stalin quotations**, *Kak lomali NEP*, 1:234–35; **discussion on Shakhty Affair**, April 1928, *Kak lomali NEP*, 1:156–92; O. I. Gorelov, *Tsugtswang Mikhaila Tomskogo* (Moscow: ROSSPEN, 2000), 200.

7. **Education discussion**, *Kak lomali NEP*, 1:193–304; Sheila Fitzpatrick, *Education and Social Mobility in the Soviet Union, 1924–1932* (Cambridge: Cambridge University Press, 1979), chap. 6; **discussion at July 1928 plenum**, *Kak lomali NEP*, 2:525–78.

8. **Collectivization trips**, Chuev, *Sto sorok besed*, 377; Rayfield, *Stalin and His Hangmen*, 148–49; E. A. Rees, *Iron Lazar: A Political Biography of Lazar Kaganovich* (London: Anthem Press, 2012), 195; R. W. Davies, *The Socialist Offensive* (Cambridge,

MA: Harvard University Press, 1980), 71, 90, 267; **Molotov**, Chuev, *Sto sorok besed*, 384, 385 ("stormy process" quotation), 386; **Yakovlev**, *Stalinskoe politbiuro v 30-e gody* (Moscow: AIRO-XX, 1995), 97; **Mikoyan**, *Kak lomali NEP*, 1:37–58; **Andreev**, *Kak lomali NEP*, 3:25–26; **Stalin's encouragement**, Chuev, *Sto sorok besed*, 377 (Stalin to Molotov quotation), *Kak lomali NEP*, 3:9 (Stalin to Mikoyan quotation).

9. **Lobbying**, James R. Harris, *The Great Urals: Regionalism and the Evolution of the Soviet System* (Ithaca: Cornell University Press, 1999), 70–104; **Kuibyshev's visitors**, G. V. Kuibysheva, *Valerian Vladimirovich Kuibyshev* (Moscow: Izdatel'stvo politicheskoi literatury, 1966), 283; **industry on Politburo agenda**, *Politburo TsK RKP(b)-VKP(b): Povestki dlia zasedanii; Katalog*, vol. 1 (Moscow: ROSSPEN, 2000) (Stalin as rapporteur, 707, 739).

10. **Mikoyan story**, A. I. Mikoian, *Tak bylo*, 289; **Tomsky comment**, *Kak lomali NEP*, 4:55; **Tomsky and Krupskaya**, Mikhail Tomskii, *Vospominaniia, stat'i, dokumenty* (Moscow: RGGU, 2001), 158; **Molotov and Bukharin**, Chuev, *Molotov*, 252–53; **applause**, *XV s"ezd Vsesoiuznoi Kommunisticheskoi Partii (b): Stenograficheskii otchet* (Moscow-Leningrad: Gosudarstvennoe izdatel'stvo, 1928); **Stalin's friendship with Bukharin**, Paul R. Gregory, *Politics, Murder and Love in Stalin's Kremlin: The Story of Nikolai Bukharin and Anna Larina* (Stanford, CA: Hoover Institution Press, 2010), 16–17; Svetlana Allilueva, *Dvadtsat' pisem k drugu* (Sankt-Petersburg, 1994), 25; Gorelov, *Tsugtswang Mikhaila Tomskogo*, 275; **Gurvich**, Zenkovich, *Samye sekretnye rodstvenniki*, 64–65; **Stalin's friendship with Tomskys**, Gorelov, *Tsugtswang*, 275 (Mishka is a particularly familiar diminutive of Mikhail).

11. **Tomsky quarrel**, Tomskii, *Vospominaniia*, 159; **Bukharin-Kamenev meeting**, Anna Larina, *This I Cannot Forget* (London: Norton, 1993), 112–13, 115; *Kak lomali NEP*, 4:152, 162–63, 188–90, 559–60; "'Prosti menia, Koba': Neizvestnoe pis'mo N. Bukharina," *Istochnik*, 1993, no. 0, 24 (Bukharin to Stalin, 10 December 1937).

12. **Stalin's handwritten note**, *Sovetskoe rukovodstvo: Perepiska, 1928–1941* (Moscow: ROSSPEN, 1999), 73; **Bukharin's shock**, Dmitrii Volkogonov, *Triumf i tragediia: Politicheskii portret I. V. Stalina* (Moscow: Novosti, 1989), bk. 1, pt. 2, 30; **Stalin on friendship**, *Kak lomali NEP*, 4:452; **campaign against Bukharin**, RGASPI, 329/2/6, ll. 58–60 (Bukharin to Stalin [August 1928]); **Bukharin's defense**, *Kak lomali NEP*, 4:151 (quotation), 187–88; **"Notes of an Economist,"** *Pravda*, 30 September 1928.

13. **Gang must be driven out**, *Pis'ma I. V. Stalina*, 220 (Stalin to Molotov [before 15 September 1929], Stalin's italics); **Bukharin not going to work**, *Kak lomali NEP*, 3:1; ibid., 4:194; **Rightists' reassignments**, *Pis'ma I. V. Stalina*, 124, 190–91; Daniels, *Conscience*, 368; Cohen, *Bukharin and the Bolshevik Revolution*, 301; Daniels, *Conscience*, 368; *Pravda*, 31 March 1931, 6; **New Year's Eve**, Roy A. Medvedev, *Nikolai Bukharin* (New York: Norton, 1980), 15, 25; Gregory, *Politics, Murder, and Love*, 65.

14. **Mikoyan quotation**, A. I. Mikoian, *Tak bylo*, 289; **Molotov**, RGASPI 558/11/767, 111–16 (letter to Stalin, 20 August 1928); **Stalin**, *Kak lomali NEP*, 3:9; **Shuisky**, Chuev, *Tak govoril Kaganovich*, 74–75; **Ordzhonikidze**, *Sovetskoe rukovodsto*, 58–59 (letter to Rykov [before 16 November 1928]; RGASPI, 74/2/43, ll. 38–39 (letter to Voroshilov, 28 October 1928); RGASPI, 74/2/43, ll. 50–51 (letter to Voroshilov, 26 June 1929).

15. **Rudzutak-Bukharin-Ordzhonikidze exchange**, *Kak lomali NEP*, 4:170; **Voroshilov on Bukharin and Right**, *Pis'ma I. V. Stalina*, 123 (8 June 1929); *Sovetskoe rukovodstvo*, 68 (Voroshilov to Stalin [March 1929]); **Kalinin**, RGASPI, 558/11/769, ll. 5–11 (Molotov to Stalin, 11 August 1930); *Pis'ma I. V. Stalina*, 198 (Stalin to Molotov, not earlier than 23 August 1930).

16. **Zhdanov**, *Revelations from the Russian Archives*, 336–37; Kees Boterbloem, *The Life and Times of Andrei Zhdanov, 1896–1948* (Montreal: McGill-Queens, 2004), 74–79; **Beria**, Amy Knight, *Beria: Stalin's First Lieutenant* (Princeton: Princeton University Press, 1993), 45; RGANI (Rossiiskii gosudarstvennyi arkhiv noveishei istorii), 5/30/4, ll. 64–79 (V. N. Merkulov to Khrushchev, 21 July 1953); S. Beria, *Beria, My Father*, 11–13; Rayfield, *Stalin and His Hangmen*, 336.

17. **Elite training**, Fitzpatrick, "Stalin and the Making of a New Elite," in Fitzpatrick, *Cultural Front*; *Pis'ma I. V. Stalina*, 156 (quotation, Stalin to Molotov, 28 August 1929).

18. **Malenkov**, A. G. Malenkov, *O moem ottse Georgii Malenkove* (Moscow NTTs "Tekhnoekos," 1992), 8–20; Zenkovich, *Samye sekretnye rodstvenniki*, 249; **Khrushchev**, William Taubman, *Khrushchev: The Man and His Era* (New York: Norton, 2003), 30–71; N. Khrushchev, *Khrushchev Remembers*, 38–42; **Pyatakov**, O. V. Khlevniuk, *Stalin i Ordzhonikidze* (Moscow: Rossiia molodaia, 1993), 67; Davies, *Socialist Offensive*, 148 (quotation); **Kaganovich quotation**, Robert W. Davies, *Crisis and Progress in the Soviet Economy, 1931–33* (London: Macmillan, 1996), 10.

CHAPTER 3. IN POWER

1. **Wonderful times**, RGASPI, 74/1/429 Ekaterina Voroshilova, "Something like a diary," entry for August–September 1955; Chuev, *Tak govoril Kaganovich*, 90–91 (moustaches), 190–91 (*vol'nitsa*); *ty*, A. I. Mikoian, *Tak bylo*, 352; **Koba**, RGASPI, 558/11/766–69; *Sovetskoe rukovodstvo*, 190–91, 280–81; **Soso**, RGASPI, 558/11/765, ll. 48–49, 57–58, 68a.

2. **Rudzutak and Kuibyshev**, *Vozvrashchennye imena*, bk. 2 (Moscow: Novosti, 1989), 144–45; Chuev, *Sto sorok besed*, 412 (Rudzutak); M. Gronskii, *Iz proshlogo... Vospominaniia* (Moscow: Izvestiia, 1991), 255–63 (Kuibyshev); **Molotov**, A. I. Mikoian, *Tak bylo*, 536; Chuev, *Tak govoril Kaganovich*, 52–53, 61; **Stalin family friends**, Allilueva, *Dvadtsat' pisem*, 25–26, 89, 107–9; **Ordzhonikidze**, Chuev, *Tak govoril Kaganovich*, 62; Chuev, *Molotov*, 250–21; **Kirov**, *Nash Mironych*, 202; Bukharin to Voroshilov [1936], RGASPI, 329/2/6, ll. 10–13; Miklós Kun, *Stalin* (Budapest: Central European University Press, 2003), 193; **Voroshilov**, *Istochnik*, 1994, no. 3, 72; **Rudzutak**, Chuev, *Sto sorok besed*, 413; RGASPI, 74/2/43, l. 38 (Ordzhonikidze to Voroshilov, October 1928); **Kuibyshev**, A. I. Mikoian, *Dorogoi bor'by*, 560–61; **Andreev**, Andreev, *Vospominaniia* (Moscow: Politizdat, 1985), 300–304; **Kalinin**, A. I. Mikoian, *V nachale dvadtsatykh*, 319–22.

3. **Polina Zhemchuzhina**, A. I. Mikoian, *Tak bylo*, 198–99; **dacha company**, *Iosif Stalin v ob"iatiiakh sem'i* (Moscow: Rodina, 1993), 161, 169–70 ("Maria Anisimovna Svanidze's Diary"); S. Mikoian, *Vospominaniia*, 28–29; RGASPI, 74/1/429 (Voroshilova, "Something like a diary," entry for August–September 1955); **Enukidze**, Simon Sebag Montefiore, *Young Stalin* (London: Weidenfeld & Nicolson, 2007), 61, 283.

4. **Polina Zhemchuzhina**, Zenkovich, *Samye sekretnye*, 274–77; Kun, *Stalin*, 270–79; Vasileva, *Kremlin Wives*, 124–49; *Stalinskoe Politbiuro v 30-e gody* (Moscow: AIRO-XX, 1995), 276; A. I. Mikoian, *Tak bylo*, 298–99; N. Khrushchev, *Khrushchev Remembers: The Last Testament* (Boston: Little, Brown, 1974), 493; **Maria Kaganovich**, Zenkovich, *Samye sekretnye*, 166; **Ekaterina Lorberg**, *Istoricheskii arkhiv*, 2000, no. 6, 212–13; Vasileva, *Kremlin Wives*, 113–26; **Dora Khazan**, Zenkovich, *Samye sekretnye*, 8; **Esfir Gurvich**, Gregory, *Politics, Murder and Love*, 58; **Kuibyshev wives**, Zenkovich, *Samye sekretnye*, 206, 210; **Valeria Golubtsova**, Malenkov, *O moem ottse, Georgii Malenkove*, 14; **Nina Beria**, S. Beria, *Beria, My Father*, 159.

5. **Krupskaya, Yakovleva, Lilina biographies**, Sheila Fitzpatrick, *The Commissariat of Enlightenment* (London: Cambridge University Press, 1970), 305, 308, 326; **Kameneva**, Michael David-Fox, *Showcasing the Great Experiment: Cultural Diplomacy and Western Visitors to the Soviet Union, 1921–1941* (Oxford: Oxford University Press, 2012), 35–46; **visual aids quotation**, Svetlana Alliluyeva, *Only One Year* (New York: Harper & Row, 1969), 403; **Voroshilova**, V. Kardashov, *Voroshilov* (Moscow: Molodaia gvardiia, 1976), 217; RGASPI, 74/1/429 (Voroshilova, letter to Raisa Samoilovna, 23 July 1954); **Khrushcheva**, Vasilieva, *Kremlin Wives*, 173–89; Sergei Khrushchev, *Nikita Khrushchev: Rozhdenie sverkhderzhavy* (Moscow: Vremia, 2010), 20; **friends of Nadya's**, Vasilieva, *Kremlin Wives*, 128; Allilueva, *20 pisem*, 108; A. I. Mikoian, *Tak bylo*, 360; Andreev, *Vospominaniia*, 298, 303–4; **letter to Maria Svanidze**, quoted in Kun, *Stalin*, 202; **Nina Beria**, S. Beria, *Beria, My Father*, 150, 246; Alliluyeva, *Only One Year*, 354.

6. **Unregistered marriage**, Zenkovich, *Samye sekretnye*, 64; Alliluyeva, *Only One year*, 45–46; Kun, *Stalin*, 275; Taubman, *Khrushchev*, 58; **Zhemchuzhina's other daughter**, Svetlana Vyacheslavovna Molotova, b. 1928, is the only daughter generally reported, but according to their 1939 census return, the Molotov household included a second daughter, Rita Aronovna Zhemchuzhina, b. 1927 (*Revelations from the Russian Archives*, 340). This is confirmed by a letter of 17 August 1948 from Zhemchuzhina to Marjorie Davies, wife of the former US ambassador, in which she reports the marriages in the same month of her two daughters, Svetlana and Sonya (*sic*), both students: RGASPI, 82/2/1595; **affairs**, Vasileva, *Kremlin Wives*, 80; Iurii Zhdanov, *Vzgliad v proshloe* (Rostov: Feniks, 2004), 308; Zenkovich, *Samye sekretnye*, 275; **young wives**, Zenkovich, *Samye sekretnye*, 177, 206–7, 210; Oleg Troianovskii, *Cherez gody i rasstoianiia* (Moscow: Vagrius, 1997), 162.

7. **Adoptions**, Simon Sebag Montefiore, *Stalin: The Court of the Red Tsar* (New York: Knopf, 2004), 12; S. Mikoian, *Vospominaniia*, 24, 29, 163; Zenkovich, *Samye sekretnye*, 167; Kardashov, *Voroshilov*, 227; Chuev, *Tak govoril Kaganovich*, 95–96; **bad influence**, A. I. Mikoian, *Tak bylo*, 198–99; **schooling**, S. Mikoian, *Vospominaniia*, 29–31; Andreev, *Vospominaniia*, 297; Larry Holmes, *Stalin's School* (Pittsburgh: University of Pittsburgh Press, 1999), 71–72, 165–68; *Revelations from the Russian Archives*, 341 (census return for Stalin household); **Svetlana's uncles**, Allilueva, *20 pisem*, 114–18; **Svetlana the boss**, *Stalin i Kaganovich: Perepiska, 1931–1936* (Moscow: ROSSPEN, 2001), 544 (Kaganovich to Stalin, 31 August 1935).

8. **Syrtsov**, *Stenogrammy zasedanii Politbiuro*, 3:176; **Molotov's indispensability**, *Pis'ma I. V. Stalina*, 247 (Stalin to Molotov, 1 September 1933); **"What stupidity!,"** *Stalin i Kaganovich*, 51 (Stalin to Kaganovich, 17 August 1931); **Rightists**, *Pis'ma I. V.*

Stalina, 217 (Stalin to Molotov ["comedy"], 30 September 1929 and 13 September 1930 ["paralyzed"]).

9. **Head of government**, RGASPI, 558/11/765, 68a (Mikoyan to Stalin [September 1930]); *Sovetskoe rukovodstvo*, 144–45 (Voroshilov to Stalin, 8 October 1930, including "leadership" quotation); Chuev, *Sto sorok besed*, 276 (Molotov's opinion); *Pis'ma I. V. Stalina*, 222–23 and RGASPI, 558/11/769, 55–62 (letters between Stalin and Molotov, September–October 1930); O. V. Khlevniuk, "Stalin i Molotov," in *Stalin, Stalinizm, Sovetskoe obshchestvo*, ed. G. Sh. Sagatelian et al. (Moscow: Institut Rossiiskoi istorii RAN, 2000), 275 (Ordzhonikidze quotation); **team positions in government**, Khlevniuk, *Politbiuro*, 79; *Stalinskoe Politbiuro*, 93.

10. **Institutional advocacy**, *Stalin i Kaganovich*, 420–21, and see note 3 in the introduction to this volume; **Stalin on budget**, Chuev, *Tak govoril Kaganovich*, 103–4; *Stalin i Kaganovich*, 57, 186, 224 (quotations); **on bureaucratic demands**, *Stalin i Kaganovich*, 72, 232, 52, 57 (quotations); **on bureaucratic tactics**, *Stalin i Kaganovich*, 68, 72 ("mousehole" quotation), 479; *Iosif Stalin v ob"iatiiakh sem'i*, 158–59 (Maria Svanidze's diary, entry for 4 November 1934: Kirov story).

11. **Ordzhonikidze**, *Pis'ma I. V. Stalina*, 82–83, 247 ("hooliganism"); RGASPI, 558/11/766, 139–42; RGASPI, 558/11/769, 68–71 ("state within a state"); *Stalin i Kaganovich*, 379; **Stalin's annoyance**, *Stalin i Ordzhonikidze*, 81–82; **defense of Pyatakov and brother**, Khlevniuk, *Stalin i Ordzhonikidze*, 37–38 and 76–82.

12. **Blatant lies**, Fitzpatrick, *Stalin's Peasants*, 62–63, 91; **letter to Nadya,** *Iosif Stalin v ob"iatiiakh sem'i*, 33 (24 September 1930).

13. **Nadya's unhappiness**, Kun, *Stalin*, 202 (quoting letter to Maria Svanidze); **flight to Leningrad**, Vasilieva, *Kremlin Wives*, 64; Tomskii, *Vospominaniia*, 158; **ill health**, Kun, *Stalin*, 214; **Industrial Academy**, N. Khrushchev, *Khrushchev Remembers*, 36–40; **critical attitude**, Vasileva, *Kremlin Wives*, 65–66; Olga Trifonova, *Edinstvennaia: Zhena Stalina* (Moscow: Astrel', 2010) (fiction, but document-based); **closed character**, Allilueva, *Dvadtsat' pisem*, 85 (quotation).

14. **Nadya's death**, Chuev, *Molotov*, 307–8; Allilueva, *Dvadtsat' pisem*, 88; **Stalin's reactions**, Kun, *Stalin*, 209–10; Chuev, *Molotov*, 309 (quotation); Chuev, *Sto sorok besed*, 250–51; Allilueva, *Dvadtsat' pisem*, 89; **letter to mother** (24 March 1934), M. Lobanov, ed., *Stalin v vospominaniiakh sovremennikov i dokumentov epokhi* (Moscow: EKSMO, 2002), 234; **death notice**, *Pravda*, 10 November 1932, 3 (note that although Kuibyshev, Kirov, and Kalinin signed as Politburo members, their wives did not; Enukidze, a non-Politburo member, signed, but four Politburo members—the bachelor Rudzutak and the three Ukrainian representatives, Petrovsky, Chubar, and Stanislav Kosior—were absent from the list); **rumors**, A. G. Solovev, "Tetradi krasnogo professor," *Neizvestnaia Rossiia* (Moscow: Mosgorarkhiv, 1993), 4:172 (entry for 9 November 1932); **funeral**, *Pravda*, 10 November 1932; Chuev, *Tak govoril Kaganovich*, 73.

15. **Famine**, *Sovetskoe rukovodstvo*, 181–84 (quotation, Voroshilov to Stalin, 26 July 1932); **Stalin's version**, Koenker and Bachman, *Revelations from the Russian Archives*, 398 (Stalin to Mikhail Sholokhov, 3 May 1933); *Istoriia SSSR*, 1989, no. 3, 46; *Stalin i Kaganovich*, 210, 273–74 ("things are terrible" quotation, Stalin to Kaganovich, 1 August 1932, Stalin's emphasis); Terry Martin, *The Affirmative Action Empire*

(Ithaca, NY: Cornell University Press, 2001), 297–98; **new leadership for Ukraine**, *Stalin i Kaganovich*, 738, 749, 760.

16. **Kazakhstan**, *Sovetskoe rukovodstvo*, 204–25; **flight from Ukraine blocked**, Fitzpatrick, *Stalin's Peasants*, 95; **"staging a famine,"** quotations from Fitzpatrick, *Stalin's Peasants*, 74–75; **"war of starvation,"** Koenker and Bachman, *Revelations from the Russian Archives*, 398 (Stalin to Sholokhov, 3 May 1933); **speech of 7 January 1933**, Stalin, *Sochineniia*, 13:198; **"eliminate malnutrition,"** Koenker and Bachman, *Revelations from the Russian Archives*, 417–18 (Kiev obkom instruction, 22 February 1933).

17. **Team's knowledge of famine**, Chuev, *Sto sorok besed*, 453–54 (Molotov quotation); http://rt.com/politics/holodomor-famine-stalin-ukraine/ (Holodomor conviction); *Sovetskoe rukovodstvo*, 249–50 (Voroshilov quotation); **Kalinin**, Golfo Alexopoulos, *Stalin's Outcasts* (Ithaca, NY: Cornell University Press, 2003) (petitions); Khlevniuk, *Master of the House* (New Haven: Yale University Press, 2009), 62–63; **retrospective comments**, Chuev, *Molotov*, 453 and 461 (quotations); A. I. Mikoian, *Tak bylo*, 294–97; N. Krushchev, *Khrushchev Remembers*, 61; Sergei Khrushchev, *Nikita Khrushchev: Reformator* (Moscow: Vremia, 2010), 30 (quotation); **repression**, J. Arch Getty and Oleg V. Naumov, *The Road to Terror* (New Haven: Yale University Press, 1999), 114–18 (text of law of 7 August); **repression called off**, Fitzpatrick, *Stalin's Peasants*, 78–79.

18. **Popular anti-Stalin sentiment**, Fitzpatrick, *Stalin's Peasants*, 289–90; **Ryutin**, Khlevniuk, *Master*, 64–66; Getty, *Road to Terror*, 52–64 (text of platform); **Stalin's complaints**, *Stenogrammy zasedanii Politbiuro*, 3:125, 3:176.

19. **Smirnov-Eismont group**, *Stenogrammy zasedanii Politbiuro*, 3:581, 3:590, 3:631, 3:635, 3:638; **Voroshilov on Rightists**, Getty, *Road to Terror*, 99–101 (text of speech to Central Committee, January 1933); **Rudzutak**, Getty, *Road to Terror*, 93; **Voroshilov on Koba**, *Sovetskoe rukovodstvo*, 241 (letter of 29 June 1933).

CHAPTER 4. THE TEAM ON VIEW

1. **Stalin report**, Stalin, *Sochineniia*, 13:282–79; **team contributions**, *XVII s"ezd VKP, 30 ianvaria–10 fevralia 1934 g. Stenograficheskii otchet* (Moscow: Partizdat, 1934), 129–32, 145–47, 150–52, 167–79, 179–88, 201–9, 224–35, 251–59, 584; **Bukharin**, Cohen, *Bukharin*, 355; **readmission of Kamenev and Zinoviev** (12 December 1933), Khlevniuk, *Politbiuro*, 102.

2. **Vote fixing**, *Tak govoril Kaganovich*, 71; **Kirov's proposed move to Moscow**, Chuev, *Molotov*, 376–77 (quotation); Khlevniuk, *Politbiuro*, 112–13; **votes against Stalin**, Lenoe, *Kirov Murder*, 128, 757; A. G. Solovev, "Tetradi krasnogo professor," *Neizvestnaia Rossiia*, 4:175 (6 March 1934, 222; Kozlov, ed. note); N. Khrushchev, *Khrushchev Remembers*, 49; A. I. Mikoian, *Tak bylo*, 592–93 (estimates of votes cast against Stalin range from 3, with 166 voting slips missing [Kozlov], or 6 [Khrushchev] to 287 [Mikoyan, citing Shatunovskaya], out of a total of 1,225 voting delegates). **General Secretary title**, Khlevniuk, *Politbiuro*, 112–13; Volkogonov, *Triumf i tragediia*, bk. 2, pt. 1, 78.

3. **Stalin cult**, Solovev, "Tetradi," in *Neizvestnaia Rossiia*, 4:156–57 (quotation), 4:173–74, 4:182 (entries for 22 December 1929 , 12 June 1933, and 7 November

1935); A. I. Mikoian, *Tak bylo*, 318; Solovev, "Tetradi," 156–57; Tucker, *Stalin in Power*, 246 (Radek quotation); Tucker, *Stalin in Power*, 248 (quotation from *Pravda*, 21 January 1934); applause ritual, *Krest'ianskaia pravda* (Leningrad), 16 November 1935, 3; **vozhdi**, Sarah Davies, *Popular Opinion in Stalin's Russia* (Cambridge: Cambridge University Press, 1999), 149–50; **wives' meetings**, Sheila Fitzpatrick, *Everyday Stalinism* (New York: Oxford University Press, 2000), 156–62; **Kaganovich**, Garros et al., *Intimacy and Terror* (New York: New Press, 1995), 184 (Shtange diary, 25 December 1936).

4. **Knights** (Rus. *bogatyri*), Davies, *Popular Opinion*, 151; **Voroshilov**, Frank J. Miller, *Folklore for Stalin* (Armonk, NY: M. E. Sharpe, 1990), 36; Dzhambul and S. Stavskii, *Stikhi i pesni* (Novosibirsk, 1938), 30; GARF (Glavnyi arkhiv Rossiiskoi Federatsii), 5446/54 (files 24, 33, 44, 57, 68, 81, 101, and 127 are labeled "Correspondence from people claiming to be relatives of K. E. Voroshilov"); **Ordzhonikidze**, Miller, *Folklore for Stalin*, 118; **Kalinin**, Miller, *Folklore for Stalin*, 134; Davies, *Popular Opinion*, 166–67 (quotation); **Kirov**, Davies, *Popular Opinion*, 178; Fitzpatrick, *Everyday Stalinism*, 185; Miller, *Folklore for Stalin*, 68, 90, 136.

5. **"Party run by Jews,"** Fitzpatrick, *Everyday Stalinism*, 186–87; **Jewish wives**, GARF, 5446/82/56, ll. 261–63 (denunciation of Zhemchuzhina, 1937); http://www .revolutionarydemocracy.org/rdv1n2/kaganfam.htm (Kaganovich family denial of marriage rumors); Chuev, *Tak govoril Kaganovich*, 19; **Caucasian prince**, GARF, 3316/16a/1446, l. 100 (July 1930); **Molotov's fiftieth**, Davies, *Popular Opinion*, 152; **place-names**, GARF, 7523/65/516 (Supreme Soviet resolutions, 1939–41); Pospelov, *Imena gorodov*.

6. **Duranty interview**, 25 December 1933, Stalin, *Sochineniia*, 13:276–81; **Wells interview** (23 July 1934), in I. V. Stalin, *Sochineniia*, vol. 1 (14), ed. Robert H. McNeal (Stanford, CA: Hoover Institution, 1967), 11–36; H. G. Wells, *Experiment in Autobiography* (London: Faber, 1984), 800–806; **Feuchtwanger interview** (8 January 1937), Lion Feuchtwanger, *Moscow 1937: A Visit Described for My Friends*, trans. Irene Josephy (New York: Viking, 1937); **Radek comment**, quoted in David-Fox, *Showcasing*, 237; **Ambassador Davies**, Joseph E. Davies, *Mission to Moscow* (London: Victor Gollancz, 1943), 83–84, 227, 230–31.

7. **Ludwig interview**, 13 December 1931, Stalin, *Sochineniia*, 13:120–21; **Stalin's languages**, Kun, *Stalin*, 146–47; Chuev, *Sto sorok besed*, 257; Wells, *Experiment*, 803; **Molotov**, RGASPI, 558/11/768, ll. 146–47 (Molotov to Stalin, 31 December 1929); Chuev, *Molotov*, 284; Chuev, *Sto sorok besed*, 107 ("diplomat" quotation); **languages**, Kaganovich, *Pamiatnye knigi*, 13–48; Sabine Dullin, *Men of Influence* (Edinburgh: Edinburgh University Press, 2008), 14; Kuibysheva, *Valerian Vladimirovich Kuibyshev*, 215; F. G. Seiranian, *G. K. Ordzhonikidze v gody sotsialisticheskogo stroitel'stva* (Tbilisi: Izdatel'stvo "Sabchota Sakar tvelo," 1986); Trotsky, *Stalin*, 395.

8. **Foreign spy networks**, Robert Service, *Spies and Commissars* (London: Macmillan, 2011); Rayfield, *Stalin's Hangmen*, 140–46; **show trials**, *Politbiuro TsK RKP(b) i Evropa* (Moscow: ROSSPEN, 2001), 211; **approval of trips**, RGANI, 3/22/70, esp. ll. 48, 65, 68.

9. **Nicolaevsky**, Boris I. Nicolaevsky, *Power and the Soviet Elite* (London: Pall Mall Press, 1965), 26–65 ("Letter of an Old Bolshevik"); Zenkovich, *Samye sekretnye*, 338–39; **Trotsky**, *Stalin i Kaganovich*, 489, 493; Volkogonov, *Triumf i tragediia*, bk. 1,

pt. 2, 167, 174; bk. 2, pt. 1, 90, 96; Deutscher, *Prophet Outcast*, 390–97; Pavel Sudoplatov, *Special Tasks* (Boston: Little, Brown, 1994), 30–31, 67.

10. **Stalin on spies**, *Stalin i Kaganovich*, 146, 225 ("our stupidity"), 269 ("all specialists spies"), 361, 364 ("forbidden to go travelling"); *Stalinskoe Politbiuro*, 146; RGASPI, 558/11/769, l. 114; **Poles arrested**, Marc Jansen and Nikita Petrov, *Stalin's Loyal Executioner* (Stanford, CA: Hoover Institution Press, 2001), 40–42; *Journal de Moscou*, *Stalin i Kaganovich*, 530, 543; **Varga Institute**, Solovev, "Tetradi," *Neizvestnaia Rossiia*, 4:178; **Molotov's tutor**, RGASPI, 82/2/1454; **German political émigrés**, Jansen, *Stalin's Loyal Executioner*, 42.

11. **Paris exhibition**, *Politbiuro TsK RKP(b)-VKP(b)*, 924; **international competitions**, *Politbiuro TsK RKP(b)-VKP(b)*, 862, 884, 897, 936; RGASPI, 17/3/983 (Politburo protocols, February 1937); *Pravda*, 2 April 1937, 1; **concern about Western reactions**, *Stalin i Kaganovich*, 414, 635; RGASPI, 82/2/537, ll. 81, 155 (Yakovlev to Stalin and Molotov, 21 March 1937).

12. **Stalin as writer (publicist)**, Evgenii S. Gromov, *Stalin: Vlast' i iskusstva* (Moscow: Respublika, 1998), 64; **spin**, *Stalin i Kaganovich*, 116; **language learning**, Kun, *Stalin*, 146–47; S. Mikoian, *Vospominaniia*, 27; Kuibysheva, *Valerian Vladimirovich Kuibyshev*, 215; **Stalin's precepts**, *Stalin i Kaganovich*, 569 ("swindlers"); RGASPI, 558/11/768, ll. 138–42 ("right on the nose"); *Pis'ma I. V. Stalina*, 245 ("spitting in the pot"); *Stalin i Kaganovich*, 545 ("quarrel" between two blocs).

13. **Foreign policy**, *Politbiuro TsK RKP(b)-VKP(b) i Evropa* (team involvement 1930–33, order of frequency: Stalin [14 times], Molotov [11], Voroshilov [8], Ordzhonikidze [7], Mikoyan [5], Kaganovich [4], Kuibyshev [2], and once each for Kirov, Kosior, Rudzutak, and Kalinin); Chuev, *Sto sorok besed*, 97–98 ("squeezed into Stalin's hand"); **Litvinov**, Chuev, *Sto sorok besed*, 97–98 ("couldn't enjoy our full trust"); Solovev, "Tetradi," *Neizvestnaia Rossiia*, 4:202–4; *Pis'ma I. V. Stalina*, 155, 161, 167; RGASPI, 558/11/768, ll. 87–89; RGASPI, 558/11/769, ll. 132–34; *Stalin i Kaganovich*, 71, 94, 107, 189, 563–64.

14. **Kuusinen**, RGASPI, 558/11/766, ll. 125–26 (Molotov to Stalin, 25 August 1926); Arvo Tuominen, *The Bells of the Kremlin* (Hanover: University Press of New England, 1983), 92, 93, 96; **Arosev**, David-Fox, *Showcasing the Soviet Experiment*, 223–26; Viacheslav Nikonov, *Molotov: Molodost'* (Moscow: Vagrius, 2005), 45; **Dimitrov and Stalin**, *The Diary of Georgi Dimitrov, 1933–1949*, intro. and ed. Ivo Banac (New Haven: Yale University Press, 2003), 69–70 and passim; **Stalin on America**, Stalin, *Sochineniia*, 13:114–15 (conversation with Emil Ludwig, 1931); **Mikoyan's trip**, A. I. Mikoian, *Tak bylo*, 300–15; Kun, *Stalin*, 296–97.

15. **Spain**, *Stalin i Kaganovich*, 681; *Stalinskoe Politbiuro*, 149, 151 ("dialectics" quotation); **Ehrenburg proposal**, *Stalin i Kaganovich*, 493, 718–19 (text); **Congress**, Katerina Clark, *Moscow the Fourth Rome* (Cambridge, MA: Harvard University Press, 2011), 177–79; http://www.gisele-freund.com/international-congress-for-the-defense-of-culture-hall-of-the-mutualite-paris-21th-of-june-1935/; **Webbs**, David-Fox, *Showcasing*, 215–19; *Politbiuro TsKP(b)-VKP(b): Povestki*, 2:303, 2:718, 2:772; **Gide**, David-Fox, *Showcasing*, 262–68.

16. **RAPP/Averbakh**, Fitzpatrick, *Cultural Front*, 104–6; Mikhail Ilinskii, *Narkom Iagoda* (Moscow: Veche, 2005), 450; *"Schast'e literatury": Gosudarstvo i pisateli, 1925–1938* (Moscow: ROSSPEN, 1997), 130–32 (Politburo resolution of 23 April

1932); **Roy**, M. N. Roy, *M. N. Roy's Memoirs* (Bombay: Allied Publishers, 1964), 538; **Kaganovich**, Evgenii Evseev, *Kaganovich* (Moscow: Iauza, 2005), 97, 101–2; **Stalin**, Katerina Clark and Evgeny Dobrenko, *Soviet Culture and Power* (New Haven: Yale University Press, 2007), 141; Tucker, *Stalin in Power*, 151–59.

17. **Gorky**, Ilinskii, *Narkom Iagoda*, 83; Gromov, *Stalin*, 151–54; **Yagoda and Gorky**, Ilinskii, *Narkom Iagoda*, 366–73, 385–88; Vitalii Shentalinsky, *Raby svobody* (Moscow: Parus, 1995), 339–46; **Maxim Peshkov's death**, Shentalinskii, *Raby*, 355–58; **Writers' dreams**, *Vlast' i khudozhestvennaia intelligentsia*, comp. Andrei Artizov and Oleg Naumov (Moscow: Mezhdunarodnyi fond "Demokratiia," 1999), 529 ("warmly and with love"); Shentalinskii, *Raby*, 120; **Stalin's telephone calls**, Shentalinskii, *Raby svobody*, 124, 239; Nadezhda Mandelstam, *Hope against Hope* (New York: Modern Library, 1999), 147.

18. **Team patronage**, Sheila Fitzpatrick, "Intelligentsia and Power: Client-Patron Relations in Stalin's Russia," in Manfred Hildermeier, ed., *Stalinismus vor dem zweiten Weltkrieg: Neue Wege der Forschung/Stalinism before the Second World War; New Avenues of Research* (Munich: Oldenbourg, 1998), 35–53, reprinted in Fitzpatrick, *Tear Off the Masks!*; Dmitrii Shostakovich, *Pis'ma I. I. Sollertinskomu* (SPB, 2006), 155–56; Chuev, *Sto sorok besed*, 314–15; N. Khrushchev, *Khrushchev Remembers: The Last Testament*, 74 (**Voroshilov**); *"Schast'e literatury,"* 273–75; RGASPI, 85/28/77 (**Kalinin**); *"Literaturnyi front": Istoriia politicheskoi tsenzury* (Moscow: Entsiklopediia rossiiskikh dereven', 1994), 27 (**Andreev**); TsGAIPD (Tsentral'nyi gosudarstvennyi arkhiv istoriko-politicheskoi dokumentatsii Sankt-Peterburga), 24/2v/2679, ll. 28–30; Aleksei Volynets, *Zhdanov* (Moscow: Molodaia gvardiia, 2013), 101, 167, 433, 528–29 (**Zhdanov**); Taubman, *Khrushchev*, 128–32 (**Khrushchev**); *Nash Mironych*, 394–96; *Byli industrial'nye: Ocherki i vospominaniia*, 2nd ed. (Moscow: Izdatel'stvo politicheskoi literatury, 1973), 35 (**Kirov**); Sergo Beriia, *Moi otets: Lavrentii Beriia* (Moscow: Sovremennik, 1994), 36, 343 (**Beria**); A. G. Malenkov, *O moem ottse*, 25 (**Malenkov**); Iu. Elagin, *Ukroshchenie iskusstv* (New York: Izdatel'stvo imeni Chekhova, 1952), 217 (**Rudzutak**); Gronsky, *Iz proshlogo*, 259–60 (**Kuibyshev**); Viktor Fradkin, *Delo Kol'tsova* (Moscow: Vagrius, 2002), 245; Chuev, *Tak govoril Kaganovich*, 105–6; Rees, *Iron Lazar*, 138 (**Kaganovich**); Fitzpatrick, "Intelligentsia and Power," 39–43 (**Molotov**); Elena Bonner, *Mothers and Daughters* (New York: Vintage Books, 1993), 123–24; *"Literaturnyi front,"* 15–16; A. I. Mikoian, *Tak bylo*, 631–34 (**Mikoyan**) ; RGASPI, f. 85, letters from Georgians; *Byli industrial'nye*, 12, 17, 189–95 (**Ordzhonikidze**); Nadezhda Mandelshtam, *Vospominaniia* (New York, 1970), 119–20 (**Ezhov**).

19. **Salons**, Shentalinsky, *Raby*, 59–50, 62–63, 66–67; Jansen, *Stalin's Loyal Executioner*, 17, 121; Vasileva, *Kremlin Wives*, 97–112; **death of Ezhova**, Jansen, *Stalin's Loyal Executioner*, 166–71; *Lubianka: Stalin I NKVD-NKGB-GUKR "Smersh"* (Moscow: Mezhdunarodnyi fond "Demokratiia," 2006), 71.

20. **"Life has become better,"** Stalin, *Sochineniia*, ed. McNeal, vol. 1 (14), 106 (speech of 1 December 1935); **Moscow Metro**, N. Khrushchev, *Khrushchev Remembers*, 64–70; *Iosif Stalin v ob"iatiiakh sem'i*, 173–75; **New Year trees**, *Khrushchev Remembers: The Glasnost Tapes* (Boston: Little, Brown, 1990), 31–32; http://atz-box.ru/stati/aznaete-li-vy/1428-istoriia-novogodnei-elki.html; **perfumes**, Jukka Gronow, *Caviar with Champagne: Common Luxury and the Ideals of the Good Life in Stalin's Rus-*

sia (Oxford: Berg, 2003), 56–60; A. I. Mikoian, *Tak bylo*, 298–99; **new suits**, Stepan Mikoian, *Vospominaniia*, 25; *Trud*, 2 July 1935, 1; **new foods**, Fitzpatrick, *Everyday Stalinism*, 90–91.

21. **Soviet Thermidor**, Leon Trotsky, *The Revolution Betrayed* (London: New Park Publications, 1967), 86–114; **end of rationing**, Khlevniuk, *Master*, 111; **Stalin and Kirov's death**, Allilueva, *Dvadtsat' pisem*, 108; Chuev, *Sto sorok besed*, 310; Lenoe, *Kirov Murder*, 251–62; **later doubts**, N. Khrushchev, *Khrushchev Remembers: The Glasnost Tapes*, 24; A. I. Mikoian, *Tak bylo*, 589–96; **Molotov on Nikolaev**, Chuev, *Sto sorok besed*, 310; **Stalin points to Zinovievites**, Lenoe, *The Kirov Murder*, 281; **deportations**, Khlevniuk, *Master*, 130; J. Arch Getty and Oleg V. Naumov, *Yezhov* (New Haven: Yale University Press, 2008), 139; **Ezhov**, Getty and Naumov, *Yezhov*, 143; **Nikolaev execution**, Lenoe, *Kirov Murder*, 358, 370; **Zinoviev and Kamenev trial**, Lenoe, *Kirov Murder*, 377–79; Getty and Naumov, *Yezhov*, 159.

22. **Stalin's friendship with Kirov**, *Iosif Stalin v ob"iatiiakh sem'i*, 168 (Maria Svanidze's diary, entry for 5 December 1934); Allilueva, *Dvadtsat' pisem*, 108; Service, *Stalin*, 294; **birthday party**, Maria Svanidze's diary, *Stalin v ob"iatiiakh*, 169–70 (entry for 23 December 1934); **ditty**, Fitzpatrick, *Stalin's Peasants*, 290–93; **Stalin's fears**, Lobanov, *Stalin v vospominaniiakh sovremennikov i dokumentakh epokhi*, 361 (quoted from Admiral I. S. Isakov).

CHAPTER 5. THE GREAT PURGES

1. **"World-historic mission,"** "'Prosti menia, Koba,'" *Istochnik*, 1993, no. 0, 23–24 (Bukharin to Stalin, 10 December 1937); **"no Fifth Column,"** Chuev, *Molotov*, 464; **Molotov**, Chuev, *Sto sorok besed*, 395; **Kaganovich**, G. A. Kumanev, *Riadom so Stalinym* (Moscow: Bylina, 1999), 78 (1991 interview).

2. **Stalin's mood**, Allilueva, *Dvadtsat' pisem*, 149; **Kaganovich and Ezhov**, Solovev, "Tetradi," *Neizvestnaia Rossiia*, 4:178; *Stalin i Kaganovich*, 702; *Stalinskoe Politbiuro*, 148, 152; **Ezhov**, Jansen, *Stalin's Loyal Executioner*, 19–20; Chuev, *Sto sorok besed*, 438; Anna Larina Bukharina, *Nezabyvaemoe* (Moscow: APN, 1989), 269–70; Mandelshtam, *Vospominaniia*, 119–20.

3. **Ezhov's rise**, Jansen, *Stalin's Loyal Executioner*, 25, 54; Getty, *Yezhov*, 204; *Stalin i Kaganovich*, 682–83; *Stalinskoe Politbiuro*, 159; Dzhambul, "Narkom Ezhov," *Pravda*, 3 December 1927, 2; **Enukidze**, RGASPI, 558/11/728, ll. 52–66 (correspondence with Stalin); Allilueva, *Dvadtsat' pisem*, 88; Edvard Radzinsky, *Stalin* (New York: Doubleday, 1996), 331; Jansen, *Stalin's Loyal Executioner*, 33–34; Roi A. Medvedev, *Chto chital Stalin?* (Moscow: Prava cheloveka, 2005), 144 (Rolland conversation); Getty and Naumov, *Yezhov*, 163 ("taking a nap" quotation); **Kremlin purge**, Getty and Naumov, *Yezhov*, 159, 161–62; RGASPI, 17/2/542, ll. 81, 83 (list of arrested persons); Zenkovich, *Samye sekretnye*, 178 (Kamenev family).

4. **Enukidze negotiations**, *Stalin i Kaganovich*, 557–58, 580, 583; RGASPI, 558/11/89; *Politbiuro TsK RKP(b)-VKP(b): Povestki*, 695; Getty, *Yezhov*, 164–65; **arrest** (11 February 1937), Khlevniuk, *Master*, 145; **Enukidze posthumously accused**, Robert Conquest, *The Great Terror* (Harmondsworth: Penguin, 1971), 514, 549; Gregory, *Politics, Murder*, 127–28; Khlevniuk, *Master*, 148; **Molotov under threat**,

Khlevniuk, *Master*, 148; Alexander Orlov, *The Secret History of Stalin's Crimes* (London: Jarrolds, 1954), 162–66.

5. **Sheinin play**, *Ochnaia stavka: P'esa v chetyrekh deistviiakh s prologom* by the Tur brothers and L. Sheinin (Moscow-Leningrad 1938); John Scott, *Behind the Urals* (Bloomington: Indiana University Press, 1989), 197–203: Sheila Fitzpatrick, *Everyday Stalinism* (New York: Oxford University Press, 1999), 203; **Stalin and trials**, RGASPI, 558/11/96, ll. 16, 31, 37, 41; RGASPI, 74/2/38, l. 82 ("bourgeois dogs" quotation); *Stalin i Kaganovich*, 631 (quotation), 638, 642–43, 666; **perlustrated materials** (October 1936), RGASPI, 558/11/96, l. 52; **"Reserve center,"** *Stalin i Kaganovich*, 631, 638; **new investigations**, Conquest, *Great Terror*, 166.

6. **Ordzhonikidze and Pyatakov**, Khlevniuk, *Stalin i Ordzhonikidze*, 67, 69; *Stalin i Kaganovich*, 631, 673; **Pyatakov's offer**, Khlevniuk, *Stalin i Ordzhonikidze*, 68–69; Jansen, *Stalin's Loyal Executioner*, 48 (the wife in question was either his second, Zinaida Vasileva, or his third, Ludmila Dityaeva, both of whom were former Oppositionists arrested in 1936; thanks to Andrea Graziosi for this information); **arrest**, Khlevniuk, *Stalin i Ordzhonikidze*, 71; **Ordzhonikidze's death**, Chuev, *Molotov*, 250–51; A. I. Mikoian, *Tak bylo*, 328–30 (quotation); Khlevniuk, *Stalin i Ordzhonikidze*, 118–29; *Khrushchev Remembers*, 84–85; *Stalinskoe Politbiuro*, 153–55; **Molotov to February–March plenum**, *Bol'shevik*, 1937, no. 8, 12–45.

7. **Military plot**, Jansen, *Stalin's Loyal Executioner*, 69–70; **friendships**, Vitaly Rapoport and Yuri Alexeev, *High Treason* (Durham, NC: Duke University Press, 1985), 274; Rees, *Iron Lazar*, 80, 194; *Molotov, Malenkov, Kaganovich, 1957* (Moscow, 1998), 69; Khlevniuk, *Master*, 218; N. Khrushchev, *Khrushchev Remembers: The Glasnost Tapes*, 27–29; S. Mikoian, *Vospominaniia*, 33, 35; A. I. Mikoian, *Tak bylo*, 553; **Voroshilov**, Radzinsky, *Stalin*, 371; *Istochnik*, 1994, no. 3, 72 (quotation); **Yakir's arrest**, Conquest, *Great Terror*, 303; **Stalin's speech** (2 June 1937), *Istochnik*, 1994, no. 3, 72–88 (text); Roy A. Medvedev, *Let History Judge* (New York: Alfred A. Knopf, 1971), 301 (quoted comment); **Molotov**, Chuev, *Sto sorok besed*, 392 (quotation); **Khrushchev**, quoted in Taubman, *Khrushchev*, 103.

8. **Tomsky's suicide**, *Stalin i Kaganovich*, 639–40; O. V. Khlevniuk, *1937-i* (Moscow: "Respublika," 1992), 199, 201; **Bukharin's poem**, RGASPI, 329/2/6, l. 93 (translation in Gregory, *Politics, Murder*, 90–91); **"shot the scoundrels,"** quoted in Gregory, *Politics, Murder*, 89; **Bukharin's trip**, Gregory, *Politics, Murder*, 83–84; **Bukharin's hunger strike**, quotations from Gregory, *Politics, Murder*, 99, 107; **Bukharin's appeals**, RGASPI, 329/2/6, ll. 10–15, and ibid. 558/11/96, ll. 22, 26 (Voroshilov); RGASPI, 329/2/6, l. 119 (Khrushchev); ibid., ll. 41–44 (Molotov); **death penalty**, Gregory, *Politics, Murder*, 120; **Bukharin's letters to Stalin**, " 'Prosti menia, Koba,' " *Istochnik*, 1993, no. 0, 24–25.

9. **Yagoda**, *Report of Court Proceedings in the Case of the Anti-Soviet "Bloc of Rights and Trotskyites," Heard before the Military Collegium of the Supreme Court of the USSR, Moscow, March 2–13, 1938* (Moscow: People's Commissariat of Justice of the USSR, 1938), 786; **Molotov comment**, Chuev, *Sto sorok besed*, 404–5; **Bukharin's final speech**, *Report of Court Proceedings*, 777, and Gregory, *Politics, Murder*, 138–40; Arthur Koestler, *Darkness at Noon*, trans. Daphne Hardy (London: Jonathan Cape, 1940), 240; **isolate families**, Chuev, *Sto sorok besed*, 415; **Bukharin's family**, Ze-

nkovich, *Samye sekretnye*, 61–66; Gregory, *Politics, Murder*, 131; **adult sons shot**, Zenkovich, *Samye sekretnye*, 176–77, 420 (Alexander and Yury Kamenev, Mikhail and Viktor Tomsky); **other punishments**, Zenkovich, *Samye sekretnye*, 337, 320–21, 420, 177 (Natalia Rykova, Leonid and Vladimir Postyshev, Yury Tomsky, Vladimir Kamenev); **orphanage,** Gregory, *Politics, Murder*, 131.

10. **Surveillance of Trotsky**, RGASPI, 558/11/96, ll. 39, 46, 50; **fate of Trotsky family**, Service, *Trotsky*, 500; Zenkovich, *Samye sekretnye*, 429–32; Deutscher, *Prophet Outcast*, 281–82; **signatures**, Chuev, *Molotov*, 514; **Kaganovich**, quoted in Rees, *Iron Lazar*, 194.

11. **Andreev**, *Vestnik APRF*, supplement to *Istochnik*, 1995, no. 1, 127; *Voprosy istorii*, 1990, no. 4, 78 (Khrushchev quotation); *Sovetskoe rukovodstvo*, 371–75; RGASPI, 558/11/65, l. 33 (reports to Stalin); Andreev, *Vospominaniia*, 218–20, 236, 301 (music); **Kaganovich**, Rees, *Iron Lazar*, 195; Mikhail Shreider, *NKVD iznutri* (Moscow: Vozvrashchenie, 1995), 64–71; **Zhdanov**, N. Kariakin, "'Zhdanovskaia zhidkost' ili protiv ochernitel'stva," in Iu. N. Afansev, ed., *Inogo ne dano* (Moscow: Progress, 1988) (quotation); S.A. Kislitsyn, *Iurii Zhdanov: Riadom so Stalinym, Sholokhovym, Il'enkovym* (Moscow: URSS, 2013), 23; **Malenkov**, Rees, *Iron Lazar*, 195; *Molotov, Malenkov, Kaganovich, 1957*, 45; Malenkov, *O moem ottse*, 33; **Mikoyan**, M. Iu. Pavlov, *Anastas Mikoian* (Moscow: Mezhdunarodnye otnosheniia, 2010), 92–93.

12. **Kaganovich**, Chuev, *Tak govoril Kaganovich*, 80 (quotation); **Voroshilov**, Vadim Rogovin, *Stalin's Terror of 1937–1938* (Oak Park, MI: Mehring Books, 2009), 151; **Zhdanov**, Boterbloem, *Zhdanov*, 161, 165; Volynets, *Zhdanov*, 214; **Khrushchev**, N. Khrushchev, *Khrushchev Remembers*, 82, 105–16; Zhores Medvedev and Roi Medvedev, *Nikita Khrushchev* (Moscow: Vremia, 2012), 124, 127; **Beria**, Knight, *Beria*, 78–86; **Central Committee**, *Khrushchev Remembers*, 572; **ministers** (People's Commissars of USSR), Roi Medvedev, *Oni okruzhali Stalina* (Benson, VT: Chalidze Publications, 1984), 26.

13. **Molotov**, Chuev, *Sto sorok besed*, 390; **Kaganovich,** *Stalin i Kaganovich*, 284 ("pupil"); **Khrushchev**, N. Khrushchev, *Khrushchev Remembers: The Glasnost Tapes*, 31 (quotation); **Andreev**, Montefiore, *Stalin*, 258 (quotation from Natalia Andreeva); **Mikoyan**, S. Mikoian, *Vospominaniia*, 30–31; **Chubar**, V. Drobizhev and N. Dubova, *V. Ia. Chubar'* (Moscow: Gosudarstvennoe izdatel'stvo politicheskoi literatury, 1963), 71.

14. **Confrontations**, RGASPI, 558/11/96, ll. 41, 43; Larina, *This I Cannot Forget*, 31, 313; Gregory, *Politics, Murder*, 113–14 (Radek quotation); Chuev, *Sto sorok besed*, 413 (Antipov quotation), 486–87; **Rudzutak**, Chuev, *Molotov*, 483–86 (quotation); Montefiore, *Stalin*, 223 ("ball gowns" quotation); Khlevniuk, *Master*, 215; **Eikhe**, Khlevniuk, *Master*, 212–13; N. Khrushchev, *Khrushchev Remembers*, 579–81.

15. **Petrovsky**, Medvedev, *Let History Judge*, 295–96; **Kosior**, Khlevniuk, *Master*, 217–18; www.alexanderyakovlev.org/fond/issues (A. N. Yakovlev papers, doc. 322: Ezhov to Stalin, 16.04.1938 on Kazimir's arrest); RGASPI, 558/11/754, ll. 112–13 (S. Kosior to Stalin, 20 April 1938); *O Stanislave Kosiore* (Moscow: Politizdat, 1989), 218–19 (quotation from A. G. Snegov); Kumanev, *Govoriat stalinskie narkomy*, 107 (interview with Kaganovich); Medvedev, *Let History Judge*, 295–96 (Kosior quotation); **Chubar**, Chuev, *Sto sorok besed*, 413–14 ("snake," 413); *Stalinskoe Politbiuro*,

167; Khlevniuk, *Politbiuro*, 229; N. Khrushchev, *Khrushchev Remembers: The Glasnost Tapes*, 35.

16. **Postyshev**, Valentin M. Berezhkov, *At Stalin's Side* (New York: Birch Lane Press, 1994), 229 (Kiev beautification); Leonid Postyshev, "Iz ukhodiashchego pro-shlogo," *Fakel* (Moscow, 1989), 202–3; N. Khrushchev, *Khrushchev Remembers: The Glasnost Tapes*, 34–35; *Pravda*, 29 May 1937, 2; Khlevniuk, *Master*, 210; Khlevniuk, *Politbiuro*, 216–23; *Stalinskoe Politbiuro*, 156–67 (text of speech of 14 January 1938, with heckling); **January 1938 plenum**, Jansen, *Stalin's Loyal Executioner*, 126; G. A. Chigrinov, "Pochemu Stalin, a ne drugie?" *Voprosy istorii KPSS*, 1960, no. 6, 92.

17. **Stalin's file**, N. Khrushchev, *Khrushchev Remembers*, 108 (quotation); Malen-kov, *O moem ottse*, 34; **Lorberg's arrest**, Vasileva, *Kremlevskie zheny*, 291–93; *Is-toricheskii arkhiv*, 2000 no. 6, 212–13; *Politbiuro i delo Beriia* (Moscow: Kuchkovo pole, 2012), 536–39 (interrrogation transcript); Chuev, *Sto sorok besed*, 315 (quota-tion); **Kalinin's letter**, *Istoricheskii arkhiv*, 2000, no. 6, 212–13; **threats to team members**, RGASPI, 558/11/762, l. 2 (Malenkov to Stalin, 22 September 1938); Malenkov, *O moem ottse*, 32; Knight, *Beria*, 78–79; *Voprosy istorii*, 1990, no. 4, 78; N. Khrushchev, *Khrushchev Remembers: The Glasnost Tapes*, 37–38; Medvedev, *Oni okru-zhali Stalina*, 149 (Mikoyan).

18. **Molotov**, RGASPI, 82/2/1439, l. 48 (tutor); Montefiore, *Stalin*, 188 (nanny); David-Fox, *Showcasing*, 301 (Arosev); Chuev, *Sto sorok besed*, 414–15 (quotation); **NKVD order**, A. I. Mikoian, *Tak bylo*, 583; **Molotov's intercessions**, RGASPI, 82/2/1439, l. 52; Montefiore, *Stalin*, 188; Chuev, *Sto sorok besed*, 420, 422; David-Fox, *Showcasing*, 301; Olga Aroseva, *Bez grima* (Moscow, 2000), 30 (quotation); RGASPI, 82/2/1453 (Mogilnaya).

19. **Kaganovich**, Chuev, *Tak govoril Kaganovich*, 79–80; Kumanev, *Govoriat stal-inskie narkomy*, 107 (interview with Kaganovich); **Mikoyan**, GARF, 120/580/680 (1937–38 correspondence, with notations); A. I. Mikoian, *Tak bylo*, 582–83; Bonner, *Mothers and Daughters*, 323–24; S. Mikoian, *Vospominaniia*, 33, 35; **Voroshilov**, Vasi-leva, *Kremlin Wives*, 84–85.

20. **Dimitrov**, Montefiore, *Stalin*, 290; **Stalin's assistants arrested**, Kun, *Stalin*, 285–88; Montefiore, *Stalin*, 266; Zenkovich, *Samye sekretnye*, 430–31 (three out of seven of Stalin's past and present secretaries were purge victims [Brezanovsky, Kan-ner, Nazeryan], and the wife of his chief assistant, Poskrebyshev, reputedly a favorite of Stalin's, was arrested in 1939 and shot in 1941); **Stalin's in-laws**, *Iosif Stalin v ob"iatiiakh sem'i*, 193; Kun, *Stalin*, 392, 409, 380, 411–15; Shreider, *NKVD iznutri*, 101; **Svanidze**, A. I. Mikoian, *Tak bylo*, 356–59; *Iosif Stalin v ob"iatiiakh sem'i*, 193; **Kavtaradze**, Montefiore, *Young Stalin*, 320; **nanny**, Allilueva, *Dvadtsat' pisem*, 97.

21. **Cynicism**, Medvedev, *Let History Judge*, 311; Montefiore, *Young Stalin*, 309; **Ezhov's fall**, Jansen, *Stalin's Loyal Executioner*, 140, 149–50, 161–65; **Ezhova's death**, Jansen, *Stalin's Loyal Executioner*, 168–71; **arrest and execution rates**, Getty, *Road to Terror*, 527–28 (around half a million arrests and 300,000 executions in 1938).

22. **Carryover rate**, Graeme Gill, *The Origins of the Stalinist Political System* (Cambridge: Cambridge University Press, 1990), 278; N. Khrushchev, *Khrushchev Remembers*, 572–73; **XVIII Congress**, *XVIII s"ezd Vsesoiuznoi Kommunisticheskoi Partii (b): 10–21 marta 1939 g. Stenograficheskii otchet* (Moscow: OGIZ, 1939), 3, 104, 211, 169; **Stalin's speech**, Stalin, *Sochineniia*, ed. McNeal, vol. 1 (14), 369; **criticism**

of Molotov, Khlevniuk, *Master*, 221; **Zhdanov's report**, *XVIII s"ezd*, 519–24; **"small-p" purging**, J. Arch Getty, *Origins of the Great Purges* (Cambridge: Cambridge University Press, 1985), 38–57, 202; **age of delegates**, Volynets, *Zhdanov*, 222; **clapping**, N. G. Kuznetsov, *Krutye povoroty: Iz zapisok admirala* (Moscow: Molodaia gvardiia, 1995), 57 (quotation).

CHAPTER 6. INTO WAR

1. **Litvinov's dismissal**, Dullin, *Men of Influence*, 232; Derek Watson, *Molotov: A Biography*, (Basingstoke: Palgrave Macmillan, 2005), 154; **bad blood between Litvinov and Molotov**, Watson, *Molotov*, 152; Maurice Hindus, *Crisis in the Kremlin* (New York: Doubleday, 1953), 48; Berezhkov, *At Stalin's Side*, 317; **Molotov's anti-Semitic outburst**, Watson, *Molotov*, 155; Berezhkov, *At Stalin's Side*, 225–26.

2. **Foreign ministry purge**, Arkady Vaksberg, *Stalin against the Jews* (New York: Alfred A. Knopf, 1994), 84–86; Chuev, *Molotov*, 332–33 (quotation); Hindus, *Crisis*, 48; **Zhemchuzhina**, RGASPI, 558/11/58, l. 99 (Stalin to Vladivostok officials, 9 May 1939); RGANI, 3/32/13, ll. 29–32; *Stalinskoe Politbiuro*, 171–72; Khlevniuk, *Politbiuro*, 242; **Molotov's abstention**, Chuev, *Sto sorok besed*, 474–75.

3. **Strang**, Richard Overy, *Russia's War* (New York: Penguin, 1998), 44–45; Watson, *Molotov*, 160 (quotation); **comment of British ambassador** (Sir William Seeds), quoted in Watson, *Molotov*, 163 and 157; **Molotov's policy preferences**, Watson, *Molotov*, 149–52.

4. **German-Soviet Nonaggression Pact**, 23 August 1939, S. Beria, *Beria, My Father*, 51–52; N. Khrushchev, *Khrushchev Remembers*, 128, 135, 139; A. I. Mikoian, *Tak bylo*, 376–77 (quotation); **Kaganovich**, Chuev, *Tak govoril Kaganovich*, 89–90 (quotation); Chuev, *Sto sorok besed*, 19 (Molotov quotation); **popular opinion**, Timothy Johnson, *Being Soviet* (Oxford: Oxford University Press, 2011), 21–22; Alexander Werth, *Russia at War* (London: Pan Books, 1964), 60–73, 83.

5. **Occupation of Eastern Poland**, N. Khrushchev, *Khrushchev Remembers*, 143–49; **Wasilewska**, N. Khrushchev, *Khrushchev Remembers*, 145; Marci Shore, *Caviar and Ashes: A Warsaw Generation's Life and Death in Marxism, 1918–1968* (New Haven: Yale University Press, 2006), 172–74, 200–202, 237–40; **Finnish War**, N. Khrushchev, *Khrushchev Remembers*, 152 (quotation), 154–55; Overy, *Russia's War*, 57.

6. **Tripartite Pact**, Watson, *Molotov*, 183–86; **Ribbentrop**, Chuev, *Molotov*, 33 (quotation); Berezhkov, *At Stalin's Side*, 46–47 (bunker story); **Hitler**, Chuev, *Molotov*, 35 (quotation); **Stalin's respect for Molotov**, Konstantin Simonov, *Glazami cheloveka moego pokoleniia* (Moscow: Novosti, 1988), 348 (quoting Zhukov).

7. **Mikhail Kaganovich**, A. S. Iakovlev, *Tsel' zhizni* (Moscow: Politizdat, 1972), 198 (quotation); G. A. Kumanev, *Govoriat stalinskie narkomy* (Smolensk: Rusich, 2005), 105–6, 556–57; N. Khrushchev, *Khrushchev Remembers*, 47–48; S. Beria, *Beria, My Father*, 165; 105–6; Chuev, *Tak govoril Kaganovich*, 78–79; *Lavrentii Beriia: Stenogramma iul'skogo plenuma TsK KPSS i drugie materialy* (Moscow: Mezhdunarodnyi fond "Demokratiia," 1999), 42–43 (1953 rehabilitation); **new cohort**, Sheila Fitzpatrick, "Stalin and the Making of a New Elite," in Fitzpatrick, *The Cultural Front* (Ithaca, NY: Cornell University Press, 1992), 149–82; **Kosygin**, Jerry Hough, and Merle Fainsod, *How the Soviet Union Is Governed* (Cambridge, MA: Harvard Univer-

sity Press, 1982), 242–44; **Gromyko**, A. A. Gromyko, *Pamiatnoe* (Moscow: Izdatel'stvo politicheskoi literatury, 1988), vol. 1; **view of Stalin**, Iakovlev, *Tsel' zhizni*, 196–97, 490–92.

8. **Assessment of German intentions**, Chuev, *Molotov*, 42; Simonov, *Glazami*, 355 (Zhukov quotation); Kumanev, *Govoriat stalinskie narkomy*, 56 (Mikoyan); Christopher Andrew and Vasili Mitrokhin, *The Sword and the Shield* (New York: Basic Books, 1999), 94 (Beria); Volynets, *Zhdanov*, 328–29; Simonov, *Glazami*, 348 (Zhdanov; note contradictory but unpersuasive testimony in S. Beria, *Beria, My Father*, 52, that Zhdanov was a Germanophile who enthusiastically supported the German alliance).

9. **German attack**, Overy, *Russia's War*, 64–65; **Stalin's reaction**, Kumanev, *Govoriat stalinskie narkomy*, 62 (Mikoyan quotation on Lenin's inheritance), 63 ("prostration" quotation: Molotov, reported by Mikoyan); Radzynski, *Stalin*, 469–72 (Ivan the Terrible); Chuev, *Sto sorok besed*, 51–2, 329–30; Chuev, *Tak govoril Kaganovich*, 88; **team meeting and visit to Stalin**, A. I. Mikoian, *Tak bylo*, 391; Kumanev, *Govoriat stalinskie narkomy*, 63–64; *Politbiuro i delo Beriia*, 20 (note the absence of Khrushchev, Zhdanov, Kaganovich, Andreev, and Kalinin from the meeting called by Beria, the first two presumably because they were not in Moscow. Andreev had come rushing up from the dacha as soon as he heard of the German attack [Andreev, *Vospominaniia*, 323], but evidently his presence was not required. The visit probably took place on June 30, after the initial meeting of the State Defense Committee on that day. According to the Kremlin office log, Stalin had been absent the two previous days.); **Molotov broadcast**, Watson, *Molotov*, 189–90; Kumanev, *Govoriat stalinskie narkomy*, 58, 481; **Stalin broadcast**, Service, *Stalin*, 449–50.

10. **Stalin head of government**, Khlevniuk, *Politbiuro*, 254 (resolution of 4 May 1941); Watson, *Molotov*, 188; **occupied territory**, Michael K. Roof and Frederick A. Leedy, "Population Redistribution in the Soviet Union, 1939–1956," *Geographical Review* (April 1979), 210; Alec Nove, *An Economic History of the USSR* (Harmondsworth: Penguin, 1972), 27; **traitors law;** Dmitri Volkogonov, *Stalin: Triumph and Tragedy* (Rocklin, CA: Prima, 1991), 427; **Stalin's panic**, Simonov, *Glazami*, 398 (quoting General, later Marshal, Ivan Konev).

11. **Kuibyshev evacuation**, Watson, *Molotov*, 192–93; A. I. Mikoian, *Tak bylo*, 417, 421; Chuev, *Molotov*, 68; Malenkov, *O moem ottse*, 42; Andreev, *Vospominaniia*, 325; **Afinogenov**, Jochen Hellbeck, *Revolution on My Mind* (Cambridge, MA: Harvard University Press, 2006), 341; **November parade**, *Pravda*, 8 November 1941, 1; Overy, *Russia's War*, 115; **Voroshilov's removal**, Chuev, *Sto sorok besed*, 63; Watson, *Molotov*, 192; **Leningrad blockade**, Overy, *Russia's War*, 105; **Zhdanov**, Volynets, *Zhdanov*, 333, 347; Malenkov, *O moem ottse*, 44 (quotation); Chuev, *Molotov*, 63–64 (quotation); A. I. Mikoian, *Tak bylo*, 562.

12. **Team performance**, Watson, *Molotov*, 195; Oleg Khlevniuk, "Stalin na voine," *Cahiers de monde russe*, 52: 2–3 (2011), 211 ("collective leadership"); A. I. Mikoian, *Tak bylo*, 465 (quotation); Kumanev, *Govoriat stalinskie narkomy*, 67–68; Simonov, *Glazami*, 347–48 (Zhukov quotation); **Molotov**, A. I. Mikoian, *Tak bylo*, 463; Chuev, *Molotov*, 63; Simonov, *Glazami*, 398; Watson, *Molotov*, 199–205.

13. **Team responsibilities**, Watson, *Molotov*, 195–96; A. I. Mikoian, *Tak bylo*, 425; Iu. N. Zhukov, *Tainy Kremlia* (Moscow: TERRA, 2000), 200, 208; Seweryn Bi-

aler, *Stalin and His Generals* (New York: Pegasus, 1969), 342; **Voznesenky**, Volynets, *Zhdanov*, 223–24; Kumanev, *Govoriat stalinskie narkomy*, 495–98; A. I. Mikoian, *Tak bylo*, 435 (quotation).

14. **Beria**, Chuev, *Sto sorok besed*, 436; Knight, *Beria*, 112–13, 118; Kumanev, *Govoriat stalinskie narkomy*, 339–41; *Riadom so Stalinym*, 432 (Ya. E. Chadaev quotation); **Malenkov**, Zhukov, *Tainy Kremlia*, 246; A. I. Mikoian, *Tak bylo*, 586; **Zhdanov**, Volynets, *Zhdanov*, 351–52; A. I. Mikoian, *Tak bylo*, 562.

15. **Khrushchev**, N. Khrushchev, *Khrushchev Remembers*, 182–89; Taubman, *Khrushchev*, 152–54, 167, 171; Kumanev, *Govoriat stalinskie narkomy*, 509–10 (Chadaev); Simonov, *Glazami*, 470–71 (Vasilevsky quotation); **Kaganovich**, Overy, *Russia's War*, 170; Kumanev, *Govoriat stalinskie narkomy*, 88, 117–18 (quotation from GKO resolution), 138, 233 (quotation from successor A. V. Khrulev), 584–85, 501–3; Chuev, *Tak govoril Kaganovich*, 52 (Kaganovich quotation); Volkogonov, *Stalin: Triumph and Tragedy*, 419 (citing I. V. Kovalev); Iurii Zhukov, *Stalin: Tainy vlasti* (Moscow: Vagrius, 2005), 127 ("out of political game").

16. **Voroshilov**, Khlevniuk, *Master*, 222; Zhukov, *Stalin*, 148–49 (quotation); A. I. Mikoian, *Tak bylo*, 463; Iakovlev, *Tsel' zhizni*, 490; **Andreev**, Kun, *Stalin*, 332; Kumanev, *Govoriat stalinskie narkomy*, 314 (quotation from I. V. Kovalev); **Kalinin**, G. K. Zhukov, *Vospominaniia i razmyshleniia* (Moscow: Novosti, 1990), 3:303; Kumanev, *Govoriat stalinskie narkomy*, 492–94 (Chadaev).

17. **Stalin on military affairs**, Chuev, *Sto sorok besed*, 271 (quotation); **Stalin's military brainstrust**, Bialer, *Stalin and His Generals*, 343; **Zhukov**, Simonov, *Glazami*, 360; **Korneichuk play** (*The Front*, 1942), Simonov, *Glazami*, 356; *Vlast' I khudozhestvennaia intelligentsia* (Moscow: Mezhdunarodnyi fond "Demokratiia," 1999), 781 (note); **Khrushchev**, N. Khrushchev, *Khrushchev Remembers*, 163 (Timoshenko quotations), 164, 211, 218; **Mikoyan**, A. I. Mikoian, *Tak bylo*, 394–98, 475; **Beria**, S. Beriia, *Moi otets* (1994), 195; Knight, *Beria*, 120; Bialer, *Stalin and His Generals*, 452; **Malenkov**, N. Khrushchev, *Khrushchev Remembers*, 196 (quotation); A. G. Malenkov, *O moem ottse*, 42; **Andreev**, Andreev, *Vospominaniia*, 330.

18. **Svetlana**, Allilueva, *Dvadtsat' pisem*, 132–38, 141–43 (quotation); Service, *Stalin*, 432–33; Zenkovich, *Samye sekretnye*, 404–5; A. I. Mikoian, *Tak bylo*, 362–63. On Morozov Sr. and Mikhoels, see chap. 8 in this volume.

19. **Stalin's instructions to sons**, Chuev, *Sto sorok besed*, 295; **Vladimir Mikoyan**, Pavlov, *Anastas Mikoian*, 182–86; **Timor Frunze**, RGASPI, 74/1/429 (Voroshilova, "Something like a diary," entry for 6 July 1945); **Yakov Dzhugashvili**, Service, *Stalin*, 430–31; Allilueva, *Dvadtsat' pisem*, 122–25; **Leonid Khrushchev**, N. Khrushchev, *Khrushchev Remembers*, 190; Taubman, *Khrushchev*, 156–58; Chuev, *Sto sorok besed*, 352; Chuev, *Molotov*, 421–22; Zenkovich, *Samye sekretnye*, 449–51; Sergei Khrushchev, *Nikita Khrushchev: Krizisy i rakety* (Moscow: Novosti, 1994), 16–17; **"Kremlin children" cases**, Pavlov, *Anastas Mikoian*, 187–88; Zenkovich, *Samye sekretnye*, 264–65, 470–71.

20. **Stalingrad**, N. Khrushchev, *Khrushchev Remembers*, 189–200 (quotation 197); **Stalin's worsening behavior**, Kuznetsov, *Krutye povoroty*, 55 (quotation); Simonov, *Glazami*, 377; A. I. Mikoian, *Tak bylo*, 466 (quotation).

21. **Security agencies**, Knight, *Beria*, 124; **Military ranks for security personnel**, *Pravda*, 11 July 1945; **Chechen deportation**, *Vainakhi i imperskaia vlast'* (Mos-

cow: ROSSPEN, 2011), 667–76; Knight, *Beria*, 126–27; **Solzhenitsyn's arrest** (9 February 1945), Liudmila Saraskina, *Aleksandr Solzhenitsyn* (Moscow: Molodaia gvardiia, 2008), 261–62; **Baltics**, Elena Zubkova, *Pribaltika i Kreml'* (Moscow: ROSSPEN, 2008), 129–45.

22. **Kiev**, N. Khrushchev, *Khrushchev Remembers*, 216 (quotations); **Leningrad**, Harrison E. Salisbury, *The Siege of Leningrad* (London: Secker & Warburg, 1969), 510, 552; **Zhdanov**, Volynets, *Zhdanov*, 346, 372–92; **Stalin's mood**, Overy, *Russia's War*, 264 (quotation); **Berlin**, Geoffrey Roberts, *Stalin's General* (London: Icon Books, 2012), 229–31.

23. **War losses**, Overy, *Russia's War*, 288; **Generalissimus**, Chuev, *Sto sorok besed*, 253; **Stalin**, Zhukov, *Vospominaniia*, 3:305 (I. Vasily's story); **Victory parade**, http://www.youtube.com/watch?v=SZ2SnuN1N5U; Zhukov, *Vospominaniia*, 3:305; Simonov, *Glazami*, 377 (quoting Zhukov); **Stalin's toast**, Stalin, *Sochineniia*, ed. McNeal, 203–4.

CHAPTER 7. POSTWAR HOPES

1. **Postwar expectations**, A. I. Mikoian, *Tak bylo*, 513; E. Iu. Zubkova, *Obshchestvo i reform, 1945–1964* (Moscow: Rossiia molodaia, 1993), 16–63; **impressing the Allies**, Lobanov, *Stalin v vospominaniiakh sovremennikov i dokumentakh epokhi* (Moscow: EKSMO, 2002), 482; Churchill, *Second World War*, 6:345; 5:330 (quotation).

2. **Flying**, RGANI, 3/22/33, l. 9 (Politburo ban, 15 September 1933); *Stalin i Kaganovich, Perepiska*, 332; RGANI, 3/22/33, ll. 3, 35 (Mikoyan's reprimand, 25 June 1933, lifted 11 May 1936); **Molotov**, Simonov, *Glazami*, 80; Bernard Bromage, *Molotov* (London: Peter Owen 1956), 214 (uniform quotation); Hindus, *Crisis in the Kremlin*, 47 (Svetlana quotation); Stalin, *Sochineniia*, ed. Robert H. McNeal, 204 (toast); Watson, *Molotov*, 217, 221, 228–30; RGASPI, 82/2/1592, ll. 40–43, 72–74 (letters to Polina, 1946–47).

3. **Beria**, S. Beriia, *Moi otets* (1994), 231–44, 245–56; Montefiore, *Stalin*; Norman Naimark, *The Russians in German* (Cambridge, MA: Harvard University Press, 1995), 350, 483, 497; **Voroshilov**, Churchill, *Second World War*, 5:306; RGASPI, 70/1/429 (Voroshilova, "Something like a diary," entries for 29 December 1945 and 17 December 1955); **Khrushchev**, N. Khrushchev, *Khrushchev Remembers: The Last Testament*, 157–76; Roi Medvedev, in Zhores Medvedev and Roi Medvedev, *Nikita Khrushchev*, 139; **Mikoyan**, A. I. Mikoyan, *Tak bylo*, 493–512; Pavlov, *Anastas Mikoyan*, 215.

4. **Language abililties**, Sergo Beriia, *Moi otets, Lavrentii Beriia: Syn za ottsa otvechaet...* (Moscow: Algoritm, 2013), 26; Alliluyeva, *Only One Year*, 390; Stepan Mikoyan, *Vospominaniia*, 27; Allilueva, *20 pisem*, 124, 128, 130–31. Sergei Khrushchev, *Khrushchev: Reformator*, 59; **Britanskii soiuiznik/Amerika**, Stalin i kosmopolitizm (Moscow: Materik, 2005), 95; Johnston, *Being Soviet*, 86–87; **Svetlana**, Allilueva, *Dvadtsat' pisem*, 128–29; Alliluyeva, *Only One Year*, 112 (quotation).

5. **Stalin's health**, Service, *Stalin*, 491; RGASPI, 558/11/97, l. 100 (foreign press, October 1945; includes the *Newsweek* report), also ll. 110, 129; **Molotov as heir**, RGASPI, 558/11/97, l. 91 (quotation); Chuev, *Sto sorok besed*, 52; **Stalin's attack** (4–7 December 1945), RGASPI, 558/11/99, ll. 86, 92–93.

6. **Mikoyan**, see chap. 6 on 1944 rebuke and sons; RGASPI, 558/11/732, l. 42 ("thieves"); **Beria**, Gorlizki and Khlevniuk, *Cold Peace*, 28; Knight, *Beria*, 135–40; Pikhoia, *Sovetskii Soiuz* (Moscow: Izdatel'stvo RAGS, 1998), 60, 73; S. Beria, *Beria, My Father*, 246; **Malenkov**, A. G. Malenkov, *O moem ottse*, 53; Gorlizki and Khlevniuk, *Cold Peace*, 27–28; **Zhdanov**, Chuev, *Sto sorok besed*, 312; Volynets, *Zhdanov*, 390.

7. **Voznesensky**, *Khrushchev Remembers*, 251 (quotation); A. I. Mikoian, *Tak bylo*, 423; Dmitrii Shepilov, *Neprimknuvshii* (Moscow: Vagrius, 2001), 390; Kumanev, *Govoriat stalinskie narkomy*, 412; Simonov, *Glazami*, 139; **Kuznetsov**, Volynets, *Zhdanov*, 224–26; Pikhoia, *Sovetskii Soiuz*, 60, 73; **future leadership**, N. Khrushchev, *Khrushchev Remembers*, 251; Pikhoia, *Sovetskii Soiuz*, 65; **Kalinin/Lorberg**, A. I. Adzhubei, *Te desiat' let* (Moscow: Sovetskaia Rossiia, 1989), 145; *Istoricheskii arkhiv*, 2000, no. 6, 212–13; **Shvernik**, Kumanev, *Govoriat stalinskie narkomy*, 138; **Bulganin**, N. Khrushchev, *Khrushchev Remembers: The Glasnost Tapes*, 39; Kumanev, *Govoriat stalinskie narkomy*, 411, 508; Zenkovich, *Samye sekretnye*, 58–60.

8. **Khrushchev**, N. Khrushchev, *Khrushchev Remembers*, 240–44; **Kaganovich**, Pikhoia, *Sovetskii Soiuz*, 77; **Andreev**, Gorlizki and Khlevniuk, *Cold Peace*, 63; Andreev, *Vospominaniia*, 268–69; **Voroshilov**, quoted Montefiore, *Stalin*, 467; Chuev, *Sto sorok besed*, 314–15; N. Khrushchev, *Khrushchev Remembers*, 308; Vasileva, *Kremlin Wives*, 86; **Zhukov**, TsKhDNISO (Tsentr khraneniia dokumentatsii noveishei istorii Samarskoi oblasti), 714/1/1149 (popular questions about Zhukov's fate, 1945–46); RGANI, 3/32/13, l. 116 (Zhemchuzhina indignant at house search); Gorlizki and Khlevniuk, *Cold Peace*, 31–32; Roberts, *Stalin's General*, 244–53.

9. **Churchill**, *Stalin i kosmopolitizm*, 31–32; **Fulton speech** ("Sinews of Peace," 5 March 1946, http://history1900s.about.com/od/churchillwinston/a/Iron-Curtain.htm; **Stalin's response** (14 March 1945), Stalin, *Sochineniia*, ed. McNeal, vol. 3 (16), 35–43; **alarm**, Zhukov, quoted in Robert Gellately, *Stalin's Curse* (Oxford: Oxford University Press, 2013), 159 (quoting Marshal Kiril Meretskov), 171; *Origins of the Cold War* (Washington, DC: United States Institute of Peace, 1991), 3–16, esp. 15–16 (Ambassador Mikhail Novikov).

10. **Soviet atomic program**, David Holloway, *Stalin and the Bomb* (Yale University Press, 1994); Knight, *Beria*, 137 (comments of physicists Yuly Khariton and Ivan Golovin); Kumanev, *Govoriat stalinskie narkomy*, 410–11 (quoted comment of D. G. Zhimerin); **Marshall Plan**, Pikoia, *Sovetskii soiuz*, 34–35 (Varga); S. Beria, *Beria, My Father*, 205; Gellately, *Stalin's Curse*, 306 (Molotov quotation); Pavlov, *Anastas Mikoian*, 226; **Cominform**, Vladislav Zubok and Constantine Pleshakov, *Inside the Kremlin's Cold War* (Cambridge, MA: Harvard University Press, 1996), 132–34.

11. **Malenkov/Zhdanov antipathy**, Alliluyeva, *Only One Year*, 394; Zhdanov, *Vzgliad v proshloe*, 123; S. Beria, *Beria, My Father*, 160; **Beria as intriguer**, Chuev, *Sto sorok besed*, 436; **bodyguards**, Allilueva, *Dvadtsat' pisem*, 134,141; S. Beria, *Beria, My Father*, 246; A. G. Malenkov, *O moem ottse*, 59; **bugging**, Molotov, Malenkov, Kaganovich, *1957*, 47; Chuev, *Sto sorok besed*, 314; Malenkov, *O moem ottse*, 59; Radzinsky, *Stalin*, 535–36; S. Beria, *Beria, My Father*, 193.

12. **Agreement/disagreement with Stalin**, Simonov, *Glazami*, 139 (Stalin's comment, quoted from postwar railways minister Ivan Kovalev), 348, 360; *Molotov, Malenkov, Kaganovich, 1957*, 121; Volkogonov, *Stalin*, 390–91; Kuznetsov, *Krutye povoroty*, 82–83.

13. **Rules on contact**, Volkogonov, *Triumf I tragediia*, bk. 2, pt. 1, 131; Sergei Khruschev, *Rozhdenie sverkhderzhavy*, 29 (quotation); Adzhubei, *Te desiat' let*, 27–28; S. Khrushchev, *Nikita Khrushchev: Reformator*, 236–38; **Beria**, Dmitrii Shepilov, *Neprimknuvshii* (Moscow: Vagrius, 2001), 33; **Khrushchev**, S. Khrushchev, *Nikita Khrushchev: Rozhdenie*, 29–30; **intelligentsia friends**, Malenkov, *O moem ottse*, 25; S. Beriia, *Moi otets (1994)*, 36; **Bulganin**, G. Vishnevskaia, *Galina* (Moscow: Rusich, 1999), 203–14; *Govoriat stalinskie narkomy*, 411 (Zhimerin); **Voroshilov**, RGASPI, 70/1/429 (Ekaterina Voroshilova, "Something like a diary," 14, 15–16, 76); **Andreev**, Andreev, *Vospominaniia*, 330.

14. **Kremlin children's education**, Sheila Fitzpatrick, "Stalin and the World of Culture," in *Totalitarian Dictatorship: New Histories*, ed. Daniela Baratieri and Giuseppe Finaldi (New York: Routledge, 2014), 75–77; **good concerts**, Alliluyeva, *Only One Year*, 390; S. Mikoian, *Vospominaniia*, 166; **gold medal**, RGASPI, 82/2/1592, l. 16. (letter to Polina [1946]); **Moscow university life**, Vladislav Zubok, *Zhivago's Children: The Last Russian Intelligentsia* (Cambridge, MA: Belknap Press, Harvard University Press, 2009), 30–31, 40, 290; Benjamin Tromly, *Making the Soviet Intelligentsia* (Cambridge: Cambridge University Press, 2014); **new generation**, RGASPI, 82/2/1592, ll. 57–60 (letter to Polina, 19 June 1947).

15. **Dinners**, Gorlizki and Khlevniuk, *Cold Peace*, 49; Milovan Djilas, *Conversations with Stalin* (Harmondsworth: Penguin, 1962), 64 (quotation), 117–35; N. Khrushchev, *Khrushchev Remembers*, 296–306 (quotation, 301); Service, *Stalin*, 524–25; Alliluyeva, *Only One Year*, 363; **late night regime**, Gorlizki and Khlevniuk, *Cold Peace*, 63–64, 196; **Zhdanov**, N. Khrushchev, *Khrushchev Remembers*, 284; Djilas, *Conversations*, 121; Dmitrii Shepilov, *The Kremlin's Scholar* (New Haven: Yale University Press, 2007), 91; **medical memo**, Gorlizki and Khlevniuk, *Cold Peace*, 63; **naps**, Service, *Stalin*, 525; Montefiore, *Stalin*, 521; **Carlsbad**, Montefiore, *Stalin*, 552; **team members' lifestyle**, Alliluyeva, *Only One Year*, 378–90; RGASPI, 74/1/429 (Voroshilova "Something like a diary," entry for 20 May 1951).

16. **Leningrad writers**, Gorlizki and Khlevniuk, *Cold Peace*, 32–33; S. Kuniaev, "Post Scriptum," *Nash sovremennik*, 1995, no. 10, 190; **Stalin's editing**, RGASPI, 558/11/732, l. 1; **MGB dossiers**, *Stalin i kosmopolitizm*, 70; **Orgburo**, "Literaturnyi front," 214, 200, 221–25; **Klyueva-Roskin affair**, Nikolai Krementsov, *The Cure* (Chicago: University of Chicago Press, 2002); **Closed Letter** (16 July 1947, text), *Stalin i kosmopolitizm*, 124; Simonov, *Glazami*, 128; RGASPI, 558/11/732, ll. 89–90; **Courts of honor**, Krementsov, *Cure*, 111–12; also V. D. Esakov and E. S. Levina, *Delo KR: Sudy chesti v ideologii i praktike poslevoennogo stalinizma* (Moscow: Institut rossiiskoi istorii RAN, 2001); **objects of anticosmopolitan campaign**, S. Borisov, *Andrei Aleksandrovich Zhdanov* (Shchadrinsk, 1998), 31; RGASPI, 17/88/819, 129–30, ll. 35–38 (Krasnodar), l. 35 (Velikie Luki); RGASPI, 17/122/326, l. 30 (Riga).

17. **Marriage to foreigners**, *Stalin i kosmopolitizm*, 107 (text of Politburo resolution of 15 February 1947); *New York Times*, 31 July 2010 (Tucker obituary); **Lina Prokofieva**, Simon Morrison, *Lina and Serge* (Boston: Houghton Mifflin Harcourt, 2013), 5–7, 249–54, 270; **Suchkov**, RGASPI, 17/121/616, ll. 20–26; *Lubianka: Stalin I MGB SSSR* (Moscow: Materik, 2007), 60–65; *Stalin i kosmopolitizm*, 729; **Britanskii soiuznik**, *Stalin i kosmopolitizm*, 547–8; Johnson, *Being Soviet*, 176; **Zhdanov's musical tastes**, Shepilov, *Kremlin's Scholar*, 95; **composers' meeting**, Alexander

Werth, *Musical Uproar in Moscow* (London, 1949); **Shostakovich's satire *(Rayok)*,** Elizabeth Wilson, *Shostakovich* (Princeton: Princeton University Press, 1994), 296– 98; **Zhdanov's laughter,** Simon Morrison, *The People's Artist* (Oxford: Oxford University Press, 2009), 29 (citing Mstislav Rostropovich and Tikhon Khrennikov); **Zhdanov's satire,** Zhdanov, *Vzgliad,* 91–92 (text).

18. **Zhdanov home life,** Alliluyeva, *Only One Year,* 390; **Svetlana/Yury romance,** Allilueva, *Dvadtsat' pisem,* 145–46; Zhdanov, *Vzgliad,* 73; **Stalin on husbands,** A. I. Mikoyan, *Tak bylo,* 363; **Svetlana and Sergo,** interview with Marfa Peshkova, http://www.mk.ru/social/interview/2012/09/06/745528-marfakrasavitsa .html; S. Beria, *Beria, My Father,* 151–52; **Peshkovas,** ibid., 191–93; Zen'kovich, *Samye sekretnye,* 25; Antonina Pirozhkova, "Ekaterina Pavlovna Peshkova," http:// magazines.russ.ru/october/2003/7/pir.html.

19. **Yury Zhdanov's career,** Gorlizki and Khlevniuk, *Cold Peace,* 40; Zhdanov, *Vzgliad,* 69 (quotation) Krementsov, *Stalinist Science,* 337 (8 December 1947); RGASPI, 17/121/639, l. 263 (17 July 1948, evidently a postdated formalization); **Shepilov,** Shepilov, *The Kremlin's Scholar,* 22, 124; **lecture,** Nikolai Krementsov, *Stalinist Science* (Princeton: Princeton University Press, 1994), 154 ("On issues of modern Darwinism," 10 April 1948).

CHAPTER 8. AGING LEADER

1. **Stalin's vacations,** calculated from log of Kremlin office visits; **Stalin aging,** Chuev, *Sto sorok besed,* 271; Kuznetsov, *Krutye povoroty,* 39, 43, 54–55; N. V. Novikov, *Vospominaniia diplomata* (Moscow: Izdatel'stvo politicheskoi literatury, 1989), 382– 83 (quotation); **"lost without me,"** Chuev, *Sto sorok besed,* 271; N. Khrushchev, *Khrushchev Remembers,* 601; **Beria,** N. Khrushchev, *Khrushchev Remembers,* 314–15; A. I. Mikoian, *Tak bylo,* 584; **Khrushchev quotations,** N. Khrushchev, *Khrushchev Remembers,* 303.

2. **Svetlana-Zhdanov marriage,** Allilueva, *Dvadtsat' pisem,* 145–46, 149; Zhdanov, *Vzgliad v proshloe,* 73–74; **Yury Zhdanov and Stalin** (on faction-fighting), Sheila Fitzpatrick, "Politics as Practice," *Kritika* 5:1 (2004), 39–40; **Svetlana's appeal to Stalin,** Allilueva, *Dvadtsat' pisem,* 150–41; **"What a fool!,"** Zhdanov, *Vzgliad* (quoting Svetlana's report); **arrests of Stalin's in-laws,** *Iosif Stalin v ob"iatiiakh sem'i,* 194; Allilueva, *Dvadtsat' pisem,* 49; A. I. Mikoian, *Tak bylo,* 361; **Stalin's paranoia,** N. Khrushchev, *Khrushchev Remembers,* 299–300, 307 (quotation); **declining competence,** A. I. Mikoian, *Tak bylo,* 521–22 (quotation); **consequences for governance,** Kuznetsov, *Krutye povoroty,* 88; Khlevniuk, *Master,* 260 ("semi-collective decision-making"); *Sovershenno sekretno,* 1990, no. 3, 13 (quotation from Central Committee Secretary Panteleimon Ponomarenko on Group of Four); Gorlizki and Khlevniuk, *Cold Peace,* 62.

3. **Jewish Anti-Fascist Committee (JAC),** G. Kostyrchenko, *Tainaia politika Stalina* (Moscow: Mezhdunarodnye otnosheniia, 2001), 430; S. Beria, *Moi otets* (1994), 56, 208, 338; Joshua Rubinstein and Vladimir P. Naumov, eds., *Stalin's Secret Pogrom* (New Haven: Yale University Press, 2001), 7–19; **Pan-Slavic Union,** Nikolai Kikishev, "Slavianskoe dvizhenie v SSSR, 1941–1948," *Khronos,* 2008, http://www .hrono.ru/libris/lib_k/kik41.php; **Crimean proposals,** Rubinstein, *Stalin's Secret*

Pogrom, 18–19; Kostyrchenko, *Tainaia politika Stalina*, 428–29; Watson, *Molotov*, 198; **Molotov's views**, Chuev, *Sto sorok besed*, 93–94; **Beria's views**, S. Beria, *Beria, My Father*, 208.

4. **Golda Meir**, Kostyrchenko, *Tainaia politika Stalina*, 417, 446, 447 (Meir quotation); RGANI, 3/32/13, l. 18; *Tainaia politika Stalina*; **JAC dissolution proposal**, Kostyrchenko, *Tainaia politika Stalina*, 365; *Stalin i kosmopolitizm*, 98–101, 194.

5. **Mikhoels murder**, Kostyrchenko, *Tainaia politika Stalina*, 392; Nataliia Vovsi-Mikhoels, *Moi otets, Solomon Mikhoels* (Moscow: Vozvrashchenie, 1977), 231–34 (text of Beria letter to Malenkov on Stalin's involvement, April 1953); RGANI, 3/32/12, l. 33; **Voroshilovs**, quotation from Kostyrchenko, *Tainaia politika*, 404; Roi Medvedev, *Okruzhenie Stalina* (Moscow: Molodaia gvardiia, 2010), 298; **Andreeva**, Gorlizki and Khlevniuk, *Cold Peace*, 102; G. Kostyrchenko, *V plenu u krasnogo faraona* (Moscow: Mezhdunarodnye otnosheniia, 1994), 137; **Zhemchuzhina's hints**, *Stalin i kosmopolitizm*, 209; RGANI, 3/32/13, l. 22 (sister's testimony); **Kaganovich**, Vovsi-Mikhoels, *Moi otets*, 195; **MGB reports**, Kostyrchenko, *V plenu*, 88–89; **"sicced a Zionist on you,"** Allilueva, *Dvadtsat' pisem*, 148.

6. **JAC dissolution**, *Stalin i kosmopolitizm*, 193–95 (Politburo resolution, 25 November 1948); RGANI, 3/32/10, l. 134 order of Bureau of Council of Ministers); **Lozovsky**, Pikhoia, *Sovetskii Soiuz*, 76; *Stalin i kosmopolitizm*, 220; Molotova, *Stalin i kosmopolitizm*, 208–9 (expulsion, 29 December 1948); Gorlizki and Khlevniuk, *Cold Peace*, 76; Chuev, *Molotov*, 552 (arrest); **Molotov**, Chuev, *Sto sorok besed*, 473 ("knees trembling"); Gorlizki and Khlevniuk, *Cold Peace*, 76 (remorse quotation); **Beria**, S. Beriia, *Moi otets* (2013), 166; **Zhemchuzhina's criticisms**, RGASPI, 589/3/6188, ll. 9–24; RGANI, 3/32/13, ll. 19, 133; Kostyrchenko, *Tainaia politika Stalina*, 447–48; **team contacts with Meir**, S. Beria, *Beria, My Father*, 170 (quotation) and Golda Meir, *My Life* (London: Weidenfeld and Nicoloson, 1975), 208–9.

7. **Molotov divorce** (end of 1948), Chuev, *Sto sorok besed*, 475; **Shamberg divorce**, Vladimir Shamberg, "Stalin's Last Inner Circle," *Harriman Review* 10:1 (1997), 32; N. Khrushchev, *Khrushchev Remembers*, 292–93; **Shambergs not on list for exile**, RGANI, 3/32/17, ll. 7–8 (memo from S. Goglidze, MGB, to Malenkov, 30 December 1952); **Molotov's and Mikoyan's replacement**, Gorlizki and Khlevniuk, *Cold Peace*, 76–77 (including Voroshilov quotation); Watson, *Molotov*, 239–41; A. I. Mikoian, *Tak bylo*, 529.

8. **Leningrad Affair**, N. Khrushchev, *Khrushchev Remembers*, 250–57; Malenkov, *O moem ottse*, 54; Zhdanov, *Vzgliad*, 304; S. Beria, *Beria, My Father*, 212–13; Chuev, *Sto sorok besed*, 434; **Stalin's role**, *Molotov, Malenkov, Kaganovich, 1957*, 49; Gorlizki and Khlevniuk, *Cold Peace*, 85; **1957 accusations**, see chapter 9; **successors**, Pikhoia, *Sovetskii Soiuz*, 65; **wedding**, M. Iu. Pavlov, *Anastas Mikoian: Politicheskii portret na fone sovetskoi epokhi* (Moscow: Mezhdunarodnye otnosheniia, 2010), 238; **Kuznetsov siblings**, S. Mikoian, *Vospominaniia*, 160–61; **arrests**, Gorlizki and Khlevniuk, *Cold Peace*, 87; *Molotov, Malenkov, Kaganovich, 1957*, 49; **investigation**, Zhores Medvedev and Roi Medvedev, *Nikita Khrushchev* (Moscow: Vremia, 2012), 149; Pikhoia, *Sovetskii Soiuz*, 67.

9. **Interrogation reports**, RGASPI, 589/3/6188 (face-to-face confrontation of Molotova with I. S. Fefer and V. L. Zuskin from JAC, 26 December 1948); RGANI,

3/32/12 and 3/32/13 (Shteinberg testimony with Stalin's circulation instruction, 3/32/13, ll. 116, 131–34, 142); **Lozovsky**, Chuev, *Molotov*, 248; N. S. Khrushchev, "Memuary Nikity Sergeevna Khrushcheva," *Voprosy istorii*, 1991, no. 11, 60; **Beria/sentence**, RGANI, 3/32/17, ll. 131–34; **Molotov target?**, Sudoplatov, *Special Tasks*, 327; **no confession from Zhemchuzhina**, RGANI, 3/32/17, ll. 131–34 (Beria, memo to Presidium, 12 May 1953); **other confessions**, RGANI, 3/32/12 and 3/32/13; **Molotov scenarios**, Valentin M. Berezhkov, *At Stalin's Side*, 341–42; N. Khrushchev, *Khrushchev Remembers*, 309; Chuev, *Molotov*, 551.

10. **Khrushchev**, N. Khrushchev, *Khrushchev Remembers*, 250; Gorlizki and Khlevniuk, *Cold Peace*, 92,103; **Bulganin**, Gorlizki and Khlevniuk, *Cold Peace*, 93–94; Chuev, *Sto sorok besed*, 323 (quotation); **collective leadership**, Khlevniuk, *Master*, 260; **team solidarity**, S. Beria, *Beria, My Father*, 239 (quotation); N. Khrushchev, *Khrushchev Remembers*, 309–10; **Malenkov as heir**, Malenkov, *O moem ottse*, 57; **Beria in trouble**, Sudoplatov, *Special Tasks*, 320; RGANI, 5/30/4, l. 98 (letter of V. N. Merkulov to Khrushchev, 23 July 1953).

11. **Molotov's standing**, Chuev, *Sto sorok besed*, 466; N. Khrushchev, *Khrushchev Remembers*, 278; Gorlizki and Khlevniuk, *Cold Peace*, 150; Simonov, *Glazami*, 80 (quotation); **message from Four to Mikoyan**, A. I. Mikoian, *Tak bylo*, 584; **Molotov on Beria**, Chuev, *Molotov*, 547 (quotation); **Molotov on Stalin's distrust**, Chuev, *Molotov*, 549 (quotation), 552; **spy accusations**, A. I. Mikoian, *Tak bylo*, 535 (Poskrebyshev quotation), 579 (Ordzhonikidze quotation).

12. **October 1952 attack**, A. A. Fursenko, "I. V. Stalin: Poslednie gody zhizni i smert'," *Istoricheskie zapiski* 3 (121) (2000), 192–93 (citing Academician A. M. Rumiantsev); Simonov, *Glazami*, 241–44; N. Khrushchev, *Khrushchev Remembers*, 279–82; Gorlizki and Khlevniuk, *Cold Peace*, 151; Pavlov, *Mikoian*, 231; A. I. Mikoian, *Tak bylo*, 574–75; **Presidium**, Fursenko, "I. V. Stalin," 193; Pikhoia, *Sovetskii Soiuz*, 94 (Voroshilov); N. Khrushchev, *Khrushchev Remembers*, 279–80.

13. **Meetings of Bureau and full Presidium** (October–December 1952 protocols), RGANI, 3/10/1- 3/10/6; A. I. Mikoyan, *Tak bylo*, 576–7; **uninvited guests** N. Khrushchev, *Khrushchev Remembers*, 309–10; A. I. Mikoian, *Tak bylo*, 579–80.

14. **Abakumov's hesitation**, Sudoplatov, *Special Tasks*, 328, 300; Pikhoia, *Sovetskii Soiuz*, 75–92; Kostyrchenko, *Tainaia politika*, 459; S. Beria, *Beria, My Father*, 213; **dropping of Zhemzhuzhina**, Joshua Rubenstein and Vladimir P. Naumov, eds., *Stalin's Secret Pogrom: The Postwar Inquisition of the Jewish Anti-Fascist Committee* (New Haven: Yale University Press, 2001), xiv–xv; **JAC trial** (transcript), Rubinstein, *Stalin's Secret Pogrom* (quotations on 226, 230); **Cheptsov's insubordination**, Rubinstein, *Stalin's Secret Pogrom*, 59–60; http://ru.wikipedia.org/wiki/Cheptsov,_Aleksandr_Aleksandrovich; **Lozovsky's appeal to Politbuto**, RGANI, 3/32/16, ll. 84–88 (7 August 1952; refused); **execution**, Rubinstein, *Stalin's Secret Pogrom*, 60.

15. **Arrests in security services**, Sudoplatov, *Special tasks*, 301; **Poskrebyshev and Vlasik**, Pikhoia, *Sovetskii Soiuz*, 94; Gorlizki and Khlevniuk, *Cold Peace*, 161 and 221n120; Sudoplatov, *Special Tasks*, 332–33; **Doctors' Plot**, Kostyrchenko, *Tainaia politika Stalina*, 632, 645; Shepilov, *Neprimknuvshii*, 229–30 (Andreev's deafness); N. Khrushchev, *Khrushchev Remembers*, 286–87; Pikhoia, *Sovetskii Soiuz*, 77 (quotation from Malyshev's notes of Stalin's statement to Central Committee, 1 December 1952); S. Khrushchev, *Nikita Khrushchev, Reformator*, 92; **Stalin and anti-Semitism**,

N. Khrushchev, *Khrushchev Remembers*, 258–69; Chuev, *Molotov*, 333; Chuev, *Tak govoril Kaganovich*, 128; S. Beria, *Beria, My Father*, 211; N. Khrushchev, *Khrushchev Remembers*, 258–69 (quotations 154, 263); A. I. Mikoian, *Tak bylo*, 536; **punishment for anti-Semitism**, Fitzpatrick, *Tear Off the Masks!*, 291–98; **feigned outrage**, scene reported by Simonov, *Glazami*, 188, and Tikhon Khrennikov, *Tak eto bylo* (Moscow: Muzyka, 1994), 177.

16. **"Blind like kittens,"** N. Khrushchev, *Khrushchev Remembers*, 601; **out of the loop**, Chuev, *Tak govoril Kaganovich*, 174–76; Chuev, *Sto sorok besed*, 435; **Kaganovich's article**, ms. in RGANI, 3/32/17, 52–92; **put-up job**, *Lavrentii Beriia*, 113 (Central Committee plenum, June 1953; voices from the Presidium shouted out confirmation); Khrushchev, dictated draft of report to XX Party Congress "On the cult of personality and its consequences" (early 1956), RGANI, 56/1/169, 43–44, and N. Khrushchev, *Khrushchev Remembers*, 601; **friendship with doctors**, N. Khrushchev, *Khrushchev Remembers*, 601 (quotation); S. Beriia, *Moi otets* (1994), 36; Andreev, *Vospominaniia*, 298.

17. ***Pravda* on Doctors' Plot**, *Pravda*, 13 January 1953; *Stalin i kosmopolitanizm*, 651–52 (texts); RGASPI, 558/11/157 (drafts, sent by Shepilov, 10 January 1953, with Stalin's comments); **Kaganovich**, Chuev, *Tak govoril Kaganovich*, 174; S. Beria, *Beria, My Father*, 166; **popular reactions**, TsKhDNISO, 714/1/1780, ll.7, 25, 39, 55–56, 67 (January 1953 reports from Kuibyshev on reactions to communiqué); RGANI, 5/15/407, ll. 33, 79, 96–97 (Central Committee agitprop department: summary of local reactions to communiqué); **Stalin in danger?**, TsKHIDNISO, 714/1/1780, l. 6; **Molotov's wife**, TsKHIDNISO, 714/1/1780, l. 99; **deportation rumors**, Sudoplatov, *Special Tasks*, 308; S. Beria, *Beria, My Father*, 244; Gorlizki and Khlevniuk, *Cold Peace*, 158–59. The only insider who fails to deny these rumors is Mikoyan (A. I. Mikoian, *Tak bylo*, 536)—but his memoirs, thanks to his son Sergo's editing, are not free from additions of urban folklore offered as insider knowledge.

18. **December 1952 Presidium**, Pavlov, *Anastas Mikoian*, 244; **lives of Molotov and Mikoyan in danger**, A. I. Mikoian, *Tak bylo*, 579–80; N. Khrushchev, *Khrushchev Remembers*, 278; **new purges imminent**, A. I. Mikoian, *Tak bylo*, 578; Pavlov, *Anastas Mikoian*, 246 (citing archival evidence); **special prison**, Pikhoia, *Sovetskii Soiuz*, 79–81; **Beria in danger**, Pikhoia, *Sovetskii Soiuz*, 74; Gorlizki and Khlevniuk, *Cold Peace*, 109–13; **Beria cult in Georgia**, RGANI, 5/30/4, ll. 125–27 (report to Molotov, 14 August 1953).

19. **Stalin's health**, Gorlizki and Khlevniuk, *Cold Peace*, 162; N. Khrushchev, *Khrushchev Remembers*, 315–20; Allilueva, *Dvadtsat' pisem*, 713; **Voroshilovs**, RGASPI, 74/1/429 (Voroshilova, "Something like a diary," 37, entry for 2 March 1953); **Berias**, S. Beriia, *Moi otets* (2013), 153; **vigil**, A. I. Mikoian, *Tak bylo*, 580; Chuev, *Sto sorok besed*, 327 (Molotov quotation); *Lavrentii Beriia*, 195–96 (Voroshilov quotation); **Beria's behavior**, N. Khrushchev, *Khrushchev Remembers*, 318 (quotation); Allilueva, *Dvadtsat' pisem*, 8–9; **team members weep**, Allilueva, *Dvadtsat' pisem*, 11, 13; N. Khrushchev, *Khrushchev Remembers*, 323.

20. **Murder hypothesis**, Chuev, *Sto sorok besed*, 327–28; Malenkov, *O moem ottse*, 62; Sudoplatov, *Special Tasks*, 333; S. Khrushchev, *Reformator*, 10; **popular rumors**, Vladimir A. Kozlov, Sheila Fitzpatrick, and Sergei V. Mironenko, eds., *Sedition: Everyday Resistance in the Soviet Union under Khrushchev and Brezhnev* (New Haven: Yale University Press, 2011), 79–80; RGANI, 5/15/407, l. 95.

21. **Meetings**, *Politbiuro Tsk VKP(b) i Sovet Ministrov SSSR, 1945–53*, comp. Khlevniuk et al. (Moscow: ROSSPEN, 2002), 436–37; **Stalin's death**, Allilueva, *Dvadtsat' pisem*, 8–9 (quotation); N. Khrushchev, *Khrushchev Remembers*, 322.

CHAPTER 9. WITHOUT STALIN

1. **New government**, *Politbiuro TsK i Sovet Ministrov SSSR*, 100–104 (protocol of meeting of 5 March 1953); *Pravda*, 7 March 1953, 1; Shepilov, *Kremlin's Scholar*, 17; Kaganovich, *Pamiatnye zapiski*, 518–19; N. Khrushchev, *Khrushchev Remembers*, 374–75; **funeral**, *Pravda*, 10 March, 1–2.; Shepilov, *Kremlin's Scholar*, 30–32, 17; Edward Crankshaw, *Khrushchev's Russia* (Harmondsworth: Penguin, 1959), 23 (quotation); Watson, *Molotov*, 245; *Lavrentii Beriia*, 167–68; **children's idealism**, S. Mikoian, *Vospominaniia*, 197 (quotations); **Polina's return**, Chuev, *Sto sorok besed*, 473–74, RGANI, 3/32/17, l. 12 (Presidium resolution, 21 March 1953); RGANI, 3/32/17, ll. 131–35 (Beria, memo to Presidium, 12 May 1953).

2. **Moscow panic**, Yevgeny Yevtushenko, *A Precocious Autobiography* (London: Collins & Harvill, 1963), 89–92; Crankshaw, *Khrushchev's Russia*, 23 ("panic and disarray" quotation); **euphoria**, Knight, *Beria*, 186 (Salisbury quotation); Crankshaw, *Khrushchev's Russia*, 23, 38 ("leathery cacti"); **disappearance of Stalin's name**, Iurii Aksiutin, *Khrushchevskaia "ottepel'" i obshchestvennye nastoreniia v SSSR v 1953–1964 gg.* (Moscow: ROSSPEN, 2004), 37; RGANI, 5/30/4, ll. 20–21; 5/15/407, l. 154 and RGASPI, 82/2/1446, ll. 73–78 (concerned citizens' letters); **criticism at plenum**, *Lavrentii Beriia*, 224.

3. **Amnesty**, Miriam Dobson, "Show the bandit-enemies no mercy!," in Polly Jones, ed., *The Dilemmas of De-Stalinization* (London: Routledge, 2006), 22–32; **rehabilitation and détente**, Pikhoia, *Sovetskii soiuz*, 122, 131; **foreign marriages**, Zubok, *Inside the Kremlin's Cold War*, 155–56; **consumer goods**, Nove, *Economic History*, 324–29; RGANI, 3/10/53, Mikoyan's report and Presidium resolution of 10 October 1953 "On increasing the production of mass consumption industrial goods and improving their quality"; **suspicions about Stalin's death**, RGANI, 5/30/6, ll. 1–2, RGANI, 5/30/5, ll. 62–65, and RGASPI, 82/2/1466, ll. 44–50, 55–56 (quotations from citizen's letters); **"blackening Stalin,"** RGASPI, 82/2/1466, l. 58; **Beria and Malenkov as Jews**, RGASPI, 82/2/1466, ll. 44–50; TsKHNIDSO, 714/1/1149, l. 88.

4. **Molotov as desired successor**, Shepilov, *Neprimknuvshii*, 249; RGASPI, 82/2/1466, ll. 26, 36, 58; **Molotov's role**, Shepilov, *Neprimknuvshii*, 249–50; **new Group of Four**, A. I. Mikoian, *Tak bylo*, 581; **Malenkov as consensus-seeker**, Shepilov, *Neprimknuvshii*, 246–47.

5. **Beria**, A. I. Mikoian, *Tak bylo*, 587 ("gone to take power"); RGANI, 5/30/4 ll.64–79 ("lent wings," letter of Merkulov to Khrushchev, 21 July 1953); *Lavrentii Beriia*, 26–27; Taubman, *Khrushchev*, 246; Pikhoia, *Sovetskii Soiuz*, 108–9; **nationalities policy**, RGANI, 5/30/6, 30–31, 44–46, 99–102; N. Khrushchev, *Khrushchev Remembers*, 329–30; RGANI, 5/30/6, ll. 11–15, 20–25; Taubman, *Khrushchev*, 249; **Beria's unilateral actions**, S. Khrushchev, *Nikita Khrushchev: Reformator*, 119; A. I. Mikoian, *Tak bylo*, 587; N. Khrushchev, *Khrushchev Remembers*, 329; RGANI, 5/30/4, ll. 31–34; *Lavrentii Beriia*, 137 (Kaganovich quotation); **Beria's scorn for party**, quoted Pikhoia, *Sovetskii Soiuz*, 110; **personality cults**, RGANI, 5/15/447, l. 56;

RGANI, 5/30/4, l. 127 (Georgia); Knight, *Beria*, 185 (Presidium resolution of 9 May 1953, proposed by Beria, banning leaders' portraits from holiday demonstrations).

6. **Beria amends Molotov text**, Shepilov, *Neprimknuvshii*, 254; **GDR discussion**, Aksiutin, *Khrushchevskaia "ottepel,"* 40–41; Shepilov, *Neprimknuvshii*, 255 (Beria quotation); A. I. Mikoian, *Tak bylo*, 584; Chuev, *Sto sorok besed*, 334–35; Zubok, *Inside the Kremlin's Cold War*, 197 (quotation); **Molotov overture**, Taubman, *Khrushchev*, 250.

7. **Plot against Beria**, N. Khrushchev, *Khrushchev Remembers*, 321–41; Shepilov, *Neprimknuvshii*, 259–67 (reporting an account Khrushchev gave him close to the event); Rees, *Iron Lazar*, 250; Chuev, *Tak govoril Kaganovich*, 65–66; A. I. Mikoian, *Tak bylo*, 587; S. Khrushchev, *Rozhdenie*, 77 (heritable property).

8. **Friends with Beria**, A. I. Mikoian, *Tak bylo*, 587; Chuev, *Sto sorok besed*, 334–35, 436; **Beria's appeals**, *Politbiuro i delo Beriia*, 19–22; **Beria's interrogations**, *Politbiuro i delo Beriia*, 58–63, 75–78, 90–95, 110–16, 151–55, 169–83, 194–97, 211–17, and 230–35; **sexual motif**, A. V. Sukhomlinov, *Kto vy, Lavrentii Beriia?* (Moscow: Detektiv-Press, 2003), 222–45; *Politbiuro i delo Beriia*, 98–104, 101–4; Nina Alekseeva, *Lavrentii Beriia v moei zhizni* (Moscow, 1996) (no confirmation of the account's authenticity); **execution**, *Pravda*, 17 December 1953; **Mikoyan's opinion**, A. I. Mikoian, *Tak bylo*, 587–88; **fate of Beria family**, S. Beria, *Beria, My Father*, 184, 273; Vasileva, *Kremlin Wives*, 185 (quotations from interview with Rada Khrushcheva); **popular opinion of Beria**, O. V. Edelman, in Kozlov et al., *Sedition*, 115; Aksiutin, *Khrushchevsiaia "ottepel,"* 47–48; RGANI, 5/15/407, ll. 74, 114, 118 (quotation); RGANI, 5/30/3, l. 74; RGANI, 5/15/407, l. 114; RGANI, 5/30/4, ll. 12, 21; RGANI, 5/15/407, l. 115; **destruction of police archives**, Pikhoia, *Sovetskii soiuz*, 124; Crankshaw, *Khrushchev's Russia*, 102.

9. **Drunk with joy**, Shepilov, *Neprimknuvshii*, 264; **Khrushchev's boasting**, Shepilov, *Kremlin's Scholar*, 274–75; Taubman, *Khrushchev*, 257 (quoting Alexei Adzhubei); Simonov, *Glazami*, 246–47; **ranking**, Shepilov, *Neprimknuvshii*, 267; **foreign travel**, N. Khrushchev, *Khrushchev Remembers*, 392–400; Malenkov, *O moem ottse*, 76–77; Zubok, *Zhivago's Children*, 92; S. Khrushchev, *Nikita Khrushchev: Reformator*, 208–9; **optimism**, Zubok, *Zhivago's Children*, 34 (quotation); **Evtushenko story**, Zubok, *Zhivago' s Children*, 59 (quoting Evtushenko); **Picasso**, RGASPI, 74/1/429 (Voroshilova, "Something like a diary," 58–59, entry for 23 July 1954); **intergenerational arguments**, S. Mikoian, *Vospominaniia*, 212–13; S. Khrushchev, *Nikita Khrushchev: Reformator*, 330; **Adzhubei**, Zubok, *Zhivago's Children*, 142.

10. **Team living arrangements**, Sergei Khrushchev, *Nikita Khrushchev: Pensioner* (Moscow: Vremia, 2010), vol. 3 of *Trilogiia ob ottse*, 26; **friendships**, Taubman, 265; S. Khrushchev, *Nikita Khrushchev: Reformator*, 103–4; S. Khrushchev, *Nikita Khrushchev: Pensioner*, 104; RGASPI, 74/1/429 (Voroshilova, "Something like a diary"), 47, 81, 85, 97–98, 107, entries for 5 October 1953, 19 and 28 September 1956, 2 September 1957; **Andreev**, RGASPI, 74/1/429 (Voroshilova, "Something like a diary"), 74, entry for August–September 1955; *Regional'naia politika N. S. Khrushcheva: TsK KPSS i mestnye partiinye komitety, 1953–1964 gg.*, comp. O. V. Khlevniuk et al. (Moscow: Rossiiskaia politicheskaia entsiklopediia, 2009), 22 (Penza question); *Lavrentii Beriia*, 207 (Andreev at July 1953 plenum); *Prezidium TsK KPSS, 1954–1964* (Moscow: ROSSPEN, 2003), 1:104, 1:925 (XX Party Congress).

11. **Malenkov**, S. Khrushchev, *Nikita Khrushchev: Reformator*, 127–28 (quotation); **worsening relations**, A. I. Mikoian, *Tak bylo*, 599–600; Taubman, *Khrushchev*, 265; Crankshaw, *Khrushchev's Russia*, 43; **ousted as head of government**, A. G. Malenkov, *O moem ottse*, 116 (Khrushchev quotation), 76–77.

12. **Popular criticism of Khrushchev**, Kozlov et al., *Sedition*, 113–14, 121, 124–25, 143–44; RGANI, 5/30/140, l. 19; RGASPI, 82/2/1466, l. 93; **Khrushchev on Molotov**, N. Khrushchev, *Khrushchev Remembers: The Glasnost Tapes*, 87 (quotation); **Molotov's criticisms**, Chuev, *Sto sorok besed*, 346 ("absurd"); Shepilov, *Kremlin's Scholar*, 311 (quotation); **Khrushchev's attack on Molotov**, Taubman, *Khrushchev*, 269 (quotations); **Zhemchuzhina and diplomats**, Bromage, *Molotov*, 183–34; **Molotov's dismissal**, Watson, *Molotov*, 257, 259.

13. **Return from Gulag**, Stephen F. Cohen, *The Victims Return* (London: I. B. Tauris, 2011), 35–36; **Natalia Rykova**, Zenkovich, *Samye sekretnye*, 338; Chuev, *Sto sorok besed*, 415; **Svanidze**, Zenkovich, *Samye sekretnye*, 406; **Mikoyan**, A. I. Mikoian, *Tak bylo*, 595–96; Cohen, *The Victims Return*, 90–91; **Molotov**, Aroseva, *Bez grima*, 256–59; **Kaganovich**, GARF, 5446/83/38, l. 98 (L. A. Sheinin's letter); Chuev, *Tak govoril Kaganovich*, 79; RGANI, 3/32/12, ll. 116–18 (L. R. Sheinin in Zhemchuzhina case); **Snegov**, Zhores Medvedev, *Nikita Khrushchev* (Moscow, 2013), 155–58; A. I. Mikoian, *Tak bylo*, 589–90; **Snegov's letter**, text in *Politbiuro i delo Beriia*, 997–1002; **Mikoyan quotation**, A. I. Mikoian, *Tak bylo*, 589–90.

14. **Enquiry to Rudenko**, S. Khrushchev, *Rozhdenie*, 71; **Shatunovskaya's charges**, Lenoe, *Kirov Murder*, 568–69, 607–8, 627; **Presidium fight**, *Molotov, Malenkov, Kaganovich, 1957*, 80; **Pospelov**, N. Khrushchev, *Khrushchev Remembers: The Glasnost Tapes*, 42; A. I. Mikoian, *Tak bylo*, 592; Fedor Burlatsky, *Khrushchev and the First Russian Spring* (New York: Charles Scribner, 1988), 102–5; Shepilov, *Kremlin's Scholar*, 133–34; **Pospelov report**, S. Khrushchev, *Nikita Khrushchev: Reformator*, 264 (quotation on Khrushchev); Taubman, *Khrushchev*, 279 (Mikoyan quotation); **Khrushchev's analysis**, N. Khrushchev, *Khrushchev Remembers*, 345; **Snegov's threat**, Taubman, *Khrushchev*, 278, quoting Sergo Mikoyan.

15. **Khrushchev's version**, N. Khrushchev, *Khrushchev Remembers*, 347–50; **official protocol**, *Prezidium TsK KPSS, 1954–1964*, 1:99–103; **Mikoyan's speech**, *XX s"ezd Kommunisticheskoi Partii Sovetskogo Soiuza* (Moscow: Gosudarstvennoe izdatel'stvo politicheskoi literatury, 1956), 1:302; **Khrushchev's speech**, N. Khrushchev, *Khrushchev Remembers*, 559–618 (text); N. Khrushchev, *Khrushchev Remembers: The Glasnost Tapes*, 43; Taubman, *Khrushchev*, 280–81; Shepilov, *Kremlin's Scholar*, 391–92; S. Khrushchev, *Rozhdenie*, 76. The draft, presented by Pospelov and Aristov on 18 February 1956 (RGANI, 52/1/169, ll. 1–28) focused on the Great Purges; Khrushchev's dictated elaboration added extensive discussion of the war and postwar (ibid., ll. 29–63).

16. **Reading of secret speech**, S. Khrushchev, *Nikita Khrushchev: Reformator*, 277; Jones, *Dilemmas of De-Stalinization*, 41–63, 65; **party loyalist letter**, RGASPI, 82/2/1466, ll. 111, 99, 93; **Georgia**, RGANI, 5/30/140, ll. 52–55; **Polish and Hungarian crises**, Taubman, Khrushchev, 289–94; S. Khrushchev, *Nikita Khrushchev: Reformator*, 289 (quotation); **plane travel**, see chapter 7; **flight to Warsaw**, S. Khrushchev, *Nikita Khrushchev: Reformator*, 290–91.

17. **Hungarian crisis**, "The 'Malin Notes' on the Crises in Hungary and Poland,

1956," *Cold War International History Project Bulletin*, nos. 8–9 (Winter 1996–97), 389–91 (Molotov quotation, 389); Mark Kramer, "New Evidence on Soviet Decision-Making and the 1956 Polish and Hungarian Crises," *Cold War International History Project Bulletin*, nos. 8–9 (Winter 1996–97), 366–69; N. Khrushchev, *Khrushchev Remembers*, 418 (quotation); Taubman, *Khrushchev*, 296; **"counterrevolution,"** S. Khrushchev, *Nikita Khrushchev: Reformator*, 292; N. Khrushchev, *Khrushchev Remembers*, 417; **Mikoyan's dissent**, A. I. Mikoian, *Tak bylo*, 598; **Presidium arguments**, Kramer, "New Evidence," 376; **Khrushchev**, Kaganovich, *Pamiatnye zapiski*, 510–15 (quotation).

18. **Picnic**, Taubman, *Khrushchev*, 309–10; S. Khrushchev, *Nikita Khrushchev: Reformator*, 417–21 (quotation 420; the speaker was Marietta Shaginyan); **Kaganovich's comment**, Kaganovich, *Pamiatnye zapiski*, 515 (quotation); **Mikoyan**, cited in Taubman, *Khrushchev*, 310; *Molotov, Malenkov, Kaganovich, 1957*, 145; **Molotov and Kaganovich**, *Molotov, Malenkov, Kaganovich, 59*, 103–4; **meeting in Bulganin's office**, S. Khrushchev, *Nikita Khrushchev: Reformator*, 421; Shepilov, *Neprimknuvshii*, 388 (note that Voroshilov, who probably would also have been invited, was in Indonesia); **Sergei's wedding**, S. Khrushchev, *Nikita Khrushchev: Reformator*, 431; **meeting 18 June**, ibid., 439–40.

19. **Move against Khrushchev**, A. I. Mikoian, *Tak bylo*, 597–99; Shepilov, *Neprimknuvshii*, 392–97; S. Khrushchev, *Nikita Khrushchev: Reformator*, 439–51; Kaganovich, *Pamiatnye zapiski*, 510–15; **hostility to Serov**, S. Khrushchev, *Khrushchev: Reformator*, 448, 454; A. I. Mikoian, *Tak bylo*, 607–9; *Molotov, Malenkov, Kaganovich, 1957*, 64 (Kaganovich); **phone-tapping**, Shepilov, *Neprimknuvshii*, 393–94; **Khrushchev's response**, Taubman, *Khrushchev*, 319–20; N. Khrushchev, *Khrushchev Remembers: The Last Testament*, 14; S. Khrushchev, *Nikita Khrushchev: Reformator*, 455–57.

20. **Central Committee plenum**, *Molotov, Malenkov, Kaganovich, 1957*, 322 (Khrushchev quotation), 108 (Zhukov quotation), 183 (quotation on Korneichuk from Aristov); **"Anti-Party Group,"** term coined by Shvernik on 19 June; S. Khrushchev, *Nikita Khrushchev: Reformator*, 450 (Molotov's anger); *Molotov, Malenkov, Kaganovich, 1957*, 66 (Voroshilov's protest); Taubman, *Khrushchev*, 324; **Voroshilov**, *Molotov, Malenkov, Kaganovich, 1957*, 423–25; Veljko Mićunović, *Moscow Diary* (Garden City, NY: Doubleday, 1980), 271 (Khrushchev quotation); **Bulganin**, *Molotov, Malenkov, Kaganovich, 1957*, 72–76, 166–67; **final statements**, *Molotov, Malenkov, Kaganovich*, 395–99 (Kaganovich), 399–402 (Malenkov), 167 (quotation on Molotov), 403–6 (Molotov); **Molotov's abstention**, S. Khrushchev, *Khrushchev: Reformator*, 473; Watson, *Molotov*, 267; **Shepilov**, Shepilov, *Neprimknuvshii*, 397–98; S. Khrushchev, *Nikita Khrushchev: Reformator*, 458–59; Taubman, *Khrushchev*, 313–14 (the addition of the more junior Shepilov may reflect Khrushchev's sense of betrayal by a former protégé); **announcement**, *Pravda*, 4 July 1957, 1–3.

21. **Popular responses**, Aksiutin, *Khrushchevskaia "ottepel,"* 225–37 (dictatorship, "chance to express opinions"), 227 ("today they drove out Molotov"), 231, 233 ("hungry for 40 years"); RGANI, 5/3/189, ll. 74–75 ("banquets"); RGANI, 3/22/189, l. 51; RGANI, 3/22/189, ll. 53–62 (anti-Semitic letter); RGANI, 5/3/189, ll. 74–75; **Sedition**, Kozlov et al., *Sedition*, 114–15 ("decent life" quotation, Kaganovich), 134

("crushed like bugs," "cared for people"); **new Presidium**, *Prezidium TsK KPSS, 1954–1964*, 1:258–59.

CHAPTER 10. END OF THE ROAD

1. **Khrushchev**, S. Khrushchev, *Nikita Khrushchev: Reformator*, 474–75 (quotation); **collective leadership under Brezhnev**, Susanne Schattenberg, "Trust, Care and Familiarity in the Politburo. Brezhnev's Scenario of Power," *Kritika: Explorations in Russian and Eurasian History* 16:4 (2015), 835–58.; **Mikoyan**, A. Sushkov, *Prezidium TsK KPSS, 1957–1964 gg. Lichnosti i vlast'* (Ekaterinburg: UrO RAN, 2009), 236–38; **Molotov's jobs**, RGANI, 5/3/189, ll. 85–92; Mićunović, *Moscow Diary*, 348–50; Watson, *Molotov*, 269; Medvedev, *Okruzhenie Stalina*, 50; **Kaganovich's job**, Medvedev, *Okruzhenie Stalina*, 215; **Malenkov's jobs**, Malenkov, *O moem ottse*, 82–85; **Voroshilov**, Medvedev, *Okruzhenie Stalina*, 305–6.

2. **Khrushchev quotation**, cited Watson, *Molotov*, 270 (from speech to XXI Party Congress); **Kaganovich quotation**, Kaganovich, *Pamiatnye zapiski*, 524; **Molotovs' return to Moscow**, Medvedev, *Okruzhenie Stalina*, 53; **Kaganovich's return**, Medvedev, *Okruzhenie Stalina*, 222; **Malenkovs' return**, Malenkov, *O moem ottse*, 86; Medvedev, *Okruzhenie*, 335; **Khrushchev's ouster**, Sushkov, *Prezidium TsK KPSS*, 239–40; Taubman, *Khrushchev*, 3–17 (quotation 16) .

3. **Anti-Khrushchev resentment**, Chuev, *Molotov*, 421–22, 433; Kaganovich, *Pamiatnye zapiski*, 519–21; **Mikoyan's New Year call**, S. Khrushchev, *Nikita Khrushchev: Pensioner*, 123–24; **Kaganovich and Molotov**, *Tak govoril Kaganovich*, 33, 38; **achievement claims**, Chuev, *Molotov*, 340–34; Kaganovich, *Pamiatnye zapiski*, 479–80; N. Khrushchev, *Khrushchev Remembers*, 3; note Khrushchev's inclusion of Stalin's defeat of the Trotskyites in the 1920s in this category in his dictated notes for speech to the XX Party Congress, 1956, RGANI, 52/1/169, 32–33; **rehabilitation of Right**, A. I. Mikoian, *Tak bylo*, 288; N. Khrushchev, *Khrushchev Remembers*, 352–53; Prezidium TsK, 760; **Bukharin supporters**, Moshe Lewin, *Political Undercurrents in Soviet Economic Debates: From Bukharin to the Modern Reformers* (Princeton: Princeton University Press, 1974); **Gorbachev rehabilitations**, Cohen, *The Victims Return*, 13; Roy Medvedev and Guilietto Chiesa, *Time of Change* (London: I. B. Tauris, 1991); Nanci Adler, *The Gulag Survivor* (New Brunswick: Transaction, 2002), 157.

4. **Arosev**, Olga Aroseva, *Bez grima* (Moscow, 2000), 260; **Stalin irreplaceable**, Chuev, *Molotov*, 261 (quotation); **Great Purges guilt**, Molotov, Malenkov, Kaganovich, *1957*, 120; **Polina**, Alliluyeva, *Only One Year*, 384, 353 (quotations); **Voroshilov on Stalin**, Medvedev, *Okruzhenie*, 307; K. E. Voroshilov, *Rasskazy o zhizni* (Moscow, 1968) ("respect" quotation); RGASPI, 84/1/6, ll. 26–27 (conversation with V. I. Stalin, 9 April 1960); **Mikoyan on Stalin**, A. I. Mikoian, *Tak bylo*, 552–58; **Khrushchev on Stalin**, Taubman, *Khrushchev*, 292 ("tragedy" quotation). Note that he made the same remark in his dictated notes for his speech to the XX Party Congress (RGANI, 52/1/169, l. 51), though it is not in the published version.

5. **Family memoirs**, see bibliography in this volume; **Ordzhonikidze**, RGANI, 5/30/4, 106–8 (renaming of city); RGASPI, 74/1/429 (Ekaterina Voroshilova, "Something like a Diary," 79, 86–87, entries for August–September 1955); **Vasily Stalin**, Allilueva, *Dvadtsat' pisem*, 161–65 ("real father" quotation); RGASPI, 84/1/6, ll.

21–30 ("never repudiated," 1960 comment to Voroshilov). Note that the fact that the summary of the Voroshilov conversation is among Mikoyan's personal papers suggests that Mikoyan was also involved in the rescue effort.

6. **Svetlana and de-Stalinization**, Allilyueva, *Only One Year*, 156–57 (quotation); S. Mikoian, *Vospominaniia*, 165; Zhdanov, *Vzgliad v proshloe*, 73; **name change and baptism**, Allilyueva, *Only One Year*, 160–61, 167, 281–84; **Tomsky and Svanidze**, Kun, *Stalin*, 416–17; RGASPI, 84/1/7, l. 33; **marriage to Singh**, Allilyueva, *Only One Year*, 36–37, 41–42, 45–46; N. Khrushchev, *Khrushchev Remembers*, 293; **defection**, Alliluyeva, *Only One Year*, 57, 114–15, 177–85; N. Khrushchev, *Khrushchev Remembers*, 293–96; **children**, S. Mikoian, *Vospominaniia*, 167; Zhdanov, *Vzgliad v proshloe*, 74; *Twenty Letters*, Allilyueva, *One One Year*, 44, 117, 205–6; Nicholas Thompson, "My Friend, Stalin's Daughter," *New Yorker*, 31 March 2014, 30; **"betrayed her father,"** S. Beriia, *Moi otets* (2013), 56; **later life**, S. Beriia, *Moi otets (2013)*; Zhdanov, *Vzgliad v proshloe*, 74; Thompson, "My Friend, Stalin's Daughter."

7. **Funerals: Voroshilova**, http://www.net-film.ru/en/film-16466/; **Voroshilov**, Medvedev, *Okruzhenie*, 307; http://www.net-film.ru/en/film-17558/; **Zhemchuzhina**, Aroseva, *Bez grima*, 262; **Khrushchev**, Taubman, *Khrushchev*, 645; S. Khrushchev, *Nikita Khrushchev: Pensioner*, 241, 274 (his protective sons had kept news of Khrushchev's death from him, to prevent him from making a sentimental gesture that might get him into trouble); **Mikoyan**, S. Khrushchev, *Nikita Khrushchev: Pensioner*, 298 (Nina Khrushcheva's diary); **Khrushchev and intelligentsia**, N. Khrushchev, *Khrushchev Remembers: The Last Testament*, 80–81; Sergei Khrushchev, *Nikita Khrushchev: Pensioner*, 135–35; Taubman, *Khrushchev*, 629, 647.

8. **Malenkov**, Malenkov, *O moem ottse*, 95–98, 104, 107–12 (monograph abstract); Medvedev, *Okruzhenie*, 336; **Molotov**, *Cold War International History Project Bulletin*, no. 4 (1994), 81–82; Medvedev, *Okruzhenie*, 62; Chuev, *Sto sorok besed*, 529–31 (readmission to party); Watson, *Molotov*, 272; Medvedev, *Okruzhenie*, 63; Chuev, *Sto sorok besed*, 551–52 (funeral).

9. **Chernenko Politburo discussion**, *Cold War International History Project Bulletin*, no. 4 (1994), 81–82; **Kaganovich funeral**, Medvedev, *Okruzhenie*, 227–28.

CONCLUSION

1. **Everyday approach**, Sheila Fitzpatrick, "Politics as Practice: Thoughts on a New Soviet Political History," *Kritika: Explorations in Russian and Soviet History* 5:1 (Winter 2004); Arch Getty, *Practicing Stalinism* (New Haven: Yale University Press, 2013); **"rules of the game,"** approach pioneered in Soviet studies by historians of science, Nikolai Krementsov, *Stalinist Science* (Princeton: Princeton University Press, 1997) and Alexei Kojevnikov, "Games of Stalinist Democracy: Ideological Discussions in Soviet Sciences, 1947–52," in Sheila Fitzpatrick, ed., *Stalinism: New Directions* (London: Routledge, 2000); **"neglecting ideology" criticism**, Stephen Kotkin, *Magnetic Mountain: Stalinism as a Civilization* (Berkeley: University of California Press, 1995), 151–52, and Igal Halfin and Jochen Hellbeck, "Rethinking the Stalinist Subject: Stephen Kotkin's 'Magnetic Mountain' and the State of Soviet Historical Studies," *Jahrbücher für Geschichte Osteuropas* 44 (1996), 456.

2. **"Totalitarianism" in Soviet history**, Abbott Gleason, *Totalitarianism: The*

Inner History of the Cold War (New York: Oxford University Press, 1995), 121–42, and Michael Geyer and Sheila Fitzpatrick, eds., *Beyond Totalitarianism: Stalinism and Nazism Compared* (New York: Cambridge University Press, 2008); **personal dictatorship**, this characterization of the system was, of course, unacceptable to Soviet writers, who followed the Leninist understanding of the early Soviet regime as a *class* (proletarian) dictatorship implemented by the Bolshevik Party to get the country through the revolutionary transition to socialism; **court politics**, Simon Sebag Montefiore, *Stalin: The Court of the Red Tsar* (New York: Knopf, 2004); Sidney Ploss, *The Roots of Perestroika* (Jefferson, NC: McFarland & Co., 2010), chapter 3, "Stalin: Onset of Court Politics," 55–80; **Muscovite analogy**, Getty, *Practicing Stalinism*; **late imperial politics**, Andrew M. Verner, *The Crisis of Russian Autocracy: Nicholas II and the 1905 Revolution* (Princeton: Princeton University Press, 1990), esp. 53–56 and 62–64.

3. **Stalin biographies**, see works by Ulam, Tucker, Volkogonov, Service, et al. in the bibliography under "Biographies, Stalin." Two important new studies, Stephen Kotkin, *Stalin: Paradoxes of Power, 1878–1928*, vol. 1 (Penguin Press, 2014) and Oleg V. Khlevniuk, *Stalin: New Biography of a Dictator*, trans. Nora S. Favorov (New Haven: Yale University Press, 2014) appeared while the present book was in press, thus, too late to be consulted. **Stalinism as institutionalized violence**, Jörg Baberowski, *Verbrannte Erde: Stalins Herrschaft von Gewalt* (Munich: C. H. Beck Verlag, 2012). **Inner circle**: The term "entourage" (*okruzhenie*) is used by Roy A. Medvedev in his *Oni okruzhali Stalina* (Benson, VT: Chalidge Publications, 1984) and *Okruzhenie Stalina* (Moscow: Molodaia gvardiia, 2010) and O. V. Khlevniuk, *Politbiuro: Mekhanizmy politicheskoi vlasti v 30-e gody* (Moscow: ROSSPEN, 1996). In a later English-language publication based on but not identical with his *Politbiuro*, he uses "inner circle": Oleg V. Khlevniuk, *Master of the House: Stalin and His Inner Circle* (New Haven: Yale University Press, 2009). **Slavish or not?** Khlevniuk, *Politbiuro*, 245 (quoting M. Lewin, *Russia/USSR/Russia: The Drive and Drift of a Superstate* [New York: New Press, 1995], 90, 266); Oleg V. Khlevniuk, "Stalin as Dictator: The Personalisation of Power," in Sarah Davies and James Harris, eds., *Stalin: A New History* (Cambridge: Cambridge University Press, 2005), 108–20 (quotations from 118); J. Arch Getty, "Stalin as Prime Minister: Power and the Politburo," in Davies and Harris, *Stalin*, 94–100. **Team-Stalin**, Stephen G. Wheatcroft, "From Team-Stalin to Degenerate Tyranny," in E. A. Rees, ed., *The Nature of Stalin's Dictatorship: The Politburo, 1924–1953* (Basingstoke: Palgrave Macmillan, 2004), 79–107; **"cabinet" analogy**, Arch Getty, "Stalin as Prime Minister: Power and the Politburo," in Davies and Harris, *Stalin*, 83–107.

4. **Great Purges**, Robert Conquest, *The Great Terror: Stalin's Purge of the Thirties* (Harmondsworth: Penguin, 1971) (the pioneering work, necessarily written without archives); Arch Getty, *The Road to Terror* (presents summary of post-Soviet archival data); Sheila Fitzpatrick, *Everyday Stalinism* (New York: Oxford University Press, 1999), chap. 8 (as experienced in towns) and *Stalin's Peasants* (New York: Oxford University Press, 1994), chap. 7 (as experienced in countryside); **team survival in Great Purges**, T. H. Rigby, "Was Stalin a Disloyal Patron?" *Soviet Studies* 38:3 (July 1986); **institutional interest in Politburo**, Sheila Fitzpatrick, "Ordzhonikidze's Takeover of Vesenkha, 1930: A Case Study in Soviet Bureaucratic Politics," *Soviet Studies* 37:2 (April 1985).

5. **Stalin's absences**, Getty, "Stalin as Prime Minister," 94–95; Wheatcroft, "From Team-Stalin to Degenerate Tyranny," 91–93; **"under Khrushchev" periodization**, for example, Iurii Aksiutin, *Khrushchevskaia "ottepel" i obshchestvennye nastoreniia v SSSR v 1953–1964 gg.* (Moscow: ROSSPEN, 2004); **implied consensus of team (without Stalin) in Stalin's last years**, Gorlizki and Khlevniuk, *Cold Peace*, 124, 133, 141, 162, 166, approach this very cautiously, due to the absence of direct evidence, but make clear that in this period, while Stalin's closest colleagues understood that Stalin constituted an "immovable road block to reform," and made no overt effort to challenge him, some or all of them nevertheless recognized the desirability of a range of changes.

6. **Opinion data**, Elena Zubkova, *Russia after the War: Hopes, Illusions and Disappointments, 1945–1957* (Armonk, NY: M. E. Sharpe, 1998); Aksiutin, *Khrushchevskaia "ottepel"*; Kozlov et al., *Sedition*; Fitzpatrick, *Tear Off the Masks!*, esp. chaps. 9–12; Sheila Fitzpatrick, "Popular Opinion in Russia under Pre-War Stalinism," in Paul Corner, ed., *Popular Opinion in Totalitarian Regimes* (Oxford: Oxford University Press), 17–32; Fitzpatrick, "Popular Opinion under Communist Regimes," in Stephen A. Smith, ed., *The Oxford Handbook of the History of Communism* (Oxford: Oxford University Press, 2014), 371–86; Sarah Davies, *Popular Opinion in Stalin's Russia: Terror, Propaganda and Dissent, 1934–1941* (Cambridge: Cambridge University Press, 1997); **objections to its use on grounds of anti-Soviet bias**, Jochen Hellbeck, "Speaking Out: Languages of Affirmation and Dissent in Stalinist Russia," *Kritika: Explorations in Russian and Eurasian History* 1:1 (2000); **postwar anti-Semitism**, Amir Weiner, *Making Sense of War: The Second World War and the Fate of the Bolshevik Revolution* (Princeton: Princeton University Press, 2001), 191–235; 287–97; Yuri Slezkine, *The Jewish Century (Princeton: Princeton University Press, 2011)*; Sheila Fitzpatrick, "The Con Man as Jew," in Fitzpatrick, *Tear Off the Masks!*, 289–98.

7. **Form of rule under Khrushchev**, William Taubman (*Khrushchev* [New York: Norton, 2003], 365) treats Khrushchev as "alone at the top" (the title of his chapter 15, on 1957–60), and quotes one insider as saying that "after 1958 Khrushchev stopped listening and surrounded himself with 'yes-men.'" In an archive-based study, the Russian scholar A. S. Sushkov (*Prezidium TsK KPSS v 1957–1964 gg.: lichnosti i vlast'* [Ekaterinburg: UrO RAN, 2009], 245–46) concludes that the announced principle of collective leadership remained unrealized under Khrushchev because of the elimination of almost anybody of equivalent weight from the inner circle, but acknowledges that the Presidium (formerly Politburo) continued to meet regularly, and that Khrushchev still "regularly discussed and decided many important questions" with a small group of leaders from the Presidium. **Brezhnev and collective leadership**, Susanne Schattenberg, "Trust, Care and Familiarity in the Politburo. Brezhnev's Scenario of Power," *Kritika: Explorations in Russian and Eurasian History* 16:4 (2015).

BIOGRAPHIES

ALLILUYEVA, SVETLANA IOSIFOVNA (1926–2011)

Daughter of Josef Stalin and Nadezhda (Nadya) Alliluyeva; history graduate of Moscow State University, married to: (1) Grigory Morozov (1944–47), (2) Yury Zhdanov (1949–52), (3) Ivan Svanidze (1957–59), (4) Brajesh Singh (1960s), (5) American architect Wesley Peters (1970s). Legally changed name to Alliluyeva in 1957, defected to the United States in 1967, returned to the USSR 1984–86 before departing again; while in the United States, published memoirs that were critical of her father. Children: Joseph (1945), Ekaterina (1950), and Olga (1971).

ANDREEV, ANDREI ANDREEVICH (1895–1971)

Son of Russian peasants, a worker who joined the Bolsheviks in 1914. A candidate member of the Politburo from 1926 and a full member 1932–52. In charge of party Control Commission 1930–31 and 1939–52; railways 1931–35; and agriculture 1943–46. Central Committee secretary 1935–46; deputy chairman of the Council of Ministers 1946–53; post-1953 member of the Presidium of the Supreme Soviet. Married to Dora Khazan (1894–1961), a student with Nadya Alliluyeva at the Industrial Academy who later held a senior position in the textile industry. Had a son, Vladimir (1919), and daughter, Natalia (1921; married Vladimir Kuibyshev).

AROSEV, ALEXANDER YAKOVLEVICH (1890–1938)

Childhood friend of Molotov, joined party in 1907. Involved in diplomatic work in 1920s, chairman of VOKS 1934–37. Arrested on 3 July 1937 and then shot. First wife, Olga Goppen, worked as a secretary to Polina Molotova; second wife, Gertrude Freund, was Czech. Daughter Olga (1925) became a well-known actress; wrote memoirs.

BERIA, LAVRENTY PAVLOVICH (1899–1953)

Georgian/Mingrelian, joined the Bolsheviks March 1917; left architecture studies to work in Cheka. Headed the Georgian GPU 1926–31, then was first secretary of Georgian and later Transcaucasian parties in 1930s; came to Moscow in 1938 to head the

NKVD (later MVD) and remained in that position until 1946; subsequently retained supervisory role over security services. Candidate member of Politburo from 1939, full member from 1946; wartime member of GKO; ran Soviet atomic project from 1944. Active reformer during post-Stalin transition, arrested by colleagues June 1953, convicted of treason in a closed military court in December, and shot. Married to Nina Gegechkori (1905–91), a chemist; their son, Sergo (1924–2000), a physicist, married Gorky's granddaughter Marfa Peshkova in 1947, and in later life wrote memoirs defending his father's memory.

Bubnov, Andrei Sergeevich (1884–1938)

Russian, son of a merchant, joined the party in 1903 as a student. With Left Opposition in 1923, then switched to Stalin's side; friend of Voroshilov's. Was in charge of education in 1930s, then arrested and shot in Great Purges. Wife Olga Bubnova ran salon with Galina Egorova and was arrested in 1937.

Budenny, Semyon Mikhailovich (1883–1973)

Served in the Cossack regiments in the First World War and in the Red Army cavalry during the Civil War; with Stalin and Voroshilov in Tsaritsyn; joined the party in 1919. Promoted to marshal in 1935 but removed from frontline posts September 1941. Member of the party Central Committee 1939–52. Folk hero, known for handlebar moustache. Second wife, Olga Mikhailova, a singer at the Bolshoi Opera, ran a literary salon and was arrested in 1937.

Bukharin, Nikolai Ivanovich (1888–1938)

Russian, son of teachers, joined the party as a student in 1906, and was an émigré in Europe and the United States before the revolution. Party theorist, admired by young Communist intellectuals in 1920s; a Politburo member 1924–29. Was personally close to Stalin in mid-1920s, headed Comintern 1926–29, and was editor of *Pravda* until June 1929, when he was removed from his posts as a Rightist. Headed a sector of the industrial ministry 1929–32 and was editor of *Izvestia* 1934–37. A defendant in the 1938 Moscow show trial, he was convicted and shot. Married to (1) Nadezhda Lukina; (2) Esfir Gurvich (daughter Svetlana born in 1924); and (3) Anna Larina (son Yury born in 1936).

Bulganin, Nikolai Alexandrovich (1895–1975)

Russian, son of an office worker, joined the party in 1917. With the Cheka, then an industrial manager in 1920s; chairman of the Moscow Soviet 1931–37. Deputy minister for defense under Stalin 1944, then minister from 1947. Full member of the Politburo from 1948. Replaced Malenkov as head of the Soviet government in 1955 and traveled internationally with Khrushchev. Close to the Anti-Party Group, though not publically condemned with them; forced to resign positions in 1958. His wife, Elena, née Korovina, was an English teacher; daughter Vera, a schoolmate of Svetlana Stalina, was a doctor and married the son of Admiral Kuznetsov 1955; son, Lev (1925), was a pilot and a friend of Vasily Stalin. Lived with de facto wife Lidia Ivanovna Ianovskaya 1944–62.

CHEPTSOV, ALEXANDER ALEXANDROVICH (1902–80)

Lawyer, head of the Central Committee's personnel department 1942–45; president of the military collegium and deputy president of the Soviet Supreme Court, holding the rank of lieutenant general 1948–57. Presiding as judge at the closed trial of the Jewish Anti-Fascist Committee in 1952, he hesitated to convict the defendants. Career ended after Marshal Zhukov denounced him in 1956 for conviction of air force leaders on fabricated evidence ten years earlier.

CHUBAR, VLAS YAKOVLEVICH (1891–1939)

Ukrainian, joined the party as a factory worker in 1907. Candidate member of the Politburo from 1926 and a full member 1935–38. Headed Ukrainian government 1923–34; from 1934 was deputy chairman of the Soviet council of ministers (Council of People's Commissars) in Moscow. Briefly headed a cellulose combine in Solikamsk before arrest in 1938; was shot during the Great Purges. Wife, Alexandra (1903–38), graduated university in 1928, worked as a light industry consultant, and was arrested with husband and shot; they had two sons, Alexei (1929) and Vladimir (1933).

CHUEV, FELIX IVANOVICH (1941–99)

Writer and publicist with Stalinist and Russian nationalist orientation. Frontline heroism was the main theme of literary works. Interviewed Molotov extensively in the 1970s and 1980s, also Kaganovich.

DZERZHINSKY, FELIX EDMUNDOVICH (1877–1926)

Polish noble family, expelled from the Vilnius gymnasium for revolutionary activity; involved in the Russian social-democratic movement from 1895; a Bolshevik from 1917. Many years in prison under the tsar; had a reputation in the party as an incorruptible ascetic. Headed the GPU/OGPU 1922–26; from 1924 also headed the supreme economic council. Nonfactional in the mid-1920s but often supported Stalin's group.

EGOROV, ALEXANDER ILYICH (1883–1939)

Russian, professional military man starting with the Imperial Army, then the Red Army in the Civil War. Joined the party in 1918, earlier in Socialist-Revolutionary (SR) Party. In the 1920s, a commander of forces in Ukraine, later Belorussia. Headed the General Staff 1935–38; marshal from 1935; first deputy minister of defense 1937–38. Arrested February 1938 and shot. Wife, film actress Galina Egorova, who ran a salon with Olga Bubnova in 1930s, was arrested in 1937.

ENUKIDZE, AVEL SAFRONOVICH (1877–1937)

Georgian, party member from 1898, secretary of the Presidium of the Central Executive Committee of the USSR (later called the Supreme Soviet) 1922–35; expelled from the party June 1935; shot during the Great Purges. Godfather of Nadya Alliluyeva.

EZHOV, NIKOLAI IVANOVICH (1895–1940)

Joined the party in 1917. Headed a Central Committee department from 1930 and the party Control Commission 1934–39; head of the NKVD 1936–38; was a candidate member of the Politburo from October 1937 and minister of water transport 1938–39. Arrested on 10 April 1939, he was shot February 1940. Married to Evgenia, née Feigenberg, formerly Khayutin and Gladun (1904–38), who held a salon and committed suicide in 1938; had an adopted daughter, Natalia Khayutina (1932).

FRUNZE, MIKHAIL VLADIMIROVICH (1885–1925)

Moldavian, joined the party in 1904. During the Civil War, a political commissar with the Red Army, then a commander in Turkestan and the Southern Fronts. Succeeded Trotsky in charge of the military January 1925, becoming a candidate member of the Politburo at the same time; died after an operation (unconfirmed rumors that Stalin had him killed). His children Tatyana (born 1920) and Timur (1923–42) were adopted by the Voroshilovs after his death.

GAMARNIK, JAN BORISOVICH (1894–1937)

Jewish, joined the party as a student in 1916. Involved in party work in the Far East and Belorussia in the 1920s, then head of the Political Administration of the Red Army 1929–37. Committed suicide when threatened by arrest in the Tukhachevsky Affair, probably after a warning from his friend Mikoyan.

GORKY, MAXIM (ALEKSEI MAKSIMOVICH PESHKOV) (1868–1936)

Russian writer, prerevolutionary financial supporter of the Bolsheviks. Defended the intelligentsia against the Cheka after the revolution, in emigration on Capri 1921–32, returned on Stalin's invitation to live in the Soviet Union, where he was feted but also closely watched. Married 1896–1903 to Ekaterina Peshkova (1876–65), who was active in the Socialist Revolutionary Party, founded the Political Red Cross in 1917, and headed Aid to Political Prisoners 1922–37. In the 1930s, Gorky's Moscow household included his son, Maxim Peshkov (1897–1934); Maxim's wife Timosha (Nadezhda Vvedenskaya), who was courted by Yagoda; and their daughter, Marfa (Svetlana Stalina's best childhood friend), who married Sergo Beria in 1947.

KAGANOVICH, LAZAR MOISEEVICH (1893–1991)

Jewish, born in Ukraine; joined the party as a worker in 1911. Political commissar in Voronezh and Turkestan during the Civil War. Candidate member of the Politburo from 1926 and a full member 1930–57. Headed the Ukrainian party 1925–30 and again in 1947. Central Committee secretary 1928–39 and concurrently first secretary of Moscow party 1930–35; in charge of railways 1935–37 and 1938–44, oil industry 1939–40, and supply 1948–52. First deputy chairman of the Council of Ministers 1953–57 and headed the committee on labor and wages. Branded a member of the Anti-Party Group, he was demoted and sent to work as an industrial manager in the Urals 1957–61. Married to Maria, née Privorotskaya, a trade union head. They had a daughter, Maya (1917), an architect, and an adopted son, Yury.

KAGANOVICH, MIKHAIL MOISEEVICH (1888–1941)

Elder brother of Lazar and a party member from 1905. Member of the party Control Commission 1927–34; deputy head of the heavy industry ministry with responsibility for aviation production 1932–36. Committed suicide under threat of arrest.

KALININ, MIKHAIL IVANOVICH (1875–1946)

Russian, peasant-born, worker, joined the RSDLP in 1898 as a founding member. A policy moderate with populist appeal, he was titular head of the Soviet state 1919–46 (chairman of All-Union Executive Committee of the Congress of Soviets until 1938 and of the Supreme Soviet from 1938). Married to Ekaterina Lorberg, Estonian fellow worker and revolutionary, who was arrested in 1938 and released after the war. Their children were Valery (1904, an engineer), Julia (1905), Alexander (1908, an engineer), Lidia (1912, a doctor), and Anna (1916, a doctor).

KAMENEV, LEV BORISOVICH (1883–1936)

Jewish intellectual, RSDLP member from 1901, a Bolshevik from 1903, working mainly underground in Russia. Opposed October seizure of power. Was a Politburo member 1919–25, a leader with Zinoviev of the Left Opposition, and chairman of the Moscow Soviet in the 1920s. Expelled from the party December 1927, he was readmitted June 1928. Arrested January 1935 on accusation of complicity in Kirov's murder, he was a defendant in the Moscow show trial in 1936, convicted, and shot. His wife Olga Kameneva (1881–1941), Trotsky's sister, was arrested in 1935 and shot, as were their sons Alexander (1906) and Yury (1921). His later partner, Tatyana Glebova, and their son, Vladimir (1929), were exiled.

KHRUSHCHEV, NIKITA SERGEEVICH (1894–1971)

Russian born in Ukraine, worker in youth, joined the party in 1918. Student at the Industrial Academy, active against Rightists in 1930, second secretary of Moscow party (under Kaganovich) 1932–35, then first secretary 1935–38. Headed the Ukrainian party 1938–47 and again 1948–49. Politburo (Presidium) candidate in 1938, full member 1939–64. Central Committee secretary 1949–53; also headed the Moscow party organization. First secretary of the party Central Committee 1953–64, also chairman of Council of Ministers 1958–64. Launched de-Stalinization campaign in 1956. Dismissed from posts October 1964. His second wife (from early 1920s) was Nina Kukharchuk. Their children were Rada (1929), a journalist married to journalist Alexei Adzhubei; Sergei (1935), an engineer, who immigrated to the United States in the 1990s and wrote extensively on his father; and Elena (1938), a lawyer. Khrushchev also had two children from his first marriage, Julia (1916) and Leonid (1917–43), a pilot and war casualty, whose wife was arrested in 1942.

KIROV, SERGEI MIRONOVICH (1886–1934)

Russian, joined the party in 1904, involved in party work in the Caucasus during the Civil War, befriending Ordzhonikidze and Mikoyan; in Baku as head of the Azerbaijan party committee 1921–26; head of Leningrad party committee 1926–34. Close friend of Stalin's from the mid-1920s; knew Nadya from youth through her father. Candidate member of the Politburo from 1926 and a full member 1930–34; appointed Central Committee secretary in 1934. Assassinated December 1934. Married to Maria Markus; no children.

KOSIOR, STANISLAV VIKENTEVICH (1889–1939)

Polish-born, eldest of four brothers active in the revolutionary movement in Ukraine, joined the party as a worker in 1907. Was involved in party work in Siberia in the early

1920s, then Central Committee secretary in Moscow 1926–28. Candidate member of the Politburo in 1927 and a full member from 1930. General secretary of the Ukrainian party 1928–38; shot in Great Purges. Second wife, Elizaveta, was arrested with her husband and died in Gulag. Their children Vladimir (1922) and Mikhail (1924) were sent to an orphanage after their parents' arrest. Vladimir died at the front in 1942.

KOSYGIN, ALEXEI NIKOLAEVICH (1904–80)

Russian, working-class background, joined the party in 1927. Chairman of the Leningrad Soviet 1938–39; minister of the textile industry 1939–40. Deputy chairman of the Council of Ministers 1940–53. Candidate and then full member of the Politburo (Presidium) 1946–53; at risk in the Leningrad Affair but survived. Candidate member of the Politburo again 1957–60, then back to full member 1960–80; also chairman of the Council of Ministers and no. 2 man to Brezhnev. His wife, Klavdia, was a cousin of Alexei Kuznetsov.

KRUPSKAYA, NADEZHDA KONSTANTINOVNA (1869–1939)

Lenin's wife and a party member from 1898. Member of the party Control Commission 1924–27 and the Central Committee 1927–39. Held a senior position in the Russian education ministry 1917–29, when she resigned with colleagues after a policy disagreement. Close to the Zinoviev Opposition in the mid-1920s.

KUIBYSHEV, VALERIAN VLADIMIROVICH (1885–1935)

Russian, military family, joined the party in 1904. Candidate member of the Politburo 1921–24 and a full member 1927–35; Central Committee secretary in 1922; head of the party Control Commission 1924–26. Headed the supreme economic council 1926–30 and Gosplan 1930–34. He married (1) Praskovia Styazhkina, an Old Bolshevik; (2) Elena Kogan, also an Old Bolshevik, who held senior positions in the Moscow Party Committee and was shot in 1937; (3) Galina Troyanovskaya, daughter of Old Bolshevik diplomat Alexander Troyanovsky; and (4) Olga Lezhava (1901), daughter of Old Bolshevik Andrei Lezhava. His son Vladimir (1917) married Andreev's daughter Natalia; his daughter Galina (1919) became an architect.

KUZNETSOV, ALEXEI ALEXANDROVICH (1905–50)

Russian, village-born, Komsomol activist promoted by Kirov, second secretary of the Leningrad party under Zhdanov from 1937, then first secretary 1945–46. Central Committee secretary and head of the cadres department 1946–49; mentioned with Voznesensky as a possible heir to Stalin. Arrested in the Leningrad Affair on 13 August 1949 and shot on 1 October 1950. His daughter Alla married Sergo Mikoyan in 1949.

KUZNETSOV, NIKOLAI GERASIMOVICH (1902–74)

Russian, sailor in the Civil War, joined the party in 1925, a military advisor in Spain 1936–37. Commander of the Pacific Fleet 1938–39, promoted to admiral in 1939, then minister for the navy throughout the war. Under a cloud in 1948 on suspicion of giving state secrets to foreigners. Returned from the Far East to Moscow as minister for the navy again 1951–56. Had a reputation for straight-talking. His son Viktor married Bulganin's daughter Vera.

LENIN, VLADIMIR ILYICH (BORN ULYANOV, 1870–1924).

Russian, son of an inspector of schools who attained personal nobility; was a university student in Kazan when elder brother Alexander was executed for revolutionary activity in 1886. Involved in the Marxist revolutionary movement from the 1880s and founder of the Bolshevik Party. In emigration 1900–1905 and 1908–17, returning to Russia after the February Revolution in the famous "sealed train" through Germany. Sidelined by strokes from mid-1922. Politburo member from its foundation in 1919 and head of the government from October 1917 until his death. Married to Nadezhda Krupskaya (*see separate entry*).

LITVINOV, MAXIM MAXIMOVICH (BORN VALLAKH, 1876–1951)

Jewish, born in the Pale, a member of the RSDLP from 1898, and a Bolshevik from 1903; spent many years in emigration. A member of the party Central Committee 1934–41; deputy foreign minister 1921–30, then foreign minister 1930–39, and the Soviet representative at the League of Nations 1934–38. Deputy foreign minister to Molotov 1941–46, serving at the same time as ambassador to the United States 1941–43. His wife, Ivy (née Low, 1876–1951), was English; their son, Mikhail, a mathematician, was the father of Brezhnev-period dissident Pavel Litvinov; their daughter, Tatyana, was a translator.

LOZOVSKY, SOLOMON ABRAMOVICH (BORN DRIDZO, 1878–1952)

Jewish, son of a rabbi, in the revolutionary movement from 1903, with the Bolsheviks from 1905 (but expelled 1914–17 after a clash with Lenin). Émigré in Switzerland and France 1908–17. Deputy minister of foreign affairs 1939–46; deputy head, then head of Soviet information and propaganda agency (Sovinformbiuro) under the Central Committee 1941–48, with supervisory responsibility for the Jewish Anti-Fascist Committee. Defendant in JAC trial in 1952, convicted despite energetic rebuttal of accusations, and shot. Daughter, Vera Dridzo, personal secretary to Krupskaya 1919–39, married Mikhail Shamberg, a friend and colleague of Malenkov's; their son, Vladimir Shamberg, married Malenkov's daughter.

LYSENKO, TROFIM DENISOVICH (1896–1976)

Ukrainian of peasant origins, agronomist, and opponent of geneticists. Although lauded by Stalin and Molotov in the late 1930s, he was despised by the intelligentsia. He survived a challenge from Yury Zhdanov in the late 1940s, and then another under Khrushchev, but lost political-scientific power in 1966.

MALENKOV, GEORGY MAXIMILIANOVICH (1901–88)

Russian, from a noble family, a gymnasium graduate with a gold medal who joined the party in 1920. Studied engineering in the early 1920s, went to work in the Central Committee office in the mid-1920s before graduation. Was the head of the Central Committee department of party organizations 1934–39, then head of the personnel department and Central Committee secretary 1939–46 and again 1948–53. A candidate member of the Politburo from 1941 and a full member 1946–57. Head of the Soviet government March 1953–55. Ousted from power as member of the Anti-Party Group in 1957. Married to Valeria Golubtsova, rector of the Moscow Power Institute from

1942. Their children were Valentina (1925), an architect, who married Vladimir Shamberg in 1948 but divorced him on Malenkov's instructions in 1949; Andrei (1937), a biologist, who later wrote a memoir that defended his father; and Egor (1938), a chemist.

MENZHINSKY, VYACHESLAV RUDOLFOVICH (1874–1934)

Polish aristocrat, cosmopolitan intellectual, and a law graduate from Saint Petersburg University in 1898. Joined the RSDLP in 1902 and the Bolsheviks in 1903; in emigration 1907–17. Headed the OGPU 1926–34. Was seriously ill in his last years, leaving Yagoda effectively in charge.

MIKHOELS, SOLOMON MIKHAILOVICH (BORN VOVSI, 1890–1948)

Actor in Moscow Jewish Theater, took over as director in 1929. Head of the Jewish Anti-Fascist Committee in 1942 and traveled to the United States, Canada, and Britain to raise money from Jewish communities in 1943. Murdered in a fake car accident on Stalin's orders January 1948; his theater closed July 1949. A cousin, Miron Semenovich Vovsi, was one of the Jewish doctors charged in the Doctors' Plot in 1952.

MIKOYAN, ANASTAS IVANOVICH (1895–1978)

Armenian, a party member from 1915, a survivor of the shooting of the 26 Baku Commissars in 1918, worked in Nizhny Novgorod and Rostov on the Don in the early 1920s. Was a candidate member of the Politburo from 1926 and a full member 1935–66. Headed the ministry of external and internal trade from 1926, then the ministry of supply from 1930, and the ministry of the food industry 1934–38. Was a member of the GKO during the war. After Stalin's death, was again trade minister and headed the Commission on Rehabilitation. Supported Khrushchev in the clash with the Anti-Party Group. Headed the Presidium of the Supreme Soviet 1964–65. Married to Ashkhen, née Tumanyan (1896–1962), with sons Stepan (1922), an aviation constructor (like his uncle Artem Mikoyan); Vladimir (1924), a pilot, killed in the war; Alexei (1925); Ivan (1927), arrested and deported during the war, along with Sergo, in the "Kremlin children's" affair; and Sergo (1929), an international relations specialist who married Alla Kuznetsova in 1949 and later helped his father write memoirs.

MOLOTOV, VYACHESLAV MIKHAILOVICH (BORN SKRYABIN, 1890–1986)

Russian, born in Vyatka Province, solid family, musical (but not related to composer who was his namesake), a student at Saint Petersburg before the war but didn't graduate. Joined the party in 1906. Was Central Committee secretary 1921–30, a candidate Politburo member from 1922, and a full member 1924–57. Headed the Soviet government (chairman of the Council of People's Commissars) 1930–41, then deputy chairman under Stalin 1941–42, and first deputy 1942–57. Negotiated the Molotov-Ribbentrop Pact in 1939. Was deputy chairman of the GKO during the war; foreign minister 1939–49, and again 1953–56 and 1941–45; minister for state control 1956–57. Ousted from the top leadership as member of the Anti-Party Group, then ambassador to Mongolia 1957–60, and head of the Soviet Atomic Energy delegation in Vienna

1960–62. Married to Polina, née Karpovskaia (party name Zhemchuzhina) (*see separate entry*); daughter Svetlana (1929) became a historian.

ORDZHONIKIDZE, GRIGORY KONSTANTINOVICH ("SERGO") (1886–1937)

Georgian, joined the party in 1903, trained as a paramedic, was briefly a student at Lenin's party school in France in 1911, member of Bolshevik Central Committee from 1912. Served in the Red Army in the Caucasus during the Civil War; was an ally of Stalin in his quarrel with Lenin over nationalities policy. Headed the party committee in Transcaucasia 1922–26, then, briefly, the Rostov committee. Chairman of the party Central Control Commission in Moscow 1927–34; candidate member of the Politburo from 1926, and a full member from 1930 until his death. Headed the supreme economic council 1930–32 and the ministry for heavy industry 1932–37. Committed suicide after a quarrel with Stalin February 1937. Married to Zinaida, née Pavlutskaya (1894–1960); adopted daughter Eteri (1923), a historian.

PETROVSKY, GRIGORY IVANOVICH (1878–1958)

Born in Ukraine in a working-class family. Active in the social-democratic movement from 1897; elected a Bolshevik deputy to the Duma in 1912. Was a candidate member of the Soviet Politburo 1926–39, president of the Ukrainian Supreme Soviet 1919–38, deputy chairman of the Presidium of the All-Union Supreme Soviet 1938–39, and deputy director of the Museum of the Revolution from 1940.

POSKREBYSHEV, ALEXANDER NIKOLAEVICH (1891–1965)

Joined the party in 1917. Worked with Stalin at the Central Committee secretariat in the 1920s, was head of the Central Committee's Secret Department in the 1930s, and, from 1935, of Stalin's personal secretariat. Dismissed by Stalin early in 1953. In 1934 married Bronislava Metallikova (1910–41), an endocrinologist, favorite of Stalin, and relative by marriage of Trotsky; she was arrested in 1939 and shot in 1941. There were two daughters, aged seven and one at the time of her arrest.

POSTYSHEV, PAVEL PETROVICH (1887–1939)

Russian, son of an Ivanovo weaver, joined the party in 1904. Fought in Siberia and the Far East during the Civil War. In Ukraine as secretary of the Ukrainian Central Committee 1926–30; in Moscow as secretary of the (Soviet) Central Committee 1930–33; back to Ukraine as second secretary (though, in fact, the top man) 1933–37; candidate member of the Politburo 1934–38. Moved to Kuibyshev as first secretary March 1937, arrested February 1938, and shot February 1939. His wife, Tatyana Postolovskaya, a party activist and signatory of Nadezhda Alliluyeva's death notice, was arrested with her husband. Their sons Leonid (1920) and Vladimir (1921) were also arrested; older son Valentin (1916) had died early.

PYATAKOV, GEORGY LEONIDOVICH (YURY) (1890–1937)

Russian, son of a sugar factory owner in Ukraine, joined the party in 1910. Held planning and economic jobs in the 1920s and was named as one of the coming men in the party in Lenin's "Testament." A prominent member of the Left Opposition, expelled from the party in 1927, then reinstated in 1928 after renouncing Trotskyism. Was deputy minister of heavy industry from 1931. Arrested in 1936, he was a leading defendant in the 1937 Moscow show trial; convicted on 30 January 1937 and shot immediately.

RADEK, KARL BERNGARDOVICH (1885–1939)

Born in a Jewish family in Lvov (Lemberg; then in Austria-Hungary), joined the party in 1903. With Rosa Luxemburg, was active in the revolutionary movement in Warsaw, leading to his expulsion from the Russian Empire in 1907. Then a student in Leipzig and Berne, associated with the left wing of Germany's Social-Democratic Party. The Bolsheviks' German expert in the 1920s, he supported Trotsky in the faction fights, was expelled from the party in 1927, and exiled. He later recanted and was readmitted in 1930. Headed the Central Committee's bureau of international information 1932–36. Arrested September 1936, he was a defendant in the 1937 Moscow show trial, receiving a ten-year sentence (all the rest got death), but died in prison.

REDENS, STANISLAV FRANTSEVICH (1892–1940)

Polish origin, a factory worker in Ukraine in his youth. A party member from 1914, member of the party Control Commission 1927–34. Head of the Ukrainian OGPU 1931–33, the Moscow regional OGPU/NKVD from 1933 to January 1938, and finally the Kazakhstan NKVD; arrested November 1938 and shot. Married to Anna Allilyueva, Stalin's sister-in-law, who was sentenced to ten years as a spy in 1948. They had two sons: Leonid (1928), arrested with the Mikoyan boys in the "Kremlin children's" affair in 1943, and Vladimir (1935).

ROKOSSOVSKY, KONSTANTIN KONSTANTINOVICH (1896–1968)

Born to Polish/Belorussian parents; father, a railway inspector, was from the Polish nobility. Volunteered for the Imperial Army during World War I, then the Red Army in the Civil War; joined the party in 1919. Arrested August 1937 as a Polish spy, then released in 1940 after Timoshenko's appeal to Stalin. Headed the Don army that captured Paulus at Stalingrad; promoted to marshal in 1944. Defense minister of the Polish People's Republic 1949–56 (removed in the Polish uprising); deputy defense minister of the Soviet Union 1956–57 and again 1958–61.

RUDZUTAK, JAN ERNESTOVICH (1887–1938)

Latvian, joined the party as a worker in 1904, became a professional revolutionary, and spent many years in prison before 1917. Served as a Central Committee secretary 1923–24; was a candidate member of the Politburo from 1923, a full member 1926–34, then a candidate again 1934–37. Was a deputy chairman of the government (Council of People's Commissars) 1926–37, simultaneously heading the party's Control Commission 1931–34. Arrested in the Tukhachevsky Affair in 1937 and shot. Had strong cultural interests (music, theater, and film) and friends in artistic circles.

RYKOV, ALEXEI IVANOVICH (1881–1938)

Russian, a party member from 1899, a Politburo member from 1922 to December 1930, deputy head of the government (the Council of People's Commissars) under Lenin, succeeding him as its chairman 1924–30. One of the leaders of the Right Opposition; later served as minister of communications 1931–36. Arrested February 1937, he was a defendant in the 1938 show trial in Moscow, convicted, and shot immediately. His wife, Nina Marshak (1884–1942), was arrested June 1937 and died in prison; daughter, Natalia (1916), was sent to Gulag. Rykov's sister, Faina, was married to the brother of émigré Menshevik publicist Boris Nicolaevsky.

SHCHERBAKOV, ALEXANDER SERGEEVICH (1901–1945)

Working-class origin, joined the party in 1918. Studied at Sverdlov Communist University in the early 1920s, then at the Institute of Red Professors in the early 1930s. Worked in the Central Committee 1932–36, concurrently serving as secretary of the newly formed Writers' Union under Gorky's chairmanship from 1934; then party secretary in Leningrad, Irkutsk, and Donetsk. Was first secretary of the Moscow party 1938–45 and a candidate member of the Politburo from February 1941. Brother of Zhdanov's wife. Died of a heart attack on the night of Victory Day.

SHVERNIK, NIKOLAI MIKHAILOVICH (1888–1980)

A party member from 1905 and a Central Committee secretary 1926–27; first secretary of the Urals party committee 1927–29. Headed the trade unions 1929–44 and again 1953–56. Chairman of the Supreme Soviet 1944–46 and the party Control Commission 1956–66. Was a candidate member of the Politburo from 1939 and a Presidium (Politburo) member 1952–53 and 1957–66. Married Maria Belaya, a Ukrainian Old Bolshevik; their daughter, Ludmila (Lyusya) (1916), was the first woman graduate of the Zhukovsky military engineering academy, specializing in television technology.

SOKOLNIKOV, GRIGORY YAKOVLEVICH (BORN BRILLIANT, 1888–1939)

Jewish intellectual, childhood friend of Bukharin, joined the party in 1905, then in emigration; earned an economics degree from the Sorbonne. Served as finance minister 1923–26, then worked in Gosplan. A candidate member of the Politburo 1924–25, he was removed as a member of the Zinoviev Opposition. Arrested July 1936, he was a defendant in the 1937 Moscow show trial, received a ten-year sentence, and died in prison. His third wife was the writer Galina Serebryakova.

STALIN, JOSEPH VISSARIONOVICH (BORN DZHUGASHVILI, 1878–1953 [BUT GAVE BIRTHDATE AS 1879 FROM THE 1920s])

Georgian, in the party from 1898 and with the Bolsheviks from 1903. Member of the Politburo from 1919; general secretary of the Central Committee from 1922 ("general" dropped from the title in 1934). From 1941 also headed the government as chairman of the Council of Ministers. First wife was Ekaterina Svanidze (d. 1907); their son, Yakov (1907–43), fell into German hands as a POW, leading to the arrest in 1941 of his wife, Julia Meltzner; he died in captivity. Stalin's second wife, Nadezhda (Nadya) Alliluyeva (1901–32), daughter of Old Bolshevik Sergei Alliluyev, was a student at the Industrial Academy in the late 1920s and died by suicide. They had a son, Vasily (1921–62), a pilot, whose second wife, Ekaterina Timoshenko, was the daughter of Marshal Timoshenko (*see separate entry*); and a daughter, Svetlana (*see* Alliluyeva), as well as an adopted son, Artem (Tomik) Sergeev (1921–2008), who became a major general of artillery.

SVANIDZE, ALEXANDER (ALYOSHA) SERGEEVICH (1884–1941)

Georgian (noble family), joined the party in 1901 and the Bolsheviks in 1904. Was well educated in Tiflis and Vienna and knew German and English. Close friend and brother-in-law of Stalin. Headed an export agency 1928–29; was a deputy trade representative in Germany 1930–31; ran the External Trade Bank 1931–35; and was deputy head of the State Bank in 1935. Arrested December 1937, he was shot in 1941. Married Maria Korona, a former opera singer, arrested with him; their son, John-Reed (Johnny) (1927–90) spent twenty years in prison and exile, returning to Moscow in 1956, where he was briefly married to Svetlana Alliluyeva (*see separate entry*).

SYRTSOV, SERGEI IVANOVICH (1893–1937)

Russian, from a white-collar family, joined the party in 1913 as a student in Saint Petersburg. Political commissar in the Red Army during the Civil War, then first secretary of the Siberian party organization 1926–29. Candidate member of the Politburo and head of the government of the Russian republic 1929–30, he lost favor when he was accused of plotting Stalin's ouster as general secretary in the Syrtsov-Lominadze Affair (1930). He was arrested in 1937 and shot.

TIMOSHENKO, SEMYON KONSTANTINOVICH (1895–1970)

Born into a Ukrainian peasant family in Bessarabia. Served in cavalry divisions during World War I and in the Red Army during the Civil War (fought at Tsaritsyn with Voroshilov and Stalin); joined the party in 1919. A marshal from 1940 and defense minister (succeeding Voroshilov) 1940–41, then deputy minister 1941–43. One of the top frontline commanders in the Second World War. Wartime friend of Khrushchev. Daughter, Ekaterina, was married to Vasily Stalin 1946–49.

TOMSKY, MIKHAIL PAVLOVICH (BORN EFREMOV, 1880–1936)

Russian, printer by trade, party member from 1904. Politburo member 1922–29, headed the central council of trade unions in the 1920s, and was one of the leaders of the Right Opposition. Deputy chairman of the industrial ministry, in charge of chemicals, from 1929, then headed the State Publishing House 1932–36. Committed suicide under threat of arrest. Wife Maria Efremova, an Old Bolshevik, was sentenced to ten years' exile after husband's death (her release was blocked by Molotov in 1954). Elder sons Mikhail and Viktor were arrested and shot in the late 1930s; son Yury (1921) was arrested with mother and exiled.

TROTSKY, LEV DAVIDOVICH (BORN BRONSTEIN, 1879–1940)

Menshevik, joined the RSDLP in 1897 and the Bolsheviks June 1917. Hero of the revolutions of 1905 and October 1917; in emigration for many years. Member of the Politburo 1919–26 and war minister 1918–25. Creator of the Red Army in the Civil War; clashed with Stalin at Tsaritsyn. Known as a ruthless disciplinarian; advocated labor conscription 1920–21. Leader of the Left Opposition after Lenin's death. Expelled from the party and deported to Kazakhstan in 1927; expelled from the country in 1929;

in exile in Turkey and later Mexico, where he was assassinated by Soviet agents. Sister Olga was married to Kamenev. Second wife was Natalia Ivanovna Sedova; their elder son Lev (1906–38) was his father's main assistant in Europe after expulsion.

TUKHACHEVSKY, MIKHAIL NIKOLAEVICH (1893–1937)
Born in Smolensk, son of an impoverished noble. Had a gymnasium education, then cadet corps; was a junior officer during World War I. Served as a volunteer in the Red Army during the Civil War and joined the party in 1918. Commander of Leningrad military district 1928–31; from 1931 was deputy head of the Military Council. Active in army modernization, he was a theorist of tank warfare. A patron of musicians, including Shostakovich. Deputy defense minister under Voroshilov from 1934, then first deputy. Charged with treason June 1937 and shot.

UBOREVICH, IERONIM PETROVICH (1896–1937)
Lithuanian peasant origin, attended university 1914–15, was a junior officer during World War I, joined the party in 1917. Fought in the Red Army during the Civil War. After being sent to Germany for higher military training 1927–28, he was deputy chairman of the Revolutionary Military Council 1930–31, and then commander successively of the Belorussian and Central Asian military districts 1931–37. Friend of Mikoyan. Charged in the Tukhachevsky Affair and shot.

VASILEVSKY, ALEXANDER MIKHAILOVICH (1895–1977)
Russian, son of a priest. NCO in World War I; served in the Red Army during the Civil War; protégé of Voroshilov and student at Frunze Military Academy in the early 1930s. Joined the party in 1938 (earlier prevented by social origin). Fought in World War II, promoted to marshal in 1943; headed the general staff 1946–49. Was defense minister 1949–53, then deputy defense minister 1953–56.

VOROSHILOV, KLIMENT EFREMOVICH (1881–1969)
Russian, born in Ukraine, son of a railway worker, Donbass miner in youth, joined the party in 1903. With Budenny, led the First Cavalry Army in the Civil War; at Tsaritsyn with Stalin; fought in the war with Poland in 1920. Defense minister 1925–40; full member of the Politburo 1925–60. Discredited as a military leader during the Finnish War and the near-fall of Leningrad in 1941. Out of favor with Stalin in the 1940s ("British spy" accusation). Headed the Soviet Control Commission in Budapest after the war, then was in arts administration. Was president of the Supreme Soviet in post-Stalin leadership. Married Ekaterina, née Golda Gorbman (1987–59); their adopted children were Petr (1914), and Frunze's daughter Tatyana (1920, a chemist) and son Timur (1923–42), a pilot, killed in the war.

VOZNESENSKY, NIKOLAI ALEXEEVICH (1903–50)
Russian, from a white-collar background, economist. Joined the party in 1919. In the 1920s, studied first at Sverdlov Communist University, then at the Institute of Red Professors, at which he taught after graduation. Received a doctorate in economics in 1935. Headed the Leningrad City Planning Commission 1935–37, then was deputy head of the State Planning Commission in Moscow from 1938. Became deputy chair-

man of the Soviet Council of Ministers in 1939, then first deputy March 1941; was a member of the GKO during World War II, a candidate member of the Politburo from February 1941, and a full member from 1947. Rumored to be under consideration by Stalin as a possible heir; was removed from all posts in connection with the Leningrad Affair March 1949, arrested in October, and shot on 30 September 1950.

VYSHINSKY, ANDREI YANUAREVICH (1883–1959)

Lawyer, Polish noble extraction, grew up in Baku, university graduate. Joined the party in 1920 (formerly a Menshevik). Prosecutor in Shakhty and three Moscow show trials; deputy prosecutor, then chief prosecutor of USSR 1931–39. After serving as first deputy foreign minister 1940–49, he replaced Molotov as minister in 1949 and remained in this position until Molotov took over again in 1953, when he reverted to first deputy. Headed the Soviet delegation to the United Nations in 1946 and was back in the United Nations after Stalin's death.

YAGODA, GENRIKH GEORGEVICH (1891–1938)

Jewish, in the party from 1907 (other sources say 1917). Grew up in Nizhny Novgorod, was a relative of Old Bolshevik Yakov Sverdlov, and knew writer Maxim Gorky from youth. Deputy head of the OGPU 1924–34, then head of its successor organization, the NKVD, 1935–36. Closer to the Rightists than to the Stalin team, also close to Gorky household after Gorky's return (in love with his daughter-in-law). A defendant in the 1938 Moscow show trial, he was convicted and later shot. Married Ida, the niece of Sverdlov and brother of Leopold Averbakh (leader of militant Russian Association of Proletarian Writers [RAPP] in the 1920s).

YAKIR, IONA EMMANUILOVICH (1896–1937)

Jewish, son of a pharmacist, studied at university in Basel and joined the party in 1917. Was in the Red Army in the Civil War and commander of the Ukrainian military district 1925–35. A friend of Kaganovich and Khrushchev, he was accused in the Tukhachevsky Affair, convicted, and shot. His wife, Sarra, publicly denounced him, presumably under pressure, then was sent to Gulag with their son, Petr, who became active in the dissident movement in the Brezhnev period.

YAKOVLEV, YAKOV ARKADEVICH (BORN EPSHTEIN, 1896–1938)

Jewish, joined the party as a student in 1913, and worked with Molotov in the Saint Petersburg underground. After a stint in the Central Committee in the mid-1920s, he headed the Agriculture Ministry 1929–34 and the Agriculture Department of the Central Committee 1934–36; from 1936, he was first deputy chairman of the party Control Commission. Never a Politburo member, he was nevertheless a frequent Politburo attendee, as a Stalin favorite, in the 1930s. Arrested October 1937 and shot. His wife, Elena Sokolovskaya, director of Mosfilm, was arrested with him.

ZHDANOV, ANDREI ALEXANDROVICH (1896–1948)

Russian, son of an inspector of schools, joined the party in 1915 as a student. Was party secretary in Nizhny Novgorod 1922–34 and then headed the Leningrad party organization 1934–44 (stayed in Leningrad during the blockade). Was a Central Committee secretary from 1934, a candidate member in the Politburo from 1935, then a full Polit-buro member 1939–48. Headed the Soviet Control Commission in Finland in 1945. Front man of cultural disciplinary campaign (*zhdanovshina*) after the war. Wife, Zi-naida, was the sister of Alexander Shcherbakov; son, Yury (1919), a chemist, headed the Central Committee Science Department 1948–53, was married to Stalin's daughter Svetlana 1949–52 (daughter, Ekaterina, born in 1950), and later became rector of Ros-tov University.

ZHEMCHUZHINA, POLINA SEMENOVNA (MOLOTOVA, BORN KARPOVSKAYA, 1897–1970)

Daughter of a Jewish tailor, born in Ukraine, joined the party in 1918 (same year that her brother and sister emigrated to Palestine). Was a political commissar in the Red Army in the Civil War, met and married Molotov. Worked as secretary of a factory party cell in Moscow 1927–32; director of the cosmetics trust 1932–36; head of the cos-metics administration of Mikoyan's Food Industry Ministry 1936–37, deputy minis-ter, then minister for fisheries in 1939; then head of textiles in Ministry of Light Indus-try 1939–48. Candidate member of the Central Committee 1939–41. Arrested for Zionism in 1949 and in exile until March 1953.

ZHUKOV, GEORGY KONSTANTINOVICH (1896–1974)

Russian, professional military, Imperial Army conscript in 1915, then in the Red Army from 1918; joined the party in 1919. During World War II, he was both a leading front-line commander (promoted to marshal in 1943) and deputy to the Supreme Com-mander, Stalin. In charge of the Soviet occupation forces in Germany 1945–46. De-moted in 1946; headed Odessa and then Urals military districts. Was first deputy minister of defense from March 1953, then minister of defense 1955–57. Candidate member of the party Presidium 1956–57, then full member June–October 1957. A key participant in the arrest of Beria and routing of the Anti-Party Group.

ZINOVIEV, GRIGORY EVSEEVICH (BORN RADOMYLSKY, 1883–1936)

Jewish, joined the RSDLP in 1901 and the Bolsheviks in 1903. Close to Lenin in emi-gration for many years before 1917. Opposed the October seizure of power. Headed the Petrograd (later Leningrad) party organization from 1918 and the Comintern from 1919, then lost both positions in 1926 as leader of the Left Opposition. Politburo mem-ber 1921–26. Arrested in 1935 on accusation of complicity in Kirov's murder. Was a de-fendant in the 1936 Moscow show trial, convicted, and shot. His first wife, Zlata Lilina (1882–1929), headed the Leningrad Education Department in the 1920s, then was ex-pelled from the party with Zinoviev in 1927. Their son, Stepan Radomylsky (1913–37), was arrested in 1936 and died in prison. His second wife, Sarra Ravich (1899–1957), was arrested in 1935 and sent to Gulag, then freed in 1954.

BIBLIOGRAPHY OF WORKS CITED

ARCHIVES (F. = *FOND*, ARCHIVAL COLLECTION; OP. = *OPIS'*, INVENTORY)

GARF (Gosudarstennyi arkhiv Rossiiskoi Federatsii)
   f. 3316 (Central Executive Committee of USSR Congress of Soviets [TSIK])
   f. 3429 (Supreme Council of National Economy of USSR [Vesenkha])
   f. 5446 (deputy chairmen of Council of Ministers of USSR):
      op. 51 (Andreev), 53 (Voznesensky), 54 (Voroshilov), 82 (Molotov), 83 (Kaga-
      novich), 85 (Malenkov), 120 (Mikoyan)
   f. 5451 (Central Council of Trade Unions of USSR)
   f. 7297 (People's Commissariat of Heavy Industry of USSR)
   f. 7523 (Supreme Soviet of USSR)
RGANI (Rossiiskii gosudarstvennyi arkhiv noveishei istorii)
   f. 3 (Politburo), f. 5 (Agitprop and General Departments of Central Committee);
      f. 52 (Khrushchev)
RGASPI (Rossiiskii gosudarstvennyi arkhiv sotsial'no-politicheskoi istorii)
   f. 17 (Central Committee of Russian/Soviet Communist Party),
   Personal papers:
   ff. 73 (Andreev), 74 (Voroshilov), 77 (Zhdanov), 78 (Kalinin), 79 (Kuibyshev), 80
      (Kirov), 81 (Kaganovich), 82 (Molotov), 84 (Mikoyan), 85 (Ordzhonikidze),
      329 (Bukharin), 558 (Stalin), 667 (Enukidze)
TsGAIPD (Tsentral'nyi gosudarstvennyi arkhiv istoriko-politicheskoi dokumentatsii
   Sankt-Peterburga)
   f. 24 (Leningrad regional party committee)
TsKhDNISO (Tsentr khraneniia dokumentatsii noveishei istorii Samarskoi oblasti)
   f. 714 (Kuibyshev regional party committee)

NEWSPAPERS

Izvestiia (central government organ)
Krest'ianskaia gazeta (Leningrad)
Pravda (central party organ)
Trud (central trade union organ)

DOCUMENT PUBLICATIONS, TRANSCRIPTS

XIII s"ezd RKP(b), Mai 1924 g. Stenograficheskii otchet (Moscow: Gosudarstvennoe izdatel'stvo polititicheskoi literatury, 1962)

XV konferentsiia Vsesoiuznoi Kommunisticheskoi Partii (b), 25 oktiabria–3 noiabria 1926 g. Stenograficheskii otchet (Moscow-Leningrad: Gosudarstvennoe izdatel'stvo, 1927)

XV s"ezd VKP(b), Dekabr' 1927 goda, Stenograficheskii otchet (Moscow: Gosudarstvennoe izdatel'stvo polititicheskoi literatury, 1961), 2 vols.

XVII s"ezd VKP, 30 ianvaria-10 fevralia 1934 g. Stenograficheskii otchet (Moscow: Partizdat, 1934)

XVIII s"ezd Vsesoiuznoi Kommunisticheskoi Partii (b), 10–21 marta 1939 g. Stenograficheskii otchet (Moscow: OGIZ, 1939)

XX s"ezd Kommunisticheskoi Partii Sovetskogo Soiuza, 14–25 fevralia 1956 g. Stenograficheskii otchet (Moscow: Gosudarstvennoe izdatel'stvo politicheskoi literatury, 1956), 2 vols.

Bol'shevistkoe rukovodstvo: Perepiska, 1912–1927, comp. A. V. Kvashonkin, O. V. Khlevniuk, et al. (Moscow: ROSSPEN, 1996)

Clark, Katerina, and Evgeny Dobrenko, with Andrei Artizov and Oleg Naumov. *Soviet Culture and Power: A History in Documents, 1917–1953* (New Haven: Yale University Press, 2007)

Foreign Relations of the United States Diplomatic Papers: Franklin D. Roosevelt; The Conferences at Malta and Yalta (Washington, DC: Department of State, 1955)

Iosif Stalin v ob"iatiiakh sem'i: Iz lichnogo arkhiva, ed. Iu. G. Murin (Moscow: Rodina, 1993)

Kak lomali NEP: Stenogrammy plenumov TsK VKP(b), 1928–29 v piati tomakh, ed. V. P. Danilov, O. V. Khlevniuk, A. Iu. Vatlin, et al. (Moscow: Mezhdunarodnyi fond "Demokratiia," 2000), 5 vols.

Koenker, Diane P., and Ronald D. Bachman, eds. *Revelations from the Russian Archives* (Washington, DC: Library of Congress, 1997)

Lavrentii Beriia: Stenogramma iul'skogo plenuma TsK KPSS i drugie materialy, comp. V. P. Naumov and Iu. Sigarev (Moscow: Mezhdunarodnyi fond "Demokratiia," 1999)

"Literaturnyi front": Istoriia politicheskoi tsenzury; Sbornik dokumentov, comp. D. L. Babichenko (Moscow: Entsiklopediia rossiiskikh dereven', 1994)

Lubianka: Stalin i Glavnoe Upravlenie Gosbezopasnosti NKVD, 1937–1938, comp. V. N. Khaustov et al. (Moscow: Mezhdunarodnyi fond "Demokratiia," 2004)

Lubianka: Stalin i NKVD-NKGB-GUKR "Smersh" 1939–March 1946, comp. V. N. Khaustov et al. (Moscow: Mezhdunarodnyi fond "Demokratiia," 2006)

Molotov, Malenkov, Kaganovich, 1957; Stenogramma iun'skogo plenuma TsK KPSS i drugie dokumenty, comp. N. Kovaleva et al. (Moscow: Mezhdunarodnyi fond "Demokratiia," 1998)

Na prieme u Stalina: Tetradi (zhurnaly) zapisei lits, priniatykh I. V. Stalinym (1924–1953 gg.), ed. A. A. Chernobaev (Moscow: Novyi Khronograf, 2008)

Origins of the Cold War: The Novikov, Kennan, and Roberts "Long Telegrams" of 1946, ed. Kenneth M. Jensen (Washington, DC: US Institute of Peace, 1991)

Pis'ma I. V. Stalina V. M. Molotovu, 1925–1936 gg., comp. L. Kosheleva et al. (New Haven: Yale University Press, 1995)

Politbiuro i delo Beriia: Sbornik dokumentov, ed. O. B. Mozokhin (Moscow: Kuchkovo pole, 2012)

Politburo TsK RKP(b)-VKP(b): Povestki dlia zasedanii. Vol. 1, 1919–29. Katalog (Moscow: ROSSPEN, 2000)

Politbiuro TsK RKP(b) i Evropa: Resheniia "osoboi papki," 1923–1939 (Moscow: ROSSPEN, 2001)

Politbiuro Tsk VKP(b) i Sovet Ministrov SSSR, 1945–53, comp. Khlevniuk et al. (Moscow: ROSSPEN, 2002)

"Posetiteli kremlevskogo kabineta Stalina," ed. A. V. Korotkov, A. D. Chernev, and A. A. Chernobaev, *Istoricheskii arkhiv*, 1994, no. 6–1997, no. 1

Prezidium TsK KPSS, 1954–1964, vol. 1, *Chernovye protokol'nye zapisi zasedanii: Stenogrammy*, ed. A. A. Fursenko (Moscow: ROSSPEN, 2003)

"'Prosti menia, Koba': Neizvestnoe pis'mo N. Bukharina," *Istochnik*, 1993, no. 0

"Protiv prisvoenii familii Stalina vozvrazhenii ne imeiu," *Istochnik*, 1996, no. 2

Regional'naia politika N. S. Khrushcheva: TsK KPSS i mestnye partiinye komitety, 1953–1964 gg., compiled O. V. Khlevniuk et al. (Moscow: Rossiiskaia politicheskaia entsiklopediia, 2009)

Report of Court Proceedings in the Case of the Anti-Soviet "Bloc of Rights and Trotskyites," Heard before the Military Collegium of the Supreme Court of the USSR, Moscow, March 2–13, 1938 (Moscow: People's Commissariat of Justice of the USSR, 1938)

Rubenstein, Joshua, and Vladimir P. Naumov, eds. *Stalin's Secret Pogrom: The Postwar Inquisition of the Jewish Anti-Fascist Committee*, trans. Laura Esther Wolfson (New Haven: Yale University Press, 2001)

"Schast'e literatury": Gosudarstvo i pisateli, 1925–1938; Dokumenty, comp. D. L. Babichenko (Moscow: ROSSPEN, 1997)

Sovetskoe rukovodstvo: Perepiska, 1928–1941, comp. A. V. Kvashonkin et al. (Moscow: ROSSPEN, 1999)

Stalin i Kaganovich: Perepiska, 1931–1936 gg., comp. O. V. Khlevniuk et al. (Moscow: ROSSPEN, 2001)

Stalin i kosmopolitizm: Dokumenty agitpropa TsK KPSS, 1945–1953, ed. D. G. Nadzhafov (Moscow: Mezhdunarodnyi fond "Demokratiia," Izdatel'stvo Materik, 2005)

Stalinskoe Politbiuro v 30-e gody: Sbornik dokumentov, comp. O. V. Khlevniuk et al. (Moscow: AIRO-XX, 1995)

Stenogrammy zasedanii Politbiuro TsK RKP(b)-VKP9(b), 1923–1938 v trekh tomakh (Moscow: ROSSPEN, 2007), vol. 1 (1923–26), vol. 2 (1926–27), vol. 3 (1928–38)

"'U menia odna nadezhda na tebia': Poslednie pis'ma N. I. Bukharina I. V. Stalinu, 1935–1937 gg.," *Istoricheskii arkhiv*, 2001, no. 3

Vainakhi i imperskaia vlast': Problema Chechni i Ingushetii vo vnutrennei politike Rossii i SSSR (nachalo XIX-seredina XX v.), ed. V. A. Kozlov (Moscow: ROSSPEN, 2011)

Vlast' i khudozhestvennaia intelligentsia: Dokumenty TsK RKP(b)-VKP(b), VChK-OGPU-NKVD o kul'turnoi politike, 1917–1953, comp. Andrei Artizov and Oleg Naumov (Moscow: Mezhdunarodnyi fond "Demokratiia," 1999)

"Vsiudu ia budu dokazat' 'svoiu nevinnovnost,'" letters of Bukharin to Stalin and Politburo members (1936), *Istochnik*, 1993, no. 2

MEMOIRS, INTERVIEWS, AND HISTORIES BY TEAM MEMBERS AND THEIR FAMILIES

ANDREEV

Andreev, A. A. *Vospominaniia, pis'ma*, comp. N. A. Andreeva (Moscow: Politizdat, 1985)

BERIA

Beria, Sergo. *Beria, My Father: Inside Stalin's Kremlin*, trans. Brian Pearce (London: Duckworth, 2001)
Beriia, Sergo. *Moi otets: Lavrentii Beriia* (Moscow: "Sovremennik," 1994)
———. *Moi otets, Lavrentii Beriia: Syn za ottsa otvechaet...* (Moscow: Algoritm, 2013)

BUKHARIN

Bukharina, Anna Larina. *Nezabyvaemoe* (Moscow: APN, 1989)
Larina, Anna. *This I Cannot Forget: The Memoirs of Nikolai Bukharin's Widow*, trans. Gary Kern (London: Norton, 1993)

KAGANOVICH

Chuev, Feliks. *Tak govoril Kaganovich: Ispoved' stalinskogo apostola* (Moscow: Otechestvo, 1992)
Kaganovich, Lazar. *Pamiatnye zapiski rabochego, kommunista-bol'shevika, profoiuznogo, partiinogo i sovetsko-gosudarstvennogo rabotnika* (Moscow: Vagrius, 1996)
Kumanev, G. A. *Riadom so Stalinym: Otkrovennye svidetel'stva; Vstrechi, besedy, interv'iu, dokumenty* (Moscow: Bylina, 1999) (1991 interview with Kaganovich)

KHRUSHCHEV

Khrushchev, Nikita. *Khrushchev Remembers*, ed. and trans. Strobe Talbott (Boston: Little Brown, 1970)
———. *Khrushchev Remembers: The Glasnost Tapes*, ed. and trans. Jerrold L. Schecter (Boston: Little, Brown, 1990)
———. *Khrushchev Remembers: The Last Testament*, ed. and trans. Strobe Talbott (Boston: Little, Brown, 1974)
Khrushchev, Sergei. *Nikita Khrushchev: Krizisy i rakety* (Moscow: Novosti, 1994)
———. *Nikita Khrushchev: Pensioner* (Moscow: Vremia, 2010), vol. 3 of *Trilogiia ob ottse*
———. *Nikita Khrushchev: Reformator* (Moscow: Vremia, 2010), vol. 2 of *Trilogiia ob ottse*
———. *Nikita Khrushchev: Rozhdenie sverkhderzhavy* (Moscow: Vremia, 2010), vol. 1 of *Trilogiia ob ottse*

KOSIOR, STANISLAV

O Stanislave Kosiore: Vospominaniia, ocherki, stat'i, comp. M. B. Pogrebinskii (Moscow: Politizdat, 1989)

KUIBYSHEV

Kuibysheva, G. V. *Valerian Vladimirovich Kuibyshev: Biografiia* (Moscow: Izdatel'stvo politicheskoi literatury, 1966)

MALENKOV

Malenkov, A. G. *O moem ottse Georgii Malenkove* (Moscow NTTs "Tekhnoekos," 1992)

MIKOYAN

Mikoian, A. I. *Dorogoi bor'by* (Moscow: Izdatel'stvo politicheskoi literatury, 1971)
————. *Mysli i vospominaniia o Lenine* (Moscow: Politizdat, 1970)
————. *Tak bylo: Razmyshleniia o minuvshem* (Moscow: Vagrius, 1999)
————. *V nachale dvatsatykh...* (Moscow: Izdatel'stvo politicheskoi literatury, 1975)
Mikoian, Stepan Anastasevich. *Vospominaniia voennogo letchikia-ispytatelia* (Moscow: "Tekhnika molodezhi," 2002)

MOLOTOV

Chuev, Feliks. *Molotov: Poluderzhavnyi vlastelin* (Moscow: OLMA-PRESS, 2000)
————. *Sto sorok besed s Molotovym: Iz dnevnika F. Chueva* (Moscow: Terra, 1991)
Nikonov, Viacheslav. *Molotov: Molodost'* (Moscow: Vagrius, 2005) [up to 1924]

ORDZHONIKIDZE

Ordzhonikidze, Z. G. *Put' bol'shevika: Stranitsy iz zhizni G. K. Ordzhonikidze* (Moscow: Istoriia grazhdanskoi voiny, 1938)

POSTYSHEV

Postyshev, Leonid. "Iz ukhodiashchego proshlogo," in *Fakel: Istoriko-revoliutsionnyi al'manakh* (Moscow, 1989)

STALIN

Allilyueva, Svetlana. *Dvadtsat' pisem k drugu* (Sankt-Petersburg, 1994)
————. *Only One Year* (New York: Harper & Row, 1969)
————. *Twenty Letters to a Friend* (New York: Harper & Row, 1967)
Lobanov, M., ed. *Stalin v vospominaniiakh sovremennikov i dokumentov epokhi* (Moscow: EKSMO, 2002)

TOMSKY

Tomsky, Yury. "Vospominaniia Iuriia Tomskogo ob ottse, 1988–89," in Mikhail Tomskii, *Vospominaniia, stat'i, dokumenty*, ed. O. I. Gorelov (Moscow: RGGU, 2001)

VOROSHILOV

Voroshilov, K. E. *Rasskazy o zhizni: Vospominaniia* (Moscow: Politizdat, 1968), vol. 1 [no further vols.]

ZHDANOV

Zhdanov, Iu. A. *Vzgliad v proshloe: Vospominaniia ochevidtsa* (Rostov: Feniks, 2004)

OTHER MEMOIRS, DIARIES, AND INTERVIEWS

Bialer, Seweryn. *Stalin and His Generals: Soviet Military Memoirs of World War II* (New York: Pegasus, 1969)

Byli industrial'nye: Ocherki i vospominaniia, comp. I. M. Danishevskii (Moscow: Politizdat, 1973)

Adzhubei, A. I. *Te desiat' let* (Moscow: Sovetskaia Rossiia, 1989)

Alekseeva, Nina. *Lavrentii Beriia v moei zhizni* (Moscow, 1996)

Aroseva, Olga. *Bez grima* (Moscow, 2000)

Bazhanov, Boris. *Bazhanov and the Damnation of Stalin*. Trans. and commentary by David W. Doyle (Athens: Ohio University Press, 1990)

Berezhkov, Valentin M. *At Stalin's Side: His Interpreter's Memoirs from the October Revolution to the Fall of the Dictator's Empire*, trans. Sergei V. Mikheyev (New York: Birch Lane Press, 1994)

Bonner, Elena. *Mothers and Daughters*, trans. Antonina W. Bouis (New York: Vintage Books, 1993)

Burlatsky, Fedor. *Khrushchev and the First Russian Spring: The Era of Khrushchev through the Eyes of His Advisor*, trans. Daphne Skillen (New York: Charles Scribner, 1988)

Byli industrial'nye: Ocherki i vospomninaniia, 2nd ed., comp. I. M. Danishevskii (Moscow: Izdatel'stvo politicheskoi literatury, 1973)

Dimitrov, Georgi. *The Diary of Georgi Dimitrov, 1933–1949*, intro. and ed. Ivo Banac (New Haven: Yale University Press, 2003)

Djilas, Milovan. *Conversations with Stalin*, trans. Michael B. Petrovich (Harmondsworth: Penguin, 1962)

Dubinsky, Rostislav. *Stormy Applause: Making Music in a Workers' State* (New York: Hill & Wang, 1989)

Elagin, Iu. *Ukroshchenie iskusstv* (New York: Izdatel'stvo imeni Chekhova, 1952)

Fradkin, Viktor. *Delo Kol'tsova* (Moscow: Vagrius, 2002)

Garros, Véronique, Natalia Korenevskaya, and Thomas Lahusen, eds. *Intimacy and Terror: Soviet Diaries of the 1930s*, trans. Carol Flath (New York: New Press, 1995)

Gromyko, A. A. *Pamiatnoe* (Moscow: Izdatel'stvo politicheskoi literatury, 1988), 2 vols.

Gronskii, M. *Iz proshlogo . . . Vospominaniia* (Moscow: Izvestiia, 1991)

Iakovlev, A. S. *Tsel' zhizni (Zapiski aviakonstruktora)*, 3rd ed. (Moscow: Politizdat, 1972)

Khrennikov, Tikhon. *Tak eto bylo* (Moscow: Muzyka, 1994)

Kumanev, G. A. *Govoriat stalinskie narkomy* (Smolensk: Rusich, 2005)

———. *Riadom so Stalinym: Otkrovennye svidetel'stva; Vstrechi, besedy, interv'iu, doku-menty* (Moscow: Bylina, 1999)

Kuznetsov, N. G. *Krutye povoroty: Iz zapisok admirala* (Moscow: Molodaia gvardiia, 1995)

Mandelstam, Nadezhda. *Hope against Hope: A Memoir*, trans. Max Hayward (New York: Modern Library, 1999)

———. *Vospominaniia* (New York, 1979)

Meir, Golda. *My Life* (London: Weidenfeld and Nicolson, 1975)

Mićunović, Veljko. *Moscow Diary*, trans. David Floyd (Garden City, NY: Doubleday, 1980)

Novikov, N. V. *Vospominaniia diplomata: Zapiski, 1938–1947* (Moscow: Izdatel'stvo politicheskoi literatury, 1989)

Orlov, Aleksandr. *Tainaia istoriia stalinskikh prestuplenii* (Moscow: Avtor, 1991)

Patolichev, N. S. *Measures of Maturity*, trans. Y. S. Shirokov and Y. S. Sviridov (Oxford: Pergamon Press, 1983)

Roy, M. N. *M. N. Roy's Memoirs*, sponsored by the Indian Renaissance Institute, Dehra Dun (Bombay: Allied, 1964)

Scott, John. *Behind the Urals: An American Worker in Russia's City of Steel*, ed. Stephen Kotkin (Bloomington: Indiana University Press, 1989)

Serge, Victor. *Memoirs of a Revolutionary*, trans. from the French by Peter Sedgwick and George Paizis (New York: New York Review of Books, 2012)

Shamberg, Vladimir. "Stalin's Last Inner Circle," *Harriman Review* 10:1 (1997)

Shepilov, Dmitrii. *The Kremlin's Scholar: A Memoir of Soviet Politics under Stalin and Khrushchev*, ed. Stephen V. Bittner, trans. Anthony Austin (New Haven: Yale University Press, 2007)

———. *Neprimknuvshii* (Moscow: Vagrius, 2001)

Shreider, Mikhail. *NKVD iznutri: Zapiski chekista* (Moscow: Vozvrashchenie, 1995)

Simonov, Konstantin. *Glazami cheloveka moego pokoleniia* (Moscow: Novosti, 1988)

Solovev, A. G. "Tetradi krasnogo professor," in *Neizvestnaia Rossiia*, vol. 4 (Moscow: Mosgorarkhiv, 1993)

Sudoplatov, Pavel, and Anatoli Sudoplatov with Jerrold L. and Leona P. Schecter. *Special Tasks: The Memoirs of an Unwanted Witness; A Soviet Spymaster* (Boston: Little, Brown, 1994)

Sukhanov, N. *The Russian Revolution, 1917: Eyewitness Account*, ed., abridged, and trans. Joel Carmichael (Oxford: Oxford University Press, 1955)

Tomskii, Mikhail. *Vospominaniia: Stat'i; Dokumenty*, ed. O. I. Gorelov (Moscow: RGGU, 2001)

Troianovskii, Oleg. *Cherez gody i rasstoianiia: Istoriia odnoi sem'i* (Moscow: Vagrius, 1997)

Tuominen, Arvo. *The Bells of the Kremlin* (Hanover: University Press of New England, 1983)

Vishnevskaia, Galina. *Istoriia zhizni* (Moscow: Rusich, 1999)

Vovsi-Mikhoels, Nataliia. *Moi otets, Solomon Mikhoels* (Moscow: Vozvrashchenie, 1977)

Vozvrashchennye imena: Sbornik publitsisticheskikh statei v 2-kh knigakh (Moscow: Novosti, 1989)

Wells, H. G. *Experiment in Autobiography* (London: Faber, 1984)

Yevtushenko, Yevgeny. *A Precocious Autobiography*, trans. Andrew R. MacAndrew (London: Collins & Harvill, 1963)

Zhukov, G. K. *Vospominaniia i razmyshleniia* (Moscow: Novosti, 1990), 3 vols.

BIOGRAPHIES

GENERAL/COLLECTIVE

Medvedev, Roi. *Okruzhenie Stalina* (Moscow: Molodaia gvardiia, 2010)

——. *Oni okruzhali Stalina* (Benson, VT: Chalidze Publications, 1984)

Vasileva, Larisa. *Kremlevskie zheny* (Moscow: Vagrius, 1992)

Vasilieva, Larissa. *Kremlin Wives*, ed. and trans. Cathy Porter (London: Weidenfeld & Nicolson, 1994)

Zenkovich, N. *Samye sekretnye rodstvenniki: Entsiklopediia biografii* (Moscow: OLMA-PRESS, 2005)

BERIA

Knight, Amy. *Beria: Stalin's First Lieutenant* (Princeton: Princeton University Press, 1993)

Sukhomlinov, A. V. *Kto vy, Lavrentii Beriia?* (Moscow: Detektiv-Press, 2003)

BUKHARIN

Cohen, Stephen F. *Bukharin and the Bolshevik Revolution: A Political Biography, 1888–1938* (New York: Alfred A. Knopf, 1972)

Gregory, Paul R. *Politics, Murder and Love in Stalin's Kremlin: The Story of Nikolai Bukharin and Anna Larina* (Stanford, CA: Hoover Institution Press, 2010)

Medvedev, Roy A. *Nikolai Bukharin: The Last Years*, trans. A.D.P. Briggs (New York: Norton, 1980)

CHUBAR

Drobizhev, V., and N. Dubova. *V. Ia. Chubar': Biograficheskii ocherk* (Moscow: Gosudarstvennoe izdatel'stvo politicheskoi literatury, 1963)

EZHOV

Getty, J. Arch, and Oleg V. Naumov. *Yezhov: The Rise of Stalin's "Iron Fist"* (New Haven: Yale University Press, 2008)

Jansen, Mark, and Nikita Petrov. *Stalin's Loyal Executioner: People's Commissar Nikolai Ezhov, 1895–1940* (Stanford, CA: Hoover Institution Press, 2001)

KAGANOVICH

Evseev, Evgenii. *Kaganovich: Satrap za spinoi Stalina* (Moscow: Iauza, 2005)

Rees, E. A. *Iron Lazar: A Political Biography of Lazar Kaganovich* (London: Anthem Press, 2012)

KHRUSHCHEV

Medvedev, Zhores, and Roy Medvedev. *Nikita Khrushchev* (Moscow: Vremia, 2012)
Taubman, William. *Khrushchev: The Man and His Era* (New York: Norton, 2003)

KIROV

Lenoe, Matthew E. *The Kirov Murder and Soviet History* (New Haven: Yale University Press, 2010)
Nash Mironych: Vospominaniia o zhizni i deiatel'nosti S. M. Kirova v Leningrade, comp. M. V. Rosliakov and V. M. Ivanov (Leningrad: Lenizdat, 1968)
O Sergee Kirove: Vospominaniia, ocherki, stat'i sovremennikov, comp. M. I. Vladimirov (Moscow: Izdatel'stvo politicheskoi literatury, 1985)

MIKOYAN

Pavlov, M. Iu. *Anastas Mikoian: Politicheskii portret na fone sovetskoi epokhi* (Moscow: Mezhdunarodnye otnosheniia, 2010)

MOLOTOV

Bromage, Bernard. *Molotov: The Story of an Era* (London: Peter Owen, 1956)
Watson, Derek. *Molotov: A Biography* (Basingstoke: Palgrave Macmillan, 2005)

ORDZHONIKIDZE

Seiranian, F. G. *G. K. Ordzhonikidze v gody sotsialisticheskogo stroitel'stva* (Tbilisi: Izdatel'stvo "Sabchota Sakartvelo," 1986)

RUDZUTAK

Trukan, G. A. *Ian Rudzutak* (Moscow: Gosudarstvennoe izdatel'stvo politicheskoi literatury, 1963)

STALIN

Baberowski, Jörg. *Verbrannte Erde: Stalins Herrschaft der Gewalt* (Munich: C. H. Beck Verlag, 2012; English translation forthcoming)
Kun, Miklós. *Stalin: An Unknown Portrait* (Budapest: Central European University Press, 2003)
Montefiore, Simon Sebag. *Stalin: The Court of the Red Tsar* (New York: Knopf, 2004)
———. *Young Stalin* (London: Weidenfeld & Nicolson, 2007)
Radzinsky, Edvard. *Stalin*, trans. H. T. Willetts (New York: Doubleday 1996)
Service, Robert. *Stalin: A Biography* (Cambridge, MA: Belknap Press, 2005)
———. *Young Stalin* (London: Weidenfeld & Nicolson, 2007)
Trotsky, Leon. *Stalin: An Appraisal of the Man and His Influence*, ed. and trans. from Russian by Charles Malamuth (New York: Grosset & Dunlap, 1941)
Tucker, Robert C. *Stalin as Revolutionary, 1879–1929: A Study in History and Personality* (New York: Norton, 1973)

———. *Stalin in Power: The Revolution from Above, 1928–1941* (New York: Norton, 1990)

Ulam, Adam B. *Stalin: The Man and His Era* (New York: Viking Press, 1973)

Volkogonov, Dmitrii. *Triumf i tragediia: Politicheskii portret I. V. Stalina* (Moscow: Novosti, 1989), 2 vols.

Volkogonov, Dmitri. *Stalin: Triumph and Tragedy*, ed. and trans. Harold Shukman (Rocklin, CA: Prima, 1992.

TOMSKY

Gorelov, O. I. *Tsugtswang Mikhaila Tomskogo* (Moscow: ROSSPEN, 2000)

TROTSKY

Deutscher, Isaac. *The Prophet Armed: Trotsky; 1879–1921* (London: Oxford University Press, 1970)

———. *The Prophet Outcast: Trotsky; 1929–1940* (London: Oxford University Press, 1970)

———. *The Prophet Unarmed: Trotsky; 1921–1929* (London: Oxford University Press, 1970)

Patenaude, Bernard M. *Stalin's Nemesis: The Exile and Murder of Leon Trotsky* (London: Faber & Faber, 2009)

Service, Robert. *Trotsky: A Biography* (London: Macmillan, 2009)

VOROSHILOV

Kardashov, V. *Voroshilov* (Moscow: Molodaia gvardiia, 1976)

YAGODA

Ilinskii, Mikhail. *Narkom Iagoda* (Moscow: Veche, 2005)

ZHDANOV

Borisov, S. *Andrei Aleksandrovich Zhdanov: Opyt politicheskoi biografii* (Shchadrinsk, 1998)

Boterbloem, Kees. *The Life and Times of Andrei Zhdanov, 1896–1948* (Montreal: McGill-Queens, 2004)

Kislitsyn, S. A. *Iurii Zhdanov: Riadom so Stalinym, Sholokhovym, Il'enkovym… "V vechnykh skitaniiakh vechnykh boreniiakh"* (Moscow: URSS, 2013)

Volynets, Aleksei. *Zhdanov* (Moscow: Molodaia gvardiia [Zhizn' zamechatel'nykh liudei], 2013)

BOOKS AND ARTICLES IN ENGLISH

Adler, Nanci. *The Gulag Survivor* (New Brunswick, NJ: Transaction, 2002)

Alexopoulos, Golfo. *Stalin's Outcasts: Aliens, Citizens, and the Soviet State, 1926–1936* (Ithaca, NY: Cornell University Press, 2003)

Andrew, Christopher, and Vasili Mitrokhin. *The Sword and the Shield: The Mitrokhin Archive and the Secret History of the KGB* (New York: Basic Books, 1999)

Carr, E. H. *Socialism in One Country, 1924–1926*, 3 vols. (London: Macmillan, 1958–64)

Carr, E. H., and R. W. Davies. *Foundations of a Planned Economy, 1926–29*, 2 vols. (London: Macmillan, 1969)

Carswell, John. *The Exile: A Life of Ivy Litvinov* (London: Faber & Faber, 1983)

Churchill, Winston. *The Second World War*, vol. 4, *The Hinge of Fate* (Boston: Houghton-Mifflin, 1950)

Clark, Katerina. *Moscow the Fourth Rome: Stalinism, Cosmopolitanism and the Evolution of Soviet Culture, 1931–1941* (Cambridge, MA: Harvard University Press, 2011)

Cohen, Stephen F. *The Victims Return: Survivors of the Gulag after Stalin* (London: I. B. Tauris, 2011)

Conquest, Robert. *The Great Terror: Stalin's Purge of the Thirties* (Harmondsworth: Penguin, 1971)

Crankshaw, Edward. *Khrushchev's Russia* (Harmondsworth: Penguin, 1959)

Daniels, Robert V. *The Conscience of the Revolution: Communist Opposition in Soviet Russia* (New York: Simon and Schuster, 1960)

David-Fox, Michael. *Showcasing the Great Experiment: Cultural Diplomacy and Western Visitors to the Soviet Union, 1921–1941* (Oxford: Oxford University Press, 2012)

Davies, Robert W. *Crisis and Progress in the Soviet Economy, 1931–33* (London: Macmillan, 1996)

———. *The Socialist Offensive: The Collectivisation of Soviet Agriculture, 1929–1930* (Cambridge, MA: Harvard University Press, 1980)

Davies, Sarah. *Popular Opinion in Stalin's Russia: Terror, Propaganda and Dissent, 1934–1941* (Cambridge: Cambridge University Press, 1999)

Davies, Sarah, and James Harris, eds. *Stalin: A New History* (Cambridge: Cambridge University Press, 2005)

Dullin, Sabine. *Men of Influence: Stalin's Diplomats in Europe, 1930–1939*, trans. from French by Richard Veasey (Edinburgh: Edinburgh University Press, 2008)

Erlich, Alexander. *The Soviet Industrialization Debate, 1924–1928* (Cambridge, MA: Harvard University Press, 1960)

Feuchtwanger, Lion. *Moscow 1937: A Visit Described for My Friends*, trans. Irene Josephy (New York: Viking, 1937)

Fitzpatrick, Sheila. *The Commissariat of Enlightenment* (London: Cambridge University Press, 1970)

———. "The Civil War as a Formative Experience," in Abbott Gleason, Peter Kenez, and Richard Stites, eds., *Bolshevik Culture: Experiment and Order in the Russian Revolution* (Bloomington: Indiana University Press, 1985)

———. *The Cultural Front* (Ithaca, NY: Cornell University Press, 1992)

———, ed. *Cultural Revolution in Russia, 1928–1931* (Bloomington: Indiana University Press, 1978)

———. *Education and Social Mobility in the Soviet Union, 1924–1932* (Cambridge: Cambridge University Press, 1979)

344 BIBLIOGRAPHY OF WORKS CITED

————. *Everyday Stalinism: Ordinary Life in Extraordinary Times; Soviet Russia in the 1930s* (New York: Oxford University Press, 1999)
————. "Intelligentsia and Power: Client-Patron Relations in Stalin's Russia," in Manfred Hildermeier, ed., *Stalinismus vor dem zweiten Weltkrieg: Neue Wege der Forschung* [*Stalinism before the Second World War: New Avenues of Research*] (Munich: Oldenbourg, 1998), and in Fitzpatrick, *Tear Off the Masks!* (2005)
————. "The Legacy of the Civil War," in *Party, State, and Society in the Russian Civil War* (Bloomington: Indiana University Press, 1989), 390–97
————. "Ordzhonikidze's Takeover of Vesenkha: A Case Study in Soviet Bureaucratic Politics," *Soviet Studies* 37:2 (1985)
————. "Politics as Practice: Thoughts on a New Political History," *Kritika: Explorations in Russian and Eurasian History* 5:1 (2004)
————. *A Spy in the Archives: A Memoir of Cold War Russia* (London: I. B. Tauris, 2014)
————. "Stalin and the World of Culture," in *Totalitarian Dictatorship: New Histories*, ed. Daniela Baratieri, Mark Edele, and Giuseppe Finaldi (New York: Routledge, 2014)
————. *Stalin's Peasants: Resistance and Survival in the Russian Village after Collectivization* (Oxford: Oxford University Press, 1994)
————. *Tear Off the Masks! Identity and Imposture in Twentieth-Century Russia* (Princeton: Princeton University Press, 2005)
Gellately, Robert. *Stalin's Curse: Battling for Communism in War and Cold War* (Oxford: Oxford University Press, 2013)
Getty, J. Arch. *Origins of the Great Purges: The Soviet Communist Party Reconsidered, 1933–1938* (Cambridge: Cambridge University Press, 1985)
————. *Practicing Stalinism: Bolsheviks, Boyars, and the Persistence of Tradition* (New Haven: Yale University Press, 2013)
Getty, J. Arch, and Oleg V. Naumov. *The Road to Terror: Stalin and the Self-Destruction of the Bolsheviks, 1932–1939* (New Haven: Yale University Press, 1999)
Gill, Graeme. *The Origins of the Stalinist Political System* (Cambridge: Cambridge University Press, 1990)
Gleason, Abbott, Peter Kenez, and Richard Stites, eds. *Bolshevik Culture: Experiment and Order in the Russian Revolution* (Bloomington: Indiana University Press, 1985)
Gorlizki, Yoram, and Oleg Khlevniuk. *Cold Peace: Stalin and the Soviet Ruling Circle, 1945–1953* (Oxford: Oxford University Press, 2004)
Gregory, Paul R., and Norman Naimark, eds. *The Lost Politburo Transcripts: From Collective Rule to Stalin's Dictatorship* (New Haven: Yale University Press, 2008)
Harris, James R. *The Great Urals: Regionalism and the Evolution of the Soviet System* (Ithaca: Cornell University Press, 1999)
Hellbeck, Jochen. *Revolution on My Mind: Writing a Diary under Stalin* (Cambridge, MA: Harvard University Press, 2006)
Hindus, Maurice. *Crisis in the Kremlin* (New York: Doubleday, 1953)
Holloway, David. *Stalin and the Bomb: The Soviet Union and Atomic Energy, 1939–1956* (New Haven: Yale University Press, 1994)

Holmes, Larry. *Stalin's School: Moscow's Model School No. 25, 1931–1937* (Pittsburgh: University of Pittsburgh Press, 1999)

Hough, Jerry, and Merle Fainsod. *How the Soviet Union Is Governed* (Cambridge, MA: Harvard University Press, 1982)

Johnson, Timothy. *Being Soviet: Identity, Rumour, and Everyday Life under Stalin, 1939–1953* (Oxford: Oxford University Press, 2011)

Jones, Polly, ed. *The Dilemmas of De-Stalinization: Negotiating Cultural and Social Change in the Khrushchev Era* (London: Routledge, 2006)

Khevniuk, Oleg V. *The History of the Gulag: From Collectivization to the Great Terror*, trans. Vadim A. Staklo (New Haven: Yale University Press, 2004), 307.

———. *Master of the House: Stalin and His Inner Circle*, trans. Nora Seligman Favorov (New Haven: Yale University Press, 2009)

Kostiuk, Hryhory. *Stalinist Rule in the Ukraine: A Study of a Decade of Mass Terror (1929–1939)* (New York: Praeger, 1960)

Kozlov, Vladimir A., Sheila Fitzpatrick, and Sergei V. Mironenko, eds. *Sedition: Everyday Resistance in the Soviet Union under Khrushchev and Brezhnev* (New Haven: Yale University Press, 2011)

Kramer, Mark. "New Evidence on Soviet Decision-Making and the 1956 Polish and Hungarian Crises," *Cold War International History Project Bulletin*, nos. 8–9 (Winter 1996–97)

Krementsov, Nikolai. *The Cure: A Story of Cancer and Politics from the Annals of the Cold War* (Chicago: University of Chicago Press, 2002)

———. *Stalinist Science* (Princeton: Princeton University Press, 1997)

Lenoe, Matthew E. *The Kirov Murder and Soviet History* (New Haven: Yale University Press, 2010)

Lewin, Moshe. *Lenin's Last Struggle*, new ed. (Ann Arbor: University of Michigan Press, 2005)

———. *Political Undercurrents in Soviet Economic Debates: From Bukharin to the Modern Reformers* (Princeton: Princeton University Press, 1974)

"The 'Malin Notes' on the Crises in Hungary and Poland, 1956," *Cold War International History Project Bulletin*, nos. 8–9 (Winter 1996–97)

Martin, Terry. *The Affirmative Action Empire: Nations and Nationalism in the Soviet Union, 1923–1939* (Ithaca, NY: Cornell University Press, 2001)

Medvedev, Roy A. *Let History Judge: The Origins and Consequences of Stalinism* (New York: Alfred A. Knopf, 1971)

Medvedev, Roy, and Guilietto Chiesa. *Time of Change: An Insider's View of Russia's Transformation* (London: I. B. Tauris, 1991)

Miller, Frank J. *Folklore for Stalin: Russian Folklore and Pseudofolklore of the Stalin Era* (Armonk, NY: M. E. Sharpe, 1990)

Morrison, Simon. *Lina and Serge: The Love and Wars of Lina Prokofiev* (Boston: Houghton Mifflin Harcourt, 2013)

———. *The People's Artist: Prokofiev's Soviet Years* (Oxford: Oxford University Press, 2009)

Nicolaevsky, Boris I. *Power and the Soviet Elite: "The Letter of an Old Bolshevik" and Other Essays*, ed. Janet D. Zagoria (London: Pall Mall Press, 1965)

Nove, Alec. *An Economic History of the USSR* (Harmondsworth: Penguin, 1972)

Orlov, Alexander. *The Secret History of Stalin's Crimes* (London: Harrolds, 1954)

Overy, Richard. *Russia's War: A History of the Soviet War Effort, 1941–1945* (New York: Penguin, 1998)

Plamper, Jan. *Stalin Cult: A Study in the Alchemy of Power* (Stanford, CA: Hoover Institution, 2012)

Rapoport, Vitaly, and Yuri Alexeev. *High Treason: Essays on the History of the Red Army, 1918–1938* (Durham, NC: Duke University Press, 1985)

Rayfield, Donald. *Stalin and His Hangmen* (London: Viking, 2004)

Reiman, Michal. *The Birth of Stalinism: The USSR on the Eve of the "Second Revolution,"* trans. George Saunders (Bloomington: Indiana University Press, 1987)

Rigby, T. H. "Was Stalin a Disloyal Patron?," *Soviet Studies* 38:3 (July 1986)

Roberts, Geoffrey. *Stalin's General: The Life of Georgy Zhukov* (London: Icon Books, 2012)

Rogovin, Vadim. *Stalin's Terror of 1937–1938*, trans. Frederick S. Choate (Oak Park, MI: Mehring Books, 2009)

Salisbury, Harrison E. *The Siege of Leningrad* (London: Secker & Warburg, 1969)

Schattenberg, Susanne. "Trust, Care and Familiarity in the Politburo. Brezhnev's Scenario of Power," *Kritika: Explorations in Russian and Eurasian History* 16:4 (2015)

Service, Robert. *Spies and Commissars: Bolshevik Russia and the West* (London: Macmillan, 2011)

Shore, Marci. *Caviar and Ashes: A Warsaw Generation's Life and Death in Marxism, 1918–1968* (New Haven: Yale University Press, 2006)

Slezkine, Yuri. *The Jewish Century* (Princeton: Princeton University Press, 2011)

Smith, Stephen A., ed. *The Oxford Handbook of the History of Communism* (Oxford: Oxford University Press, 2014)

Thompson, Nicholas. "My Friend, Stalin's Daughter," *New Yorker*, 31 March 2014

Tromly, Benjamin. *Making the Soviet Intelligentsia: Universities and Intellectual Life under Stalin and Khrushchev* (Cambridge: Cambridge University Press, 2014)

Vaksberg, Arkady. *Stalin against the Jews*, trans. Antonina W. Bouis (New York: Alfred A. Knopf, 1994)

Viola, Lynne. *Peasant Rebels under Stalin* (New York: Oxford University press, 1994)

Weiner, Amir. *Making Sense of War: The Second World War and the Fate of the Bolshevik Revolution* (Princeton: Princeton University Press, 2001)

Werth, Alexander. *Russia at War* (London: Pan Books, 1964)

Wheatcroft, Stephen G. "From Team-Stalin to Degenerate Tyranny," in E. A. Rees, ed., *The Nature of Stalin's Dictatorship: The Politburo, 1924–1953* (Houndsmill: Palgrave Macmillan, 2004)

Wilson, Elizabeth. *Shostakovich: A Life Remembered* (Princeton: Princeton University Press, 1994)

Zubok, Vladislav. *Zhivago's Children: The Last Russian Intelligentsia* (Cambridge, MA: Belknap Press at Harvard University Press, 2009)

Zubok, Vladislav, and Constantine Pleshakov. *Inside the Kremlin's Cold War: From Stalin to Khrushchev* (Cambridge, MA: Harvard University Press, 1996)

BOOKS AND ARTICLES IN RUSSIAN

Aksiutin, Iurii. *Khrushchevskaia "ottepel" i obshchestvennye nastroeniia v SSSR v 1953–1964 gg.* (Moscow: ROSSPEN, 2004)

Chigrinov, G. A. "Pochemu Stalin, a ne drugie?" *Voprosy istorii KPSS*, no. 6, 1960

Dzhambul and S. Stavskii. *Stikhi i pesni* (Novosibirsk, 1938)

Esakov, V. D., and E. S. Levina. *Delo KR: Sudy chesti v ideologii i praktike poslevoennogo stalinizma* (Moscow: Institut rossiiskoi istorii RAN, 2001)

Fradkin, Viktor. *Delo Kol'tsova* (Moscow: Vagrius, 2002)

Fursenko, A. A. "I. V. Stalin: Poslednie gody zhizni i smert,'" *Istoricheskie zapiski* 3 (121) (2000)

Gromov, Evgenii S. *Stalin: Vlast' i iskusstva* (Moscow: Respublika, 1998)

Kariakin, N. "'Zhdanovskaia zhidkost' ili protiv ochernitel'stva," in Iu. N. Afansev, ed., *Inogo ne dano* (Moscow: Progress, 1988)

Khlevniuk, O. V. *1937-i: Stalin, NKVD i sovetskoe obshchestvo* (Moscow: "Respublika," 1992)

———. *Politbiuro: Mekhanizmy politicheskoi vlasti v 1930-e gody* (Moscow: ROSSPEN, 1996)

———. "Stalin i Molotov: Edinolichnaia diktatura i predposylki 'oligarkhizatsii,'" in *Stalin, stalinizm, sovetskoe obshchestvo: K 70-letiiu V. S. Lel'chuka*, ed. G. Sh. Sagatelian et al. (Moscow: Institut Rossiiskoi istorii RAN, 2000)

———. *Stalin i Ordzhonikidze: Konflikty v Politbiuro v 30-e gody* (Moscow: Rossiia molodaia, 1993)

———. "Stalin na voine," *Cahiers de monde russe* 52:2–3 (2011)

Kostyrchenko, G. V. *Tainaia politika Khrushcheva: Vlast', intelligentsia, evreiskii vopros* (Moscow: Mezhdunarodnyeotnosheniia, 2012)

———. *Tainaia politika Stalina: Vlast' i antisemitizm* (Moscow: Mezhdunarodnye otnosheniia, 2001)

———. *V plenu u krasnogo faraona: Politicheskie presledovaniia evreev v SSSR v poslednee stalinskoe desiatiletie; Dokumental'noe issoledovaniia* (Moscow: Mezhdunarodnye otnosheniia, 1994)

Kuniaev, S. "Post Scriptum," *Nash sovremennik*, no. 10, 1995

Lenin, V. I. *Polnoe sobranie sochinenii v 55-i tomakh*, 5th ed. (Moscow: Gosudarstvennoe izdatel'stvo politicheskoi literatury, 1958–70)

Medvedev, Roi. *Okruzhenie Stalina* (Moscow: Molodaia gvardiia, 2010)

———. *Oni okruzhali Stalina* (Benson, VT: Chalidze Publications, 1984)

Medvedev, Roi A. *Chto chital Stalin? Liudi i knigi, pisatel' i kniga v totalitarnom obshchestve* (Moscow: Prava cheloveka, 2005)

Pikhoia, R. G. *Sovetskii Soiuz: Istoriia vlasti, 1945–1991* (Moscow: Izdatel'stvo RAGS, 1998)

Pospelov, E. M. *Imena gorodov: Vchera i segodnia (1917–1992); Toponomicheskii slovar'* (Moscow: Russkie slovari, 1993)

Shentalinsky, Vitalii. *Raby svobody: V literaturnykh arkhivakh KGB* (Moscow: Parus, 1995)

Stalin, I. V. *Sochineniia*, 13 vols. (Moscow: Gosudarstvennoe izdatel'stvo politicheskoi literatury, 1948–52)

———. *Sochineniia*, 3 vols. (vols. 14–16), ed. Robert H. McNeal (Stanford, CA: Hoover Institution, 1967)

Sushkov, A. *Prezidium TsK KPSS, 1957–1964 gg. Lichnosti i vlast'* (Ekaterinburg: UrO RAN, 2009)

Trifonova, Olga. *Edinstvennaia: Zhena Stalina* (Moscow: Astrel', 2010)

Zhukov, Iu. N. *Tainy Kremlia: Stalin, Molotov, Beriia, Malenkov* (Moscow: TERRA, 2000)

———. *Stalin: Tainy vlasti* (Moscow: Vagrius, 2005)

Zubkova, E. Iu. *Obshchestvo i reformy, 1945–1964* (Moscow: Rossiia molodaia, 1993)

———. *Pribaltika i Kreml'* (Moscow: ROSSPEN, 2008)

INDEX

foreigners, contact with, 95–99, 148, 192–93, 322
Forster, E. M., 105
Fourth International, 98
France, 97, 101, 145, 149
French Revolution, 21, 40, 115, 140
friendship, 57, 65, 108, 274, 286 n. 12
Frunze, Mikhail, 70; biography of, 320
Frunze, Tanya (daughter of Frunze, adopted by Voroshilov), 70, 187, 237, 320, 329
Frunze, Timur (son of Frunze, adopted by Voroshilov), 70, 165, 320, 329
funerals, 264–65, 267–68; Kalinin's, 179; Khrushchev's, 265, 313 n. 7; Lenin's, 20; Mikhoels's, 204; Stalin's, 221, 224–26; Zhdanov's, 184

Gamarnik, Jan, 121, 137, 162; biography of, 320
Geneva Summit (1955), 236
Genghis Khan, 56, 84
Georgia/Georgians, 17, 19, 29, 89, 95, 110, 139, 187, 195, 220, 231, 246; in central leadership positions, 8, 16, 30, 65, 66, 317, 319, 325, 327; nationalism in, 38
Germany, 101, 136, 143, 149–50, 152, 173, 232, 299 n. 8, 328, 331; attack on Soviet Union of June 1941, 151–52; Embassy of, 39; German Democratic Republic (GDR, East Germany), 174, 232, 233; Federal Republic of, 232; intelligence service of, 121–22; invasion of Poland by, 147; policy toward, 143–44, 147–48, 172; refugees from, 98; reparations from, 183; Soviet Military Administration (SVAG) in, 180
German-Soviet Nonaggression Pact, 147–48, 324
Getty, J. Arch, 272, 273, 275
Gide, André, 105
GKO. See State Defense Committee
Glinka, Mikhail, 194
Goldshtein, Boris (Busya), 99–100
Golubtsova, Valeria (wife of Malenkov), 68, 239, 323–24
Gomułka, Władysław, 246–47
Gorbachev, Mikhail, 260, 265, 267–68
Gorbman, Golda. See Voroshilova
Gorky, Maxim, 89, 107–8, 195, 327, 330; biography of, 320; health of, 107
Gorlizki, Yoram, 6, 280

Gosplan. See State Planning Commission
Great Fatherland War. See Second World War
Great Purges, 3, 4, 7, 108, 110, 113–42, 198, 206, 207, 212, 236, 261, 270, 272, 273, 274; after-effects of, 192; arrests and executions in, 128, 140, 243, 245, 259, 297 n. 21; impact on team, 65, 160; individual victims of, 124, 131, 133, 140, 212, 318, 319, 320, 322, 325, 326, 327, 328, 329, 330, 331; responsibility for, 243–44, 260
Gromyko, Andrei, 151, 267
Gulag, x, 46–47, 125, 134, 158, 192, 199, 226, 228, 235; releases from, 241–42, 263
Gurvich, Esfir (2nd wife of Bukharin), 54–55, 66, 68, 125, 318
Gurvich, Svetlana (daughter of Bukharin), 54, 125, 318

Harriman Averell, 174, 175–76
health of leaders, 18–19, 41, 97, 107, 116, 131, 133, 141, 155, 161, 169, 175–76, 178, 179, 180, 189–90, 197, 219, 222
Hemingway, Ernest, 236
Higher Party School, 69
Hindus, Maurice, 143
Hitler, Adolf, 2, 145, 147, 149, 152, 167, 183
Hoover, Herbert, 61
Hull, Cordell, 104
Hungary, 174, 180, 246, 329
Hungarian Revolution, 246–48
Huxley, Aldous, 105

ice cream, 104, 111, 133
Ignatiev, Semyon, 217
India, 263–64
Industrial Academy, 62–63, 68, 79, 80, 317, 327
industrialization, 4, 8, 35, 43, 47–48, 52–53, 63, 103, 259, 274
Institute of Red Professors, 49–50, 62, 68, 107, 157, 327, 329
Institute of World Economy, 99
intellectuals, Communist, 107; European, 105–6; Jewish, 200; in party leadership, 24, 27, 51, 62; hostility toward, 49
intelligentsia, Russian/Soviet, 106–10, 217, 228, 248, 265; postwar disciplining of, 178, 191–94; team contacts with, 186–87,

intelligentsia (*cont.*)
191; team's children and, 187–88, 195, 263
interests, representation of, 74–77, 274
Israel, 200, 202–3
Italy, 101, 149, 167
Ivan the Terrible (Tsar), 152
Izvestiia (newspaper), 100, 237, 266, 318

Japan, 97, 100, 145, 149, 181
Jewish Anti-Fascist Committee (JAC), x, 200–202, 204, 205, 207, 212, 218, 324; trial of, 215–16, 319, 323
Jews, 200–205, 212, 216–17, 219, 222, 242; American, 200–202; as "bourgeois nationalists," 207, 217–18; in central leadership positions, 16, 17, 24, 94, 102, 144, 151, 215, 320, 321, 323, 326, 327, 330, 331; emigration of, 201; Jewish question, 276–77; Jewish wives of leaders, 68; rumors of deportation of, 219; survivors of German occupation, 168. *See also* anti-Semitism; Doctors' Plot; Israel
journalists, 101, 163; foreign, 95, 98–99, 176, 193

Kaganovich, Lazar, 3, 16, 17, 32, 36, 41, 51, 62, 63, 64, 73, 80, 87, 89, 96, 98, 111, 112, 116, 120, 140–41, 147, 150–51, 186, 190, 199, 249, 257, 265, 277, 299 n. 9, 319; and "Anti-Party Group," 249–53; biography of, 8, 26–27, 320; bullying style of, 65; in collectivization, 51; contacts with intelligentsia of, 107–8, 110; contacts with military of, 162; and culture, 105, 107–8, 110; death of, 267, 268; and de-Stalinization, 244; fall of, 5, 7; family and social life of, 26, 238, 258, 267; and famine of 1932–33, 83; and foreign policy, 152, 232; friends of, 66, 121, 138, 162–63, 330; in Great Purges, 126, 127–28, 132, 133; on Great Purges, 115, 129; as Jew, 94, 218, 242, 253, 257; and Jewish question, 199, 202, 203, 218; memoirs of, 258–59; as Moscow leader, 75; post-1957 fate of, 255–56, 258; in post-Stalin leadership, 222, 224, 229, 231, 233, 239, 242, 248; in postwar leadership, 209, 213; and railways, 76, 160; in Second World War, 153, 154–55, 158, 159–60; as secretary of

Central Committee, 90, 91; on Spanish Civil War, 104–5; and Stalin, 64, 67, 71, 73, 91, 92, 99, 100, 101, 119, 129, 138, 261; on Stalin, 32, 75, 76, 104–5; as Stalinist, 243, 251; and Stalin's legacy, 259; and trade unions, 58, 59; and Ukraine, 179–80
Kaganovich, Maria (wife of Lazar), 68, 81, 320
Kaganovich, Maya (daughter of Lazar), 70, 187, 237, 267, 320
Kaganovich, Mikhail (brother of Lazar), 26, 150–51, 261; biography of, 320–21
Kaganovich, Yury (adopted son of Lazar), 70, 104, 320
Kalinin, Mikhail, 3, 5, 11, 15, 17, 28–29, 32, 34, 56, 60, 71, 72, 89, 91, 92, 96, 110, 141, 170, 260, 299 n. 9; biography of, 29, 321; in collectivization, 51–52; death of, 179; friends of, 66; in Great Purges, 129, 133–34; health of, 133, 141, 179; as party "proletarian," 24; as "peasants' friend," 84–85; places named for, 13, 94; political troubles of, 36, 61; popular image of, 29, 54, 94; in Second World War, 154–55, 161; and Stalin, 65, 94; and Supreme Soviet, 75, 117; and wife's arrest, 133. *See also* Lorberg, Ekaterina
Kamenev, Lev, 16, 18, 20, 27, 34, 35, 112–13, 124; biography of, 321; expulsion from party of, 41; in faction fights of 1920s, 41; marriages of, 70; meeting with Bukharin of, 56–57, 59–60; readmission to party of, 89; rehabilitation of, 260; relatives of, 118; and Stalin, 33, 65; trials and execution of, 117–18, 123
Kameneva, Olga, 69, 103, 118, 321, 329
Kapler, Alexei, 164
Karpovskaya, Polina. *See* Zhemchuzhina, Polina
Kavtaradze, Sergo, 139
Kazakhstan/Kazakhs, 125, 182, 240; famine in, 82; Trotsky's exile to, 41
Kennedy, John (US President), 112
KGB. *See* security organs
Khachaturian, Aram, 193
Khazan, Dora (wife of Andreev), 28, 63, 68, 69, 80–81, 129, 133, 203, 317
Khlevniuk, Oleg V., 5–6, 272–73, 280
Khrulev, General Andrei, 163

Molotov, Vyacheslav (*cont.*)
130, 259; in Second World War, 152–58;
and security services, 208; and Stalin, 5,
46, 53, 61, 65, 66, 67, 78, 79, 92, 100, 101–
2, 118–19, 145, 150, 157, 161, 173, 176–
77, 181, 185, 186, 211, 219, 225; on Stalin,
31, 80, 115, 132, 135, 197, 260–61; as
Stalinist, 243, 248, 251, 261; as Stalin's
heir, 176–77, 210, 229, 246; and Stalin's
legacy, 259; Trotsky on, 26; and Zhemchuzhina, 144–45, 204, 208, 211, 225–
26, 241
Molotova, Polina. *See* Zhemchuzhina, Polina
Molotova, Svetlana, 8, 71, 173, 173–74, 179,
187, 188, 190, 198, 261, 288 n. 6, 324
Molotov-Ribbentrop Pact. *See* German-
Soviet Nonaggression Pact
Montefiore, Simon Sebag, 5, 271
Morozov, Grigory, 164, 175, 204, 317
Morozov, Joseph, 164, 204
Moscow: in Great Purges, 128; Moscow
Metro, 111; Moscow Soviet, 19, 318, 321;
perspective from, 34–35; political leader-
ship of, 63, 75, 155, 236, 320, 321, 327; in
Second World War, 154–55, 157
Moscow Art Theatre, 99, 106
Moscow Jewish Theater, 164, 200, 324
Moscow State University, 9, 175, 184, 188,
195
Moscow trials. *See* show trials
Mukhitdinov, Nuriddin, 251
music, 173, 329; Andreev as lover of, 8, 127;
as team recreation, 68, 188; Zhdanov's at-
tack on (1948), 193–94
Mussolini, Benito, 2

Nagy, Imre, 246–48
name changes, 13, 94–95, 262, 267–68, 317,
263, 317
nationalities policy, 19, 29, 199, 226, 227–28,
230–31, 325
Neizvestny, Ernst, 265
Nevsky, Alexander, 155
New Economic Policy (NEP), x, 22, 44, 260
Nicholas II (Tsar), 272
Nicolaevsky, Boris, 97–98, 123, 327
Nikolaev, Leonid, 112–13
NKVD. *See* security organs
Novikov, Nikolai, 198
Novodevichy Cemetery, 80, 265, 267, 268

October. *See* Revolution of October 1917
OGPU. *See* security organs
Oistrakh, David, 100
Old Bolsheviks, x, 17, 21, 64–65, 97, 102,
110, 131, 229, 242, 253, 328
oligarchy, 19, 273
one-party rule, 16, 21
Oppositions/Oppositionists, 22–23, 33–34,
35, 37, 41–42, 45, 53, 103, 106, 108, 125,
259–60, 321, 322; defeat of, 39–42; exile
of, 46. *See also* Left Opposition; Rightism
Ordzhonikidze, Eteri, 70, 187, 325
Ordzhonikidze, Grigory (Sergo), 3, 5, 17, 31,
34, 51, 54, 56, 57, 60, 61, 65, 68, 71, 74, 89,
90–91, 92, 93, 102, 104, 129–30, 184,
262; biography of, 8, 9, 29–30, 325; and
Bukharin, 59–60; conciliatory impulses
of, 36, 59; death of, 65, 120–21; defense of
subordinates by, 78, 120, 121, 128; dislike
of faction-fighting of, 34, 40–41; family
loyalty of, 78, 120; foreign travel of, 96–
97; friends of, 30, 34, 57, 59, 66, 86, 87,
118, 121; health of, 41; image of, 93; and
industrial ministries, 47, 74–75, 77; Lenin's criticism of, 19; and party Control
Commission, 41, 53; as patron, 110;
places named for, 94–95; Politburo disagreements of, 73, 77; and Stalin, 65, 67,
77–78, 79, 120, 211–12; volatility of, 6, 77
Ordzhonikidze, Zinaida (Zina), 69, 81, 140,
262, 325

parades, 6; May Day, 13; Victory (1945), 170,
180–81
Paris Exhibition of 1935, 99
Pasternak, Boris, 105, 107, 108–9
patronage, 108–10, 270, 281 n. 6, 293 n. 18,
329
Paulus, General Friedrich, 166–67, 326
peasants, 10, 22, 81; departure from village
of, 45, 48, 78, 108; "peasant voice" in lead-
ership, 29; policies toward, 32, 43, 44, 45,
199, 214, 228; and Stalin, 81, 83, 84–85
People's Commissariats. *See* ministries of
Soviet government
Peredelkino, 107
Persimfans, 106
Pervukhin, Mikhail, 252
Peshkov, Maxim, 108, 320. *See also* Vvedens-
kaya, Nadezhda